BITTER HARVEST

BITTER HARVEST

*A History of California
Farmworkers, 1870–1941*

CLETUS E. DANIEL

University of California Press

Berkeley • Los Angeles • London

University of California Press
Berkeley and Los Angeles, California

University of California Press, Ltd.
London, England

Library of Congress Catalog Number 82-50506
ISBN 0-520-04722-2

Printed in the United States of America
1   2   3   4   5   6   7   8   9

*This book is dedicated to the memory of
my father, who worked with his hands.*

Contents

Illustrations

Preface

This book is about power and the lack of it. More particularly, it is a history of the powerlessness of an occupational group: the men, women, and children who worked for wages in the fields and orchards of California from the late nineteenth century to the end of the 1930s. It is also a history of how and why, in an age notable for the equalizing tendencies that organization and reform promoted in the power relationship between industrial workers and their employers, the powerlessness of farmworkers not only persisted but became more profound and immutable.

In the course of researching and writing this book I have incurred innumerable debts. Many are owed to librarians and archivists whose names are unknown to me. Their contributions were plainly indispensable to the book's progress and completion. Equally important was the early guidance and encouragement given to me by my teachers in the History Department at the University of Washington, particularly that given by Robert E. Burke, Otis A. Pease, and Wilton B. Fowler. I regard the opportunity I had to learn the historian's craft from these able and generous teachers as perhaps the most fortuitous of my professional career. It has also been my good fortune to have several colleagues at the New York State School of Industrial and Labor Relations at Cornell University who have not only allowed me to go on at great length about this book at various stages of its progress, but also offered many wise and useful suggestions for its improvement. In this regard I am especially indebted to James A. Gross, Roger R. Keeran, and Maurice F. Neufeld.

For the generous financial assistance they provided during the research for the book, I express my deep appreciation to the Woodrow Wilson National Fellowship Foundation, the National Endowment for the Humanities, the American Council of Learned Societies, and the New York State School of Industrial and Labor Relations.

I am also grateful to Joyce Wright, who not only typed and retyped the manuscript, but helped me in at least a dozen other ways that facilitated the research and writing of this book.

My greatest debt is to my family: to my son, Jacob, and my daughter, Danielle, who helped me to keep my work on this book in perspective; and to my wife, Helen, who unfailingly encouraged and supported me at every stage of my work, and who in the end makes this and everything else worthwhile.

Finally, I acknowledge my special indebtedness to those who inspired this book: the hundreds of Mexican farm laborers who worked alongside me in the lettuce fields of the Salinas Valley during the summers of my childhood. They were among my first heroes, and my admiration for them has not diminished. They showed and taught me compassion, and they never permitted the wretchedness of their lives to rob them of their dignity. Their names are unremembered, but their faces and their singular heroism are indelibly etched in my memory.

CLETUS E. DANIEL

Ithaca, New York

BITTER HARVEST

1

The Erosion of
Agrarian Idealism

From the earliest days of the American republic farming has been regarded as an especially honored occupation. Farming was not just an occupation but a way of life, one singularly fitted to promote and safeguard those values of self-reliance, freedom, industry, simplicity, and thrift celebrated and presumably practiced by the agrarians who largely composed this country's founding generation. In his *Notes on Virginia,* Thomas Jefferson, America's foremost and most influential celebrant of Arcadian values, wrote:

> Those who labor in the earth are the chosen people of God, if ever He had a chosen people, whose breasts He has made His peculiar deposit for substantial and genuine virtue. It is the focus in which he keeps alive that sacred fire, which otherwise might escape from the face of the earth. Corruption of morals in the mass of cultivators is a phenomenon of which no age nor nation has furnished an example.[1]

Though Jefferson was a gentleman farmer, more intimately familiar with the duties of the overseer than with those of the actual toiler, he nonetheless emphasized—as did his chief collaborator, James Madison—that the surest guarantee of democratic institutions and a wholesome national life consisted in the maintenance of an agricultural economy whose mainstay was the yeoman farmer working his own land on a scale commensurate with the labor power that he and his family represented.[2] Thus it was not simply the agrarian life that Jefferson and others cherished and promoted, but farming on a small scale by self-sufficient citizens who were in the greatest degree possible the masters of their individual economic fates.[3]

In contrast to the idealized and even romanticized family farm, which supposedly nurtured democracy, southern plantation agriculture

15

stood condemned, not just because its slave-labor base gave moral offense, but also because it was farming on a scale that engendered values of class and caste that were antithetical to those that Jefferson and his adherents extolled. Throughout the nineteenth century persistent agitations ensued for public land policies that would afford privileged access to the small family farmer and discourage large-scale agricultural enterprises that at once commercialized and demeaned life on the farm. The most pointed debate generated by the controversy over small- versus large-scale farming occurred at mid-century, before the ultimate approval of the Homestead Act in 1862. During the congressional debate preceding the law's enactment, an advocate of the family farm hearkened unabashedly to the agrarian ethic of Jefferson when he declared, "Instead of baronial possessions, let us facilitate the increase of independent homesteads. Let us keep the plow in the hands of the owner. Every new home that is established, the independent owner of which cultivates his own freehold is establishing a new republic within the old, and adding a new and strong pillar to the edifice of the state."[4]

Even when it was most dutifully observed and practiced, the "small is better" ideal embodied in the Homestead Act did not, of course, result in the establishment of a farming economy in which every person who toiled on the land did so as an independent, self-employed agrarian entrepreneur. Yet despite the corruptions of purpose that often marred its administration and the increases that occurred in both tenancy and bonanza farming toward the end of the century, the law did reinforce and legitimize the family farm as the typical agricultural unit in the northern states, and helped to extend that pattern throughout much of the upper midwestern and plains regions opened to settlement after its passage.[5]

Because of the statutory emphasis and popular approbation enjoyed by the idea that the "real" American farm was one operated on a small enough scale to require, for the most part, only the labor that the farm family could supply, those who worked for wages in the areas dominated by family farming were generally regarded as fledgling yeomen, apprenticed on the land as they made their way up the rungs of the agricultural ladder to the level of bona fide freeholders. Whether or not the agricultural ladder symbolized a real rather than an illusory process of upward mobility, and the evidence is far from conclusive still, farm laborers were popularly viewed as an impermanent, transitory element within the agricultural population, one that was necessary to the rural economy but continuously being transformed and dissipated by it.

President Theodore Roosevelt's Commission on Country Life noted that a scarcity of experienced farm labor was the perennial result of this process, but argued that as long as "the United States continues to be a true democracy," farm employers would simply have to accept the fact that the farm laborer of one season might well be the tenant or independent farm operator of subsequent seasons.[6]

While farm laborers certainly enjoyed no special esteem within the small-scale family-farming economy, they were seldom looked upon as a disadvantaged group. The real or imagined impermanence of their economic status discouraged any tendency to regard them as a pitiable class. Probably of more importance, though, was the simple fact that what the "haves" had in most family-farming regions was insufficiently grand to make for much contrast between them and the "have nots." Hard physical labor was the common denominator among all those whose lives were invested in small-scale farming, whether farmer, farm wife, farm child, or hired farm laborer. Since the farm laborer generally worked beside his employer, ate at the same table, and perhaps even slept under the same roof, the differences in status and lifestyle between employer and employee were often hard to discern. The Commission on Country Life, seeking to impress upon the nation the homogenizing effect of farmwork on social relationships in family-farming regions, abandoned descriptive terms with class or status connotations and referred to all those who labored in small-scale agriculture simply as "land-workers."[7]

If farming on a small scale discouraged the growth of rigid class divisions between farmers and their hired laborers, the social and psychological climate on the large-scale commercial farm promoted impenetrable class and caste lines that admitted of not the slightest ambiguity. For this kind of agriculture no analogies were to be found in the bucolic world of Jefferson's noble and solitary freeholder. Rather, this was the kind of agriculture for which analogies of scope and character were more readily and instructively drawn from the domain of the ante-bellum plantation master. This was the kind of agriculture that evolved easily and not unnaturally from a pattern of monopolistic landholding that dated from the earliest days of settlement. This was the kind of agriculture that drew plain and ineradicable economic battle lines between farm employer and hired laborer. This was, its exceptional varieties notwithstanding, California agriculture from the late nineteenth century onward.

The large-scale agriculture of California did not represent a departure from the dominant family-farming tradition in America for the simple reason that California was never a part of that tradition. For other western regions, territorial status and then statehood meant the coming of social, political, economic, and intellectual processes of acculturation that would displace the wilderness with a rustic facsimile of civilization. California, with nearly a century of development under successive Spanish and Mexican colonial administrations behind it, entered the Union in 1848 to be Americanized rather than civilized. And, given the rapidly changing character of the nation during the middle decades of the nineteenth century, Americanization no longer meant the benign imposition of political, social, and economic values and practices associated with an increasingly anachronistic revolutionary past, but rather a callous, often ruthless transformation that dictated an allegiance to new mores consistent with the nation's evolution toward a capitalistic and industrialized future.

For the most part the reorientation of California proceeded rapidly under American rule. The gold mania at mid-century, which saw hordes of old and new Americans descend on the state in very short order, played a particularly important role in the quick transformation of California from a placid Latin colony with strong pastoral inclinations to a bustling, self-consciously special and resourceful state where American aspirations and enterprise flourished on an exaggerated scale. As one contemporary observer of that momentous time somewhat ruefully noted, the discovery of gold had attracted "such a mixed and heterogeneous mass of energetic, daring, and reckless men as had never before invaded any part of the continent, except, possibly, in the conquest of Mexico."[8]

Within a few short years the Americanization of California was so far advanced that the political and economic life of the state revealed few vestiges of its colonial heritage. One glaring exception, however, was to have a profound and enduring impact on California's agricultural development: the pattern of landownership that survived from the state's colonial past.

Long before the Treaty of Guadalupe Hidalgo ceded California to the United States, the colonial land policies of both Spain and Mexico had promoted, through grants of massive tracts of land to favored individuals and families, conditions under which the ownership and control of much of the best land rested with a relatively small colonial aristocracy. To be sure, the Americanization of California after 1848 brought rapid and substantial changes to this system of landownership. Yet the essential change, frequently achieved by fraudulent means, consisted of a displacement of the original owners by Anglo newcomers intent on putting to profitable uses the millions of rich acres that their predecessors had been content to devote primarily to pastoral pursuits. Significantly, the monopolistic pattern of landownership established earlier was left largely undisturbed, and its perpetuation became one of the controlling factors in the development of agriculture in California. For while family farming of the traditional American variety gained a foothold in the state during the last half of the nineteenth century and the early decades of the twentieth, the inability of small farmers to gain access to vast tracts of the state's most arable land helped to forestall the development in California of an agricultural economy and rural society dominated by the small-scale family farm.[9] And just as the family farm did not come to typify agricultural production in California, neither did the hired man associated with small-scale farming ever come to typify the agricultural wage earner in the state.

That farming in California differed in scale and in spirit from the traditional family farming that was at once livelihood and lifestyle for its adherents in middle America was apparent at a very early stage. In his seminal *History of California,* published in 1890, Hubert Howe Bancroft wrote: "For size of farms California exceeds every other state, and it is a peculiarity favored by her speculative spirit, which delights in operations on a large scale."[10] Bancroft noted further that the dominant mentality in California agriculture was akin to that found in "mining and other chance efforts" in the state, one revealing above all a hope of realizing a "rapid acquisition of wealth."[11] Notably absent from this mentality was an integrated conception of farming as a social end as well as an economic means.[12]

Yet, paradoxically, the highly commercialized, even industrialized farms or ranches that emerged by the end of the nineteenth century as the characteristic type of agriculture in California had begun only a generation before as a counter to bonanza farming, which the new agricultural entrepreneurs had condemned as harmful to the development of small-scale family farming consistent with American ideals and traditions. That the advocates of traditional agrarian values became in a relatively brief time the operators of "farm factories" that embodied the commercial ethic of modern industrial America revealed not an insincerity of conviction so much as an inability or unwillingness to cling to abstract social ideals in the face of economic imperatives that arose out of the country's headlong and seemingly inexorable rush toward what appeared, by most definitions, to be progress.

The erosion of the family-farming ideal in California was a slow process, neither readily discerned nor readily acknowledged by that growing population of farmers in the state who before the 1890s had criticized large-scale agriculture as unwholesome and un-American. Using a brand of rhetoric with which Jefferson himself would surely have felt at ease, agrarian orators at the annual meetings of the California State Agricultural Society inveighed against the twin evils of monopolistic landholding and large-scale farming, detailing with undisguised resentment the social, political, and economic harm visited upon the state when such circumstances combined to deny family farming its rightful hegemony over the countryside. Delivering the annual address before the society in 1865, John F. Morse, a devotee of agrarian values, advised his listeners that if agriculture was "the most perfect criterion by which to estimate the . . . honesty, the virtue, and contentment of the people," then conditions in California offered considerable cause for alarm. Voicing a sentiment that found expression in virtually every gathering of the society from the 1850s through the 1880s, Morse warned:

> Free and untrammelled agricultural homes, cultivated and kept in order by the men who own the soil, are the sources of the most indestructible national wealth. And in our country there is but one thing that can militate against this great national desideration. That is the tendency to a monopoly of soil, the holding of more land than can be properly managed, and the introduction of lease-ridden estates. Oppressive monopoly in anything is a curse to society and dishonor toward God and man. But if monopoly must exist, let it live anywhere rather than in the husbandry of our country.[13]

The appearance in California of farming enterprises on a truly mammoth scale revealed in a particularly graphic way, Morse suggested, that "there are no monopolists so arrogant, so dictatorial, so dangerous to the peace and perpetuity of the State, as the overgrown . . . nabobs of the soil." His concern, clearly, was that agriculture on so large a scale retarded, if it did not block entirely, the development of the small family farms that "constitute the true glory and security of a nation or State." Upon reciting the socially and spiritually enriching characteristics of family farming on a small scale, Morse announced: "This is the kind of agriculture we want in California."[14] Charles F. Reed, in his presidential address before the society in 1869, reiterated these criticisms of land monopoly and large-scale agriculture, and declared: "Our public domain, our lands in general, should be divided up into small farms or parcels, each one of these to become the home and homestead of a family, dependent for a livelihood upon the cultivation of that homestead."[15]

The particular focus of such criticisms was the bonanza wheat-farming operations that had first appeared in the state on the heels of the gold rush, and which by 1889 were producing in excess of 40 million bushels on 2.75 million acres, making California the second largest producer of wheat in the nation.[16] The agrarian critics of large-scale wheat farming found in its methods and motives, and in the speculative psychology of its practitioners, little with which advocates of family farming could identify. Rather, they saw in bonanza wheat farming the same single-minded, get-rich-quick. orientation that had been revealed in the behavior of gold miners throughout much of the 1850s. Indeed, if the mother lode symbolized the initial discovery of the state, wrote one prominent farmer, then surely the appearance of bonanza farms marked "the second discovery of California."[17] The wheat lands that had come to dominate agriculture in the San Joaquin and Sacramento valleys by the 1880s were too frequently, he complained, "farmed . . . by absentee owners from their offices in San Francisco, or by telephone from offices in neighboring towns; farmed often solely as the mine is worked."[18] Another advocate of family farming insisted that "large farming is not farming at all. It is mining for wheat. In one point of view, it is a manufacturing business in which clods are fed to the mill and grain appears in carloads. Such farming holds the same relation to society as does a manufacturing corporation."[19]

The "relation" of large-scale agriculture to society was, in fact, at the heart of the agrarians' criticism of the big wheat farms. True to their Jeffersonian ideals, they argued that the essential purpose of agriculture was to create secure homes of independent farm families that would in community constitute the bedrock of a genuine republican society. And plainly, the bonanza wheat farmers were not home builders. Like the miners, they contributed their intelligence and industry to the extraction of wealth only, giving no thought to the long-run developmental needs of the state. The contrast between these two approaches to farming could not have been framed more starkly or couched in a more compelling and self-serving moral context. Family farming on a small scale gave life to humane and enduring society, while large-scale farming created only personal fortunes. While, as one agrarian observed, the vision of the large-scale farm operator was limited to "only the sterner features of the guild: the order, the machine, the minimum of expense, the maximum of product," that of the family farmer encompassed "the school house, the church, the library, the social circle, the moral influence, the intelligence that lays at the base and foundation of the political and governmental fabric."[20]

Yet if agrarians objected to large-scale farming on the basis of what it failed to contribute to the state's development, they were still more critical and resentful of the active harm caused by enterprises that they believed to be inherently antisocial. For beyond its failure to serve the higher social and political purposes of agriculture, bonanza farming was, the agrarians charged, responsible for several derivative evils as well. Because the big wheat farms occupied tens of thousands of acres of the best land in the state's principal agricultural regions, they perpetuated the tradition of monopolistic landholding dating from California's colonial past. As long as huge tracts of land were tied up in the "mining of wheat," agrarians argued, the small family farms that alone constituted the ultimate social salvation of the state could not be had. Further, the opponents of large-scale farming claimed that the relatively slow growth of the state's population after the flush fifties had passed was attributable almost entirely to the discouraging effect that bonanza agriculture had on potential immigrants seeking lives on the land. Was it surprising, the agrarians asked rhetorically, that neither native-born Americans nor European immigrants displayed much interest in migrating to California, given "the fact of our large individual land holdings, and an indisposition to subdivide and sell?"[21]

Still another charge lodged against the large-scale wheat farmers was that their operations had not only commercialized agriculture to the point of blurring the once obvious distinction between farm and factory, but had also given the state's agriculture so pronounced a one-crop character as to make the entire farm economy of California vulnerable to the vagaries of a notoriously unstable international grain market. On the bonanza farms, one critic noted, "fortunes come and go with the seasons."[22] Not until the "incessant agricultural monotone of wheat, wheat, wheat" was silenced and the farms of California became diversified, producing first to meet the farm family's needs and then for sale to local markets, would the agriculture of the state be on a firm and stable foundation, the agrarians argued. Where diversified farming had gained a foothold in the state, wrote General N. P. Chipman, a leading advocate of traditional agriculture, conditions contrasted sharply with the social and institutional poverty of large-scale, one-crop farming. Moving from the large-scale wheat farm to the diversified family farm was, he insisted, like passing from wilderness to civilization. "The transformation is as sudden and striking as from the desert to the oasis. Pass from the wheat region of the great San Joaquin to the mixed farming of San José, and you pass from agricultural darkness to agricultural light; from a land of apparent desolation to one of plenty."[23] To the authentic American farmer, Chipman asserted, large-scale wheat farming offered "nothing to inspire one with a pride in his calling." In contrast, the family farmer was elevated in both mind and spirit by the fact that "diversified farming calls out the best intelligence we possess." And though the monetary rewards realized by the wheat grower might be greater than those achieved by the family farmer, Chipman concluded, the latter's "attachment for and pride in his calling deepens with the years as they pass, and he becomes a positive factor in the civilizing and ennobling influences of his occupation rightly followed."[24]

The agrarians' final and most profound objection to large-scale farming was that, because of its reliance on cheap, seasonal wage labor, it introduced class divisions that were abhorrent to all true Jeffersonians. Because advocates of family farming in California tended to embrace the traditional notion that the legitimate scale of agricultural enterprise was naturally determined by the amount of labor that the family itself could provide, they were suspicious of any farming that was done on a scale so large that wage labor was indispensable to its operation. Of course agrarians in the state did acknowledge a legitimate role for hired labor in agriculture. Indeed, they believed that most farmers needed during their busiest seasons of the year more labor than family members alone could provide, and that hired hands offered the most sensible solution to these needs. Yet as the agrarians saw it, the workers on whom family farmers relied during their busiest seasons were not a class apart, but were members in good standing of an undifferentiated rural class for whom arduous agricultural labor was a transcending fact of life.

The agrarians' vision of a classless rural society derived not only from an abstract idealism, but from a common, if often romanticized, recollection of the hired laborer's status within the farming economy of the East. This benign stereotype appeared regularly in the speeches of agrarians before the State Agricultural Society during the late nineteenth century. "In the Eastern States," went a fairly typical assertion, "farm laborers are a part of the family; they eat at the table with their employers—they are self-respecting citizens of the Republic."[25] The typical eastern farm, said another agrarian, was a model of social equality, "where father, mother, sons, and daughters all toiled; where labor was honorable and honored; where the hired man and the hired maid were called 'help,' and sat in equal honor at the farmer's long harvest table."[26] Although in the East disharmony and conflict ruled the relations between factory owner and factory hand, observed another admirer of that region's farming, there was "little discontent there among farm laborers, because of the small farms and the close relations between the farmer and his employee."[27]

If supporters of family farming in California painted too rosy a picture of the social relations on the small-scale farms of the East, they had no need of hyperbole in depicting the class divisions and social maladies bred by their own state's large-scale agriculture. The dependence of large-scale commercial agriculture on a large force of cheap seasonal labor was fairly well established by the 1850s. Indians, impressed into the farm work force by discriminatory vagrancy laws, were a major source of such labor throughout the 1850s, and their numbers were augmented by disappointed gold miners and by some Chinese who had been driven out of the mining camps by whites determined to enforce their exclusive racial privilege in the goldfields.[28] While bonanza wheat farms employed the largest crews of farmworkers, an increasing number of large fruit orchards and farms devoted entirely to the growing of such specialty crops as hops became equally dependent on an abundant supply of casual laborers readily available for work in the busy seasons but able to move on when the demand for their labor fell at season's end to virtually nothing. So enthusiastic were many bonanza farmers and other speculators about the present and future profitability of large-scale agriculture in California that on several occasions during the 1850s they called for the establishment of a full-blown plantation economy in the state, complete with a black slave-labor force imported from the South. In addition to wheat and the other crops already being grown on a large scale in the state, such labor-intensive crops as cotton, coffee, tea, and tobacco might, these enterprising boosters argued, be grown in California's fertile valleys with equal facility and remunerative advantage if only an adequate supply of slave labor could be had. When it became apparent to them that antislavery feeling in the state was too strong to permit them to implement their schemes, they looked about for some other equally suitable source of cheap labor.[29]

If agrarians were upholding traditional values by believing that farm work was honorable and that farmworkers should be honored, the values that shaped bonanza farmers' attitudes toward agricultural labor were plainly of the new commercial age. From the first they tended to regard labor only as a factor of production, and sought through any means available to reduce the costs of labor to the lowest levels possible. Seldom, if ever, were California's major farm employers willing to let the natural mechanisms of an unfettered labor market determine those costs. Rather, they sought to influence the supply of labor in ways that would guarantee that farmworkers were available in adequate numbers when they were needed and at a cost that would not endanger the profits that constituted the fundamental motive of large-scale agriculture.

The bonanza farmers' unwillingness to buy their labor on the basis of supply and demand, as urban employers were forced to do, was largely due to their belief that they could never successfully compete for labor with their counterparts in the cities and towns of the state. This belief was rooted in a self-serving and somewhat arcane analysis of the state's labor market concocted from equal parts of their own homespun price theory, a convenient notion of the special character of agricultural employment, and an expedient racist folklore that would come to enjoy the status of a self-evident truth in agribusiness circles during the twentieth century. Farm employers insisted as early as the 1850s that they were at a disadvantage in trying to compete with the state's urban employers for wage labor that was perennially scarce as long as the lure of the goldfields remained strong. The different market conditions affecting the two groups were cited with particular frequency and emphasis by farm employers seeking to explain their disadvantaged position. They noted, for example, that because urban employers in the state generally operated in local markets, they were able to exercise considerable control over prices, and so were in a position to pass on to their customers the relatively high wages commanded by labor. In contrast, the products of California's large-scale agriculture were usually sold, farm employers argued, in national or international markets, at prices determined by forces far beyond their control. Thus, while high labor costs might pose no threat to the ultimate profitability of an urban business, they were likely, agricultural employers concluded, to have a very severe effect on their own economic well-being, because such cost increases invariably eroded their profits.

Their alleged inability to pay wages comparable to those offered by urban employers was only the first of the reasons that California's large-scale farmers regularly cited in support of their contention that they were uncompetitive in the state's labor market. Of equal importance were the competitive disadvantages that derived from what farm employers claimed was the special character of employment in commercial agriculture. They noted, for example, that even when the wage disparity between industrial and agricultural work was not a dissuading factor, employment on bonanza farms was usually less attractive to workers than city jobs because it was seasonal, and typically involved very long hours, working conditions that were harsh, and living conditions that were at best primitive and at worst nearly intolerable. It was in the nature of things, they argued, that farmwork was seasonal, and that the hours were long and the working conditions uncongenial. Insofar as poor living conditions were concerned, most farm employers denied that they were so bad as their detractors maintained. But even when the more candid among them acknowledged the fact that the living conditions farmworkers faced were generally poor, they insisted that farm employers could not reasonably be expected to make large expenditures to improve conditions given the relatively brief periods that their farms were homes to workers. In short, farm employers conceded that employment in large-scale agriculture was less desirable than most of the work that urban employers in the state offered to job seekers.

Finally, large-scale farm operators argued that they were unable to compete for the available wage labor in the state because that labor was overwhelmingly white, and most of the work that needed to be done on bonanza farms had come to be regarded as not suitable for whites. Even if the wages and working and living conditions were comparable to those available in the cities and towns, farm employers insisted, white wage earners simply would not take jobs they regarded as onerous or accept the degraded economic and social status associated with such work. The reasons assigned to these supposed biases against farmwork on the part of whites were varied. That part of the white labor force composed of disappointed gold seekers and other transients generally was, the employers claimed, so slothful and irresponsible that its members found any work onerous, and especially any work that took them far from the saloons and gaming dens that were their preferred habitat. The more responsible and industrious class of white labor in the state disdained farm employment, farm employers said, because of expectations of upward mobility. Those workers had come to California seeking better lives for themselves and their families, and if they sought lives on the land, employers asserted, it was as independent farmers rather than as dependent farmworkers. Similarly, European immigrants arriving in the state did not, one spokesman for large-scale farmers wrote, "come to California to continue the peasant life they lived in over-populous Europe, but to become land-owners and tillers of their own soil."[30] Given this unwillingness among most white wage earners to accept jobs on California's bonanza farms except under the most pressing economic circumstances, what was more reasonable, employers asked, than that they should look to other races as the most likely sources from which an adequate supply of seasonal farm labor might be recruited? The interest that many of the state's farm employers expressed in black slave labor during the 1850s was an early reflection of this mentality, but it was even more emphatically revealed in their attitudes toward California's growing population of Chinese immigrants. Once farm employers saw that they could not import slaves, Chinese labor seemed the logical alternative. Indeed, one of their spokesmen insisted in 1854 that logic as well as an inexorable destiny dictated that Chinese farmworkers should "be to California what the African has been to the South."[31]

Farm employers saw in the Chinese, as they would see in a succession of nonwhite groups in subsequent decades, a work force ideally suited to their needs. Chinese workers were, employers insisted, docile, industrious, trustworthy, and reliable. Moreover, they were said to be experienced at agricultural tasks, to live very simply, to be willing to accept seasonal employment, to be employable through "gang bosses" or labor contractors who also provided immediate supervision, to be available in unlimited numbers if actively recruited, and, most important, to work for wages lower than any other group of laborers in the state was willing to accept. Throughout all of the these arguments ran the same theme. Chinese workers, because they were not white, did not, indeed could not, have aspirations or expectations comparable to those that white workers might reasonably harbor or consider a matter of right on the basis of their whiteness alone. As farm employers saw it, Chinese workers offered the perfect solution to the central dilemma of California's large-scale agriculture. They provided the cheap labor power that was indispensable to its success but were immune to the democratizing forces of tradition, circumstance, and social contract that afforded the lowly just enough opportunity for advancement to keep the popular expectation of upward movement alive. Not without reason, the big farm employers in California believed that the agricultural industry they envisioned could not be erected on a secure basis if the cheap labor that was the most essential prerequisite for its success was forever being siphoned away by real or imagined promises of even modest preferment. The path to industrial security lay in the recruitment of a work force whose estrangement from the social and cultural mainstream was so profound and unalterable as to render it captive economically. In Chinese laborers the advocates of large-scale farming saw, if not slaves, at least the practical equivalents of slaves. Like the post–Civil War freedmen, whose technical freedom was rarely a serious impediment to their practical enslavement within the agricultural economy of the New South, Chinese farmworkers—and many

27

of the other groups of nonwhite farmworkers who would succeed them—would not be slaves, but as they would be locked into a single occupational status by powerful social, political, and economic forces that they could not reasonably hope to resist, their freedom would plainly be more illusory than real. To those who questioned the morality of this logic, farm employers replied that it was not the puny will of man but immutable nature that had ordained that the relationship of the Chinese to whites be one of servant to master. As William Blackwood, a leading farm employer in the state, observed with apparent guilelessness, "the laborers of China are born to servitude—it has become ingrained in their natures. They never seek to rise above it."[32] And, lest anyone suggest that man might somehow undo nature's plan in this regard, Blackwood added that "no power of any government [could] effect a change in this respect." "The simple and only question affecting our welfare, in connection with the Chinaman, is," Blackwood suggested, "Can we use him profitably in developing our industries without contamination?"[33] Using his own and his fellow farm employers' initial experiences with Chinese workers as his guide, Blackwood unhesitatingly answered in the affirmative. To those who still remained doubtful, Blackwood suggested a reassuring analogy. "As a class of laborers," he noted,

> the Chinese in California have heretofore occupied precisely the same position in the body politic that the peasantry of Europe do at home. The Chinese in California have no voice in governmental affairs: neither have the peasantry of Europe. The Chinese of California live on or near the lands of their employers: so do the peasantry of Europe. The Chinese are sober, temperate, and industrious: so are the peasantry of Europe. The Chinese in California do not aspire to rise above the position of common laborers: neither do the peasantry of Europe. The Chinese do not seek to affiliate socially with the better class in California: neither do the peasantry of Europe seek such social affiliation there.

With "a large class of cheap laborers in large supply," Blackwood prophesied, it would be "beyond the powers of an ordinary mind to compute" just how far California's large-scale agricultural enterprises "could be profitably pushed, or the amount of wealth these industries would create in the state. . . . With such a class of laborers around him, the farmer, the orchardist or vineyardist [could] retire to rest at night feeling secure."[34]

Yet if the thought of Chinese farmworkers available in abundant supply induced feelings of security and contentment among California's largest farm employers, it excited profound disquietude among a majority of the state's agrarian population. To the agrarians Chinese farmworkers personified the social and economic corruption of traditional American values that they believed large-scale agriculture promoted. If farm employers saw special advantages in the foreignness of Chinese laborers, agrarians saw with equal clarity special horrors. Never, they agreed, could or should a group so utterly different from themselves in culture, aspirations, ideas, and a thousand other ways be assimilated into the rural society of California. That the leaders of large-scale agriculture in the state had come to regard Chinese labor as indispensable to their economic well-being was to agrarians definitive proof of the socially destructive character of bonanza farming.

The advocates of family farming had expressed their unalterable opposition to the use of Chinese labor even before the dangers they depicted had materialized to any significant degree. At no time during the period from 1850 to 1870, despite the histrionic and grandiose conjurations of bonanza farmers, did Chinese workers constitute more than 10 percent of the state's seasonal farm-labor force.[35] Not until the 1870s, when thousands of Chinese workers previously employed in the construction of the western end of the first transcontinental railroad began to seek new jobs, did the composition of the state's agricultural work force indicate a heavy dependence on Chinese labor by bonanza farmers.[36] Agrarians condemned the use of Chinese wage earners less out of concern over the current extent of the practice than out of fear of what it presaged for their own hopes of building a family-farming economy. In the course of his recitation on the glories of small farms and the evils of big farms before the 1870 meeting of the State Agricultural Society, A. A. Sargent, a politician who sought to exploit the fears of his audience, expressed an opinion of Chinese farm labor that more authentic agrarian spokesmen reiterated annually at the society's conventions. Voicing the particularly grave fears that agrarians harbored regarding the long-range implications of bonanza farming's labor requirements, Sargent declared:

Many have seen a solution of the labor question in the employment of Chinese, who furnish a fair article of labor, skilled and unskilled, [for wages] at which white men cannot subsist. This may be a temporary relief to capital, and may forward enterprises that else would halt indefinitely. But I am not able to concur in the opinion that the immigration in large numbers of this people is desirable. A slower growth of a community, with the elements in it only of Christian civilization, seems to me far preferable to rapid development by an alien, heathen population. Would not twenty-five stalwart German or Scandinavian emigrants, with their families, be better for the real interests of the State than the whole Chinese population of [Sacramento]? If the object of society is merely to accumulate wealth in the hands of an upper class, and have the laborer the mudsill—if American civilization and republican institutions could coexist with such a theory and practice—then it might be well to crowd every avenue of labor with Asiatics, and rejoice in the cultivation of the last inch of soil . . . by the adroit Chinese to the exclusion of white labor.[37]

Like the increasingly vitriolic attacks on Chinese workers by organized labor and other groups in California's principal cities and towns throughout the 1870s, the vocal assaults launched by agrarians were blatantly racist and chauvinistic. Yet if agrarians were not above framing their arguments in ways calculated to excite the baser instincts of the state's white population, they always made it plain in the end that their essential objection was not to the Chinese themselves, but to those developments and circumstances that threatened to make a large, dependent wage-labor force a permanent fixture of agricultural life in California. A seasonal farm-labor force comprised exclusively of whites, while it might have given less offense to the racial sensibilities of agrarians, was an equally loathsome prospect socially because it, too, would succor large-scale agriculture to the detriment of family farming and traditional rural values. While such agrarian proponents as A. A. Sargent freely indulged a racist rhetoric of the vilest sort, they also emphasized that the whole economics of large-scale farming affronted the "American way." Suggesting an "imperative" truth that "the capitalist" would do well to keep in mind, Sargent said:

The safety and well being of society depends on the intelligence and comfort of the laboring classes. . . . They are the workers, and by their numbers, under our form of government, they are the ones who choose rulers and determine the destiny of the Republic. They cannot fulfill the duties of citizenship on the wages of peons or coolies. Their relation to the State demand[s] of them education and virtue, which are only to be expected of those who have the means furnished by a fair share of the profits of capital in exchange for their labor and skill to bring education, comfort, and advancement within their reach. This has been the American theory. . . . It has fostered independence of labor; it has prevented class distinctions; it has been the parent of virtue, intelligence, and patriotism; it cannot be superseded and this country remain a Republic, where rights and benefits are reciprocal.[38]

As the mainly urban-based agitation for exclusion of the Chinese from California gained momentum during the late 1870s, agrarians took full advantage of the opportunity it afforded them to attack large-scale agriculture as a magnet for undesirable immigrants. Where large-scale farming was entrenched, they argued, labor could be neither dignified nor independent. Speaking of the big farms that relied most heavily on Chinese and other wage labor, one agrarian spokesman recited the full range of social destruction that large-scale agriculture threatened. "Such farming as this," he told those in attendance at the 1880 meeting of the San Joaquin Valley Agricultural Association, "may enrich the particular owner, but it introduces a feudal system. It makes the State a wilderness, and brings society back to the barbarism of the mediaeval age. It destroys homes and the family. It breeds tramps and idlers. It destroys churches and schoolhouses. It would in time present the great, beautiful valleys of our State as treeless, verdureless plains."[39] Speaking before the same agricultural society at its meeting the year before, another critic of large-scale farming had insisted that the agrarians' belief "that the mammoth farms of California are as great an evil as the immense landed estates of the English nobility" was too charitable an assessment of the situation. After all, he noted, the "aristocratic domains" of the English supported a tenantry, at least, while the "home evil" lacked even this modest compensatory feature.[40]

If urban agitators tended to regard Chinese exclusion as an end in itself, agrarians saw it only as an important first step toward the eventual dismantling of California's large-scale agricultural industry. The ultimate remedy for the remaining problems facing the state's rural society, including the problem of class divisions, was, of course, the same Jeffersonian medicament that agrarians had prescribed from the beginning: small-scale, diversified family farming. "Small farming," one particularly ebullient agrarian wrote, "is the panacea for about all the ills of life. It is a solution of all the most vexed problems of political economy. In that country where the people who own the land cultivate it, and govern it, the doctrines of Malthus, Ricardo, and Adam Smith, and all the philosophers who have endeavored to accommodate the science of government to the use of the class that had conquered States and monopolized its lands, will not apply." The same spokesman estimated that with the exclusion of the Chinese and the decline in large-scale agriculture which he hoped it would bring about, the "happy time" was surely not far off when "in California, every man who is willing to till the land shall have as much, and no more, than he can advantageously cultivate."[41] Similarly, Charles Wetmore, an agrarian from Alameda County, argued that the state's "only salvation from Chinese and tramps" lay in a concerted program to induce "industrious families to settle upon and cultivate small five and ten-acre homes."[42] Another, and somewhat more romantic, devotee of small, diversified farming claimed that "such farms . . . would transform the Valleys of the San Joaquin and Sacramento, the great plains of Salinas and Santa Clara. Like the fruitful plains of Lombardy, nestled beneath the Julian Alps, they would literally blossom like a rose, for fruitful gardens produce everything that ought to be demanded to make men happy and build up a State."[43] Still another agrarian promised that with the decline of large-scale agriculture and the rise of a rural economic structure in which the land was "owned in small tracts and occupied and worked by the owners," a time would soon be at hand when "all conflict between labor and capital [would be] adjusted; their differences all reconciled and ended."[44]

With the passage of the Chinese Exclusion Act of 1882, agrarians not only looked forward to fundamental changes in the character of the state's agriculture, but suggested how the transition from large- to small-scale farming ought to be effected. As early as the 1860s, and even before, agrarians had argued that the best interests of California agriculture would be served by the drastic reduction, if not outright abandonment, of extensive cereal crops, especially wheat, and the substitution of fruit crops intensively cultivated on otherwise diversified, small-scale family farms.[45] Among the several benefits that its proponents expected from such a change was the subdivision into small farms of the huge tracts of land previously devoted to wheat; a displacement of the migratory labor force by nonseasonal, local labor drawn largely from the ranks of the farmers' own children; and an increase in diversified farms that still had the capacity to generate a modest cash income from the sale of the fruits whose cultivation was especially well suited to California's mild climate. In short, what the agrarians hoped the change would at last introduce into the state's rural society was the conviction that farming ought to be a way of life rather than simply an instrument of capitalist enterprise and profit.[46]

During the 1880s agrarians seldom missed an opportunity to promote small-scale horticulture and viticulture as alternatives to large-scale wheat farming. And with increasing frequency and confidence they claimed that the structural and psychological transformation necessary to the ultimate well-being of the state's farm life was in process. In its official report to Governor R. W. Waterman for 1887, the State Board of Agriculture stated that "a great revolution is rapidly but quietly taking place, whereby the larger land holdings are breaking up, and being sold . . . in small tracts to families that are seeking homes, where they can till the soil three hundred and sixty days in each year, and reap the result of their labor with less output than anywhere else in the civilized world. It is here . . . that the blanket-carrying tramp laborer is being driven out, and his place supplied by laborers who own the land they till." As a consequence of this change, the board reported, the state's "extensive grain fields . . . will be transformed into paying orchards, vineyards, and garden spots, thereby creating an increased demand for good land throughout the State, and the building up of a happy and prosperous community."[47] In the same year, an equally hopeful prognosticator observed before a crowd gathered at the Butte County Citrus Fair: "The most cheering feature in California's future prosperity is that the large tracts are cutting up into small farms, and the laborers and not the landlords, own the farms."[48]

In point of fact, a transformation of considerable magnitude was discernible in the major farming districts of the state during the 1880s. Wheat and other cereal farming, which had dominated California agriculture during the preceding thirty years, declined in importance as the cultivation of fruits, especially oranges and grapes, and vegetables was greatly expanded. In 1879 the combined value of cereal crops in the state was nearly $70 million, a figure that represented just over 96 percent of the total value of all agricultural production in California for that year. The value of all the fruits, nuts, and vegetables produced was less than $3 million, or only 3.9 percent of the total value of all agricultural products.[49] The statistics for 1888, less than a decade later, revealed dramatic changes in the relative values of extensive and intensive crops. The aggregate value of cereal crops had fallen to $49 million, while the value of crops produced just in the orchards and vineyards of the state had jumped to $25 million, or slightly more than 50 percent of the value of the entire crop of cereals for that year. Moreover, the latter crops were grown in an area equal to only about 9 percent of that devoted to cereals.[50] Increases in the production of some fruit crops were nothing short of spectacular. For example, the production of citrus fruits in the state was of so little consequence in 1880 that no precise figures were compiled, yet by 1886 California growers were exporting nearly 27 million pounds of oranges and lemons. The increased production of dried fruits during the 1880s was similarly impressive. Only 220 pounds of raisins had been shipped from the state in

1874, but by the end of the 1880s nearly 18 million pounds were being exported annually. The amount of vegetables being exported to both national and international markets in 1889 was ten times greater than the total for 1880.[51]

The changes that occurred in the 1880s were a source of considerable satisfaction to proponents of small-scale agriculture. Yet because of the intensive nature of the fruit and vegetable cultivation that displaced cereal crops, and also because of the generally unalloyed commercial mentality that the growers of these new crops tended to adopt, the agrarians' dream of an agricultural economy typified by diversified family farms operating on a scale commensurate with the labor power of the family members alone was no closer to being realized than it had been in the heyday of "King Wheat." Indeed, with the rise of horticulture, which agrarians had exalted as the most hopeful basis for a small-scale family farming economy in California, the possibility that traditional agricultural values would ever govern the state's rural society was irretrievably lost.

That fruit and vegetable farming in California were pursued on the same highly commercialized and specialized basis that wheat farming had been was a function both of changing economic and technological circumstances directly affecting the state's agricultural status and of newly evolved personal and social values that simultaneously deflated the civic idealism that underlay the agrarian notion of the good society and heralded the arrival of a marketplace mentality more nearly consistent with the asocial, mechanistic tenets of capitalism. In large measure, the industrialization of California's fruit and vegetable farms resulted from a very rapid market expansion brought about by new and improved methods of transportation. The first transcontinental railroad linking California to the population centers of the Midwest and East was completed in 1869, but it produced no dramatic changes in the state's agriculture largely because its principal product, wheat, was still more cheaply transported by water than by rail. In the 1880s, however, the Southern Pacific line was extended into the heart of the new citrus-growing regions of Southern California, and the development of refrigerated boxcars made possible the shipment of perishable products to distant eastern markets. With these developments fruit and vegetable farming on a commercial scale experienced a boom of such dimensions as to dwarf even that sparked by the discovery of gold. With new markets creating a seemingly insatiable demand for the fruits and vegetables of the state's irrigated fields, orchards, and vineyards, the profitability of such farming appeared to be guaranteed. The nearly simultaneous development of new and improved canning and drying techniques permitted California farmers not only to sell all of the fresh produce they could grow, but to profit as well from an equally strong and enduring demand for processed fruits and vegetables. And in the absence of any really formidable market competition, especially insofar as fruit production was concerned, most growers appear to have eagerly subscribed to the belief expressed by one of their number that "it is possible . . . for us to become the orchard of the whole world."[52]

The transforming powers of intensive agriculture were revealed with particular force in Southern California, which had experienced a comparatively languorous development before the 1880s. As the cultivation of citrus fruits proceeded, the region underwent an almost instantaneous commercial awakening. Los Angeles, its leading town, grew in population from only 11,000 inhabitants in 1880 to 30,000 by 1884.[53] Los Angeles County's population increased from just over 33,000 in 1880 to more than 117,000 by 1888. In the neighboring county of San Bernardino, where farmers embraced the new citrus culture no less single-mindedly, population grew from under 8,000 to more than 25,000 over the same brief span of years.[54] Similar rates of growth were experienced throughout the region of citrus culture south of the Tehachapi Range, and there was no doubt, according to one of the area's prominent growers, that the orange deserved recognition "as the cardinal factor in the development of Southern California from the census-enumerator's standpoint."[55]

While the spectacular record of growth compiled in the orange-growing counties of Southern California was unequaled, the new emphasis on horticultural enterprise elsewhere in the state was no less pronounced, and the overall result was a dramatic transmutation of California's agricultural landscape. Even more important, however, was the fact that the rise of commercial horticulture tested the mettle of agrarianism as it had not been tested before, and the failure of traditional farm values to withstand the mounting economic pressures of the modern industrial era marked the true beginnings of the age of agribusiness in California.

That the idea of small-scale family farming lost out to agribusiness in California is hardly surprising. Because the closest it ever really came to achieving concrete dimensions in the state was in the idealized recollections of transplanted easterners who had known its virtues in a different place and time, small-scale farming as a way of life remained largely an abstraction, alluring but intangible. In contrast, fruit and vegetable farming on a commercial scale revealed in measurable terms its economic profitability almost at once. Also, because agrarians had been among the earliest and most enthusiastic boosters of horticulture, and had initially emphasized the apparent differences rather than the essential similarities between this new kind of agriculture and the bonanza wheat farming that typified the old pattern of large-scale enterprise, they tended not to recognize the nature of the choice confronting them. The most easily understood measure of the magnitude of wheat farming was, of course, the acreage it occupied, and on that basis the horticultural pattern that emerged in the 1880s clearly represented a reduction in scale. Yet when scale was measured in such terms as land value, level of capitalization, degree of irrigation necessary, and labor requirements, it was plain beyond any doubt that what the commercial fruit and vegetable farming of the 1880s lacked in spatial extent it more than made up for in concentration of economic resources and intensity of operation. Thus the tradition of large-scale commercial agriculture established by wheat farmers in the 1850s was reinforced and perpetuated by the rise of fruit and vegetable farming, whose size and entrepreneurial inspiration differed in character and ambience but in the end was of a kind with what it displaced.

At the annual meetings of the state's important agricultural organizations, where the agrarian critics of large-scale farming had previously held forth so regularly and eloquently, the success of fruit and vegetable farms throughout California was greeted with general approbation. Only rarely during the late nineteenth century was the agrarians' abiding concern with bigness and the social evils of commercialized agriculture raised in the context of fruit and vegetable farming. Frederick Cox, in his presidential address to the 1891 convention of the State Agricultural Society, reviewed in the customary fashion the progress of California farmers during the year just ending, but, significantly, departed from that governing format long enough to sound a warning against what he believed to be a dangerous tendency among too many of the state's new horticulturists. While noting that California was "destined to be the foremost State of the Union in the production of the fruits of the temperate and sub-tropical climes," and that "the future profits of horticulture [were] certainly assured," Cox nonetheless saw a clear and present "danger . . . attending this enthusiasm." "The desire to possess land and the ambition to engage in large enterprises," he warned, "forestalls the judgment and deadens the ear to the voice of prudence." This infectious preoccupation with bigness was abroad in the farming regions of California, Cox argued, and had fostered a "tendency to enlarge the area of individual ownership of orchards and vineyards." Repeating the criticism that agrarians had leveled earlier against the wheat farmer, Cox asserted: "The man who is planting, or has planted his hundreds of acres of fruit, is not a horticulturist in the true meaning of the word," but "simply a gambler for quantity and not for quality," and thus "a detriment to the State." The true hope of California agriculture rested with "the orchardist of a few acres," who cherished the original agrarian dream that "the pursuit of horticulture may be the happy means of dotting the land with small holdings, which will be the seat of happy homes, whence shall proceed a generous brood of men and women reared amid the most congenial environments, perfect types of American manhood and womanhood, and fitted for every duty and performance of life. This hope will be frustrated if the tendency to large orchards is not resisted."[56]

But those in attendance at the society's 1891 meeting were clearly in no mood to contemplate the suggestion implicit in Cox's warning that the scale of fruit and vegetable farming had to be bridled somehow if the state's agriculture was going to escape those socially destructive influences that they had previously attributed to large-scale one-crop farming. While Cox's admonition was still echoing through the meeting hall, other speakers were taking up the convention's dominant litany, emphasizing with hard statistics and well-turned phrases both the realized and potential riches that fruit and vegetable farming on a commercial scale was capable of producing.

It is more than a little ironic, if not particularly surprising, that a group that had so readily discerned and criticized a speculative, get-rich-quick mentality among others was unable or unwilling to recognize a tendency in the same direction within its own ranks. More than simply revealing an acquisitive capacity, however, the tendency among California's fruit and vegetable farmers to turn their backs on the agrarian ideals they had formerly espoused so devoutly reflected a process of change in fundamental social values that affected not just those on the farm, but the whole society during the late nineteenth century. Though physically isolated from the midwestern and eastern population centers that experienced the most immediate and profound social and economic consequences of industrialization, the farming population of California was not insulated from the changes in values wrought by industrial society. Indeed, in one important sense, the state's farming class was particularly vulnerable to those changes. The farming populations of the East and the Old Northwest could look to community traditions that were several generations old to buffer the impact of changes accompanying the new economic order; because of Califor-

nia's relative youth and its incongruous colonial past, its agriculturalists had few social conventions that were mature enough or formidable
enough to serve as moderating forces. Where diversified family farming was really a way of life and contributed to the establishment and
maintenance of a community order productive of large social profits,
the likelihood of its complete abandonment in favor of unmitigated
commercial farming, even though the latter offered greater economic
rewards, was remote. As commercialism grew in such areas, the family
farm tended to place a somewhat greater emphasis than in former times
on generating a cash income, but without going so far as to forsake its
essential social purpose. Thus when agrarian and capitalist values
clashed in the older family-farming regions of the country, what tended
to emerge was a variable synthesis of old and new rather than an
incontestable triumph of the new over the old.

In stark contrast, the abstract agrarianism that arose in California as a
counter to bonanza farming, lacking the force and durability that de-
rives from both longevity and widespread practical adherence, was
simply not strong enough to retain the allegiance of a farming population to whom the imposing benefits of commercial horticulture were
being demonstrated in real terms on every side. The nature of the
choice facing those who had earlier professed agrarian values—the
choice between broad social interests and individual economic gains—
was particularly important given the changes that were gradually taking
place in the American definition of success during the late nineteenth
century. Before the industrial era, agrarians tended to measure success
largely in social terms. The family farmer, despite the economic self-
sufficiency that his lifestyle and orientation emphasized, was judged a
success or failure mainly on the basis of how completely he had merged
his motives and interests with those of the community. Thus in his
pursuit of success the small-scale family farmer tended, despite contrary pretensions, to give reinforcement to collectivist rather than individualistic values. And while the individual farmer normally realized
only a very modest economic reward, society presumably prospered
from such a system.[57]

With the rise of industrialism and a concomitant tendency toward the
atomization of preindustrial society, the idea of success defined in
community terms was challenged by a new definition that emphasized
individual economic accomplishments above all else. In the capitalist
environment that industrialization energized and reinforced, agrarian
ideals were plainly anachronistic, and to the extent that they retained
faithful adherents, it was only at an ever increasing individual econom-

ic sacrifice. In those family-farming regions of the country where traditional agrarian values were most firmly rooted, this new definition of success insinuated its way into the popular mentality only haltingly, and was softened and rendered less compelling in the process. In California, the hopeful rhetoric of a generation of agrarian evangelists notwithstanding, this more "modern" measure of success not only gained a ready acceptance, but tended as well to legitimize and make sense of the state's earlier history. When measured against the preindustrial standards of the eastern family-farming regions, the pattern of large-scale commercialized agriculture that established itself so rapidly in California gave the state's farming a distinctly aberrant character. And it was this pronounced tendency to deviate from the norm that fostered the early development of an outspoken agrarian sentiment in the state. Yet if large-scale farming was at variance with traditional agrarian values, it was entirely consistent with those modern industrial values that were rapidly gaining preeminence as the nineteenth century drew to a close. Indeed, in California the nation was afforded its first look at agriculture in truly modern dress: an enterprise that still had content in common with traditional farming, but which revealed a oneness in motives, methods, and sense of unadulterated economic purpose with the burgeoning industrial order.

2

In Search of a Peasantry

The telltale vocabulary of economic individualism was, of course, hardly foreign to the ears of Californians. It was, a generation of disgruntled agrarians believed, the mother tongue of gold miners, land speculators, and bonanza farmers. And from the late nineteenth century onward it was increasingly the language of the state's agricultural population as well. As the economic viability of the new horticulture was demonstrated in ever more unequivocal terms, the yearly convention proceedings of California's leading agricultural societies revealed a steadily diminishing concern with social questions and a growing preoccupation with the business and technical aspects of farming. Consistent with this new emphasis was the promotion and glorification of a new agricultural archetype whose approach to farming revealed the amalgam of technical expertise and business acumen that personified the modern practitioner. And just as the yeoman had served as the personal emulative symbol of traditional family farming, the new agribusinessman became a role model for farmers striving to succeed in the increasingly commercial environment of California agriculture.[1]

For an industrial role model the state's agribusinessmen looked to the city and to the modern corporation. Speaking of the steps that California's farmers needed to take in concert if they were "to keep abreast of the progressive, competitive spirit which marks every department of human effort," and thus avoid being "left behind in the great race of life," one advocate of modernization implored agribusinessmen in San Luis Obispo County to do "as the capitalists, the corporations, the great trusts are doing." If the state's farmers were to "inaugurate an era of progress and prosperity," he declared, they needed to unite in "intelligent cooperative effort for the promotion of their interests." Agribusinessmen must follow the lead of their urban counterparts and "study well the lesson which is being taught by the corporation: in unity, in intelligent corporation, there is *strength*; in divided effort there is weakness." Embracing a social philosophy that Horatio Alger might well have endorsed, he concluded: "We are the architects of our own fortune; if we prove to be masters of the situation, an era of prosperity hitherto unparalleled in our experience awaits us."[2]

Other spokesmen at farmers' meetings suggested that farming as an economic enterprise could not achieve full assimilation into the commercial mainstream of modern America until it shook off its traditional image and dressed itself for business. Edward Wickson, a popular and influential professor in the College of Agriculture at the University of California, advised farmers in 1889 that "agriculture must be disclosed . . . in the true light of its progressive character and its possibilities." Emphasizing that the "spirit of progress [had] breathed" upon farming, Wickson argued that its practitioners needed to convey the message that modern agriculture was no longer "ruled by tradition and fable as it once was." As captivating and idyllic as those traditions might still seem to some, he noted, they were irrelevant to most California farmers, who understood that insofar as agriculture was concerned, there was "only one way now for it to go forward, and that is by exercising the same spirit, the same ceaseless activity, the same earnest desire for better understanding and fuller knowledge which have achieved success in commerce and manufacturing industries." Once the state's agribusinessmen had come to share and be guided by this essential "secret of the onrush of our commercial and manufacturing industries," Wickson insisted, the historic distinction between the businessman and the farmer and the ideas that governed their realms of life would begin at last to lose its force and its validity.[3]

Both the expressions and the actions of the state's agribusinessmen during the late nineteenth century indicate their basic agreement with Wickson and others that much could be gained by adapting the orientation and techniques of urban commerce and industry to rural enterprise. In particular, farmers evinced a growing interest in finding ways to bring more order and efficiency to their work, and thereby to eliminate waste and increase productivity, as well as generally reduce the level of unpredictability to which their inherently unpredictable businesses were subject. Thus the application of scientific methods to what was with increasing frequency referred to as the "profession of agriculture" became especially important with the development and expansion of horticulture on a commercial scale. By the end of the 1890s a close, mutually beneficial relationship was well established between large-scale farmers and the faculty of the College of Agriculture at the University of California, with the latter not only providing technical expertise but serving as a conduit for those ideas and practices of urban industry and commerce that the state's agribusiness community was moving to adopt.

The rapid development of a modern business mentality among California's large-scale farmers was further disclosed by their keen interest in organizing themselves in ways that would promote greater efficiency in and control over the production, transportation, and "orderly marketing" of commonly grown crops.[4] Farmers' groups organized along occupational and regional lines had appeared very early in the state's history, and, as in the case of the State Agricultural Society and the district associations affiliated with it, had generally devoted themselves to the discussion, advancement, and protection of the larger political and economic interests of California's rural population. It was within these organizations, for the most part, that the debate over the ideal structure, size, and character of the state's current and future agriculture had raged. The new farmers' organizations that began to appear toward the end of the century were not designed to displace or even to compete with the existing bodies, but were organized strictly along commodity lines and concerned essentially with the protection and promotion of the common business interests of farmers engaged in the growing and selling of a particular farm product. Fruit growers took the lead in this movement. Beginning in the early 1880s, large-scale orchardists held annual meetings to discuss various matters of mutual concern.[5] Later in the decade, more particularistic cooperative organizations were founded to advance and protect the interests of those engaged in the production of specific fruit crops. The earliest and most important of these organizations appeared in the citrus-growing regions of Southern California in the mid-1880s, and, after a somewhat shaky start, several finally merged to become in 1893 the Southern California Fruit Exchange. With the expansion of citrus culture to other parts of the state, the organization soon changed its name, becoming in 1905 the California Fruit Growers' Exchange.[6] By 1910, J. W. Jeffrey, the state commissioner of horticulture, was telling those in attendance at the California Fruit Growers' Convention that such cooperative organizations were required in every branch of commercial agriculture in order "to centralize [its] demands and efforts" and "promote the general welfare of its business." If the state's agribusinessmen were going to succeed in the modern business world, Jeffrey argued, those groups producing California's major commercial crops

should each have a league or a protective committee of some kind authorized and supported for the purpose of handling every proposition that has a general bearing upon the prosperity of the business, and to whom all could look in times of danger, or in the promotion of any measure of benefit to the whole industry. I earnestly recommend that this convention take up this matter of trades representatives, and urge every industry to make provision for the handling of its difficulties through some plan that will bring its every element into harmonious and effective action in the promotion of all its trade interests, and in protection from its perils.[7]

The state's agribusinessmen apparently saw the merit in Commissioner Jeffrey's proposal. By 1920 growers' cooperatives were an established feature of virtually every branch of commercial agriculture in California.[8]

In the absence of any very formidable dissuasive factors, either social or economic, the industrialization of California agriculture and its attendant attitudinal transformation were largely accomplished by the beginning of the twentieth century. Family farms could, of course, be found in nearly every rural locality in the state, as could an ideological and emotional disposition toward farming that revealed that at least a residue of unreconstructed agrarianism had survived into the new age of agribusiness. Plainly, however, agrarian ideas had become anachronous in the leading agricultural districts of the state, and after 1900 family farming survived only as a marginal appendage of a rural economy dominated in fact and in spirit by agribusinessmen as single-minded in their pursuit of profits as the most unwavering urban capitalist. The California farmer, more than "all others of his class," noted one agribusinessman, "has grown farthest from the idea of merely trading the products of his land for the necessities of life." In contrast to the traditional American farmer, he continued, the "grower" in California had "chosen to enjoy the modern conveniences and diversions of life," and thus had accepted "the necessity of placing his business upon an industrial basis as firm and attractive as possible."[9]

That agriculture, which had emerged as California's leading industry by 1900, developed on so highly industrialized a basis was a fact of enormous influence in shaping the subsequent history of the state.[10] Few aspects of California's development in the twentieth century were unaffected by its distinctive pattern of agriculture, and no problem was more directly linked to the rise of industrial farming than that of agricultural labor relations. The special irony of this latter fact, of course, is that one of the blessings that was supposed to flow from the displacement of bonanza wheat farming by fruit and vegetable farming was the elimination of the farm-labor "problem" in California. And that irony is heightened by the fact that with the rapid mechanization of the state's large-scale wheat farms during the last quarter of the nineteenth century, most of the labor problems that agrarians had earlier condemned bonanza farmers for creating were disappearing as machines did more and more of the work that gangs of migrating laborers had performed previously. To the extent that California agriculture depended on a large, highly mobile wage labor force in the 1890s, it was the labor requirements of large-scale fruit and vegetable farming rather than those of bonanza wheat farming that perpetuated and increased that dependence.[11]

With the rapid growth of the commercial fruit and vegetable industry during the 1880s and early 1890s and the emergence of an agribusiness mentality consistent with its spirit and purpose, the nature of the long-standing debate over the character and status of agricultural labor in the state changed in fundamental ways. As long as the farm-labor question had been addressed as an adjunct of the larger controversy over large-scale wheat farming versus small-scale family farming, the answer was readily apparent. Within the leading agricultural circles in the state a clear consensus existed that virtually all farm-labor problems would be solved when small family farms that were largely self-sufficient in labor power displaced big farms that were not. As horticulture on a commercial scale began in the 1880s to demonstrate its handsome profitability, however, interest in solving farm-labor problems by eliminating the need for a dependent wage-labor force quickly waned. Thus at their annual meetings it became less common for agricultural spokesmen to repeat the conventional agrarian wisdom, which held that a permanent class of farmworkers had no rightful place in a genuinely healthy rural society, and more common for them to suggest the implementation of various reform measures that would moderate, if not eliminate, the most disagreeable and degrading aspects of employment in large-scale agriculture without disestablishing the class barrier that had earlier been erected between the state's farm employers and farmworkers. As one critic of past employment practices on California's big farms declared in 1887, the social consequences of large-scale agriculture would be rendered less onerous if employers improved working conditions enough to attract labor of a better quality. At the heart of the farm-labor problem, so this critique suggested, was the fact that "the farm laborers of California have not been treated as they are in older parts of the country. They are required to furnish blankets, and sleep in straw. They are fed in moving hotels, on wheels, under a burning sun. There are no home comforts afforded here to the farm laborer." It

followed that there would be an "observable . . . change in the character of the people who offer themselves for employment in rural pursuits" only after the conditions of labor in agriculture reflected an
understanding by employers that "every employment first attracts the
character of the people willing to engage in that employment. Make the
employment of men brutal, and you must depend upon a brutalized
class to fill the positions it offers, a class that will become more
embruted by the character of its treatment."[12]

Others, while agreeing that better working conditions would probably ease the situation, insisted that farm employers could not hope to
attract and retain labor of a desirable character until they alleviated the
problem of extreme seasonality. Using the example of Senator Leland
Stanford's vineyard of 3,900 acres, purportedly the "largest operation
of its kind known," William H. Mills noted in an address before the
1890 convention of the State Agricultural Society that while the
vineyard required 700 workers for a three-week period at the height of
the harvest season, it provided annual employment for only 70 workers. His extrapolation from those figures led him to conclude that
commercial vineyards throughout the state afforded annual employment to 3,500 workers, but demanded ten times that number for the
brief period of the harvest. The rationalization of the state's farm-labor
market, Mills argued, could be achieved only through greater diversification of California's agricultural industry.[13]

The rigid economics of large-scale commercial agriculture, however, discouraged farm employers from making those adjustments that
might have made farm employment attractive to a more stable class of
workers or eased the problem of seasonality. Among the prevailing
conditions of labor, low wages were probably the single most important factor in keeping workers of the character they desired out of the
state's fields and orchards. Yet, just as bonanza wheat farmers had
done a generation before, the operators of commercial fruit and vegetable farms clung tenaciously to the argument that because of the labor-
intensive character of their businesses and the fact that labor costs,
unlike transportation and other fixed costs, were the only large operating expense over which they exercised control, a higher wage structure
would pose an obvious and unacceptable threat to profits.[14] For what
agribusinessmen regarded as equally compelling economic reasons,
diversifying their farms as a means of reducing seasonality of employment was not a viable option. By the end of the 1880s, land devoted to
the intensive cultivation of such cash crops as oranges and hops was

45

valued at between \$300 and \$500 per acre. The same land devoted to diversified farming, said agribusiness spokesmen, would have much less than half that value per acre.[15]

Hugh M. LaRue, a leading proponent of industrialized agriculture in California, reminded those advocating crop diversification:

> In considering this question of diversified farming, we should not overlook the fact that the most profitable production of a soil and climate is that which is most aided by natural forces. The profits of any line of agriculture are ascertained only by the standard of the money value of its products. The question in its latest and best analysis, is how much value in dollars can be raised by devoting a certain number of acres to a given product.[16]

In short, LaRue was arguing that the state's farmers, like all businessmen, were obliged by the first principle of capitalism to use their productive means for the purpose of maximizing profits.

Despite their unwillingness to diversify or to abandon the low wage structure on which California's large-scale agriculture was founded, commercial fruit and vegetable growers were not unwilling to explore alternative means of ameliorating the worst social effects of the farm-labor system. For example, when a labor shortage threatened in the mid-1880s, most farm employers appear to have resisted the rather considerable temptation to push for a resumption of Chinese immigration, even though Chinese workers were widely regarded as the ideal source of cheap labor when economic criteria alone were considered.[17] Had depressed economic conditions in the cities of the state not sent waves of urban laborers into the countryside in search of work during much of the 1880s and 1890s, some farm employers might have been persuaded to look once again to the Orient. Most, however, appear to have concluded, without betraying visible signs of regret, that the era of cheap Chinese labor had come to an end. Just after Chinese immigration had been legally terminated, one agribusiness spokesman noted, in a peculiarly economical panegyric, that "it supplied a manual labor which could be obtained from no other source. Now that its increase has been arrested, we must accept the fact that as a labor element it is in the way of ultimate extinction."[18] It is likely that the editor of the *Pacific Rural Press* was expressing a sentiment shared by a majority of California's farm employers when he observed that while the cessation of Chinese immigration would "imply a new domestic policy for many of the farmers and fruit-raisers of this State," it "should not be viewed as a calamity." Summoning up an appropriate measure of optimism, he concluded: "It may be inconvenient at first, but after a few years no doubt the places now held by the Chinese will be filled by a more desirable laboring population."[19]

While a few farm employers were suggesting toward the end of the 1880s that Mexicans, southern blacks, or Japanese workers ought to be imported to augment the diminishing supply of Chinese laborers, most fruit and vegetable growers endorsed the verdict, originally pronounced by agrarian critics of bonanza farming, that things would not be right on California's farms until the labor power necessary to their operation was performed by white workers recruited from the ranks of European immigrants and native Americans "back East."[20]

Yet in espousing an idea that had long been at the core of the agrarian strategy for the social rehabilitation of California agriculture, farm employers were not forsaking the commercial values that were increasingly gaining their allegiance and shaping their behavior. The agrarians' central assumption had always been that white immigrants attracted to the state would bring not only their labor, but an invincible resolve to employ that labor on their own small-scale family farms. When farm employers began in the 1880s to adopt the view that white workers constituted the ultimate solution to their labor problems, they neither contemplated nor desired changes in the highly commercial structure of the state's agricultural industry or in the basic relationship between themselves and the dependent wage earners who labored for them. Unlike those who hoped that an influx of white labor would have a therapeutic effect on the state's deviant agriculture, the fruit and vegetable growers who were emerging as the primary employers of farmworkers in California wished only for a cheap and reliable labor force free of the social and racial characteristics they found offensive in the Chinese and tramp laborers on which commercial agriculture had previously relied.

Most farm employers, however, did recognize that if they were to achieve their goal, substantial modifications had to be made in the industry's labor system. Interestingly, the alternative system that gained the widest support among employers was, at least to the extent that it contained distinct elements of paternalism, similar to those being developed in the manufacturing sector by pioneering welfare capitalists. As outlined by Charles Wetmore, a leading vineyardist and critic of the bonanza farmers' labor policies, the new system was to end migrancy through the establishment by employers of communities of farmworkers and their families in close proximity to the large-scale farms that required their labor for a portion of each year. "The great defect" in the existing farm-labor system, Wetmore argued, was that it failed to encourage "well established village communities." Because farm employers had not endeavored "to secure a permanent population," they sought, at the expense of the social well-being of the state, to satisfy their labor needs by relying on "nomadic supplies." Too often, Wetmore wrote, the "proprietors of large estates have been content to herd their workmen as they would their cattle." Yet the new class of agribusinessmen had learned little from the unhappy experience of earlier bonanza farmers in their dealings with labor, according to Wetmore. "No provision has been made," he observed, "for the accommodation and convenient settlement of that class of people on which our fruit industries must depend for successful operation." "Within easy walking distance of surrounding vineyards and orchards," wrote Wetmore, "small villages for the accommodation of the laboring classes should have been established. All the conveniences for such useful citizens, suitable to their necessities and economies, should have been thought of in proper time." His investigations on behalf of the state's Board of Viticultural Commissioners, however, led him to conclude that "the farmer who erects suitable cottages for the accommodation of such people is the rare exception, and no associated effort to provide village accommodations has been inaugurated." Alluding to the difficulties that farm employers were likely to encounter as the Exclusion Act whittled away the supply of Chinese labor, Wetmore warned that there was "no time to lose in making proper arrangements for the reception of a more reliable class of working people."

While Wetmore did not hesitate to chastise farm employers for their failure to develop a viable labor system, neither was he reluctant to suggest a specific corrective. "Let me suggest the remedy," he wrote,

and trust to the good sense of all practical viticulturists and horticulturists to act in the matter. Let those who have some spare capital organize in each community companies for the encouragement of villages of working people. Purchase suitable tracts of the most fertile land, located centrally with reference to the district to be benefited; divide the same into lots of one acre or less; plant their borders with useful trees, according to the place, but especially the mulberry, if practicable; provide the means of obtaining water for irrigating garden vegetables, whether by ditches, steam power, or wells; erect cheap, comfortable cottages on a number of them at once, and keep a supply of such tenements always ready for occupants; offer to rent these lots at a low rate, sufficient to pay ordinary interests on the investment, with the privilege of purchase at a fair price after one or two years' occupation and approval of the industrious character of the tenants; grant long time, with low interest, to the purchasers, if desired by them; and let the agent of the company be active in securing employment for the tenants. Then notify the immigration agents, merchants, Consuls, and others in San Francisco, that you have homes ready for people to occupy in the center of communities where labor is required for at least six months in the year.

The farm employer who operated on an especially large scale should, Wetmore added, "prepare as soon as possible to build similar cottages on portions of his land suitable to the wants of simple-minded people—where they may practice household economies, raise their chickens, feed a pig, and cultivate vegetables." Once the farmworker villages were established, he warned, farm employers would be well advised to avoid being "so foolish as to incorporate . . . any misdirected notions of controlling the habits of these villagers beyond what the proper administration of law and the preservation of public peace require." Having undertaken such a program, Wetmore concluded, "we may honestly invite that class to come to us which we need; without it, we shall struggle for a long time with the labor problem."[21]

The need for a new labor system that incorporated features conducive to the permanent settlement of white farmworkers and their families in the leading agricultural districts of the state appears to have been readily acknowledged by most farm employers.[22] The plan formulated by Charles Wetmore, however, was not without its critics. The most outspoken opponent of the program was William Blackwood, an orchardist who had argued strenuously both before and after the passage of the Exclusion Act that large-scale agriculture in California could not survive on a profitable basis in the absence of an adequate supply of cheap Chinese labor. Any plan based on the belief that whites, whether from Europe or the eastern states, would agree to settle permanently on the employers' lands as a dependent peasantry was, Blackwood insisted, both misguided and potentially dangerous to the maintenance of large-scale commercial agriculture in the state. Beyond the costs associated with the plan, which he said would pose a threat to the employers' profits, Blackwood feared that the agrarians were correct in their long-held belief that if large numbers of white families settled in the state's farming regions, their latent desire to become independent freeholders would sooner or later manifest itself in the destruction of large-scale agriculture in California. Suggesting the scenario that this calamitous subversion was likely to follow, Blackwood wrote:

Those large vineyardists who now contemplate the cottage tenant plan will probably soon find, to their cost, that their tenants have discovered that they, instead of the vineyardists, are masters of the situation. Just when their services cannot possibly be dispensed with, a strike will be organized, and new and vexatious concessions will be demanded. To save his year's production, the vineyardist is compelled to concede. In law he has no redress; he cannot enforce a specific performance of their contract with him. Another year, other and still more onerous demands are made; till in the end he is ruined, and his cottage tenants have probably divided up his great vineyard among themselves.[23]

Whether Wetmore's farmworker settlement plan imperiled California's industrialized agriculture in the ways and to the extent that Blackwood feared remained an unresolved question because no serious effort was undertaken to implement it. The plan was born out of a common expectation among farm employers that the Chinese Exclusion Act would sharply reduce the supply of farm labor available to them. When the anticipated labor shortages failed to materialize, farm employers lacked the economic incentives to participate in the extraordinary recruitment program Wetmore envisioned. Throughout the 1880s and 1890s the number of Chinese farmworkers in California did steadily decline, but depressed economic conditions in the state's cities and towns during much of that period permitted farm employers to avail themselves of a large pool of unemployed urban laborers. The likelihood of a farm-labor shortage was further reduced by the entry of a growing number of Japanese immigrants into the agricultural work force from the late 1880s onward.[24]

Not until the turn of the century did renewed fears of a farm-labor shortage generate enough anxiety among employers that they were finally willing to launch a concerted drive to recruit families of white workers on a basis similar to that suggested by Charles Wetmore nearly two decades earlier. Fruit growers meeting in convention toward the end of 1900 responded to reports of a farm-labor shortage during the recently concluded harvest season by passing a resolution authorizing a special farm-labor committee "to devise ways and means" of augmenting the existing agricultural work force.[25] One speaker, Isidor Jacobs, reminded his fellow agribusinessmen that the need for a thoughtful plan to recruit a class of permanent white farmworkers had been recognized many years earlier, but noted that no useful efforts "in this direction" had been made. "Are we," he asked, "to persist in this inaction until the problem becomes so serious as to mean heavy loss to our fruit interests?" Farm employers would do well, Jacobs concluded, to develop a strategy to bring to their communities the "hundreds and thousands of men and women east of the Rockies who would be glad of the chance of living in this State, and who would make their living as well in California as they do in the East."[26]

The committee of five farm employers appointed to explore ways of solving a labor problem made increasingly acute by the revival of the state's urban economy and the continued expansion of labor-intensive agriculture lost little time in adopting Jacobs's suggestion. In its report to the convention a year later, the committee indicated that it had succeeded in persuading the Southern Pacific Railroad to "put into effect a colony rate for home-seekers," and claimed that "several thousand people" were attracted to the state as a result. The committee further reported that, in cooperation with San Francisco business interests, it had formed and provided a year's funding for an organization called the California Colony Association, whose purpose was to induce "bona fide colonists" to settle in California's major agricultural districts. Already, the committee asserted, the organization had located over eight hundred families in various parts of California, and had persuaded the railroad to extend its colony rate.[27]

Yet despite the successes the committee reported, fear of a severe shortage of farm labor quickly deepened to the point of exciting within agribusiness circles between 1902 and 1906 an extended and often acrimonious debate that concluded with the emergence of an agricultural labor policy from which the last vestiges of social purpose had finally been expunged. In its earliest stages the debate revealed sharp differences of opinion within the ranks of the state's largest farm employers over the question of whether a combination of social and economic criteria, or economic criteria alone, ought to shape and govern their labor policies. In its last stages the debate made plain the fact that, whatever social preferences they might express, farm employers in California were above all else businessmen. And as consumers of labor in an extremely labor-intensive industry, they found the seductive logic of cheap labor too alluring to resist.

The major impetus for the debate was provided by H. P. Stabler, a leading fruit grower from the upper Sacramento Valley, who delivered a paper at the Twenty-seventh Fruit-Growers' Convention, in December 1902, calling for an industry-wide effort to attract to California young white families in the principal agricultural states of the East. "Labor is the problem of the twentieth century," Stabler asserted in his opening remarks. "Labor is the greatest factor of expense in any industrial enterprise, and this is particularly true of the fruit business of

California." Largely as a result of the expansion of the fruit industry in the state, farm employers had not, Stabler noted, been able to find enough labor of acceptable quality to meet their needs. While he agreed that it was the availability of Chinese laborers that had made possible the development and growth of a large-scale horticultural industry in the state, he argued that it was no longer realistic for farm employers to advocate their continued employment, given the demonstrable antagonism toward the Chinese in California. "Whether or not Chinese exclusion has been a benefit to the horticultural interests of California is a mooted question among fruit-growers," he said. Conditions had to be met "as they exist," and "in casting about for an increased supply of labor . . . the Chinaman is not to be considered."

In making his case, however, Stabler went beyond simply suggesting the political difficulties associated with the employment of Chinese farmworkers. Speaking of both Chinese workers and the growing population of Japanese labor that was gaining a foothold in the agricultural work force, he acknowledged that while there were "some arguments to be advanced in favor of their employment," they were "not ideal as workers in our industry. Their lack of intelligence, their lack of interest in the welfare of our business, besides numerous other arguments, might be cited," Stabler said, "to prove that their employment is not essential to the best success of fruit growing."

What was essential to the ultimate prosperity and soundness of labor-intensive farming in the state, according to Stabler, was a wage-labor force composed of young white men and women born to an agricultural life. "It is an axiom of industry," he asserted, "that the best workers are born on the soil. . . . An intelligent, thrifty, energetic, steady, young white man who was raised on a farm can do more work than any laborer a fruit-grower can secure. . . . His familiarity with the ways of the country, with the methods of business, . . . and the important fact that he is acquainted with manual labor, make him the ideal employee in an orchard."

As to where such labor might be found, Stabler said, "A shortage in the home supply compels us to ask the farmer lads of the agricultural districts of the Eastern States to come to California to better their conditions by employment in our orchards and vineyards." In addition to the natural attractions that California possessed as a "new country with a mild climate," the main inducement to potential immigrants from the East ought to be the promise of advancement toward an ever brighter economic future in a growing industry. It would, Stabler told his colleagues be selfish of us to expect them to accept our offer of employment if the only inducement held out was the dollar a day and board usually paid orchard workers. The further fact that after two or three years spent in an orchard or vineyard will fit the earnest and energetic young men for places as foremen at better wages, eventually leading to positions as superintendents and managers, at salaries equal to men in similar capacities in commercial houses, will induce many of them to come to California.

The strategy that Stabler proposed differed from those suggested by earlier advocates of white farm labor more in scope and detail than in character. While his predecessors had tended to focus their concerns on a single region or crop, Stabler proposed a comprehensive effort that would encompass the needs and interests of the entire agribusiness community in California. "The best prospect at hand of relieving the present stress of the labor supply," he advised, "is an organized effort to induce a large immigration of young men from the agricultural districts of the Eastern States." "I am persuaded that a united effort on our part would result in a large immigration of a desirable class of settlers" who, Stabler declared, would jump at the chance "to make 'Westward Ho!' their watchword."

I would ask this convention, through its Chairman, to appoint a committee of fifteen, representing the various fruit districts of the State, to adopt such measures as will induce a sufficient supply of workers to come to the Coast in time for the next harvest. By working in conjunction with the Transportation Companies, State Board of Trade, the California Promotion Committee, the Sacramento Valley Development Association, the San Joaquin Commercial Association, the Coast Counties Association, canners, packers, hop-growers, dairymen and other bodies, much may be accomplished to relieve the labor situation before next season.[28]

Although Stabler assured his listeners that his scheme was "feasible," many farm employers considered unrealistic any plan that sought to introduce social considerations into the making of farm-labor policy; the objective conditions of industrialized agriculture, they believed, dictated that economic factors alone should govern the employers' course of action regarding labor. In response to the Stabler plan, A. N. Judd, a leading fruit grower from Watsonville, declared, "We are confronting a condition, not a theory. The condition is this: We have degraded a certain class of labor, and there is not a man who lives in any agricultural locality who wants to get in and do this work." The time had come when farm employers needed to "bury any previous prejudices" and discuss their common labor problems realistically. Because of the working and living conditions that necessarily prevailed in their industry, Judd told his colleagues, white workers of the type that the Stabler plan might attract would surely strive to escape the degraded conditions confronting farm labor in California at the earliest opportunity. Low wages, disagreeable living conditions, and seasonal employment that kept most farm laborers moving from crop to crop in search of work opportunities were hard and immutable facts of the state's agribusiness economy, whether or not employers wished it so. Given those realities, Judd insisted, the only sensible course was to abandon the delusion that white farm labor could be lured to California and concentrate on finding workers whose expectations were commensurate with the very limited benefits that employment in large-scale agriculture conferred. Past experience, Judd observed, taught that only Chinese laborers were suitable for the state's agricultural industry. Reading from a memorial to the United States Congress that the Pajaro Valley Fruit-Growers' Association of Watsonville hoped to have the convention endorse, Judd declared: "We have learned by long experience that the Chinaman gives satisfaction as a common laborer in the business where his services are most needed. He is industrious, patient, docile, and generally reliable." If California farm employers were to succeed in finding labor adapted to their "peculiar wants," Judd concluded, Congress would have to act as the memorial implored, and amend the Exclusion Act "to admit a sufficient number of common laborers from China to supply our urgent and pressing necessities in that regard."

In the discussion that followed Judd's remarks, most speakers rejected his arguments and endorsed the Stabler plan. Beyond their commonly expressed belief that any attempt to amend the Exclusion Act would meet with certain defeat, given the overwhelming public sentiment against such a course, those who joined the debate tended to concur in Stabler's central contention that the labor question in California could be satisfactorily and definitively answered only through the employment of white workers drawn from farming regions in the East. And when one of the plan's supporters proposed its adoption by the convention, his motion carried easily by a voice vote.[29]

Acceptance of the Stabler plan did not, however, silence employers who favored renewed Chinese immigration. Raisin growers from the Fresno area, in particular, argued strenuously that Chinese labor was indispensable to their industry because neither white nor Japanese farmworkers had proved to be satisfactory. Whites, they insisted, were simply not willing to do the work required under prevailing conditions, and the Japanese were too ambitious to be their own masters and too willing to strike for higher wages at harvesttime to be suitable employees. The Fresno contingent offered a resolution stating that it was "the sentiment of the fruit-growers of California that the Chinese Exclusion Act should be so amended as to admit farm laborers in restricted numbers," but it was tabled without discussion because of "the lateness of the hour."[30]

Not until the final day of the convention, and after a considerable amount of behind-the-scenes maneuvering had apparently taken place, was action finally taken on the resolution in favor of renewed Chinese immigration. By a vote of 33 to 20 the convention approved a recommendation by its resolutions committee that the Congress be asked to amend the Exclusion Act in order that a "restricted" number of Chinese farmworkers might be admitted into the country. For the proponents of Chinese labor this "victory" was obviously a hollow one. It is likely that the resolution's ultimate passage was no more than a conciliatory gesture by supporters of the Stabler plan, who understood not only that they had carried the day insofar as the development of a new labor policy was concerned, but also that any entreaty to Congress on behalf of so unpopular a cause was certain to receive an unsympathetic response.[31]

The fifteen-member committee authorized by the convention to develop a plan of action that would result in the attraction of thousands of white farm families into the state's agricultural regions acted immediately to discharge its responsibility. Directed by H. P. Stabler, to whom the chairmanship had quite naturally fallen, the committee was absorbed in planning its campaign within less than a week following the convention's adjournment. Calling itself the California Employment Committee, and backed by funds contributed by farm employers and the San Francisco–based California Promotion Committee, the Stabler committee began in early February 1903 to send into "the thickly populated agricultural districts in the East," and in time even to Europe, the first of several groups of carefully chosen farm employers charged with the task of "delivering stereopticon lectures and distributing a vast amount of literature of a character intended to induce young farmers and others to come to California to reside." A preliminary report on the committee's activities presented to fruit growers meeting in Los Angeles only three months later indicated that emissaries of agribusiness interests in California had made attractive overtures to potential immigrants in virtually every state east of the Rockies. Having done its part, the committee concluded, it was now time for farm employers in the state to come forward with guarantees of "work and comfortable living accommodations" to the "hundreds of young men and families" who were likely to accept the general offers of employment being so liberally extended by its envoys. One supporter of the committee's work noted that a "very important feature" of the report was its emphasis on the need to offer prospective farmworkers more than wages alone. "If we are going to invite farm labor to come from the East to our shores," he warned, "we require more than employment to make those who come want to stay here."[32]

The disquieting belief that wages alone would not be sufficient to attract and retain labor of the desired character was confirmed during the 1903 harvest season. When H. P. Stabler reported the campaign's progress to the Twenty-ninth Fruit-Growers' Convention in early December he was forced to admit that only 917 easterners had actually been placed in jobs during the harvest season, and that many of them had since returned home. Since farm employers and canneries had listed more than 9,000 harvest-season job openings with the California Employment Committee, the campaign's relative inefficacy was plainly evident. Yet while those who had doubted the plan's practicability from the beginning undoubtedly felt vindicated, the Stabler committee's ready inference was that employers had simply not sweetened their offers enough or in the right ways to make employment in California's agricultural industry worth enduring the hardships that a cross-country move posed for most immigrants. After analyzing the early results of the campaign, Stabler said, his committee had determined that farm employers would have to offer "special inducements" to prospective immigrants if greater progress was to be realized. And, he hastened to add, his committee and the California Promotion Committee had "evolved a plan" that, in addition to being "thoroughly practicable," provided just that extra something needed to "almost entirely solve the problem of help in the harvest season." The essential feature of the new plan was an arrangement whereby farm employers would agree to lease or sell "on easy terms five, ten, and fifteen-acre pieces of land to men with families who will agree to assist the fruit-grower and farmer in his harvest, while acquiring homes of their own." Such a provision was, Stabler concluded, just the "special inducement" required to guarantee ultimate success, since

the original plan of our committee, which contemplated securing young men from the agricultural districts of the Eastern States to assist fruit-growers in their operations, could only at best be a temporary solution to the help problem. The young men thus obtained would in all likelihood drift to various parts of the State and would not become permanent residents of any one district.

The plan of securing men with families and locating them in homes of their own is a far better solution of the help problem than any other plan that has been submitted to our committee. In some districts of the state this feature is not entirely novel, as it has been tried in a small way and has proven satisfactory both to the growers and to the homeseekers.[33]

The Stabler committee apparently saw in this new plan of recruitment the clear outlines of a panacea. Few farm employers, however, shared that vision. So slight was the employers' response to the committee's proposal during the 1904 harvest season that its report at year's end betrayed a distinctly recriminatory tone. "In order to attract a better class of young men and families from the East," the report stated, "this committee desires to insist that the fruit-growers and farmers of California must arrange for caring for these newcomers in a manner better than the conditions now existing on many of the farms, orchards, and vineyards of California." Reiterating the sanguine argument it had made a year earlier, the committee wrote:

We feel that our troubles in securing efficient help will be largely overcome when we have in proximity to the orchards, vineyards, and farms a permanent class of settlers, rather than the transient help on which we now depend for carrying on so much of our work. In fact, we have discovered that very many farmers in the East are anxious to come to California when they can be assured of securing small tracts, and developing them, securing employment in bearing orchards and vineyards in the vicinity.[34]

The committee was, the report concluded, irrevocably "devoted to bringing into our State families of agricultural workers who desire permanent homes." Its increasingly plaintive appeal to farm employers was that they demonstrate in concrete ways an equally passionate devotion to the same ideal.

The leaders of California's rural society willingly embraced the social ideal that the eastern recruitment plan was designed to promote. As businessmen and employers, however, they were simply unable to find economic reasons sufficiently compelling to justify the extraordinary measures that the committee had urged upon them. They apparently had less difficulty seeing as good business sense, however disagreeable it may have been on other grounds, the advisability of continuing their reliance on workers whose chronic powerlessness, whether it was a function of minority racial status or pronounced socioeconomic alienation, tended to foster a debilitating occupational inertia that had long redounded to the economic advantage of employers in industrialized agriculture.

Plainly, at that moment when rhetoric was no longer a viable substitute for action, most farm employers in California indicated a strong disinclination to abandon familiar labor practices in favor of a new policy that necessitated real economic risks but promised only theoretical, and highly ambiguous, social benefits. The plan of action urged on employers by the Stabler committee ultimately provided for such a test of their values, and at the 1906 fruit growers' convention they made their choice.

When the labor question came up at the 1906 convention it was not, as it had been in the recent past, because of the California Employment Committee's need to report its progress. Instead, it came up because the committee's opponents felt the time had come for a showdown. Early in the convention, opponents of the eastern recruitment program offered a resolution calling on the Congress to amend the Exclusion Act to permit Chinese labor again to enter the country. When one member objected that the resolution was out of order, its proponents moved to suspend the convention rules and proceed with a discussion and vote. Opponents of the resolution, believing that it ought to be referred to the proper committee, again objected, declaring that the question involved was too momentous and controversial to be dealt with in so precipitate a manner. As one member argued: "If there is any resolution that should be referred to the Committee on Resolutions that is the one."[35] Convinced that they would prevail when the resolution was finally voted upon, and hopeful that such a gesture might placate some of their opponents, the resolution's sponsors ultimately agreed to pursue their goal through the convention's normal procedures.

While the proponents of renewed Chinese immigration had accurately gauged their voting edge, they did not succeed in escaping a bitter debate on their way to ultimate victory. When the Committee on Resolutions emerged from its deliberations it placed two reports before the convention, one endorsed by a solid majority of its members calling for the resolution's adoption, the other backed by a small but vocal minority still loyal to the ideal of a farm-labor force composed of white families permanently settled in close proximity to the large-scale farms that employed them. In addition to the crudely chauvinistic arguments on which opponents of Chinese immigration had traditionally relied, the authors of the minority report insisted that the Chinese Exclusion Act was "an expression of the will of the nation," and that lifting the barrier it imposed would not only "lower the standard of living [of] American labor," but also mean that those "families that now camp in our orchards and vineyards to earn wages with [the] view of buying homes of their own will be driven from the fields in despair." The plain-spoken but evidently persuasive counterargument advanced by advocates of the majority report was that large-scale commercial agriculture in California simply could not be sustained on a profitable basis in the absence of a reliable labor force suited to its "peculiar wants." After a brief, acrimonious exchange between the contending factions, the chairman of the convention cut off the debate and called for a vote. It was, he declared, "useless to discuss this question" because "every man has made up his mind." In the vote that followed, 43 employers endorsed the majority report's call for a resumption of Chinese immigration, while 26 voted to leave the Exclusion Act unamended and, presumably, to persist in the effort to recruit white farmworkers from the East.[36]

While the vote revealed that farm employers remained deeply divided, it was nonetheless definitive, for it not only marked an end to the debate that had raged since 1902, but also effectively ended a much more protracted and far-reaching controversy regarding the proper relationship between farm labor and the land that had occupied those involved in developing and directing the state's agriculture for more than half a century.[37] J. W. Jeffrey, the state commissioner of horticulture, was not unmindful of the central place that the "labor question" had long occupied in the deliberations of California's agricultural leadership when he endeavored in 1909 to review the history of farming in the state since the mid-nineteenth century. "The farm-labor problem," he noted, had been "one of the most exasperating" confronting the state's farmers over the years, and it was "with great reluctance" that he sought to make sense of the "tangle of social, political, industrial and racial elements" that combined to make it so formidable. Suggesting a particularly apt simile, Jeffrey described the farm labor problem as being

> like the rainbow colors revolving upon a disk. You can make the color white, or any shade into black, or every color its own, by the way you turn the circular plate. I am not sure that this comparison is good, for there are many growers here who have been trying for years to make the labor

question show white, and are convinced that it will require a different revolution from any that has been tried to make it show up in anything but somber hue. But to me the lights and shadows of this issue are sufficiently bewildering even if we could bring it down to the economics of the farm alone. And when the farm-help question is carried into sand-lot discussion, into argument sociological, ethnological, and everything but simply logical, a Philadelphia lawyer could not untangle the skein.[38]

Yet as difficult and enduring as the farm-labor problem had been, Jeffrey felt that one important truth had emerged from farmers' efforts to resolve it: that "one can not be sure of anything at this time upon the vexatious question of farm labor, except that it must be finally worked out upon economic lines." His reconstruction of the main lines of development in the state's farming industry revealed clearly his own belief that the structure and character of California agriculture was determined by inexorable economic forces over which the individual farmer exercised no control. This economic determinism was distinctly implied in Jeffrey's argument:

Fruit growing has not been a growth in California altogether if we consider the building up of correlative enterprises along with it in the rural districts, such as manufacturing, mercantile, and other subsidiaries. On the contrary, fruit production has become, in many lines, an accretion of large enterprises but little dependent upon each other in husbandry and dependent upon labor in large quantities but a portion of the time. If horticulture had been a steady, slow development, as was agriculture east of the Mississippi, we would have been far behind our present achievement, but there would be no labor problem.

"If," he concluded,

in looking down closely into this industry, we find that it could not have been developed in any other way, and that it must be continued along the lines of large individual holdings, instead of being cut up into multitudes of very small farms dependent less and less upon hired help—if large capital is to be essential to our continued progress in fruit production, then we must look to the cheapest and most effective peripatetic labor that can be procured.[39]

As a self-avowed "progressive" in an industry that he pridefully claimed was becoming infused with an abiding progressive spirit, Jeffrey believed he was on solid ground in asserting that a rational farm-labor policy would emerge only when empiricism rather than emotion guided the state's agricultural employers in their actions, and when economic efficiency rather than social accommodation was their transcending ambition.[40]

Though they might have stated it differently, the vast majority of farm employers in California had by 1910 come to agree with Commissioner Jeffrey's matter-of-fact declaration that the only appropriate labor policy was one that was compatible with the economic imperatives of industrialized agriculture. What this newly arrived-at consensus meant in practical terms was that farm employers in the state had accepted as incontrovertible truth the belief that industrialized agriculture could not nourish and perpetuate itself without a captive peasantry to supply the immense labor power it consumed. Since they readily acknowledged that a peasantry in the Old World mold was intolerable in a democratic society, most farm employers in California opted for its practical equivalent: a labor force whose economic immobility was a function less of bald politico-legal inhibitions than of de facto social disaffection and racial discrimination. Thus the special benefit that derived from a farm-labor policy that capitalized on the powerlessness of socially marginal groups was that is afforded farm employers nearly exclusive access to a large force of workers whose common occupational torpor was maintained without resort to coercive schemes that would have directly affronted America's democratic sensibilities.

Yet if such a labor system did not violate the letter of America's democratic covenant, there were those with agrarian credentials who believed that it plainly did violence to its spirit. At almost precisely the same time that California's agribusiness community was forging the consensus that would govern labor relations in the state's industrialized agriculture for the next half century, the Country Life Commission, which was appointed by President Theodore Roosevelt to inquire into the character and quality of farm life in the United States, was concluding, among other things, that only where agriculture was organized on a basis that permitted and even encouraged the steady advancement of hired farm labor to higher levels of economic independence were the interests of democracy being served. Of particular importance, the commission argued, was the need for an agricultural labor policy whose effect would be to strengthen the individual farmworker's attachment to the land. "The best labor," its report insisted, "is resident labor." Where agriculture was being practiced in ways that discouraged the integration of farm laborers into the social fabric, "it is certain that farming must be so modified and organized as to meet the labor problem at least half way." More specifically, the commission concluded,

"Such reorganization of agriculture must take place as will tend more and more to employ the [farm laborer] the year round and tie him to the land. The employer bears a distinct responsibility to the laborer, and also to society, to house him well and to help him to contribute his part to the community welfare."[41]

Not surprisingly, the contrast between a farm-labor policy of the type that the Country Life Commission found consistent with American values and the labor system that agribusinessmen in California had resolved to employ was so extreme as to provoke a considerable volume of comment. Surely among the best-informed commentators was William Beard, a member of the Country Life Commission whose special familiarity with the complexion and operation of industrialized agriculture in California derived in part from his close personal observation of it in action in the Sacramento Valley, a center of large-scale farming where he had lived for many years. Rather than directing his criticisms just toward the labor practices associated with industrialized agriculture in the state, Beard focused on what he believed was the pernicious orientation that farming on a large scale had spawned, especially the tendency among agribusinessmen to become so preoccupied with economic considerations that their interest in the social implications of their common employment practices withered to the point of cynical indifference. Many residents of the California countryside, he noted in an address before the State Agricultural Society, "wonder what this country life movement is all about." Rural people felt this uncertainty, he suggested, because "they know the farmers are prosperous, more prosperous than ever before, and fail to see where anything is particularly wrong when farmers are making money faster than ever before in the history of farming in this country." Yet as accurate as this perception of the California farmer's economic condition might be, Beard declared, it entirely missed the point because "prosperity is not the answer to the country life problem." "On the contrary," he insisted, prosperity was "often the largest factor in the development of the very conditions of which complaint is made." That agriculture in California was and would continue to be highly profitable, he said, was "certain." Yet, he warned: "We must not be content . . . with assurance of prosperity merely. The problems of country life must not be confounded with economic problems. The country life problem is of educational, social and other advantages, of suitable environment, of ideals; the economic problems are of dollars and cents." A "degree of prosperity," he agreed, was "essential to the development of a satisfying life in either the city or the country," but "prosperity alone is often a bar to the development of the best country life." Success in agriculture was not, Beard insisted, measured "from the standpoint of the welfare of the farmer only," but also in terms of the value of the farmer's "contribution to the welfare of the nation at large." Repeating a quintessential tenet of agrarianism that a majority of the state's farmers had themselves endorsed a generation earlier, Beard stated, "A home owning population on the land is and must be the real foundation of the greatness of this republic." And in a pointed reference to industrialized agriculture's growing dependence on nonwhite farm labor, he added that it was "essential" that this farming population remain "distinctly American."[42]

The deficiencies in rural life which William Beard observed in California resulted in large part from the failure of social objectives whose merit was widely acknowledged in agricultural communities to achieve practical adherence when they conflicted with even more alluring economic potentialities. Indeed, the conundrum facing California agriculturalists from the mid-nineteenth century onward was how to pursue farming enterprises on the most profitable bases possible without doing irreparable harm to the texture and morale of the state's rural society. That most farm employers in California genuinely wanted to achieve such an equilibrium is revealed in the time and effort they spent searching for ways and means to displace, reform, or otherwise rehabilitate a farm-labor system that they had long regarded as socially dysfunctional. In light of this long-standing concern, the decision that most agribusinessmen had arrived at by 1906, in favor of abandoning further efforts to forge a socially viable labor policy, necessitated the formulation of a compelling new rationale. And since the labor system to which they had resigned themselves directly contradicted the ideal they had proclaimed only a few years before, farm employers felt an especial need to come up with a self-satisfying explanation of the dissonance that such critics as William Beard were quick to point out. Farm employers gained the relief they sought, and escaped whatever moral discomfort their seeming exploitation of marginal people may have caused them, by embracing and assiduously cultivating the same racial and social myths that bonanza farmers in the state had indulged fifty years earlier—myths that made their labor policy appear to comport with the natural order of things. Hence, Chinese workers (and the Mexican, Filipino, and other nonwhite laborers who would succeed them in the state's fields and orchards) were, employers insisted, naturally suited to agricultural work by reason of their relatively small physical stature, ability to tolerate hot weather, native stoicism, and innate lack of ambition.[43] The group of mainly footloose, single white males who supplied a substantial portion of the labor on which industrialized agriculture relied were, employers believed, likewise consigned to the farm work force by a mechanism of natural selection. The growing conviction among farm employers that white laborers of a decent character simply would not stoop, either literally or figuratively, to work for wages in large-scale agriculture persuaded them that those whites who did end up in the migratory labor stream were fit for nothing better. "The unhappy occupants" of this "poor white caste," as Sidney Coryn, San Francisco newspaperman, described them,[44] were destined to endure the degradation of seasonal agricultural employment because, employers concluded, their collective social degeneracy forestalled their economic elevation to legitimate "white men's work."[45]

If the argument that farm employers advanced to justify their reliance on socially marginal workers failed to disarm critics, it succeeded in equipping agribusinessmen with a socioeconomic exegesis around which they could close ranks and from which they could derive increasing comfort, as what began as self-serving rationalization quickly metamorphosed into rigid orthodoxy. The orientation toward labor that governed the thinking of California's agribusinessmen by the era of World War I was the antithesis of the view that their agrarian antecedents had espoused in the course of damning the socially bankrupt labor practices of bonanza wheat farmers. Above all, the agrarians had emphasized, employment in agriculture should neither deprive the farmworker of his individuality and personal dignity nor consign him to a permanent subclass outside the mainstream of rural society. Yet as industrialized agriculture in the state matured, it fixed the relationship between farm employer and farm laborer so that precisely those circumstances obtained. By the twentieth century, employment in California's large-scale agriculture had come to mean irregular work, constant movement, low wages, squalid working and living conditions, social isolation, emotional deprivation, and individual powerlessness so profound as to make occupational advancement a virtual impossibility. To the typical large-scale farm employer in California, seasonal farm laborers had become faceless, nameless units of production. They were pairs of hands, indispensable to the success and profitability of the employer's business but with no greater affinity for the land than the urban factory operative had for his work station.[46]

Like every other aspect of his business, the farm employer's labor policies were at once a testimony to his desire for modernity and evidence of his belief that the only agricultural traditions deserving of his allegiance were those able to meet the test of the balance sheet. Only in his public rhetoric did vestiges of agrarianism survive, and even that became a reflection of the employer's modern business sense. Aware of the important role that public opinion played in shaping a political environment conducive to the advancement and protection of his economic interests, the agribusinessman was never hesitant to employ the sacrosanct vocabulary of Jefferson or to affect the deameanor of the beleaguered yeoman if it was politically cost-effective to do so. Thus in 1910, when California's farm employers demanded the passage of an alien land law that would reverse the movement of growing numbers of Japanese immigrants up the agricultural ladder, from the position of dependent farmworker to that of independent farm owner, they did so in the name of selfless agrarianism. "The occupancy of the land of this State by citizens who are freeholders and homebuilders is," they proclaimed, "the ideal condition of rural life, and greatly to be desired." This desire could hardly be realized, they declared, with the "land and its products . . . coming into possession of alien persons, incapable of citizenship and incapable of assimilation."[47]

When combined with the diligent lobbying methods that California agribusinessmen, like organized businessmen everywhere, were practicing with growing sophistication as the twentieth century progressed, the agrarian posturing they were able to affect with such plausibility made them an especially formidable political force in both state and national affairs.[48] And given their determination to have cheap foreign labor, farm employers became ever more mindful of the need to maintain their political influence at the highest level possible if they were to succeed in promoting federal immigration policies that afforded them access to farm labor of the desired character. Yet even when they struck their most earnest agrarian pose and practiced their most astute political manipulations, success was not, of course, certain. For example, as ardently as they pressed for a resumption of Chinese immigration between 1906 and the end of World War I, farm employers failed to make even modest headway in their drive to breach the Exclusion Act. When they brought their political influence to bear on behalf of more realistic goals, however, agribusinessmen found the federal government willing to favor them as it did no other class of employers.

After relying mainly on white transients, a nearly constant supply of jobless urbanites, and a shrinking pool of Chinese and Japanese workers from early in the century until the 1917 harvest season, farm employers, anticipating severe labor shortages as the wartime manpower drain increased, warned that agriculture could make its vital contribution to the war effort only if its special labor needs were met. The clear preference of agribusinessmen in 1917, as in the preceding ten years, was for changes in federal immigration laws that would permit the importation of Chinese farm labor. Many of those who participated in the labor discussions that dominated the Fiftieth Fruit-Growers' Convention hoped that the wartime emergency might arm them with just the sort of extraordinary leverage they needed to overcome decades of uncompromising popular opposition to a resumption of Chinese immigration. Other delegates, convinced that even the special pressures generated by the war were not enough to mitigate anti-Chinese feeling, argued that political realism dictated the importation, not of Chinese, but of West Indian, Puerto Rican, or Mexican farm labor. In response to the special pleadings of large-scale cotton and sugar-beet interests in the Southwest, the federal government had agreed just after the country entered the war to ease restrictions on the importation of agricultural workers from Mexico. Believing that still more generous concessions might be won, a group of delegates favoring the importation of Mexican labor argued that the state's agribusinessmen should not paint themselves into a corner by their uncompromising insistence on renewed Chinese immigration. And while some employers complained that Mexican workers were less efficient and docile than the Chinese, the convention finally voted, with obvious reluctance, to ask the government "to permit the introduction of sufficient Chinese or other farm labor" to meet the wartime needs of California agriculture.[49]

In resigning themselves to the fact that Chinese labor was finally and irreclaimably beyond their reach, farm employers in California displayed a curiously high degree of anxiety. They had been denied access to new supplies of Chinese workers for more than thirty years, and the very small number still to be found in the farm labor force in 1917 hardly constituted an indispensable resource. What appears to have generated the employers' disquietude was a somewhat vague but nonetheless deep-seated fear of separation from an abstract ideal rather than an actual resource. No class of labor had come closer to meeting the industry's definition of ideal farmworkers than had the Chinese. Chinese workers had long been, in fact, the standard against which all other farm laborers were measured. And though employers had for many years seriously contemplated a redefinition of their ideal, by 1906 the old economic definition had reemerged as the only one they considered workable, and thus no other farmworkers measured up to the Chinese.

The preference of farm employers for Chinese workers was rooted not in any particular knowledge or appreciation of the Chinese culture or national ethos, but in their awareness of the extent to which powerful social and political forces historically combined in California to render the Chinese economically and occupationally powerless. In effect, the attachment of farm employers was not to a distinct national group but to those characteristics of powerlessness that the Chinese revealed in a greater degree than had any other group of farmworkers with whom agribusinessmen were familiar. And with an equally myopic focus on what was essential to them, farm employers expressed a lack of enthusiasm for Mexican labor in 1917 not because they felt any particular disdain for Mexicans as an ethnic group, but because they feared that as farmworkers Mexicans might not be vulnerable in an equal degree to that aggregation of social and other forces that had tended to guarantee the powerlessness of Chinese laborers.

In a relatively short time, however, those doubts were dispelled. As agribusinessmen took increasing advantage of the federal government's liberalized immigration policy toward Mexico, and of the heavy flow of illegal immigration across a notoriously porous border, their early diffidence gave way to a marked enthusiasm for Mexican farmworkers.[50] By the mid-1920s Mexicans not only had become mainstays of the agricultural labor force, but had displaced the Chinese in the employers' conception of ideal farmworkers. This change in attitude derived from two simple facts: Mexicans were available in abundant supply, and employers soon realized that social, political, and economic forces combined to render Mexican farmworkers as powerless as they had the Chinese a generation before.[51]

When the California Department of Agriculture analyzed the composition of the state's farm-labor force in 1928, it discovered that while industrialized farming continued to employ laborers from a wide variety of racial, ethnic, and national groups, Mexican workers were unrivaled both in numbers and in the degree to which they fulfilled the fundamental desires of farm employers. In response to investigators' questions, employers expressed an overwhelming preference for Mexican workers, whom they described as available, tractable, and cheap.[52] In the end, what employers saw in Mexican farmworkers were the telltale signs of powerlessness, and they were at once satisfied and relieved. Moreover, they were now persuaded that large-scale agriculture in California could not survive without Mexican labor, and they resolved to use their political power and influence to ensure that it remained available to them. And despite active repatriation programs and the federal government's adoption of administrative policies to stanch the flow of legal immigrants from Mexico, farm employers were able to avail themselves of a large pool of Mexican labor that was continually supplemented by illegal immigrants, who moved across the border with relative ease even when restrictionist pressures were being applied with the greatest intensity.[53]

On the eve of the 1930s industrialized agriculture in California had arrived at a stage of structural maturity and economic vitality that was unmatched in any other farming region of the country.[54] Consistent with its industrial character, large-scale commercial farming in the state shared in the relative prosperity that the nation's urban economy experienced in the 1920s rather than in the decline and demoralization that plagued the country's agricultural sector throughout the decade. And agribusinessmen were not at all reluctant to attribute a very considerable measure of their industry's success to the fact that they had developed labor policies that gave them absolute control over wages, hours, and most other conditions of employment.

Yet as robust as the economy of industrialized agriculture had been in the 1920s, the calamitous nosedive that the national economy took at the end of the decade sent California's large-scale farming industry plummeting toward a depression more enervating and destructive than any it had previously known. Like most industries, agribusiness entered a period of severe retrenchment. And because farm employers exercised more control over labor costs than any others, they sought for the most part to carry out the cost cutting necessitated by rapidly faltering economic conditions largely at the expense of their wage-labor force. It was at just such a time of economic crisis that the advantages that derived from the employers' strategy of amassing a powerless labor force ought to have yielded its greatest benefits. Thus it is all the more surprising that when California's disadvantaged farm-workers were confronted by employers bent on imposing still more oppressive working conditions, they responded not with the docility and weakness for which they had long been prized, but with an angry militancy that would plunge the state into a decade of labor conflict more turbulent and savage than the American countryside had ever experienced.

For California's farm employers, the bitter irony of the 1930s was that the ferocity that attended labor relations in agriculture until the eve of World War II was a direct product of their laborious efforts to create a farmworker population whose most enduring and praiseworthy characteristic was its powerlessness. Had employers been willing or able to contemplate a less one-sided power relationship with labor when pressures for such a realignment began to mount at the beginning of the decade, they might well have spared themselves and much of the state's rural population the worst effects of the conflict that later engulfed industrialized agriculture. Yet farm employers had locked themselves into a labor-relations policy that could tolerate neither flexibility nor compromise, and so virtually guaranteed that when workers demanded a role in determining wages and working conditions, they would respond with almost total intransigence.

That farm employers in the state would adopt a siege mentality in response to such pressures for change was predictable given their open disregard for labor as their campaign to ensure a powerless work force came to apparent fruition. And the resultant unilateral labor policies, reinforced by discontinuity of employment and strong racial and social prejudices, produced worker-employer relations that were callously impersonal. So far had farming in California moved from the agrarian concept of the honorable and coequal farm hand that George P. Clements, director of the agricultural department of the Los Angeles Chamber of Commerce and one of the industry's most respected authorities on farm labor, could declare in 1926, "The old fashioned hired man is a thing of the past. He has left the farm. There is no place for him, and the farmer, who does not wake up to the realization that there is a caste in labor on the farm, is sharing too much of his dollar with labor."[55] The individual farmworker so viewed was more a commodity than a human being; more an expendable cog than a productive partner. Thus to permit the farm laborer to have a say in fixing the terms under which he worked not only contradicted the logic of the employers's perception of their relationship, but threatened to undermine the economic foundation on which industrialized agriculture was erected. Farm employers had convinced themselves, much as their counterparts in the nation's mass-production industries had done, that their labor policies were dictated by economic forces that were inherently rational, if not always humane in their effects. When farmworkers rebelled against the system in the 1930s, employers tended to regard their rebellion as an irrational assault against the natural order. To give in to workers' demands, to permit labor costs to be influenced by what amounted, in the employer's mind, to incoherent political factors, was to court economic disaster. In explaining the agribusinessman's inability to accommodate his workers' desire for a voice in the determination of wages and conditions, Charles Teague, a citrus grower and prominent spokesman for industrialized agriculture, commented, "He cannot change his way of doing business without going out of business altogether."[56] With this powerful sense of economic vulnerability influencing their attitude toward change, agribusinessmen tended to see in the demands of their workers not just a challenge to the prerogatives of the employer, but a threat to the survival of their industry. Resisting labor's demands thus became much more than a matter of simply preserving the status quo. It became, in effect, an unconditional struggle for economic self-preservation, with abject ruin awaiting those who lacked the will to persevere, and thus to survive.

3

Organization and Reform:
The Progressive Era

Whatever the differences of race, national origin, language, and psychology that existed among farmworkers in California from 1870 to 1930, working for wages in industrialized agriculture normally conferred membership in an unhappy fraternity whose cohering force was a kinship of powerlessness. Except for the relatively small number of hired men who were permanently employed on the state's large farms, a worker's presence in the migratory farm-labor force could usually be regarded as conclusive evidence of his powerlessness to escape what was commonly acknowledged to be the most disadvantaged and degraded occupational status in California.

The barriers that were interposed between agricultural workers and their advancement to better jobs varied with the categories into which they fell. The overriding explanation of the captive occupational status of nonwhite farmworkers lay in the fact that they were distinct racial minorities in a society that simply would not tolerate their free and equal participation in the economic life of the state. Though white workers in the agricultural wage-labor force were exempted from the singular abuses visited on their nonwhite counterparts, the episodic depressions that plagued the state's urban economy or their own emotional or social incapacity rendered them equally powerless to overcome the obstacles before them and to find secure places for themselves in the economic mainstream. In the end, however, the cause of the individual worker's occupational immobility was overshadowed by the fact of it. Whether his position in the farm labor force was a function of race or social marginality was of little significance. The transcending implication of the typical farmworker's occupational status was that he was usually powerless to do anything about it.

A natural consequence of the farmworker's fixed status was the emergence of an industrial-relations structure that afforded the employer nearly absolute power in deciding the terms and conditions of employment. Already favored with labor-market conditions that usually guaranteed them a surplus, farm employers exploited the added advantages that derived from the workers' chronic powerlessness to maximize their profits by minimizing labor costs. The result was a pattern of low wages, oppressive working conditions, and unspeakably bad living conditions that became increasingly invulnerable to change as employers adopted the view that such a labor system was not only necessary to the survival of their industry but also reflective of a process of natural selection that at once explained and legitimized it.[1]

For the most part, the industrial relations that prevailed in California's labor-intensive agricultural industry were enormously advantageous to its growth and prosperity. Among the less wholesome byproducts of the highly impersonal and exploitative labor policies that the state's farm employers followed was a powerful undercurrent of worker discontent that surfaced often enough after 1900 to give industrial relations in agriculture a notably volatile and conflictful character.[2]

With few exceptions, the challenges that farmworkers mounted against the authority of agricultural employers before 1930 were unorganized, spontaneous reactions to abnormally poor wages or conditions by small groups of workers employed on a single "ranch" or in a single locality. More often than not, only a single racial or ethnic group was involved. The usual object of these brief risings was to force adjustments of one or more of the immediate conditions of work. Seldom during this period were the workers involved motivated by a conscious and purposeful desire to establish their right of collective participation in the process by which wages and conditions were fixed or to create formal organizations through which they might bargain with the boss on other than an ad hoc basis.[3]

During the late nineteenth century farm employers were never confronted with a serious organized challenge to their authority. Chinese farmworkers worked for particularly low wages and under especially harsh conditions, but made few significant attempts to force their employers to grant improvements. This apparent docility gave rise to a widely held belief among employers that Chinese workers were ideal for their industry because, as disagreeable as working and living conditions in industrialized agriculture might be from the standpoint of most "American" workers, they were enough to satisfy the stunted aspirations of such nonwhite aliens as the Chinese. While such an analysis undoubtedly gained reinforcement from racist assumptions that enjoyed wide currency throughout all segments of the state's white population, the reluctance of Chinese farmworkers to challenge prevailing conditions probably had much less to do with the satisfaction they derived from their work than with other factors more suggestive of their fundamental powerlessness. For example, the labor-contracting system under which the Chinese worked tended to make their employers inaccessible to them. One of their own countrymen typically functioned not only as the agent through which their labor was sold, but as the immediate supervisor of the workers he was supplying. The system thus insulated the employer from the workers he employed and significantly limited their capacity to bring pressures to bear on him directly. Probably even more important, however, in explaining the relative tractability of Chinese farmworkers was the fact that the risks associated with aggressive challenges to the employer's control were so grave, given the palpable hostility that confronted them on all sides, that they saw no certain advantages but many real dangers in pursuing such a course. Thus, in the end, the marginal circumstances of their lives militated against boldness, against jeopardizing what was for many Chinese immigrants the single opportunity for work and livelihood available to them in an otherwise inimical atmosphere.[4]

During the same period, white workers in the agricultural labor force usually displayed no greater proclivity for militancy in the face of exploitative working conditions than did the Chinese. For the most part, whites in the farm-labor pool were transients for whom work in large-scale agriculture was a disagreeable expedient. Most had not yet come to think of themselves as permanent members of an agricultural proletariat, and so tended not to adopt collective approaches to their common problems. To the extent that white workers rebelled against the harsh conditions they found on California's big farms during the late nineteenth century, it was mainly as individuals, and the form of that rebellion was usually the "strike in detail," an action that consisted, as one writer described it, of nothing more than the disgruntled individual worker "simply drifting off the job."[5] While this form of rebellion might well have disrupted the employer's operation temporarily, it posed no threat to his power because it was unorganized, highly individualistic, and, to the extent that it represented an effort to flee rather than challenge the authority of the boss, essentially escapist. Perhaps the most lasting effect of the strike in detail was to create a popular image of white farmworkers as shiftless and irresponsible, unable by reason of their collective depravity to tolerate the discipline imposed by any kind of honest employment.[6]

Not until the turn of the century, when Japanese workers established themselves as an important new source of agricultural labor, did farm employers in California come face to face with laborers with enough solidarity and common purpose to force even a modest sharing of control over wages and working conditions. That the Japanese should have emerged as an especially difficult group for agricultural employers to control was more than a little ironic. When significant numbers of Japanese first began to arrive in the state at the end of the 1890s, it was at a time of threatened labor shortages throughout California's leading agricultural regions, prompting newly heartened employers to hail them as ideal surrogates for the increasingly ephemeral Chinese. And their initial experiences with Japanese farmworkers tended to reinforce that cheering first impression. Having come almost exclusively from their homeland's agricultural class, Japanese farmworkers were usually highly skilled at the types of jobs waiting for them on California's industrialized farms. And to the further delight of employers, they typically worked through labor contractors and appeared willing to accept wages as low as or lower than those of any other group in the farm-labor pool. There was a method in this seeming docility, however, as the Japanese were not long in making clear.[7]

The favorite method by which Japanese farmworkers enhanced their own bargaining power was as simple as it was effective. Through well-organized labor "associations" that initially functioned as contracting agencies, Japanese workers accepted wages far enough below the prevailing standard to drive all other farmworkers out of the area. Once their control of the local labor market was firmly established, Japanese workers waited until crop conditions were at a critical stage to threaten a withdrawal of their labor unless momentarily vulnerable farm employers raised wages or made other improvements in the existing labor contract. Suddenly forced to negotiate with a Japanese labor contractor who was more a bargaining agent for the workers he supplied than an independent, self-interested middleman, farm employers usually had little choice but to grant wage and other concessions if they hoped to avert a strike and save their crops.[8] Such militancy quickly produced in many of those farm employers who had earlier championed the Japanese both deep disenchantment and a nostalgic longing for the good old days of unrestricted Chinese immigration. In a typical lament, one obviously cheerless farm employer reminded his colleagues at the 1907 California Fruit-Growers' Convention that "the Chinese when they were here were ideal. They were patient, plodding, and uncomplaining in the performance of the most menial service. They submitted to anything, never violating a contract. The Japanese now coming in are a tricky and cunning lot, who break contracts and become quite independent. They are not organized into unions, but their clannishness seems to operate as a union would."[9]

Yet as distressing as such uppity behavior surely was to a farm employer with a fast-ripening crop on his hands, Japanese farmworkers had no strong desire to establish a collective bargaining tradition so durable and formidable as to pose a permanent threat to the hegemony of the state's agricultural employers. The reason, if professed ideal had not so readily succumbed to racial partisanship, ought to have warmed the hearts of authentic agrarians everywhere that the agricultural ladder continued to be celebrated as a symbolic expression of economic egalitarianism. For, in the best agrarian tradition, most Japanese immigrants worked unceasingly to advance themselves as rapidly as possible from the status of dependent laborer to that of independent farm owner. And if so dramatic a transformation proved unattainable, Japanese workers endeavored, at the very least, to ascend to the intermediate position of farm tenant.

Rather than gaining them the respect and approbation of their fellow agriculturalists, however, the ambition of the Japanese aroused a rapidly mounting opposition to their presence in the countryside. Anti-Oriental feeling had been in relative remission in the state for a generation, but as the Japanese attained visible success both in their dealings with farm employers and in their strivings toward a higher place in the agricultural hierarchy, Californians demonstrated that their long neglect of the racist vocabulary and methodology so artfully employed against the Chinese had not appreciably dulled their aptitude for nativist vituperation. By 1907 enough political pressure had been generated to cause the federal government to adopt a restrictionist policy toward further Japanese immigration. And to discourage the acquisition of farmlands by Japanese already in California, the state legislature enacted a few years later a patently discriminatory alien land law. Advocates of the law hoped that it would not only impede the movement of Japanese up the agricultural ladder, but drive those who had already attained higher rungs back into the farm-labor force. The law was circumvented with a minimum of ingenuity, however, and those Japanese farmers who were ultimately forced off the land tended to gravitate toward urban occupations rather than return to the agricultural wage-labor population.[10]

Although Japanese farmworkers continued to work in industrialized agriculture long after restrictionist policies were introduced, farm employers found them steadily less bothersome as their numbers dwindled markedly after 1907. That employers were relieved rather than distressed by a steady decrease in the size of the Japanese labor force available to them is in large part attributable to their unhappy experience with workers too intractable to fulfill the particular expectations that the state's agribusinessmen had of hired labor. Yet the reaction of farm employers may well have been less sanguine had not the decline in the numbers of Japanese farmworkers been more than compensated for by a nearly simultaneous swelling of the farm-labor force by thousands of white workers who were unable to find jobs in California's economically infirmed urban centers between 1908 and 1917.[11]

If labor-market conditions tended to favor employers during the decade preceding the country's entry into World War I, however, labor relations in industrialized agriculture did not continue along the generally tranquil path they had earlier traveled. Both the frequency and the scale of agricultural labor disputes increased, and the planning and organization apparent in many of them reflected an important change in the character of the challenges farmworkers in California were mounting against employers. In part, the development of more volatile relations between farm employers and their workers resulted from changes in the composition of the farm-labor force, particularly a sharp increase in the employment of whites, many of whom had a greater appreciation for organized collective action than earlier migratory farm laborers had. Of still greater importance, though, was the fact that California's agricultural proletariat, after decades of seeming invisibility, had at last attracted the attention of the American labor movement.[12]

The labor movement that "discovered" the migratory farmworker in the West around 1909 had two very distinct and antithetic wings. The American Federation of Labor (A.F. of L.) tended to look upon the unorganized casual farm laborer as a potential threat to its organizational security in California's cities and towns; the Industrial Workers of the World (IWW, or Wobblies) saw in the otherwise pitiable figure of the disinherited bindle stiff a likely recruit into the advance guard of a revolutionary cadre whose professed mission was the deliverance of the working class from the "wage slavery" of capitalism. Neither organization had a particularly sure understanding of either the economics of large-scale agriculture or the patterns of employment that prevailed on California's labor-intensive farms. Nonetheless, each resolved to advance its own special interests by organizing the state's previously neglected farm-labor force. What was never quite so plain was just what advantages would accrue to the workers themselves as a consequence of the exertions on their behalf by these outside labor organizations.

Given the pronounced craft bias that shaped the thinking of A.F. of L. policy makers from the organization's founding in 1886, the federation's expressions of interest in unskilled or semiskilled migratory farmworkers could never be accepted at face value. In what was perhaps the A.F. of L.'s first suggestion of an organizational interest in hired farm laborers, Samuel Gompers argued in the early 1890s that he was compelled to reject a Populist proposal of a political alliance between workers and farmers because the latter were too often employers of wage labor that was likely to be recruited into the federation's ranks.[13] Yet rather than disclosing a sincere interest in farmworker organization, Gompers's position was, in fact, part of a fairly transparent stratagem to ensure that the voluntarist, nonpartisan political philosophy espoused by the federation's leadership remained uncompromised. An equally heavy aura of disingenuousness surrounded nearly every subsequent reference to farmworker organization that the A.F. of L. was to make, including those made by its spokesmen in California.

While the difficulties associated with the unionization of migratory farmworkers were always many and complex, the ultimate barrenness of the A.F. of L.'s organizational record in industrialized agriculture was largely attributable to the fact that the federation, despite its fulsome rhetoric, cared little in the end whether or not agricultural unionism was a success. This essential ambivalence toward farmworker organization was discernible throughout the entire period of the federation's activity on behalf of farm unionism in California before World War I.

From the beginning, the A.F. of L.'s central motive in organizing agricultural workers had to do with self-protection rather than workers' solidarity or class mission. In 1903 the Central Labor Council of Los Angeles passed and sent on to the national headquarters of the A.F. of L. a resolution calling for the organization of the state's migratory farmworkers regardless of race or nationality. The council's reasoning was explicit. Such organization would afford "the most effective method of protecting the American workingman and his standard of living," since it would discourage nonwhites in the local farm-labor force from "scabbing on white people," especially those in urban trades.[14]

The California State Federation of Labor, which assumed responsibility for most of the subsequent A.F. of L. efforts to organize migratory labor, adopted resolutions favoring farmworker organization almost yearly after 1903. In 1908, at the suggestion of Andrew Furuseth, president of the International Seamen's Union and a firm believer in the thesis that unorganized migratory labor constituted a threat to urban unionists, a few halting steps were taken by the Oakland Central Labor Council to determine how agricultural workers might be most effectively organized. Also at Furuseth's urging, the national convention of the A.F. of L. adopted in the same year a resolution instructing its executive council to devise an organizational methodology applicable to migratory farm labor.[15] The timing of the resolution was greatly influenced by a growing concern within the federation that the Wobblies would make good on their loudly proclaimed intention to organize western farmworkers. Indeed, had there been no other argument to commend such a course, the IWW's interest in farm labor was reason enough to cause so implacable a foe of radicalism as Andrew Furuseth to push for a counteractive A.F. of L. campaign.[16]

Despite the urgency that appeared to attend the federation's decision, little action of real consequence to agricultural workers in California or other western states resulted from the 1908 resolutions, or from those passed regularly at its national conventions through 1913. The unwillingness of the A.F. of L.'s national leadership to pursue an energetic campaign of farmworker organization appears to have been due in part to a simple lack of funds, but the most important barrier to action was a basic lack of interest in the project among the very cautious men who comprised the federation's executive council. In debates on the convention floor in 1909, a number of delegates expressed the opinion that efforts to organize farm laborers were very likely to antagonize American farmers, a group with whom the A.F. of L. desired to establish friendly relations, and from whom, the federation hoped, important support could be elicited for its union-label campaign. One delegate, revealing a fundamental ignorance of prevailing economic relationships between workers and employers in industrialized agriculture, went so far as to argue that the burden of organizing farm laborers ought to be borne by farmers rather than by trade unionists. The A.F. of L.'s leadership painlessly resolved the question by delegating full responsibility for the organization of farmworkers to the individual state federations, thus allowing those intent upon organizing agricultural labor to proceed as far as their own resources permitted, while letting those state bodies that doubted the usefulness or propriety of such campaigns continue their policies of aloofness and neglect.[17]

Only in California did a campaign worthy of note develop, but its focus shifted almost at once from farmworkers to the relatively less disadvantaged white workers employed in canneries and packing sheds, a group of workers whose classification as genuine agricultural labor was subject to considerable qualification. Among the much larger class of migratory field and orchard labor, a very large proportion of which was nonwhite, little was attempted and nothing was accomplished.[18]

From 1910 until 1914, the period of its most intense activity, the state federation employed methods of organization among migratory labor that reflected an appalling ignorance of the collective nature and habits of casual agricultural workers. J. B. Dale, the organizer assigned by the state federation to unionize farm labor, conducted a campaign distinguished only by its extraordinary ineptitude. Throughout the entire four years of the campaign, Dale confined his activities to the major cities of the state, ignoring the rural districts where the workers he was seeking to organize were employed. His strategy, as he explained it before the U.S. Commission on Industrial Relations in 1914, was to talk with farm laborers "in town, where they are on Sunday."[19] If he was in fact able to confront actual agricultural workers, and the available evidence strongly suggests that he was not, probably no time or place less conducive to successful organization of such people could have been chosen. More often than not, Dale's contact with migratory farmworkers came during periods of unemployment, when they congregated in cities, hoping to take advantage of the usually meager social and relief services there. During such periods farm laborers tended to be both economically and psychologically unreceptive to the idea of unionization. Not only were they unemployed, and thus unable or unwilling to stretch their meager stakes to include initiation fees and dues, however modest, but they were also removed from the poor wages and harsh working conditions that might have heightened their receptivity to an organizer's arguments. Dale freely admitted his failure to attract genuine agricultural workers into the ranks of the A.F. of L. Yet he apparently never questioned the applicability of his organizing methods to migratory farm labor. In a remark that revealed his essential ignorance of economic realities in large-scale agriculture, Dale blamed an uncooperative attitude among California farm employers for the ultimate frustration of his organizational work.[20]

Beyond the weaknesses in organizational tactics that afflicted the state federation's campaign, its most serious deficiency from the beginning was the halfhearted and dispirited nature of its implementation and prosecution. Try as they might, the self-absorbed and racially fastidious craft unionists who devised and managed the campaign simply could not bring themselves to regard farmworkers as full-fledged members of the same wage-earning class within which they presumed to exercise special prerogatives and discharge special responsibilities as a self-designated aristocracy. Any enthusiasm for farmworker organization that did exist within the state A.F. of L. at the campaign's launching dissipated quickly. As their organizing drive began to lose the modest momentum it had initially enjoyed, federation leaders at both state and national levels spoke less and less of the need for worker self-help and more and more of the need for legislation that would ease or eliminate some of the worst abuses associated with employment in California's industrialized agriculture. New laws establishing sanitation standards in farm-labor camps and job-information bureaus to assist migratory agricultural workers in securing the fullest possible employment each year were the legislative remedies that federation spokesmen emphasized in particular, although they always dutifully reiterated the A.F. of L.'s first dictum, that organization remained the only sure and proper road to a definitive amelioration of the problems confronting farmworkers.[21]

In demonstrating their willingness to let government supply solutions to problems affecting farmworkers, A.F. of L. leaders were exempting agricultural labor from the federation's guiding philosophy of voluntarism. In effect, federation leaders were persuaded that the most expedient way to discharge the responsibility they had too readily assumed was to assign farmworkers to the same category that the A.F. of L. set aside for women and children in the labor force. This category's special utility lay in its capacity to accommodate those groups of workers whose powerlessness the A.F. of L.'s white male leaders conveniently considered to be impossible to remedy because it derived from an inherent inability to appreciate and practice those techniques for self-betterment and self-protection which all other classes of workers under the federation's banner relied upon to empower themselves. The A.F. of L.'s tradition of opposing governmental intervention in the affairs of workers and employers was rooted in the voluntarist assumption that the only kind of power worth having was that which the workers themselves created in the workplace through their own collectivity. If farmworkers were, as a class, inherently devoid of those instincts for collective enterprise essential to successful unionization and the ultimate alleviation of their powerlessness, and that was the conclusion the federation promptly drew from its initial experiences with agricultural labor in California, then government intervention became not only a legitimate action but perhaps the only realistic means of improving working conditions in agriculture. Yet, whatever its rationale, the A.F. of L.'s steady deemphasis of farmworker organization in favor of legislative palliatives involved considerably more than a mere substitution of one tactic for another. As long as the federation, no matter how reluctantly, had pursued its strategy of organization, it was addressing directly the problem of farmworker powerlessness. As it gravitated away from an economic strategy and toward a political one, its focus necessarily shifted from the underlying problem facing agricultural wage earners to just the most visible symptoms of that problem. When the state A.F. of L. finally abandoned its interest in farmworkers in 1916, it did so without having accomplished any of its own organizational goals, and without having redressed in even the slightest degree the imbalance of power that existed between employers and workers on California's industrialized farms.

The A.F. of L. was plainly out of its element when it ventured into the countryside and the inhospitable realm of large-scale agriculture. For the Industrial Workers of the World, which had spent the years immediately following its founding in 1905 struggling to survive a series of wrenching internecine squabbles, the discovery of a degraded class of farmworkers and other casual laborers in the western states gave its revolutionary mission the human focus that would dominate the organization throughout much of its brief but turbulent history. In ideology, if not in every other way, the IWW was the antithesis of the A.F. of L. And probably in no other arena of common activity was that fact more emphatically documented than in their respective campaigns of farmworker organization in California. The IWW had been founded, at least in part, for the purpose of offering American workers an anti-capitalist alternative to what Wobblies disparagingly described as the accommodationist craft unionism of the A.F. of L. When it came to organizing farmworkers employed in industrialized agriculture, the IWW vehemently and endlessly dissented from the A.F. of L.'s assumption that the congenital helplessness of farmworkers made them a naturally dependent, and thus unorganizable, class. Possessed of an almost evangelical passion, the IWW resolved to use its well-stocked arsenal of revolutionary slogans and promises to break through a barrier of cynicism and distrust created by decades of neglect and mistreatment, thereby disclosing the truth of its belief that there existed within the ranks of migratory farmworkers in California a spirit of rebelliousness as fervent and uncompromising as any that could be found in industrial America.[22]

The question of just how much influence the IWW ultimately gained among California farmworkers is impossible to answer with precision. The ambivalence of western Wobblies toward the goals of conventional unionism rendered the normal indices of successful organization generally useless. While the numbers of dues-paying members and of chartered and functioning local unions served as fairly accurate gauges of the A.F. of L.'s importance within a regional work force, they were much less reliable measures of the IWW's true strength among agricultural laborers. Yet, whatever the actual membership of the organization at the height of its appeal, it is difficult to imagine that by 1917 there was anywhere in California a group of farmworkers or employers who had not, either directly or indirectly, felt the influence of the IWW.

The organizational ideal of the IWW found expression in its ambitious advocacy of "One Big Union" as the repository of all labor power. Despite the color-blindness that this vision promoted, Wobblies found themselves unable in the end to dispel the myths or allay the fears that had combined to keep the agricultural labor force in California strictly segregated along racial lines. Unlike the A.F. of L., however, which was earnestly striving to banish the Japanese from the state when it was not simply ignoring them, the IWW strove to enlist the support of Japanese workers. During the most intense phases of the anti-Japanese agitation in California, editorials condemning racism and lauding the "class consciousness" of Japanese farmworkers regularly appeared in the *Industrial Worker*. White workers who rebelled at the notion of accepting Japanese laborers as their equals in the working class were reminded that "a yellow skin is to be preferred a thousand times to a yellow heart."[23]

Although Japanese farmworkers appear to have been friendly toward the Wobblies, even cooperating with them on a few occasions, they were very rarely persuaded to join the organization. The reason for their reluctance is not difficult to discern. They had nothing to gain, in practical terms, from affiliation with the IWW, and much to lose. Having demonstrated time and again that their rather euphemistically described "labor associations" were in fact formidable vehicles for economic protection and advancement, Japanese workers were understandably reluctant to abandon the strength and solidarity that derived from their racial homogeneity in order to become members of a far larger group that was hopelessly heterogeneous, and thus much less likely to achieve an equally effective capacity for collective action. The success that the Japanese had attained in their numerous confrontations with California farm employers was well known to the IWW, and the solidarity they evinced during such disputes was much envied by Wobbly organizers. In testimony before the U.S. Commission on Industrial

Relations in 1914, George Speed, an experienced Wobbly organizer in the state, described Japanese farmworkers as having "a far better sense of organization than . . . the native American," and praised their ability to "act more solid together than do the natives."[24] In addressing himself to the problem of IWW policy toward the Japanese, a field organizer in Fresno emphasized the same point by suggesting that Wobblies could learn far more from Japanese farmworkers than they could teach them. Combining a succinct statement of fact with a bit of sage advice, this organizer wrote: "The Japanese are organized, they are past masters in the art of bringing John Farmer to his knees. My advice is learn the tactics used by the Japanese. Go thou and do likewise."[25]

Beyond the fact that they had nothing to gain in terms of greater economic strength by joining the IWW, most Japanese farm laborers appear to have been in fundamental disagreement with the Wobblies' revolutionary objectives. While Wobblies sought to destroy capitalism in America, the Japanese aspired to better their relative economic position within the existing capitalist system. It was this basic conflict of ultimate aims, perhaps more than anything else, that militated against lasting cooperation between Wobblies and Japanese farmworkers.[26]

Despite their inability to win the allegiance of the Japanese and most other nonwhite farmworkers, Wobblies found the white migrants who had come to dominate the state's farm-labor force by 1910 not only willing to listen to their revolutionary preachments, but hungry for any ideological formula that posited the innate wickedness of the socioeconomic order that created a laboring class as disadvantaged and degraded as themselves. Indeed, it is unlikely that any other class of workers in the country possessed a greater natural affinity for the IWW's unique brand of alienated radicalism. Mainly unencumbered single males with neither constraining familial responsibilities nor strong geographic loyalties, white farmworkers were entombed in a subculture of material, social, psychological, and spiritual poverty from which avenues of escape into the American promised land of independence and affluence were, realistically speaking, nonexistent. They were, as Carleton Parker described them, "the finished product of an economic environment which seems cruelly efficient in turning out human beings modeled after all the standards which society abhors."[27] To the IWW, itself "a psychological by-product of the neglected childhood of industrial America,"[28] the migratory agricultural worker was someone neither deserving of pity nor requiring moral uplift, but instead a living, incontrovertible proof of the malevolence and essential degeneracy of capitalism in the United States. These workers were, in the IWW's view, the "soldiers of Western industry, out of whose sinews and brain the enormous wealth of the West is distilled."[29] Yet they were, manifestly, workers to whom the product of labor was almost wholly denied. As Wobbly writer Walker Smith insisted, they were "the real proletarians," people who "truly" had "nothing to lose but their chains." "It is to this class," argued Smith, "turned down by the A.F. of L., that the I.W.W. must turn for material to organize."[30]

What the IWW held out to the migratory farmworker was not only the promise of a new life, but also, through an involuted social Darwinism, absolution from responsibility for the moral, social, and economic debasement of his past. The power of such an appeal among workers with so disadvantaged a background and so bleak a future is not difficult to understand. Among the thousands of migratory farm hands who had come to regard the American dream as a cruel hoax, the conviction grew, as one writer observed, that "the last single hope of rehabilitation and human dignity lay in the revolutionary programme of the I.W.W."[31]

Not unlike the A.F. of L., which viewed the organization of migratory farmworkers as a means of protecting urban unionists from potential scabs and strikebreakers, the IWW initially approached the task of farmworker organization out of perceived self-interest. Many Wobblies feared that the success of their entire movement, including the final overthrow of the wage system, would be constantly in jeopardy if so large a group as the agricultural work force was neglected by the organization.[32] In his report to delegates attending the Second Convention of the IWW in Chicago in 1906, Secretary-Treasurer William Trautmann stressed the importance of bringing farmworkers into the Wobbly fold. The strategy he proposed emphasized the role of timber workers as a link between the industrial working class and the agricultural labor force. Because timber workers were migrants, regularly forced to seek short-term employment in agriculture, Trautmann suggested that they were uniquely suited to carry the message of industrial unionism and class solidarity to those workers engaged primarily in farmwork.[33]

Despite the intentions expressed at the 1906 convention, however, no organizational work appears to have been undertaken among farm laborers in California for three years, a fact surely related in some degree to the internal wrangling that convulsed the IWW during that period. Finally, in 1909, several IWW locals were established in scattered farming areas of the state. The first local chartered was in Redlands, a region of intensive citrus cultivation east of Los Angeles.

Shortly thereafter locals were established in the Imperial Valley, a vast, exclusively agricultural area on the Mexican border, and, after a rather halting start, in Fresno, the commercial center of the great San Joaquin Valley.[34]

Despite these early organizational successes and the singular amenability of so many of the state's farmworkers to its militant proselytizing, the IWW never really established itself as a genuine labor organization among California's agricultural work force. While Wobbly organizers succeeded in "fanning the flames of discontent" throughout the state's leading agricultural districts, they failed, and miserably so, in the more important work of fashioning the collective discontent of farmworkers into a viable instrument of economic change, much less revolution. Although there are innumerable reasons for this frustration, each seems in the end to be traceable to the IWW's failure to subordinate its agitational function to a more exacting, if perhaps less exhilarating, labor-union function. Examples of this failing dominate the organization's record among California farmworkers at least through 1915.

In the spring of 1910, Wobblies congregated in Fresno and shouted their determination to organize the army of agricultural "wage slaves" in the San Joaquin Valley. Taking up their positions on street corners throughout the town, Wobbly soapbox orators opened their organizational campaign by alternately bombarding those who would listen with impassioned attacks on the "master class," instructing them in the virtues of industrial unionism and the inexorable power of a united wage-earning class, and describing, with an unaffected religiosity, the workers' paradise that lay on the far side of that final general strike which every action of the IWW was supposed to promote and bring nearer. Local authorities acted to halt these meetings. And although the efficacy of street-corner oratory as an organizational method was always more illusory than real, Wobbly class warriors, led by Frank Little, immediately abandoned their goal of union building in order to do battle over the principle of free speech.[35]

The Fresno free-speech fight, with its attendant police terror and vigilantism, raged for several months, finally ending early in 1911 with a compromise settlement providing for limited free speech. With characteristic hyperbole the IWW proclaimed a complete victory.[36] Yet as praiseworthy as the Fresno fight was as an exercise in defense of the principle of free speech, when it is judged in the context of the IWW's avowed mission in the San Joaquin Valley—the organization of farmworkers—the contest can hardly be regarded as a signal advance. Whatever the real or imagined advantages that flowed from the free-speech "victory," they were not translated into gains in farmworker organization. The thousands of agricultural workers who were unorganized and exploited when Wobblies began their agitation in Fresno in 1910 remained no less unorganized and exploited when Wobblies departed the city in 1911.

The Fresno fight indicated perhaps more than anything else that the IWW, in California agriculture at least, was unable to function as an instrument of both revolution and trade unionism at the same time. To such Wobblies as Frank Little, for whom the overthrow of capitalism was not simply a radical's dream but a realistic goal that every day of class struggle brought closer, free-speech fights like the one at Fresno afforded the opportunity to expose to public view the integrated economic, political, social, and institutional power of the "master class" in the full bloom of its wickedness. Alongside so seemingly grand and essential a confrontation, the task of organizing valley farmworkers in order that they might bargain with farm employers from a position of strength was likely to seem mundane and tangential to the cause of revolution.[37] Perhaps this partially explains why so few Wobblies remained in Fresno at the close of the struggle to avail themselves of the free speech they had won, and why so many, including Frank Little, immediately departed for the Mexican border and participation in Mexico's infant revolution.[38]

The Fresno episode was neither isolated nor uncharacteristic. In the aftermath of the Wheatland hop pickers' strike in 1913,[39] as well as in a dozen other less notable incidents, Wobblies sought to further the cause of farm unionism not through on-the-job organization, but through a special brand of inflammatory political agitation liberally sprinkled with threats of sabotage and arson.[40] Although few Wobblies seem in fact to have had the stomach for the depredations they threatened, they nonetheless succeeded in fixing in the public's mind an image of the IWW that hardly enhanced its reputation as a labor union and surely facilitated the work of those who lobbied for federal suppression of the organization in 1917.[41]

Not until the end of 1915, when the failure of the IWW's campaign among California farmworkers became fully apparent, were the soapbox orators and political propagandists who had led it displaced by Wobblies oriented more toward on-the-job organizational methods and economic direct action. To emulate the success that the newly formed Agricultural Workers' Organization, No. 400, had achieved among migratory harvest hands in the Midwestern wheat belt during the summer of 1915, Wobblies in California worked during 1916 to adapt the

AWO's system of floating job delegates to the special requirements of their region. Whatever opportunities for actual organization existed in the state during the 1916 harvest season, however, were largely squandered as a result of internal wrangling over the question of direct affiliation with the AWO. Many California Wobblies apparently feared that affiliation with the AWO would cost them the autonomy they had previously enjoyed. After a brief and vacuous effort to establish an identical but entirely independent farmworkers' organization, the larger IWW locals were forced, again by Wobblies representing the on-the-job membership, to seek charters from the AWO. Thus it was not until the 1917 harvest season that Wobblies in California were finally prepared to undertake an organizational campaign that promised results translatable into real economic power on the job. The change came too late. That summer the government's wartime assault on the IWW shattered the organization's capacity to give further direction to the agricultural labor movement in the state.[42]

An anemic postwar effort by the IWW to resurrect its organizing campaign among California farmworkers came to nothing because of the state's newly enacted criminal syndicalism law and the public's militant antiradicalism. Also, internal disorders continued to rack the organization, and the unattached bindle stiffs who had predominated in the prewar farm-labor force were rapidly being displaced by migrant families, whose present-minded mentality was singularly unaccommodating to millennial visions.[43]

With the disappearance of IWW activists from the farming centers of California, the agricultural labor movement in the state lapsed into quiescence. Throughout the 1920s agricultural wage earners labored in almost total anonymity, partaking of none of the fabled prosperity of the period. The pattern of extreme seasonality, very low wages, and miserable living conditions that had long characterized employment in industrialized agriculture in the state remained undisturbed during the decade.[44] Yet the IWW had plainly left its mark. Though the Wobblies had failed miserably to organize and emancipate the state's farmworkers, they had aroused deep fears and left a legacy of virulent antiradicalism and antiunionism among the groups that controlled the political economy of California's large-scale commercial agriculture.[45]

Though the threat of unionism was the most formidable and disturbing challenge they faced in the period before World War I, farm employers had to contend as well with mounting pressures exerted by reformist political forces in the state. As in the country generally, a strong reform sentiment was growing in California throughout the prewar era, and the highly visible abuses visited upon the state's farm-workers soon attracted the attention of progressive political elements concerned both with the plight of the rural working class and the undesirable social consequences of the labor policies followed by most agribusinessmen. The modest reforms that progressives sought, mainly during the liberal administration of Governor Hiram Johnson, involved no direct interference by the state in agricultural labor relations. Like progressives elsewhere, California reformers were motived less by a desire to increase the power of labor than by the desire to curb the power of employers, whose labor practices they considered to be detrimental to the social and economic well-being of the whole state. Thus, while they had no desire to force farm employers to share control over wages and conditions with their employees, many progressives were convinced that the public welfare would be usefully served if the state set certain limits beyond which employers could not go in the exercise of their unilateral authority. As George Mowry, a leading historian of progressivism in California, has noted, "many progressives were eager to clip the wings" of the state's employing class, but "they had little intention of strengthening the power of organized labor."[46]

Because in many areas of the state farm employers were part of the political coalition on which the progressive movement depended for its essential support, reform proposals that promised to protect farmworkers against many of the worst abuses they faced on the job were ignored. And even where relatively modest labor reforms were concerned—child labor, women's hours, workmen's compensation—organized farm employers insisted that they not apply to farm labor.[47] When more ambitious pro-labor elements proposed in 1914 the adoption of the eight-hour day in all industries, agitated farm employers quickly organized a Farmers' Protective League through which they launched a massive, and ultimately successful, campaign to defeat the proposal.[48]

In the end, the only success that progressives concerned with conditions of farm employment could claim resulted from the work of a state agency whose original charter contemplated no direct involvement in such matters. At the time of its creation by the state legislature in 1913, the Commission of Immigration and Housing was envisioned as a social welfare agency whose ministrations would facilitate the assimilation of immigrants into the social and economic life of the state.[49] Its mission was abruptly altered, however, when the so-called Wheatland riot brought to public attention the unspeakably demeaning conditions of employment on California's industrialized farms.[50]

The Wheatland episode revealed at once the pathology of labor relations in industrialized agriculture and the desperation of the disinherited class impressed into the service of the agribusiness economy. If the Wheatland conflict's deeper implications escaped most of its contemporary analysts, identifying its immediate causes required no special powers of discernment. In advance of the 1913 summer picking season, the Durst brothers' hop ranch, one of the largest employers of farm labor in California, advertised for workers throughout the state, and in Oregon and Nevada as well, making attractive offers of employment to all migrants interested in coming to the upper Sacramento Valley town of Wheatland for the August hop harvest. In response to this solicitation approximately 2,800 men, women, and children arrived at the Durst ranch in late July, only to find that there was work for no more than 1,500 pickers. Once in place, the extremely heterogeneous work force—more than two dozen nationalities were represented—discovered living and working conditions so extraordinarily degrading and exploitive as to incite deep anger and restiveness.[51] Sensing the opportunity before them, a small number of pickers who were familiar with the teachings of the IWW acted to consolidate the workers' anger into an instrument of direct action. With overwhelming support from the workers to embolden them, a committee of hop pickers drafted and submitted to Ralph Durst a list of demands incorporating a wage increase and improvements in both working and living conditions. While Durst agreed to some of the demands, he flatly refused to increase wages or to alter certain working conditions. Moreover, he sought to break the threatened strike by removing from the scene the man who had emerged as the obvious leader of the workers, Richard "Blackie" Ford. When a local constable called on by Durst to assist in this goal failed to produce a warrant, an angry crowd of workers refused to permit Ford's arrest. Shortly thereafter Durst telephoned authorities in the nearby town of Marysville, reporting with little regard for accuracy that lawless and riotous hop pickers had taken control of his ranch. In response to Durst's fearsome entreaty, the Yuba County sheriff and a hastily assembled group of heavily armed deputies proceeded to Wheatland.

Upon their arrival in late afternoon, authorities found not the rampaging mob that Durst had described, but a peaceful crowd of about two thousand men, women, and children gaily singing the Wobbly standard, "Mr. Block." The crowd's peaceable temperament notwithstanding, the sheriff, two deputies, and Edward Manwell, the Yuba County district attorney, waded into the assembly, intent on arresting Blackie Ford and dispersing the meeting. As they approached the platform where Ford was standing, the sheriff shouted a dispersal order. To lend emphasis to the command, a shot was fired in the midst of the crowd. Rather than sobering the crowd, the shot touched off a brief but furious battle. In all, perhaps as many as twenty shots were fired. When the fighting stopped, four persons lay dead: District Attorney Manwell, a deputy sheriff, a young English hop picker who had been standing nearby, and a Puerto Rican worker who, after disarming one of the lawmen, killed both Manwell and the deputy, only to be killed himself by another member of the posse. At the close of the fighting the authorities beat a hasty retreat to Marysville. Hop pickers by the hundreds also left the area as quickly as they could assemble their belongings. When six companies of National Guardsmen dispatched to the area by Governor Hiram Johnson arrived in the early hours of August 4, they found the Durst ranch relatively depopulated.[52]

If the initial reaction of Yuba County authorities to the Wheatland riot was one of shock, that feeling quickly gave way to an intense desire to wreak vengeance upon those responsible for the deaths of Manwell and the deputy sheriff. Yet it became apparent at once that they were less interested in determining who had fired the fatal shots than in punishing the IWW. Within a day of the incident Ralph Durst was quoted as saying that while "the officers might have been a trifle hasty, I will lay the blame upon a few people who . . . call themselves I.W.W.s."[53] On August 7, a coroner's jury, with Ralph Durst as its principal witness, ruled that the deaths had occurred at the hands of "rioters incited to murderous anger by I.W.W. leaders and agitators." The jury then instructed county lawmen to do all in their power to find and arrest Blackie Ford and "other guilty parties," meaning those conspicuously involved in efforts to organize hop workers on the Durst ranch before the riot.[54]

A manhunt of extraordinary proportions ensued. Conducted for the most part by Burns detectives in the employ of Yuba County, the search for the Wheatland agitators spread throughout the West. Armed with John Doe warrants and heedless of legal niceties, the Burns men made dozens of arrests on little or no evidence, and then sought through threats, intimidation, beatings, torture, and bribery to gain confessions that might implicate Ford and the other prominent activists at Wheatland in a conspiracy to murder Edward Manwell, if not in the actual killing itself.[55] In the end the search produced four men regarded by county authorities as ringleaders of the alleged conspiracy: Blackie Ford, Herman Suhr, Walter Bagan, and William Beck. Tried for murder in an atmosphere poisoned by virulent anti-IWW feeling, Ford and

Suhr were convicted and given life sentences. Bagan and Beck, who ultimately proved to be of no interest to the prosecution, were acquitted.[56]

Beyond providing what Carey McWilliams later described as "the first California labor cause célèbre,"[57] the Wheatland episode afforded progressives the fullest opportunity they were to have to apply their reformist palliatives to conditions of employment in agriculture. The vehicle of this progressive intervention was the newly created Commission of Immigration and Housing, which was empowered by Governor Johnson in late 1913 to undertake an investigation of the causes of the Wheatland uprising.[58] When the commission issued its report early in 1914, it was immediately apparent that the agency intended to interpret its gubernatorial mandate so broadly as to encompass far more than investigatory powers. Having concluded that the "real cause" of the Wheatland riot was to be found in the "inadequate housing and the insanitary conditions under which the hop pickers were compelled to live," the commission resolved to defuse the highly volatile situation affecting relations between farm employers and migratory workers by enforcing minimum standards of health and sanitation in the hundreds of labor camps that dotted the landscape of industrialized agriculture.[59]

That the Commission of Immigration and Housing sought to use its Wheatland investigation as the basis for a statewide campaign of labor-camp inspection and improvement is largely attributable to the opportunistic disposition of the small group of ardent progressives to whom Governor Johnson entrusted the agency's uncertain fortunes. Chaired by Simon J. Lubin, a Sacramento merchant with impeccable progressive credentials, the commission represented a cross section of the reform coalition that had carried Johnson to victory in 1910.[60] Of still greater significance, however, was the fact that the commission was dominated by progressives from the northern part of the state, who tended to be more liberal than their Southern California counterparts when it came to social questions,[61] and who tended to believe that labor unrest in agriculture would persist until farm employers, whether of their own volition or as a result of governmental compulsion, acknowledged their moral obligation to afford farmworkers fair and humane working and living conditions.

The man selected by Lubin and his fellow commissioners to translate the commission's vision of a conflict-free labor relations system on the farm into a functioning reality was Carleton H. Parker. In Parker the commission found an executive secretary who in many ways personified the progressive tradition of the early twentieth century. Trained in

Two views of the living conditions confronting hop pickers on the Durst ranch near Wheatland at the time of the riot there in 1913. Photos: California Commission of Immigration and Housing.

A view of the model camp built on the Durst brothers' ranch in 1914 in response to
the camp sanitation campaign of the Commission of Immigration and Housing.
Photo: California Commission of Immigration and Housing.

engineering at Berkeley and in labor economics at Harvard and the University of Heidelberg, Parker valued order and rationality in the search for solutions to society's problems and sympathized with the human wreckage that a largely unregulated capitalist economy left in its wake.[62]

In undertaking an investigation of the Wheatland episode, Parker sought to organize and interpret the empirical evidence the commission staff amassed within the context of his own personal theory of the ecological and psychological causes of labor unrest.[63] Relying heavily on the ideas of both Sigmund Freud and economist Thorstein Veblen, whom he regarded as his intellectual mentors, Parker brought to his analysis of the Wheatland conflict an abiding conviction that the deep worker hostility that exploded with such tragic consequences on the Durst ranch was the "natural psychic outcome of a distressing and anti-social labor condition." Impressed by the powerlessness of California's floating population of agricultural laborers, Parker wrote of the typical casual farmworker: "His condition is one of mental stress and unfocused psychic unrest, and could in all accuracy be called a definite industrial psychosis. He is neither willful nor responsible, he is suffering from a stereotyped mental disease."[64] Thus the resort to violence by farmworkers at Wheatland was most profitably understood not as a willful assault against the established order, Parker insisted, but "as ordinary mental disease of a functional kind, a sort of industrial psychosis";[65] a "psychic ill-health generated by the worker's experience."[66] The central implication of Parker's analysis was that farmworkers were, because of their utter powerlessness, victims rather than victimizers, the human proof of just how "mentally insanitary" and "psychopathological" the environment of "modern industrialism" had become.[67] "As a class," he wrote, "the migratory laborers are nothing more or less than the finished products of their environment. They should therefore never be studied as isolated revolutionaries, but rather as, on the whole, tragic symptoms of a sick social order." Insofar as California's migratory farmworkers were concerned, Parker concluded, "nurture has triumphed over nature, the environment has produced its type."[68]

Once having come to this "new realization of the irrational direction of economic evolution,"[69] Parker argued, the "militant minority"[70] upon whom society necessarily relied to give both expression and dimension to its latent reformist impulses needed to take the all-important step from dispassionate social diagnosis to practical activism. "The labor mind in America," he wrote, "is in profound unrest, and it is imperative that those Americans on whom falls the duty of thinking and planning accept such facts as all-determining and do not misuse the moment by useless if admirable moral indignation."[71] Determined that his fellow Californians must "know more of the meaning of progress,"[72] Parker resolved in early 1914, while the more shocking revelations of farmworker mistreatment which his Wheatland investigation produced were still fresh in the public's mind, to remedy what he saw as a "mal-adjustment between a fixed human nature and a carelessly ordered world" by reordering the environment that governed the lives of those employed in industrialized agriculture; by forging what he later described as "a new standard of normality."[73]

With the release of its Wheatland findings in February 1914, the Commission of Immigration and Housing began, under Carleton Parker's direction, a widely publicized campaign to marshal support for its contention that if labor troubles of the kind that had developed on the Durst ranch were to be avoided in the future, farm employers would have to bring the housing and sanitation standards in their labor camps up to the minimum levels recommended by the commission. Beyond alluding to the moral responsibility of employers toward labor, the commission "pointed out that a sanitary camp meant an increase in the willingness and efficiency of the laborer, and that it was in the employer's own pecuniary interest, as well as that of humanity, to have a sanitary and livable camp."[74]

The minimum standards that the commission sought to enforce represented a compromise between genuinely decent conditions and what could reasonably be expected of farm employers who were not obliged by law to comply with the agency's recommendations. In its official report to Governor Johnson at the end of 1914, the commission described the minimum standard it had established as being "sufficiently high to insure results, but not so expensive and so impracticable as to deter employers of labor from adopting it, since employers had to be persuaded, rather than compelled by law, to make the improvements suggested."[75] In light of its inability to compel employers to accept its recommendations, the commission sought to exploit a heightened public awareness of the generally deplorable conditions that existed in the state's farm-labor camps as a means of pressuring otherwise invulnerable employers to make needed improvements. Recounting these early efforts, which it described as "educational in character," the commission noted: "Old prejudices, old habits of thought had to be broken down before a new practice could be initiated. Employers had to be persuaded not only that the improvements sought were necessary to the health and general well-being of the workers, but that good camp conditions meant a more contented, more stable and more efficient labor supply."[76]

Whether or not employers actually put aside "old prejudices" in favor of new habits is problematical. Less uncertain is the fact that enough agribusinessmen responded to the commission's urgings to bring about a measurable improvement in the quality of farm-labor camps throughout the state. To be sure, many "recalcitrant employers," as the commission described them, "considered the new demands unreasonable or visionary."[77] Yet many others not only made the suggested improvements, but publicly endorsed the reformers' main contention that improving the environments of labor camps had a theraputic effect on employment relations in industrialized agriculture and increased worker productivity as well.[78] In the citrus-growing regions of Southern California the commission found farm employers especially amenable to labor-camp reform. Similarly, hop growers in the northern part of the state reacted positively to the commission's recommendations, including, ironically, the Durst brothers.[79] In the Imperial Valley and the Sacramento delta region, as well as in several other isolated farming districts, the commission encountered attitudes among farm employers ranging from indifference to intransigence.[80]

On the whole, however, the commission expressed considerable satisfaction with the overall response of farm employers, and claimed an impressive record of improvement in labor-camp housing and sanitation over several years. In the early 1920s, with the rapid dissipation of progressive sentiment and the growing dominance of business and agribusiness over the state's political life following World War I, the commission found itself operating in an atmosphere markedly less conducive to reform. By 1923 conservative political opposition to an activist commission had mounted until the agency not only was unable to carry on its work in behalf of further labor-camp reforms, but was powerless to halt a process of retrogression that wiped out most of the improvements of earlier years by the end of the decade. A governmental reorganization in 1927 deprived the commission of its independent status and effectively eliminated its power to influence conditions of employment in industrialized agriculture.[81]

Though the campaign of labor-camp improvement undertaken by the Commission of Immigration and Housing in 1914 generally failed to achieve permanent gains, the commission established a reputation as a friend and protector of the migratory farmworker. When it came to farmworker organization, however, the commission, manifesting an antipathy toward trade unionism that was not uncommon among progressives, was much less friendly to those who prescribed unionism as the only certain antidote to the powerlessness of agricultural laborers.[82] Because the militant IWW was the union most actively preaching the gospel of collective action to California farmworkers before World War I, the commission's antiunionism has sometimes been mistaken for simple antiradicalism.[83] To be sure, the commission's progressive leadership was not unmindful of the singular vulnerability of an avowedly revolutionary labor organization, and in discouraging the unionization of farmworkers it did not hesitate to employ the hoary but unfailingly affecting rhetoric of antiradicalism. Notwithstanding this tactical opportunism, the antiunionism of commission progressives derived from a purposeful ideological disposition rather than from an objection to the particular character of a particular labor organization.

Both Simon Lubin and Carleton Parker, the two men most responsible for shaping the commission's labor policies, shared with leading progressives throughout the state a belief that while unionism was a natural and understandable response to the exploitive genius of organized capital, it was a symptom of serious economic infirmity that ought to disappear once reformers succeeded in putting the house of capitalism in order. Unions were, in short, a "temporary expedient representing the necessity of one class standing against another" only until such time as the nation had progressed "beyond the questions of class and caste."[84] In assessing what he regarded as the common attitude of reformers in the state toward unions and other institutional manifestations of class, historian George Mowry has written: "The California progressive . . . wanted to preserve the fundamental patterns of twentieth-century industrial society at the same time that he sought to blot out, not only the rising clash of economic groups but the groups themselves, as conscious economic and political entities." When reduced to its simplest instincts, progressivism in California tended to be prolabor but antiunion. The "progressive mentality," Mowry wrote, "sought to aid the underprivileged individual while it frowned upon the rise of organized labor as a bargaining social group."[85]

Plainly, the activities of the Commission of Immigration and Housing revealed this peculiar duality. In early 1914, when Carleton Parker was still endeavoring to enlist support for the commission's proposed program of labor-camp improvement, he promised that among the benefits that were likely to flow from such a program was an undermining of the IWW's efforts to organize farmworkers. In an enthusiastic letter to Governor Johnson at the time the commission was releasing its Wheatland report, Parker wrote:

> The Immigration Commission now has the funds, the men and the organization to clean up this abuse [labor camp conditions] this coming summer, insure a decent standard of comfort to the seasonal worker and take away the argument and talking weapon of the agitator. The most important labor problem in California is that of the seasonal agricultural laborer on whom the I.W.W. plan to concentrate this summer. I am convinced that our opportunity here is real and vital and our service will be as imperative and essential to the farmer and employer as to the farm laborer.[86]

As always, Parker's humane environmentalism led him to the conclusion that only when working and living conditions in industrialized agriculture were elevated to a level of decency would unionism, strikes, sabotage, and other evidences of individual and collective alienation cease to flourish within the farm-labor force. His principal fear was that farm employers would refuse to recognize the causal relationship between poor conditions and the spirit of revolt that had revealed itself with tragic clarity at Wheatland, and which, he believed, was rapidly welling up within workers' ranks throughout California. The unhappy but likely consequence of intransigence on the part of the employer, Parker predicted, would be the unionization of his workers. "Difficult though organization of these people may be," he warned, "a coincidence of favoring conditions may place an opportunity in the hands of a super leader. If this comes, one can be sure that California would be both very astonished and very misused." Referring specifically to the IWW but implicitly to unionism in general as a phenomenon of class rebellion, Parker declared, "There will be neither permanent peace nor prosperity in our country till the revolt-bases of the I.W.W. are removed, and till that is done the I.W.W. remains an unfortunately valuable symptom of a diseased industrialism."[87]

As initially outlined by Parker, the antiunionism of the Commission of Immigration and Housing was entirely benign, emphasizing the eradication of the "revolt-bases" on which he and his fellow reformers believed the IWW's organizational appeal was founded. Soon, however, the agency embraced a more activist antiunion strategy. As Wobblies intensified their agitation during the summer of 1914, Parker, with Lubin's blessing, launched a covert campaign of surveillance, sending undercover agents into the countryside "to hobo" around in order to collect intelligence relating to IWW activities.[88] Although Parker, because of his outspoken criticism of farm employers, was forced to resign his commission post in the fall of 1914, his modest anti-IWW effort was greatly expanded during the 1915 harvest season. In addition to undertaking a more elaborate program of surveillance,[89] the commission encouraged Governor Johnson to enlist the support of other western governors in making a secret appeal to the federal government for suppression of the IWW. In the end, an investigation by the Department of Justice led federal officials to conclude that action of the kind the governors contemplated was unwarranted. By 1915, however, the antiunionism of the Commission of Immigration and Housing had clearly become more forceful. And while its initial attempt to promote federal suppression of the IWW was frustrated, the commission supplied the bulk of the evidence adduced to justify the massive crackdown on Wobblies by the Department of Justice in 1917.[90]

Had a labor organization of less radical reputation and provocative demeanor been leading the campaign to organize California farmworkers between 1914 and 1917, the commission's bias toward unionism might well have been expressed with greater subtlety and indirection. Yet given the progressives' view that unionism was incompatible with a socially wholesome and rational system of industrial relations, it is unlikely that the commission would have viewed even a moderate farmworker union as other than a symptom of economic malaise or pursued with less conviction the belief that genuine reform dictated the eventual abandonment of such organizational instruments of class conflict. Equally unlikely is the notion that the commission's antiunion proclivities constituted the primary reason for the IWW's inability to bring its organizing campaign among California farmworkers to fruition. Certainly Wobblies in the state, divided as they were over questions of both tactics and objectives, made the largest contributions to the campaign's ultimate failure. Yet, no matter how kindly and well-intentioned its motives, the progressivism embodied in the activities of the Commission of Immigration and Housing did pose a barrier to collective action by farmworkers, and thus tended to place reformers, whether they chose to be there or not, on the side of less selfless and high-minded opponents of agricultural unionism.

Once farm employers understood that the reforms contemplated by the commission did not really threaten their control of essential labor-relations policies, they had little reason to oppose them. But when progressives shifted their attention from the narrow issue of agricultural labor relations to the much wider range of social and economic problems resulting from the domination of the state's farm life by large-scale, labor-intensive operations, employers were confronted by reform proposals of an infinitely more menacing character. Bringing to their analysis of industrialized agriculture the same values of order and progress that governed their thinking generally, progressives found little of a socially redeeming nature in a farming system that discouraged the participation of the family farmer as it tended to invite ever greater concentration of landownership. Throughout the period of World War I, leading social reformers in the state, resurrecting many of the arguments that agrarians had employed without success at the end of the nineteenth century, advocated the development of land and settlement policies that would facilitate the establishment of family farms while forestalling the further rise of agribusiness. Among the most outspoken proponents of such policies were the members of the Commission on Land Colonization and Rural Credits, a special agency created in 1915 to investigate the land-tenure system in California. Comprised of such leading progressives as Harris Weinstock, Chester Rowell, and Elwood Mead, the commission issued a report in 1916 which was highly critical of the pattern of landownership fostered by industrialized farming, and recommended that large landholdings be broken up so that family farmers might have access to small tracts. Emphasizing its belief that such new farms were desirable primarily for social reasons, the commission stated: "It must be made clear . . . that such homes afford not an opportunity *to make money,* but an opportunity for those who have money to get the most out of life."[91]

In response to the commission's recommendations, the state legislature appropriated funds for two relatively modest experimental settlement projects designed to help democratize California's rural economy by promoting family farms. Under the guidance of Elwood Mead, a devoted agrarian reformer, the settlements at Durham, in Butte County, and Delhi, near the San Joaquin Valley town of Turlock, were launched in 1918 with high enthusiasm, and represented what Carey McWilliams later described as "a daring innovation in American land policy."[92] But inept planning, inadequate funding, and unfavorable economic and political conditions in the 1920s caused the projects to collapse.[93]

Other reform schemes designed to promote the displacement of industrialized farms by small-scale family farms gained attention during the same period, but none was able to attract enough support to overcome the opposition mounted by well-organized agribusiness interests. A refurbished single-tax proposition, sponsored by agrarian reformers who hoped, rather naively, that large-scale agriculture could be taxed out of existence, was resoundingly defeated at the polls in 1916, and again two years later. Once it began to look beyond the immediate abuses faced by farmworkers to the adverse effects that the irrational labor-market conditions fostered by industrialized farming were having on the whole of California society, the Commission of Immigration and Housing also proposed sweeping agrarian reform. After surveying the options available to the state for alleviating the worst social problems created by the labor routine of large-scale agriculture, the commission concluded in 1919 that "the only possible, final solution of this evil seems to be the abolishment of the whole system that requires an army of migratory workers."[94] Not surprisingly, the abolition of "the whole system" did not follow. Indeed, by 1927 the commission, its reformist energies and statutory authority long since dissipated, had resigned itself to the fact that an army of migratory workers was indispensable to the well-being of California agriculture, and was struggling to do nothing more than keep a reasonably accurate statistical record of the social and economic injuries the system continued to inflict.[95] To the extent that the commission remained interested and involved in the political debate surrounding the labor practices of industrialized agriculture in the 1920s, it was only to register its opposition to the unrestricted immigration of Mexican farmworkers.[96]

Though labor conditions and employment relations in industrialized agriculture had been subjects of obvious and often intense concern to California progressives, the reform era passed without the question of farmworker powerlessness ever having been addressed directly. With the return to a more conservative, business-oriented political and economic climate in the state during the 1920s, the "labor question" in agriculture lost most of the currency it had enjoyed throughout the preceding decade.

Yet, if the oppressive circumstances of farmworkers' lives attracted relatively little attention in the 1920s, the decade nonetheless witnessed significant changes in agricultural labor relations as farm employers worked to rationalize and control the labor situation in their industry.[97] Their efforts were encouraged by the domineering labor policies being forged by industrial employers and by the banks, utilities, railroads, processors, and other urban interests that greatly expanded their investments in agribusiness throughout the decade.[98] In the mid-1920s the largest farm employers in the state, on both regional and commodity bases, led a movement to establish cooperative labor bureaus, designed largely to formulate and enforce common wage agreements that would eliminate competition for labor and thus reduce even further the already meager power of agricultural workers to influence wages and working conditions.

As commercial farming expanded in California during the 1920s, the demand for cheap labor increased greatly. The newly established labor bureaus sought to ensure both that the free flow of farmworkers from Mexico remained uninterrupted and that existing supplies of labor would be efficiently used. The largest, and probably the most effective, of the specialized farm-labor cooperatives was the Agricultural Labor Bureau of the San Joaquin Valley.[99] Founded in 1926 by several county farm bureaus, chambers of commerce, and farm employers' associations representing raisin, fruit, and cotton growers in the San Joaquin Valley, it both facilitated the orderly expansion of agribusiness in its own region and served as a model for labor bureaus elsewhere in the state.[100]

To the degree that collective action among farm employers extended their control over labor-market and working conditions, it necessarily exacerbated the powerlessness of the state's farmworkers. The growth of farm employers' organizations tended to widen still further the chasm between employer and employee in industrialized agriculture. Whatever vestiges of personalism and mutual interest remained in agricultural labor relations before the development of such employers' organizations rapidly disappeared as the movement gained momentum. Yet at the same time that such developments in the 1920s tended to compound and intensify the disadvantaged status of farm labor in California, they also increased the likelihood that when agricultural workers finally began to contemplate how they might most effectively counter the organized power of employers, they would themselves turn to collective action. And if such efforts toward collective action were to achieve any success, they would have to match the scale of organization forged by the employers. Thus, while the changes in agricultural labor relations that the 1920s ushered in tended to encourage unionism, they also ensured that the task of farmworker organization, which had always been enormously difficult, would be even more formidable in the years ahead. No longer would it be possible for aspiring farm unionists to think in terms of a single farm, a single employer, and a single group of racially homogeneous workers. From the 1920s onward the objective circumstances of industrial relations on the farm dictated that if unionism was to be successful, organization would have to proceed on a regional basis, among a vast farmworker population composed, by employers' design, of disparate and often antagonistic racial, ethnic, and linguistic elements.[101]

If the idea of unionism gained new adherents among the state's farmworkers during the 1920s, the practice of unionism remained virtually unknown to them throughout the decade. Union activity was discouraged both by an excess supply of labor and by changes in the composition of the farm-labor force, especially the displacement of potentially militant single males by entire families of somewhat more timorous and economically inexperienced Mexican immigrants. The obvious power of farm employers and their allies and the disinclination of the A.F. of L. to organize farmworkers were additionally important reasons for the failure of an agricultural labor movement to materialize. Had poor wages and miserable living conditions alone been enough to promote worker organization, the fields and orchards of California would surely have been rife with unionism in the 1920s. Unlike many urban employers, who were pioneering various welfare and employee representation schemes designed to mollify their workers and thus forestall the rise of independent unionism, farm employers, with few exceptions, sought to squeeze the last measure of profit out of their businesses by cutting labor costs to the bone.[102]

As the "golden" decade of the 1920s was moving toward its unexpectedly ignominious end, few workers anywhere in America were laboring under conditions as materially unrewarding, as physically arduous, or as psychologically oppressive as were those employed on California's industrialized farms. In one very important sense, however, farmworkers were closer to the mainstream of the American working-class experience than the visibly marginal circumstances of their lives tended to suggest. For, when the degree of control exercised by the individual worker over his or her own working life is used as a measure, it is difficult to argue persuasively that California's agricultural proletariat was demonstrably more disadvantaged than the mainly unskilled and semiskilled workers in America's mass-production industries. Despite the profligate boosterism of the business class and the flourishing of welfare capitalism across the industrial spectrum, workers in the nation's basic industries found that by the time the legendary prosperity of the 1920s had percolated down to their level, the floodtide of affluence described on the country's editorial pages had become a barely perceptible trickle. And when it came to the development of a capacity for collective economic action, industrial workers had compiled no less dismal an organizational record during the decade than had California farmworkers. For the most part, the A.F. of L. had demonstrated no more interest in organizing industrial labor than in organizing farmworkers.[103]

Yet, with the precipitate decline of capitalism to the brink of ruin in the early 1930s, forces were set in motion which ensured that the historic community of status between industrial and agricultural workers would not long endure. As the events of the 1930s would abundantly attest, however, it was not for lack of trying that farmworkers in California would ultimately fail to overcome their powerlessness, when so many of their urban counterparts were succeeding.

4

Communists on the Farm

Since low wages, irregular employment, harsh and abusive working conditions, and an utterly degraded standard of living had been the prevailing facts of the California farmworker's life for decades, the rise of an agricultural labor movement in the state at the beginning of the 1930s was due to more than a simple desire among workers to alleviate particularly oppressive features of their generally desperate economic situation. Rather, it was the product of a gradual realization among Mexican workers, who comprised a majority of the farm-labor force, that only through organization were they likely to mitigate their endemic powerlessness. Whatever other purposes it was destined to serve, the emergence of a militant disposition among Mexican farmworkers shattered the employers' comforting stereotype of the amiable and accommodating if somewhat dim-witted and disease-prone peon consigned by the infallible logic of nature to precisely that station which best served the interests of California's industrialized agriculture. This "new" Mexican was a product less of a dramatic transformation than of a slow process of acculturation. Throughout the 1920s farm employers and their allies continued to indulge their stereotypical assumptions regarding Mexican farmworkers. Repeating the popular thinking of the decade, a prominent Pasadena physician declared, "The Mexican is a quiet, inoffensive necessity in that he performs the big majority of our rough work, agricultural, building, and street labor. They have no effect upon the American standard of living because they are not much more than a group of fairly intelligent collie dogs."[1] Dr. George P. Clements, the manager of the agricultural department of the Los Angeles Chamber of Commerce and an influential authority on Mexican labor, couched his "expert" appraisal in more temperate terms, but expressed essentially the same point of view. Writing in the mid-1920s, Clements said of the typical Mexican immigrant working in agriculture:

He is ignorant of values; he knows nothing of time; he knows nothing of our laws; he is as primitive as we were 2,500 years ago. He does not know our language, the result being that he becomes a petty criminal through ignorant violations and a prey for every unscrupulous scoundrel in the country. He rarely if ever takes out his citizenship, mixes in politics, or labor squabbles unless directed by some American group. He is the most tractable individual that ever came to serve us.[2]

Yet the events of the late 1920s and early 1930s that made it necessary for the state's agribusinessmen to reform their opinions of Mexicans indicated that time and experience had indeed imparted an appreciation of the group-interest militancy that was an indispensable prerequisite to worker organization. "That the Mexican immigrants are beginning to orientate themselves in California," wrote one State Bureau of Labor Statistics official, "is evidenced by the fact that they have begun to organize into unions for the purpose of improving living and working conditions in the land of their adoption."[3]

The rising ethnic pride and class consciousness that coalesced into a campaign to organize Mexican farmworkers first revealed itself in Los Angeles in 1927, when representatives of several mutual-aid societies in Southern California met to discuss ways of improving the lot of Mexican laborers. Early in 1928, with the support of interested consular officials and the encouragement of the Regional Confederation of Labor in Mexico, the Los Angeles Federation of Mexican Societies established the Confederación de Uniones de Obreros Mexicanos (CUOM), an organization whose avowed purpose, despite the revolutionary rhetoric that infused its constitution, was to promote bread-and-butter unionism among Mexican workers. Beyond improving wages and working conditions, the particular desire of the two to three thousand Mexican workers who belonged to local unions that affiliated with the CUOM in 1928 was to eliminate or reform the exploitive labor contracting system that governed employment in large-scale agriculture.[4]

Louis Bloch, an official of the State Bureau of Labor Statistics who specialized in agricultural labor relations, saw in the founding of the CUOM a challenge to both the authority and the assumptions of farm employers. "The fact that Mexican laborers are beginning to organize into unions," Bloch argued, "is significant from the standpoint of those employers who look upon Mexican laborers as tractable and docile persons. It appears probable that, if these labor unions will be able to retain and enlarge their membership, they will make attempts to secure

Parent and child at work in California's industrialized agriculture (1930s). Photo: Bancroft Library, University of California, Berkeley.

better wages and working conditions to justify the existence of their organizations."[5]

The first evidence of the new worker activism that Block described was not long in revealing itself. At the southernmost end of the state, Mexican farmworkers had provided most of the labor power necessary to the operation of the Imperial Valley's highly industrialized agriculture almost from the beginning of the century, when massive irrigation efforts transformed the region from a barren desert into a fertile garden of unexcelled productive capacity. By the late 1920s the Imperial Valley was one of the leading vegetable- and melon-growing areas in the country. And with its large-scale production, absentee corporate ownership, labor-intensive crops, and seasonal reliance on an army of nonwhite migrants, the valley's agriculture represented industrialized farming in its most extreme and unalloyed form.[6]

For those employed on the valley's farms, mainly Mexicans and a large minority of Filipinos by the late 1920s, conditions were as oppressive as those faced by farmworkers anywhere in America.[7] Until 1928 the discontent of the valley's farmworkers had usually remained submerged, although sporadic labor troubles had appeared often enough to give farm employers in the region some reason for concern.[8] On the eve of the cantaloupe harvest in the early spring of 1928, Mexican farmworkers, in apparent response to the upsurge of interest in unionization among their countrymen in other parts of Southern California, formed the Workers Union of the Imperial Valley (La Unión de Trabajadores del Valle Imperial).[9] With the assistance of Carlos Ariza, the Mexican vice-consul at Calexico, and the support of local mutual-aid societies, the union succeeded in attracting a membership of roughly 1,200 workers by early May. The union acted immediately to bring about improvements in wages and working conditions, but its respectful overtures to area melon growers were rejected out of hand. The union's leadership had apparently not contemplated any action so direct and forceful as a strike, but a few dozen rank-and-file militants rejected their leaders' conciliatory posture and struck several farms just as the harvest was getting under way. Employers and local authorities joined forces to smash the strike almost immediately, but not without suffering the unsettling realization that Mexican farmworkers might not be the docile, uncomplaining beasts of burden that they had so confidently described them as being for more than a decade.[10]

Despite its brevity, and the fact that only a relative handful of the Imperial Valley's farmworkers were directly involved, the 1928 cantaloupe workers' strike was significant in that it revealed both a militant spirit and a firm expectation among Mexican laborers that their new union ought to be a fighting organization rather than simply another mutual-aid society. The strike also disclosed, however, that the new unionism among Mexican farmworkers was not without serious defects. The strike was completely unplanned, and thus devoid of the strategical and tactical considerations that might have enhanced its effectiveness. While the strikers deserved high marks for their militancy and courage, especially in light of the violent antiunionism they confronted, those laudable characteristics counted for little in the absence of an equally impressive measure of leadership. The other major weakness revealed by the strike was that the pronounced ethnic consciousness of the Mexican unionists, which derived as much from irremediable cultural differences as from a conscious choice, isolated them almost entirely from the non-Mexican farmworkers in the valley. This was particularly damaging to the potential success of farm unionism in the Imperial valley because it tended to increase the estrangement of the large minority of Filipino workers in the region from the Mexican majority. And given the reputation for militancy and radicalism enjoyed by Filipino workers, it appears likely that had their cooperation been solicited, the strike would have posed a much more formidable challenge to farm employers.[11]

The task of uniting the farmworkers and giving effective organizational focus to the palpable discontent that surged through their ranks in the Imperial Valley during 1928, as well as in California generally throughout the 1930s, was fraught with problems of staggering complexity. Both the A.F. of L. and the IWW had proved unequal to the challenge of organizing California's agricultural proletariat and abolishing its historic powerlessness, the former because of a lack of will and the latter because of a lack of coherent vision. Toward the end of 1929 the Communist Party of the United States, having proclaimed itself the new best hope of America's toiling masses, resolved to try its hand at accomplishing that task. And though they, too, were destined to fail in the end, in the early 1930s the Communists did provide the forceful leadership that was conspicuously absent in earlier organizing efforts among the state's farmworkers. Once fully joined, this volatile combination of farmworker militancy and radical leadership produced one of the most turbulent and eventful chapters in the history of agricultural unionism in the United States.

The decision that resulted in the appearance of a Communist-led agricultural labor movement in California was not made in response to signs of growing restiveness among the state's farmworkers but grew out of a policy promulgated half a world away by revolutionary tacticians at the highest levels of the Communist Party of the Soviet Union. Early in 1928 Soviet leaders determined that the interests of international communism were not being adequately served through the existing policy of having national Communist parties around the world "bore from within" the established trade unions of their respective countries. Communist trade unionists practicing the methods of the united front had failed to gain control of the labor movements of the most highly developed capitalist countries, and thus had failed to rally the world's workers either to the defense of the Soviet Union or to the cause of revolutionary communism. And so the united-front policy was abandoned in favor of a strategy of dual unionism, which provided for the establishment of Communist-led labor movements independent of the existing noncommunist trade unions in the capitalist countries.[12] The essential task of the new Communist labor movement was not to engage in a debilitating competition with the conservative trade unions for the allegiance of skilled tradesmen, but to organize the masses of semiskilled and unskilled workers in the basic industries who had traditionally been ignored or given inadequate attention by the established craft unions. Among those unorganized workers who were expected to become the backbone of the Communist labor movement were agricultural wage earners.[13]

The need for organizational work among agricultural workers in the capitalist nations had been recognized by international Communist leaders as early as 1920. As part of its agrarian "thesis," the Second Congress of the Communist International (Comintern) advised its multinational constituency that it was the "fundamental task" of each nation's "town proletariat" to educate and organize the "agricultural proletariat . . . in order to win it over to the side of the Soviet power and of the dictatorship of the proletariat."[14] Agrarian organizers were instructed to assist farmworkers, and, if possible, small farmers and tenant farmers, too, in establishing rural unions that could function in concert with the revolutionary unions among the urban working class. Once effected, this marriage of rural and urban workers was expected to "guarantee in full the success of the proletarian revolution."[15]

Despite the Comintern's directives, Communist trade unionists in the United States entirely ignored agricultural workers during the 1920s. Throughout most of the decade the Communists' labor arm, the Trade Union Educational League, had its hands full simply trying to maintain a tenuous influence on the fringes of unions affiliated with the A.F. of L.[16] Even when the Fourth Congress of the Red International of Labor

Unions (Profintern) officially sanctioned the independent organization of unorganized workers in 1928, the Communist Party, U.S.A., its leadership deeply divided over the wisdom of dual unionism and the ultraleftism of the so-called Third Party, made no immediate effort to establish its influence among farmworkers. Not until the founding of the Trade Union Unity League (TUUL) in Cleveland in the late summer of 1929, and after "the sharpest pressure of the Comintern and Profintern" had been applied,[17] was the organization of farmworkers finally discussed, and then only in the larger context of the party's overall tasks among the unorganized masses. The presence at the TUUL meeting of a "handful of agricultural worker delegates from the Far West," actually representing a small group of Mexican sugar-beet workers from Colorado, did result in the formation of the Agricultural Workers Industrial League (AWIL). Since, however, such workers' leagues were, in TUUL leader William Z. Foster's view, "not yet strong enough to function as unions," the AWIL was described as being no more than a union "in embryo."[18]

Although the TUUL had shown its willingness to pay lip service to the idea of organizing agricultural wage earners, the organization concentrated its efforts almost exclusively among the industrial work force.[19] Thus when in January 1930 the Communist Party became involved in its first real farmworker struggle, it was not a case of diligent organizational work finally bearing fruit, but a product of sheer opportunism.

On the first day of 1930, Mexican and Filipino farm laborers, increasingly dissatisfied with declining wages and the miserable working conditions in the lettuce fields of the Imperial Valley, walked off their jobs at several farms in the vicinity of Brawley. Within a few days what had started as a spontaneous, uncoordinated protest among a few hundred workers had become a full-fledged strike involving an estimated 5,000 field laborers. Because most of the Mexican workers, who constituted a majority of the strikers, belonged to the Mexican Mutual Aid Society of the Imperial Valley, the quasi-union that had succeeded the Workers Union of the Imperial Valley following the cantaloupe pickers' strike in 1928, that organization reluctantly assumed leadership of the strike. Its leaders sought the assistance of Edmundo Aragón, the Mexican consul at Calexico, in arranging a meeting with leaders of the Western Growers Protective Association, an employers' organization representing vegetable and melon growers in the valley. Predictably, Aragón's polite entreaties to the affected employers were ignored.[20]

As they had done two years before, growers mobilized their forces, which included city, county, state, and federal authorities, in order to crush the strike before it had time to gain real momentum. Imperial County Sheriff Charles Gillett, an enthusiastic enforcer of the growers' antilabor program, immediately set about his strikebreaking task by insisting that no strike existed. On January 2, 1930, the *Calexico Chronicle* reported that Gillett had arrested a correspondent from a Spanish-language newspaper in Los Angeles for writing that a strike was on in the Imperial Valley. The sheriff, the report continued, had declared that there was no strike. The *Brawley News,* however, seemingly less willing to jeopardize its credibility, reported on the same day that the offending newsman had been arrested "on suspicion of being identified in some way with the effort of Mexican and Filipino field workers in this vicinity to establish a wage scale." Suggesting the seriousness with which growers and valley authorities actually viewed the situation, the *News* further reported that federal immigration officials had promised "wholesale . . . roundups" of all Mexicans involved in the strike. Somewhat disconsolately, though, the paper informed its readers: "Filipino workers identified with the labor movement could not . . . be apprehended by immigration authorities, as the Philippines belong to the United States."[21]

With strikers getting little effective leadership from the cautious Mexican Mutual Aid Society, with intimidating threats being made by immigration officials, and with the ubiquitous Sheriff Gillett appearing throughout the valley to break up strikers' meetings and arbitrarily arrest all "troublemakers," the strike seemed destined to collapse as rapidly as it had begun. But the sudden appearance in the region of three energetic, if not particularly knowledgeable, Communist organizers from the TUUL quickly altered the strike's course. Whether or not it was due to their presence alone, within a day or two of their arrival new life had been breathed into the strike. And although in the end their efforts led to nothing more than the prolongation of a strike that was doomed from the start, TUUL organizers were effective enough to force growers and their supporters to admit publicly that the lettuce workers' strike was, as the *El Centro Press* noted on January 10, "much more serious than was at first suspected." More important still was the fact that the involvement of Communist organizers in the Imperial Valley lettuce strike marked the beginning of a new period of conflict in agricultural labor relations in California.

Ironically, Communist organizers first learned of the Imperial Valley strike, and the new opportunities it afforded them, through a brief article in the back pages of the *Los Angeles Times,* the most staunchly antilabor, antiradical newspaper in the state. Upon learning of the strike, the "leading elements" of the Los Angeles branch of the TUUL convened a "hurried conference" and decided to send a representative to the Imperial Valley to "investigate the situation." Frank Waldron, the young TUUL member selected to carry out the mission, reported after a brief visit to the region that the Mexican Mutual Aid Society was not providing the militant leadership the situation demanded, and that Communist organizers were needed if a "bona fide" workers' organization was to revive the rapidly faltering strike.[22]

Waldron and two other party members who had earlier been involved in organizing unemployed workers in the Los Angeles area were instructed by district TUUL leaders to proceed at once to the Imperial Valley. Neither Waldron, who as Eugene Dennis was destined to assume the leadership of the American Communist Party after World War II, nor his accomplices, Harry Harvey and Tsuji Horiuchi, had organizing experience among farmworkers. The trio nevertheless borrowed a car, gathered food and other provisions, and set out for the strike scene.[23]

Upon arriving in the town of Brawley, in the heart of the strike region, the three men made contact with local sympathizers and hastily formed a branch of the Agricultural Workers Industrial League. During their first few days in the strike area, the men were careful not to advertise their presence. The enthusiastic reception they apparently received from the small groups of strikers they initially met with, however, convinced them at once that the organizational opportunity before them held considerable promise. Recalling the initial strategy that he and his fellow organizers followed while hiding in Brawley's squalid Mexican barrio, Harry Harvey later said:

We had to keep ourselves under cover as much as possible. It was necessary for us to sleep during the day and to work among the laborers during the night. After dark we would immediately scoot around the shacks and hovels of the workers who were always glad to see us. They warned us against the stool pigeons, gave us information, and let us know the temperature of the workers in the various fields, just how hot or cold they were toward the strike. The workers we visited would arrange little meetings of the strongest union elements among the workers and out of these we would set up committees. When we would have a meeting at a Mexican home a guard would be posted outside. They would take you out the back way and come out in front three or four doors down. In talking to these splendid rank-and-file representatives of the working class one was heartened. No sacrifice, in the matter of getting them better living and working conditions, seemed too great to make. After these nocturnal

113

visits we would . . . spend the rest of our time mapping a campaign, arranging work for our committees, and running off strike bulletins or leaflets on an old mimeograph.[24]

After several quiet days of preliminary organizational work, Waldron and Harvey finally surfaced to conduct the AWIL's strike agitation among a wider circle of workers, including Filipino laborers. Making effective use of their mimeograph machine, the organizers soon flooded the strike region with a variety of handbills and leaflets imploring workers both to support the ongoing strike and to join the AWIL. To promote the latter goal an attractive list of AWIL strike demands was drawn up and widely distributed throughout the valley. Included among the twelve demands on the rather ambitious list were a minimum hourly wage of 50 cents for all workers, with higher pay for more difficult or skilled work; a guarantee of at least four hours' pay any time workers were called to the fields; an eight-hour day with time and a half for overtime and double time for Sundays and holidays; abolition of the labor contracting system; recognition of the AWIL; no work for children under sixteen; no discrimination on the basis of race, sex, or union membership; improved housing provided by employers; and the establishment of a hiring hall under the exclusive control of the AWIL—in effect, a closed shop.[25]

Although it is clear that Communist organizers sought to establish the AWIL as the only farmworker union in the Imperial Valley, it is equally clear that they saw the necessity of building the union's appeal around fundamental issues involving wages and working conditions, and not around abstract ideological arguments that had little meaning to these deprived workers. Consistent with this emphasis, in the preface to their list of demands the organizers declared: "All of us agricultural workers in Imperial valley are working under the most miserable conditions, treated not like human beings, but like animals. Wages are far below what one needs to live on and support a family. It is time that we get together in order to fight for better conditions."[26]

By bringing their agitation into the open, Communist organizers succeeded in briefly revitalizing a strike that growers and others had claimed was on the verge of collapse. Strikers and other workers apparently reacted enthusiastically to the AWIL's militant appeals, and endeavored during the second week of January to implement the union's many suggestions for strengthening the strike.[27]

By revealing their presence in the valley, however, AWIL organizers also provoked vigorous counteractions by growers and their supporters.

Moreover, those intent on breaking the lettuce workers' strike were now able to proceed in the name of selfless Americanism rather than in the less noble and altruistic cause of simple antiunionism. Growers, public officials, and newspapers wasted little time in dusting off the time-worn but still moving and efficacious anticommunist phraseology born out of the frenzied patriotism that had gripped America during and after World War I.[28]

In response to the growing clamor for all-out repression of radical "agitators" in the valley, arrests of strikers mounted rapidly. An especially vigorous manhunt was launched to apprehend AWIL organizers once their activities came to light, and on January 12 the inevitable arrests were made. The three were charged with vagrancy and placed in separate jails, where each was interrogated and roughly treated over several days. The efforts of authorities were particularly directed toward forcing the men to confess that they had planned to blow up lettuce sheds in the valley. Despite much mistreatment, each steadfastly denied the existence of such a plan.[29]

As soon as the men were jailed, the International Labor Defense began a legal campaign to gain their release. And because its directors believed that possible violations of First Amendment rights were involved in the case, the Southern California branch of the American Civil Liberties Union also sent representatives into the valley to investigate the circumstances of the organizers' arrests. After arriving in the strike region from Los Angeles, the ACLU representatives quickly determined that the civil liberties of the arrested Communist organizers had indeed been violated, and proceeded to the office of Sheriff Gillett to register an indignant protest. In doing so they unwittingly availed themselves of a firsthand demonstration of the prevailing mood among growers and authorities in the Imperial Valley. Before the Reverend Clinton J. Taft and his associate had even finished voicing their protest, Sheriff Gillett was on his feet, punching, kicking, and shoving the two men through the door of his office and out into the street, where he continued to vent his rage, cursing his terrified victims and challenging them to slug it out with him. In describing the encounter several days later, Taft readily conceded that Gillett's office "richly merits the description which he himself has given it on the upper left hand corner of his official envelopes: 'The lowest-down sheriff's office in the world (57 feet below sea level).'"[30]

Despite the publicity generated by their encounter with Sheriff Gillett, the ACLU's emissaries failed to persuade local authorities to free Waldron, Harvey, and Horiuchi. Finally on January 16 Leo Gallagher, a Los Angeles attorney representing the International Labor Defense, succeeded in getting the arrested AWIL organizers released on bail. By then, however, the lettuce workers' strike was approaching collapse, and the organizers' release failed to slow its rapid deterioration. Because they monitored all communications sent out of the valley by Western Union, local authorities were able to learn in advance of plans by the Workers' International Relief to bring food and other supplies to the strikers, and effectively blocked all relief efforts. Without relief from the outside, strikers with families to feed, and most Mexican workers fell into that category, had no choice but to return to work.[31]

In addition to the aid rendered by local, state, and federal authorities, growers also received invaluable assistance from leaders of the Mexican Mutual Aid Society. These men, mainly merchants and small businessmen, had never been enthusiastic about the strike, and reacted bitterly to the AWIL's efforts to take control of it.[32] When they failed to forestall the Communist takeover, they sought to salvage their organization's badly damaged reputation among employers by cooperating in the drive to smash the strike and wreck the AWIL. As a start, the society's leaders issued a public warning to Mexican workers that unless they severed all ties with Filipino strikers, they would face immediate deportation.[33] Soon afterward, in cooperation with the Mexican consul at Calexico and federal immigration officials, the society's leaders began a campaign to repatriate strikers by promising them that free land would be given to them in Mexico if they agreed to return home. In truth, little or no land was available to strikers who accepted the offer, but the large number of workers who returned to Mexico did not discover that fact until it was too late. At the same time that efforts were under way to repatriate strikers, Mexican officials friendly to Imperial Valley growers were reportedly recruiting new immigrants below the border to fill the labor vacuum created by the flow of former strikers southward.[34]

Under so many pressures, the strike finally collapsed. On January 23 the *Daily Worker* reported that AWIL leaders in the valley had reluctantly concluded that since most Mexican strikers had either left the region or been persuaded by leaders of the Mexican Mutual Aid Society to return to work, it was necessary to abandon the strike in order to protect the minority of Filipino strikers from further harm. At the same time that they called off the lettuce strike, however, AWIL organizers announced that they would launch a second strike in late spring, when the valley's cantaloupe harvest was due to begin. While admitting that the lettuce strike had failed, they insisted that the invaluable experience that had been gained from that encounter would virtually guarantee the success of the projected cantaloupe workers' struggle.[35]

Although Communists familiar with conditions in the Imperial Valley tended to attribute the collapse of the lettuce workers' strike to the strikebreaking activities of local authorities and the Mexican Mutual Aid Society, they recognized that a lack of careful prestrike planning had also contributed to its failure. With their own failures in mind, AWIL organizers resolved to prepare the ground for the spring cantaloupe strike with extreme care. Additional TUUL organizers were recruited from Los Angeles and San Francisco, and a series of workers' meetings was begun in order to perfect strike plans and to form various strike committees.[36]

Filipino farmworkers, whom Communist organizers had come to consider the most militant element in the Imperial Valley's agricultural labor force, were the earliest and most enthusiastic supports of the AWIL's strike agitation, although large numbers of Mexican laborers also unhesitatingly lent themselves to the new venture.[37] AWIL organizers had hoped that white workers, too, could be persuaded to join their ranks, and when a spontaneous strike broke out on February 11 among white packers and trimmers employed in lettuce sheds throughout the valley, the opportunity the Communists had sought appeared to be at hand. AWIL spokesmen immediately pledged their solidarity with the striking shed workers and promised to assist them in winning the wage demands that had prompted the walkout.[38]

From the beginning, however, the striking shed workers made it plain that they wanted nothing to do with the AWIL. When a Communist organizer who had been active in the earlier fieldworkers' strike tried to address a meeting of striking shed workers, he was dragged out of the hall by several American Legionnaires who were in attendance. Only the presence of several hundred Mexican and Filipino field laborers gathered outside the meeting hall prevented the angry legionnaires from carrying out a threat to beat their hapless captive.[39] After little more than a week the shed workers' strike ended when employers agreed, at the suggestion of Charles Connell, the regional head of the U.S. Conciliation Service, to establish a slightly higher wage scale for shed work. The employer's willingness to give favorable consideration to Connell's suggestions reflected in part their recognition that the timing of the shed workers' walkout had left them extremely vulnerable to crop losses. It also reflected the fact that Connell had pledged himself to assist employers in their efforts to thwart the AWIL's plan to conduct a strike during the melon harvest. Connell had assisted in the

117

successful drive to break the January lettuce strike, and he resumed his helpful activities as soon as the AWIL began its new strike agitation.[40] Finally, employers pursued a conciliatory course in the shed workers' strike in order to ensure the continuing unwillingness of white workers to support Mexican and Filipino field laborers in any future labor struggles in the region.[41]

The failure of AWIL organizers to recruit white shed workers was viewed as only a minor setback, and did not affect efforts to rally support for the melon strike. During March, AWIL organizers, operating out of a shack in Brawley which served as the league's official headquarters, moved from town to town throughout the valley, organizing and conducting mass meetings among Mexican and Filipino workers. At these meetings workers were encouraged to contribute their ideas regarding strike demands and tactics, and to select district field committees that would coordinate strikers' activities once the struggle was under way. Organizers apparently felt that decentralizing the leadership of the strike not only offered tactical advantages, but also helped to impress upon workers the AWIL's interest in rank-and-file involvement in all phases of prestrike activity.[42]

While the tasks of planning and promoting the cantaloupe strike were controlled entirely by the AWIL and the auxiliary relief and legal defense arms of the Communist Party, the ACLU sought to dissuade employers and local authorities from employing the extralegal strikebreaking tactics to which they had resorted earlier by publicizing those tactics as widely as possible. Bringing the plight of disadvantaged farmworkers in the Imperial Valley to the attention of the nation was not an easy task. When Roger Baldwin, the ACLU's founder and executive director, asked Bruce Bliven, the liberal editor of *The New Republic,* to publish a lengthy article exposing the gross violations of workers' civil rights during the lettuce strike, Bliven refused: "When we have to get the whole world into eight pages a week, an invasion of civil liberty has to be a little more outrageous than this, to command so much space."[43] Bliven did offer to print a 300-word editorial decrying the mistreatment of Imperial Valley workers. The editors of *The Nation,* to whom Baldwin made a similar overture, proved equally unwilling to devote the pages of their magazine to an article by the Reverend Taft relating his eyewitness account of the lawless behavior of farm employers and their allies during the January strike. While Baldwin was able to make full use of the ACLU's own publicity channels, he found himself unable to generate much concern among a wider circle of liberals over the obscure troubles of two such distinctly marginal groups as nonwhite farmworkers and militant Communists, especially when they were centered in a place as remote from the nation's economic and political vortex as the Imperial Valley.

Because the AWIL made little or no effort to keep its strike plans confidential, wide publicity attended the activities of Communist organizers during the entire period of their agitation. The responses of growers, authorities, and most valley citizens to sensational local newspaper reports of prestrike doings were predictably hostile. Any threat to the region's multimillion-dollar melon crop was viewed as a direct threat to the personal well-being of every citizen in the valley. That Communists were behind the agitation provided an additional, if essentially superfluous, justification for prompt and untempered suppression. The prevailing community spirit was typified in a letter to the editor of the *Brawley News* by a local minister, who, after briefly reviewing the menacing tenets of communism and surveying the economic dangers a strike would pose, proposed that the "best" citizens in the valley immediately organize themselves for the purpose of stopping the agitation while there was still time to do so.[44]

Although authorities originally sought to play down the activities of Communist organizers by reassuring the public that complete tranquillity had reigned in the valley since the collapse of the January lettuce workers' strike, privately they were increasingly apprehensive. The true depth of their concern was first revealed in late January, when the *Brawley News* reported that valley authorities had requested that Governor Clement C. Young call out the National Guard to aid them in quelling "communistic activities" in the region. The American Legion official who leaked the news to the press reported that authorities had decided to request the state's assistance in preventing Mexican and Filipino field laborers from attending meetings at which "assertedly objectionable sentiments were voiced," presumably by AWIL organizers. Apparently embarrassed by the disclosure that they were seeking outside help, city and county officials denied any knowledge of the request to Governor Young, and continued to insist in their public statements that quiet prevailed on the labor front in the valley.[45]

The strategy that authorities ultimately adopted to combat the AWIL menace was one that initially generated no publicity. In response to intense pressure from the major farm employers in the region, Imperial County District Attorney Elmer Heald finally decided to crush the farmworker movement by using the state's well-tested criminal syndicalism law against the Communist leadership of the AWIL. With the expert assistance of Captain William Hynes of the Los Angeles Police

Department's notoriously antilabor "Red Squad," Heald secured the services of three professional labor spies. The three were instructed to infiltrate the AWIL, to gain the confidence of Communist organizers in the valley, and then to collect evidence that would facilitate the criminal syndicalism prosecutions that Heald intended. So successful were the spies in establishing themselves within the AWIL that not long after entering the valley they were included among a small, select group of farmworkers taken to Los Angeles by veteran organizers to join the Communist Party. Thus, during the busiest weeks of the AWIL's campaign, Heald was able to monitor virtually every activity of Communist organizers and to keep abreast of the latest planning for the impending melon workers' strike.[46]

Ironically, Communist organizers guessed very early that authorities were seeking a pretext to use the criminal syndicalism law against AWIL leaders. The *Daily Worker* reported on January 30 that the mysterious appearance of rumors of a planned campaign of property destruction by Communists in the valley was undoubtedly part of a scheme to defeat the AWIL's efforts "legally." That Communists apparently did nothing to counter the authorities' strategy suggests that they were confident that their activities among farmworkers in the valley did not constitute a violation of the state's criminal syndicalism statute.

For the most part, Communist organizers behaved, as they had during the January lettuce strike, in ways consistent with their declarations that the essential purpose of the melon strike was to improve wages and working conditions. As new organizers who had not been involved in the earlier strike entered the valley to give assistance to the AWIL, however, they apparently brought with them the greatly heightened sense of revolutionary obligation that derived from the American Communist Party's loudly proclaimed intention to implement the Communist International's new ultrarevolutionary "line" by politicizing every "struggle" of the American working class, whether or not it had genuine political implications. Thus, as AWIL leaders implored farmworkers to join the union and support its fight for better wages and conditions in the melon fields, they also prompted workers to "fight against the danger of imperialist war," to "establish a workers and farmers government," and to "defend the Soviet Union."[47] While there is no evidence to suggest that the AWIL succeeded in convincing Mexican and Filipino farmworkers that they ought to include the defense of the Soviet Union among their personal priorities, the infusion of revolutionary political rhetoric into the melon-strike agitation undoubtedly lent credence to employers' assertions that the valley's labor troubles were rooted in the subversive intentions of Communist troublemakers rather than legitimate workers' grievances.[48]

The inevitable showdown between the AWIL and antiunion forces came in mid-April. Late in March the AWIL had announced that a conference of all agricultural workers in the Imperial Valley would be held on April 20 in El Centro. At that conference, AWIL spokesmen advised, final preparations for the cantaloupe strike would be made and the first steps taken to form a "national industrial union in agriculture."[49] On the evening of April 14, while preliminary meetings were being held in various parts of the valley, city, county, and state law-enforcement officials began a massive roundup of AWIL leaders and militant farmworkers. Meetings were raided throughout the valley, as were the several AWIL offices that had been established. Scores of workers were arrested, and what authorities described as "incriminating" evidence was seized. At El Centro alone more than 100 persons were arrested at a single workers' meeting. Additional arrests were made for several weeks afterward, especially of suspected AWIL officials who had evaded the April 14 dragnet. The initial charge lodged against those arrested was conspiracy to destroy the Imperial Valley's cantaloupe crop. Bail was fixed at the prohibitively high figure of $40,000 per man, although the normal bail for such charges in the rest of the state ranged from $500 to $3,000. After much effort, the International Labor Defense finally persuaded the presiding judge to reduce the bail, but $15,000 was as low as he would go.[50]

Most of the arrested workers were released within a few days. Only those identified by District Attorney Heald's undercover agents as leaders of the farmworker agitation remained in custody. On April 30 the Imperial County Grand Jury returned a blanket indictment against sixteen suspected Communists, charging them with three separate violations of the state's criminal syndicalism law: conspiracy to commit criminal syndicalism, belonging to an organization that advocated criminal syndicalism, and advocating criminal syndicalism. The International Labor Defense, with the help of ACLU lawyers from Los Angeles, assumed responsibility for defending those named in the indictment.[51]

With the arrest of the AWIL's most active organizers, agitation for the cantaloupe strike quickly died out. Communists outside the valley made a halfhearted effort to keep the strike agitation alive by encouraging farmworkers to select new leaders from their own ranks to carry on the work begun by AWIL organizers, but since valley authorities had forcefully demonstrated their unwillingness to tolerate any further efforts to promote a strike, potential leaders were understandably reluctant to come forward.[52]

During the six weeks between the arrests of AWIL leaders and the start of their trial, Communists in the southern part of the state were forced to abandon their organizational efforts in favor of legal defense work on behalf of the eleven men finally selected by District Attorney Heald to stand trial in El Centro.[53] Apparently convinced that there was no possibility of gaining a dismissal or reduction of the charges against their clients, the two attorneys engaged by the ILD to handle the case devoted their energies almost entirely to a vigorous but finally unsuccessful effort to win a reduction of the defendants' bail from $15,000 to $5,000. As a result of their failure, only one man, Frank Spector, was free on bail during the pretrial period. That Spector was the one defendant for whom bail was arranged is not surprising. As a leading functionary of the International Labor Defense in the United States, Spector was not only the highest-ranking party member facing prosecution in the Imperial Valley case, but also the person best qualified by experience and training to organize political and economic support around the country for himself and his fellow defendants. To the unmasked chagrin of Imperial Valley authorities, Spector was busy throughout California both before and during the trial organizing well-publicized political protests against the criminal syndicalism prosecutions and the continuing exploitation of farmworkers in the region.[54]

The El Centro trial began on May 26 in the court of Judge Von H. Thompson, an outspoken anticommunist prominent in American Legion affairs. After several days a jury consisting of nine men and three women was selected to hear the case. Because farmworkers were, for a variety of legal and economic reason, ineligible for jury service, the panel was composed mainly of farmers and merchants, each of whom, the ACLU charged, admitted a strong bias against Communists.[55]

Once the jury was impaneled, District Attorney Heald asked that charges be dropped against two of the eleven defendants before proceeding to make the state's case against the remaining nine. The only testimony offered in evidence against the defendants came from the three professional labor spies in Heald's employ. In succession, each took the stand to testify that the defendants had conspired to destroy the valley's melon crop, and had counseled farmworkers to use violence and terrorism in accomplishing that goal. In addition, each informer dutifully testified that the defendants had intimated that their ultimate goal in promoting a strike was to effect the destruction of capitalism and the overthrow of the government of the United States. To complete the prosecution's case, Heald sought to convince the jury that proof of membership in the Communist Party, as in the IWW, was enough in itself to justify conviction of the defendants under the state's criminal syndicalism law. To assist him in establishing this point Heald called upon Captain Hynes, the Los Angeles cop who had supplied the labor spies upon whose testimony the state's case was based. Certified by the court as an expert on revolutionary doctrines, Hynes advised the jury that the sole objective of the Communist Party, U.S.A., and thus of all its individual members, was the violent overthrow of the government of the United States. Since each of the nine defendants freely admitted to being a party member, Heald suggested to the jury that the application of elementary syllogistic logic would propel them toward the inescapable conclusion that the accused were guilty as charged.

Though they believed from the start that a fair trial was impossible under prevailing circumstances, defense attorneys endeavored nonetheless to refute the state's charges. Individually and collectively, the defendants denied the prosecution's allegations that they had conspired to destroy the valley's melon crop or that they had advocated the use of sabotage and terrorism by valley farmworkers. The charges made by Heald's "hirelings" were, defense attorneys argued, fabricated in every detail, products of a crude conspiracy by growers and authorities to deny farmworkers their right to organize and strike for better wages and working conditions. The highly emotional but irrelevant issues of communism and violent revolution, the defense insisted, were merely part of a tired subterfuge introduced by growers and their cohorts to conceal the true nature of the economic struggle going on in the valley.[56]

Defense attorneys were essentially correct in their assertion that authorities in the valley had acted to destroy the AWIL not because it was led by Communists, but because it threatened to become an effective farmworkers' union capable of conducting a successful strike.[57] Heald had admitted as much long before the trial began, and openly confirmed it again soon after the trial ended.[58] Yet at the same time the defense was arguing that the Communist issue was a political red herring, designed to divert attention from the underlying economic causes of worker militancy in the valley, leaders of the ILD were insisting that the defendants and their attorneys give the trial the fullest possible political significance by using it as a forum for the vilification of capitalism and the celebration of proletarian virtue and power. R. W. Henderson, the principal defense attorney and one of the state's most experienced lawyers in handling criminal syndicalism cases, argued that the ILD's strategy was counterproductive, but informed

Roger Baldwin that despite his advice, the defendants had insisted on "hewing to the line" and letting "the chips fall where they may."[59]

To members of the jury, whose individual economic well-being was inextricably bound in one degree or another to the agricultural economy of the valley, and thus to the major growers in the region, it mattered little in the end whether the suppression of the AWIL and its agents was a product of crass economic self-interest or of genuine patriotism. As their verdict would attest, jury members believed that the strikebreaking scheme hatched by employers and local authorities was fully justified as an act of self-preservation against upsetting ideas carried by men who were "outsiders" literally as well as figuratively. In testimony before a congressional hearing some months after the trial, District Attorney Heald noted that the fundamental objection of valley citizens to the El Centro defendants was that they were "not only not residents of [the] valley, but not a single one of them ever had a job in Imperial County, ever worked there, never did a day's work—not a single one of them ever did a day's work in Imperial County."[60]

Late in the afternoon of June 13 the Imperial Valley criminal syndicalism cases went to the jury. After little more than an hour of deliberation, the jury filed back into the courtroom to announce that the defendants had been found guilty on all counts. Conviction on each count carried a penalty of from one to fourteen years in prison. The five veteran Communists among the defendants were given prison sentences of three to forty-two years each. The single Filipino defendant received a somewhat less severe sentence of two to twenty-eight years. For the three Mexican defendants, none of whom was a citizen of the United States, sentencing was held in abeyance pending the issuance of deportation orders.[61]

When news of the Imperial Valley convictions and sentences reached Los Angeles and San Francisco, a storm of protest was raised in radical and liberal circles. The trial was denounced as an obvious frame-up, and valley growers and authorities were castigated by Communists, Socialists, and liberals alike for their heavy-handed treatment of AWIL leaders specifically and their systematic exploitation of farmworkers in general. At protest meetings held throughout the state, the "Imperial Valley outrage," as one writer labeled the whole affair, was condemned as a transparent but brutally effective effort by farmer-capitalists hidden behind a veneer of anticommunist respectability to crush the labor movement in California agriculture.[62]

On the legal front, the trial's outcome touched off a court battle that continued for nearly three years. It also brought to light a fundamental conflict between the Communist-controlled International Labor Defense and the ACLU over the questions of how and with what motives the process of appeal ought to be approached. Before the original trial had begun, ACLU spokesmen claimed that the Imperial Valley cases constituted the most serious contraventions of First Amendment freedoms that had taken place anywhere in the country during 1930.[63] As the ILD made plain its intention to use the Imperial Valley trial as a propaganda forum, however, the national leaders of the ACLU became increasingly reluctant to lend their organization's influence and resources to what they feared would degenerate into a cynical ideological circus. While the trial was still in progress Roger Baldwin cautioned local ACLU officials in Los Angeles that they should focus their concern on defending the right of workers to organize rather than on safeguarding the activities of individual Communist organizers.[64] Once the trial had concluded, Baldwin felt that his earlier concern that the ILD might seek to politicize it had been confirmed. Thus when Communist leaders in New York asked the ACLU to cosponsor an appeal of the Imperial Valley convictions, Baldwin declined on the grounds that he no longer believed that civil liberties were at issue in the case.[65] Finally, at the urging of Felix Frankfurter and Alfred Bettman, an Ohio attorney who specialized in criminal syndicalism cases, Baldwin agreed to give limited support to the ILD's appeal, although he still refused to provide the financial help that was the Communists' greatest need.[66]

After a delay of many months, the appeals of the Imperial Valley trial and its verdict were finally argued during March 1931 before the Fourth District Court of Appeals in Fresno. From the defense's point of view, the appeals produced mixed results. The conviction of Frank Spector, the most prominent of the Imperial Valley prisoners, was reversed on all counts because, the court concluded, the prosecution had failed to produce evidence that he had been present in the valley before the time that he was indicted. The convictions of the remaining defendants were overturned on two counts because of a defectively drawn indictment. But the court upheld the Imperial Valley jury's original finding that the men had advocated criminal syndicalism, and also denied the appellants' request for a new trial. The ILD's plan to appeal to the United States Supreme Court was dashed when R. W. Henderson, the attorney who had handled the case from its beginning, finally resigned over the long-standing differences between himself and Communist leaders regarding the extent to which the original trial and its appeals ought to be politicized in keeping with Communist Party policy. For more than a year the campaign to free the Imperial Valley prisoners continued, but the agitation shifted from the courts to the offices of the state's parole authorities. By the fall of 1932, each of the prisoners had served enough of the five-year sentences ultimately fixed by the State Prison Board to become eligible for parole. With undisguised reluctance, the board finally agreed to parole the men one at a time until the last prisoner was released in early 1933. Two of the men, Tsuji Horiuchi and Carl Sklar, were subsequently deported to the Soviet Union. None of the remaining prisoners returned to the work of farmworker organization upon being released.[67]

As important as the legal campaign on behalf of the Imperial Valley prisoners was to them, many Communists regarded it as having less long-term significance than a companion political movement begun at the same time to bring about the repeal of California's criminal syndicalism law. To those Communists familiar with the history of the criminal syndicalism law's application, the Imperial Valley case had from the beginning been a source of especial concern, particularly in terms of its potential implications.[68] When the El Centro jury determined that the revolutionary objectives of the Communist Party's program constituted an incitement to criminal syndicalism, and therefore that membership in the party was a crime, what had previously been a nagging concern among Communists was transformed into a deep fear that the state's criminal syndicalism law might be used to crush their organization in the same manner that it had been employed a few years before to destroy the IWW. With the announcement of the Imperial Valley verdict, efforts began in Los Angeles and San Francisco to organize an initiative campaign to repeal the state's criminal syndicalism law. Alone and in cooperation with various liberal groups and the State Federation of Labor, Communists sponsored numerous public protest meetings and gathered thousands of signatures on petitions calling for the law's abolition.[69] Convinced that the law posed a threat to the party as long as it remained on the books, Communists continued their drive against it even after the appeals court decision in mid-1931, since in reversing those criminal syndicalism convictions based on proof of Communist Party membership alone the court had not actually addressed itself to the question of the party's legality under the law. Long after the last of the Imperial Valley prisoners had gained his freedom, the Communists drive to repeal California's criminal syndicalism law remained active. And although their own campaign to kill the law did not succeed, their years of political groundwork may well have contributed to the ultimate removal of the law from the statute books during the 1950s.[70]

If the Imperial Valley struggle succeeded in generating vigorous legal and political activities in defense of agricultural unionism in California, it failed to provide an equally forceful stimulus for further organizational efforts among farmworkers, even though most Communists believed that the AWIL's experience in the region confirmed the party's official position that America's "rural proletariat" was ready and willing to be molded into a powerful new instrument of revolutionary change.[71] To an important extent the failure of the AWIL to resume its campaign of farmworker organization derived from its inability to put effective new organizers into the field to replace those eliminated by the El Centro prosecutions. Communist ambitions in agriculture remained very much alive, but like the IWW before it, the party found itself much more successful in producing spokesmen who could analyze the tactical deficiencies of the Imperial Valley campaign than in attracting organizers willing and able to carry on the difficult and dangerous work of union building out in the fields and orchards.[72]

Despite bold promises to organize the entire farm-labor force in California, the AWIL's actual record during 1931 and much of 1932 was devoid of real accomplishment. Throughout the period, most of the organizational work undertaken by Communists in California was among the growing body of unemployed workers. It should perhaps be noted that because farmworkers made up a disproportionately large segment of the total unemployed population in California, they did have considerable contact with Communist organizers. The circumstances of such contact, however, were plainly not conducive to the building of a viable agricultural workers' union.[73]

To the degree that Communists were active among farmworkers in California during 1931 and the first half of 1932, they tended to follow a rather passive organizational strategy. Organizers for the Agricultural Workers' Industrial Union (AWIU), the new name that the AWIL adopted in early 1931, made few if any concentrated efforts to recruit a large, permanent membership. Instead, AWIU leaders sought to advance the union's fortunes by taking advantage of the spontaneous strikes provoked by steadily declining wages and deteriorating working conditions.

The first of the two opportunities that presented themselves to the AWIU during this period was among cannery workers in the Santa Clara Valley who had walked off their jobs in July 1931 in response to a 20 percent reduction in wages. As soon as AWIU organizers learned of the walkout, they were in San Jose, working to wrest control of the strike from the American Labor Union, a small independent union formed a few months earlier by the predominantly Italian cannery workers in the region. Communists apparently experienced little difficulty in gaining the influence they sought. In recognition of their activities among this new constituency, organizers again changed the name of the organization, this time to the Cannery and Agricultural Workers Industrial Union (CAWIU), the name by which it would be known for the remainder of its career. Once in control of the situation, CAWIU leaders endeavored to organize mass picketing of struck canneries by the 2,000 workers involved in the strike. When employers responded by bringing in gangs of scabs under the armed guard of local police and deputized American Legionnaires, numerous violent clashes resulted. Several CAWIU leaders were arrested during these picket-line battles, and when strikers organized mass marches to protest the arrests, local authorities and vigilantes responded with further violent attacks. Given the employers' determination to break the strike by force, the CAWIU's demands—a wage increase of 10 cents an hour, time and a half for overtime, free transportation to work for women employees, no discrimination against union members, equal pay for equal work, and formal recognition of the union—failed to receive a hearing. Convinced after several days of fruitless struggle that their cause was hopeless, and disillusioned with the CAWIU and its leadership, strikers finally returned to work without having won a single demand. Its new name notwithstanding, the CAWIU's influence among workers in California's canning industry came to an abrupt end with the collapse of the Santa Clara Valley strike.[74]

CAWIU activity was at a low ebb for almost a full year following the Santa Clara Valley dispute. While union leaders patiently awaited the outbreak of another spontaneous farmworkers' strike, they did almost nothing to recruit new members or to retain old ones. As a result, the CAWIU was without a membership by early 1932. Critics within the party were quick to attribute the union's weakness to its passive organizing policies, but their criticisms had no immediate effect.[75] And although most critics outside the party had no desire to see the CAWIU's organizational record improve, they observed the same weakness in the union's approach to organization. One of the most interesting of these outside commentaries was offered by E. P. Marsh, an official of the U.S. Conciliation Service, who wrote of CAWIU organizers after seeing them in action during the San Jose cannery strike: "These followers of Bill [William Z.] Foster wouldn't know what to do in case they won a strike and had to establish and stay with an organized group; causing unrest and hatred of established government, demonstrations and clashes with authority, is their immediate goal rather than the prosaic, detailed work of carrying on the non-spectacular work of an every day union."[76]

In May 1932 the CAWIU was briefly spurred into action by another spontaneous farmworkers' strike in central California, this time among 1,500 Mexican, Filipino, and Puerto Rican pea pickers in the vicinity of the San Mateo County community of Half Moon Bay. The workers' principal grievance was one typical of the period. At the beginning of the harvest, area farmers announced that the piece rate for picking a sack of peas was being reduced from 75 cents to between 40 and 50 cents. Although they were unorganized, pea pickers in the region immediately withdrew their labor in protest against the wage cut. Only a few hours after the walkout began, CAWIU organizers were on the scene. They encountered no resistance in assuming leadership of the strike, since none had previously existed. Demands for restoration of the old wage rate and improved working and living conditions were quickly formulated by CAWIU leaders and presented to local farmers. Employers wasted little time in making clear their intention to break the strike by force. Calls for help broadcast throughout the country brought a small army of police and special deputies, mainly farmers, into the strike region. Strikers were advised that unless they immediately returned to work, they would be evicted from employer-owned labor camps and replaced by imported scabs. Strikers were further warned that attempts to hinder new workers from entering the fields would not be tolerated. Under these pressures, and realizing that the strikers were unprepared for a long, difficult struggle, the CAWIU reluctantly called off the strike after only twenty-four hours. For the second time in less than a year, the CAWIU's efforts to capitalize on a spontaneous farmworkers' strike ended in abject failure.[77]

With the collapse of the pea pickers' strike, CAWIU leaders appear to have recognized at last the impossibility of building a strong agricultural labor movement on spontaneous, wholly unplanned uprisings. While the embarrassing defeats that the CAWIU had suffered at San Jose and Half Moon Bay promoted a growing internal disenchantment with its opportunistic strategy, it seems likely that increasingly harsh criticisms of the union's organizing tactics from high party circles were an equally important factor in persuading its leaders to reevaluate their methods. CAWIU leaders were surely stung by such comments as those by Harrison George, a leading authority on the Communist Party's agrarian program in America, who described as "inexcusable" the union's failure to realize even modest organizational gains from the several agricultural strikes in which it had been involved since 1930.[78] Equally embarrassing to CAWIU leaders was the *Western Worker's* assertion in May 1932 that, despite the widespread discontent and militancy that deteriorating agricultural wages and working conditions had generated among California's farmworkers, the union was "dead" in virtually every section of the state.[79]

Yet whatever the subsidiary factors that contributed to the renovation of its tactics and the regeneration of its enthusiasm for the work of farmworker organization, the CAWIU was finally forced to become a more effective organization during the latter half of 1932 mainly because of the influence exerted by one man, the new district organizer to whom the fortunes of the Communist Party in the far western states were entrusted at the beginning of 1931.

In Sam (Samuel Adams) Darcy, Communists in California gained a district organizer as resourceful and effective as any who served the American party during the 1930s. Though only in his mid-twenties when he assumed control of District 13, which encompassed California, Nevada, and Arizona, Darcy was already a seasoned and accomplished Communist leader. He was, according to Orrick Johns, a party member who worked under him during the early 1930s, a fearless front-line fighter and "an adroit tactician, quick and sure," but also a leader who was "thoroughly at home in theory." Recalling the character of Darcy's leadership, Johns wrote: "He was implacable and immovable in carrying out a decision, once it was made, and he made decisions that were not easy to carry out. He was a slave driver, but a convincing one." Yet Johns insisted that while Darcy used his authority unhesitatingly ("I have seen him whip a dozen rebellious leaders into line, some of whom thought they had better intellects than his"), he was not an authoritarian personality. "If he gave what seemed an arbitrary order," Johns wrote, "he made it clear to us just why he gave it." As district organizer, Darcy was authorized to enforce the strict discipline that was the party's essential strength. And for Johns and his fellow party members in San Francisco "there was an element of dread simply in the title." Despite the trepidation fostered by this seeming omnipotence, however, Johns concluded: "Darcy was a human being, and, if he seemed unreasonable and tough, there is no doubt that he was beloved by the rank and file. I can remember, after taking criticism from others that I thought was unjust, for mistakes in work that had cost me sleepless nights and long days, a word from Darcy in his office would wipe out the irritation and give me new courage."[80]

Sam Darcy was born in the Ukraine in 1905 and as a small child was brought by his family to the United States. Growing up in the fetid ghettos that enclosed New York City's garment district, Darcy took easily and naturally to the anticapitalist ideologies that suffused the politically congested world of the Jewish needle trades workers, because they, more than the native American doctrines of economic individualism and free enterprise, offered plausible and personally reassuring explanations of the wage earner's degraded status in the "land of opportunity."[81]

With the development of an American communist movement following World War I, Darcy found his ideological home. Even as a teenager he won recognition within party circles for his intelligence and energy, and after a few years of prominent work in the Young Communist League he became one of the select group of American Communists sent to the Soviet Union for study and training at the Lenin Institute. Returning home in early 1929, Darcy arrived at a time when the American party was convulsed by savage internecine power struggles.[82] It was also a time, however, when leadership opportunities were multiplying as former leaders who had lost their fights for position and authority either were vanquished or voluntarily abandoned the party in favor of an assertedly higher and purer expression of Marxist-Leninist consciousness. For the rising young Communist who had not taken part in the fierce battles that determined who would lead the American Communist Party in the 1930s, the principal danger was that his work would be too effective, too flamboyant, and revealing of too much ambition to suit those perched, always somewhat precariously, at the top of the leadership pyramid. Because Darcy was both visibly talented and unabashedly ambitious, he was not long in offending the distinctly paranoiac sensibilities of leaders who had only recently ascended to the highest positions of authority within the American party. During the initial phase of the party's national campaign to organize the Depression era's growing army of unemployed workers, Darcy antagonized Earl Browder, in particular, by enhancing his personal stature through the leading role he played in planning and organizing the largest and most widely publicized of the early mass demonstrations of the unemployed, that held in New York City on March 6, 1930.[83] Relations between Darcy and some leaders, including Browder, were also probably strained as a result of the undisguised contempt he frequently exhibited toward those national party functionaries whom he disdainfully described as "middle-class rejects who couldn't make it in the bourgeois world."[84]

Browder was not long in making known his displeasure with Darcy's too enterprising and conspicuous activism. Shortly after the March 6 demonstration Darcy was suddenly placed in charge of the International Labor Defense, and thereby effectively isolated from the affairs of the national office. Still not convinced that he had really succeeded in neutralizing his young antagonist, however, Browder sought in late 1930 to put even greater distance between Darcy and the New York headquarters by exiling him to what was widely regarded as one of those dead-end posts reserved for errant party functionaries: district organizer of District 13, the most geographically remote extremity of the entire Communist network.[85]

After the heady environments of Moscow and New York City, the comparatively listless atmosphere surrounding the work of the Communist Party in California and the remainder of District 13 induced a mild case of culture shock in Darcy when he and his wife, Emma, arrived in San Francisco on Christmas Eve, 1930. He found a district organization that was in a complete shambles, a district-wide membership of fewer than 300, a treasury that amounted to $6, and a dispirited leadership deprived of its most energetic elements six months earlier by the El Centro criminal syndicalism convictions. On Christmas Day, when he paid his first visit to the district headquarters of the party, in a rough working-class neighborhood "south of the slot" (south of Market Street) in San Francisco, he found a shabby storefront whose matching interior was "a dark recess littered with dirt." Darcy also had that day his first contact with the membership of Branch 1 of District 13 of the Communist Party, U.S.A.: thirty or so drunks and derelicts sprawled on the floor and on a few rickety benches, sleeping peacefully and reeking of "canned heat." As he soon discovered, the essential advantage of party membership in the minds of many of the area's less encumbered denizens was that it guaranteed a warm place to "flop" on cold winter nights. The full-time "staff" charged with overseeing the less than dynamic affairs of District 13 was composed of three devoted but demoralized party members who did little to hide their initial feelings of resentment toward the brash young New Yorker exiled into their midst by a national office that had in the past pursued a policy of studied indifference to their situation.

Despite the innumerable difficulties he faced in trying to rehabilitate the thoroughly dilapidated organization he had inherited, Darcy also saw a rich opportunity before him. As a result of the national leadership's disinterest in District 13, he had a free hand in deciding how and toward what ends the new energies he was able to generate within the California party would be used. And he wasted no time in giving form to his ambitious personal vision of the party's mission in the Far West.

Beyond the immediate custodial responsibilities that occupied him as a result of the district's organizational disarray, Darcy regarded the organization of unemployed workers and the state's agricultural wage earners as the most urgent task facing the Communist Party in California. His emphasis on the unemployed was a natural consequence of the country's rapidly deteriorating economic situation, and conformed entirely with the program of the party nationally. When it came to farmworkers, however, Darcy believed, correctly, that notwithstanding the party's sporadic endorsement of an agrarian strategy that contemplated, among other things, the unionization of America's rural proletariat, nothing beyond vacuous rhetoric had been expended by the national leadership in behalf of agricultural organization. The brief involvement of Communists among farmworkers in the Imperial Valley was the result less of a coherent organizational program than of a still smoldering interest in agricultural unionism that had survived from the era of IWW activism in rural California. And once deprived by the El Centro convictions of those organizers who had been most responsive to the Wobbly legacy, the campaign of farmworker organization that the district leadership had impetuously launched at the beginning of 1930 was within a year drifting aimlessly under the irresolute and inept direction of party officials who were simply unable to translate their intentions into effective organizing tactics.

Though Darcy had no previous experience with farmworkers or familiarity with the special characteristics of employment relations in California's industrialized agriculture, his astuteness as an organizer compensated for what he initially lacked in specialized knowledge. And while he realized early on that the organization of migratory farmworkers posed enormous problems, he soon discovered that the state's agricultural laborers were, precisely because of their utter poverty and social debasement, "willing to fight the battle of nothing-to-lose." He also realized that the party's only hope of success in organizing agricultural laborers lay in a strategy that deemphasized its own political self-interest in favor of immediate improvements in the wages and working conditions of the workers. Finally, Darcy concluded that if farmworkers were to be unionized by the party, the actual work of organizing them had to be done by members who were themselves from the working class; middle-class members, he believed, tended to eschew intimate tactics in favor of lectures designed to inform laborers of their revolutionary obligations in the face of capitalist oppression.

133

And so Darcy launched an intensive program to recruit and train organizers who, because of their own class background and experience, were able to relate to the state's farmworkers even if they were not actually from the ranks of the agricultural labor force.[86]

Convinced as a result of its sorry record in 1931 that drastic changes were needed in both the structure and the orientation of the CAWIU, Darcy began early in 1932 to exert pressure on the union's leadership to develop a new approach to organization that would be based on careful study, thorough preparation, concentrated effort, and the fullest possible degree of worker involvement at the grass roots level in the union's decision-making processes. Much like the Wobblies nearly two decades earlier, Communist leaders began to express in increasingly direct language their conviction that too much emphasis had been placed on empty propaganda and not enough on real organizational work centered around the basic demands with which agricultural workers were most concerned.[87]

Darcy's influence was clearly in evidence at the annual District 13 Convention of the Communist Party, U.S.A., held in July. In keeping with the party's policy of "self-criticism," convention delegates dwelt at length on the faults and weaknesses of the CAWIU's previous work among farmworkers, and the union's leaders were chastised for their consistent failure "to apply the Party line properly." Specifically, CAWIU leaders were chided for their dismal organizational record following the Santa Clara Valley cannery strike, their reluctance to share the union's leadership with newer members drawn from the rank and file, and their tardiness in recognizing the deficiencies in a union-building policy based on the exploitation of spontaneous strikes rather than thoughtful and diligent farmworker organization. But surely the unkindest rebuke of all came when, in summary, the district leadership censured CAWIU leaders for having failed during the preceding two years to conduct themselves as "serious minded revolutionaries."

Having administered the prescribed reproofs, the convention endorsed several principles meant to serve as basic guidelines for the union's future course. CAWIU leaders were instructed to build the union through strong mass organization, and not by feeding off spontaneous workers' uprisings; to select a major industrialized farming region as a "concentration point," and to put their "best forces" to work establishing an organizational stronghold from which the union's power and influence could later radiate; and to promulgate, with rank-and-file assent, a set of concrete workers' demands in advance of the harvest season, and then to impede the harvest until those demands were met.[88]

Whether out of eagerness to redeem themselves in the eyes of their comrades or because they had been inspired by the convention's directives, CAWIU organizers responded immediately to the challenge before them. On July 18 a conference of all CAWIU members was held in San Jose to map a new strategy for the months ahead and to put the union on a more businesslike footing. After perfunctory admissions of past errors, union leaders reviewed in detail the deteriorating conditions of employment in industrialized agriculture in California. The draft resolution adopted by the conference when it concluded its work reflected the union's dutiful intention to implement the district convention's directives. The CAWIU would maintain its headquarters in San Jose and concentrate its organizational efforts among farmworkers in the Santa Clara, Salinas, and Pajaro valleys. As the resolution sought to make clear, however, the union's policy of concentrated effort did not mean that agricultural workers in other areas of the state would be neglected. In addition, conference delegates agreed that the union's leadership had to reflect the various elements of its membership in terms of race, nationality, sex, and age. Finally, they agreed that patient and thorough organization was an absolute prerequisite to any economic action, and that all strikes and other union activities must be intended to enforce only "concrete" demands—that is, those involving wages, working conditions, and union recognition. To ensure that every farmworker could afford membership in the CAWIU, the conference established the lowest possible initiation fees and montly dues. The initiation for an employed worker was 50 cents; an unemployed worker paid only 10 cents. Monthly dues for a working member were set at 30 cents, while jobless members paid only 5 cents. Membership books were 5 cents for everyone. In a final gesture of ideological conformity, the conference resolution reiterated the CAWIU's desire to cooperate with small farmers and urban workers in advancing the political objectives of the Communist Party.[89]

During the months following the San Jose meeting, CAWIU organizers were conspicuously active throughout the three-valley region selected by the conference for special attention. Though somewhat less visible, additional organizers were actively working on behalf of the union in various other rural areas of the state. Not having launched their new campaign until the summer harvest season was well under way, however, CAWIU organizers found themselves working almost exclusively among unemployed farmworkers during the late fall of 1932. As a result, gains in union membership were disappointingly small. Yet despite their failure to enroll large numbers of agricultural workers, CAWIU organizers remained active, mainly in organizing hunger marches and protests against inadequate government relief policies, but also selling the idea of unionism to farmworkers whenever the opportunity presented itself.[90]

The first real indication of the effectiveness of the CAWIU's efforts came in mid-November, when tree pruners struck near the Solano County town of Vacaville, a fruit-growing district midway between Sacramento and San Francisco. The strike began on the fruit ranch of the area's largest grower, Frank H. Buck, who only a few days before had won election to Congress on the Democratic ticket headed by Franklin D. Roosevelt. At the beginning of the pruning season, and just before the election, Buck had announced publicly that he intended to pay his workers $1.40 for an eight-hour day. While the daily wage for the same work and hours had been $3.50 as recently as 1928, Buck's offer appeared positively generous alongside the $1.25 being offered by other orchardists in the area. Moreover, Buck allegedly promised local farmworkers that if elected he would raise their pay even further. On November 8 Buck was elected, apparently receiving the support of almost every farmworker in the district who was eligible to vote. Two days later, after securing the agreement of other important farm employers in the area, Buck announced that beginning November 14 the wage for tree pruning would be cut to $1.25 for a nine-hour day, a rate even lower than that originally contemplated by most of his fellow growers.[91]

Buck was apparently unaware that the CAWIU had been actively organizing workers in the vicinity of Vacaville for several months. A handful of young organizers from Sacramento had entered the area in August mainly to organize unemployed farmworkers, but by the time Buck and his fellow orchardists announced their plans to cut wages, the CAWIU had gained sufficient influence among local farmworkers to allow it to call the first prearranged strike in its three-year history.[92]

On November 14, the day the reduced wage rate went into effect, 400 Mexican, Filipino, Japanese, and white tree pruners walked off their jobs. According to union spokesmen, 250 of the workers had joined the CAWIU before the strike began, and the others were quickly signing up. The strike demands issued by the union generally conformed to those it had enumerated in previous strikes: a daily wage of $1.50; an eight-hour day; no evictions of strikers from employer-owned housing pending settlement of the dispute; a guarantee of no discrimination on the basis of race, sex, or union activity; and formal recognition of the CAWIU by employers. In response, the affected employers, who adamantly refused to deal with the union throughout the strike, offered $1.20 for an eight-hour day.[93]

Almost totally lacking in essential resources, the CAWIU was at once forced to rely on outside help to sustain the strike. Within a few days the communist Workers' International Relief had pledged its full support to the striking workers and their families. Likewise, the International Labor Defense immediately offered its services to strikers arrested during the numerous clashes that occurred when employers and local authorities sought to transport scabs through the union's militant picket lines or to break up strike meetings. The first confrontation took place on November 21, when strikers tried to barricade the main street of Vacaville to prevent the passage of trucks carrying scabs toward the orchards on the outskirts of town. Police quickly moved in and arrested six strike leaders, but when a large mob of pickets surrounded the outnumbered authorities, they were persuaded to release their prisoners. During the many violent clashes that followed, those strikers who were arrested fared less well.

As in earlier agricultural labor disputes in the state, city and county authorities threw their full weight behind employers' efforts to undermine and break the strikers' resistance. The fact that the mayor of Vacaville was himself one of the largest orchardists in the region no doubt facilitated the especially close cooperation between employers and public authorities which manifested itself during the strike.[94]

Employers also succeeded in attracting the support of much of the area's white citizenry, mainly through fervent anticommunist appeals and by exploiting the racial antagonisms that had long smoldered in the region. In an apparent effort to arouse community feeling against the strikers, employers and local newspapers charged on several occasions that the CAWIU was advocating and practicing sabotage. Although the union vehemently denied the accusations, its denials had little effect in cooling the passions aroused by such charges. At a large anticommunist rally organized on December 2 by farmers, local businessmen, and the American Legion, whose members were prominently arrayed on the side of the employers throughout the strike, citizens of Vacaville and the surrounding countryside heard local leaders angrily denounce the CAWIU as an instrument of Communist subversion. They also heard the same leaders suggest a resort to "Judge Lynch" in combatting the "red" agents who were using the strike to advance their "anti-American" master plan. A local churchman advised his fellow patriots

137

that "a real menace confronts this community which must be met in the good old American way." The speaker who followed, a judge from a nearby town, instructed his audience that "the good old American way" meant adopting "the system that is used south of the Mason and Dixon line."[95]

Local vigilantes took the suggestion to heart. Three days after the rally, while the town's police chief was, according to the *Western Worker,* "conveniently absent," a band of masked men, in possession of all the necessary keys, entered the Vacaville jail, opened cells holding several strike leaders, and dragged them to waiting automobiles. At a remote spot several miles away the terrified strikers were beaten, given crude haircuts, doused with red paint, and abandoned with a warning that unless they immediately left the country, a more definitive punishment awaited them. Local authorities, to whom the CAWIU assigned responsibility for the kidnappings, made no effort to identify or arrest the vigilantes.[96]

Despite the efforts of employers, law-enforcement officials, and vigilantes to break the strike, the CAWIU was reasonably successful in keeping scab labor out of struck orchards during the early weeks of the dispute. Presumably to protect male strikers from further physical assaults, the mass picket lines maintained by the CAWIU during the latter stages of the strike consisted mainly of women and children. Such a strategy in no way compromised the effectiveness of the picket lines, since the women strikers had earlier shown themselves to be among the most militant and fearless participants in the struggle.[97]

As the weeks passed and the union's meager resources were finally exhausted, however, the strikers' ability and will to continue the fight weakened. The several forms of intimidation used by local antilabor forces also took their toll. Many Filipino strikers, faced with increasing threats of violence, were in time forced to flee the region for their own protection. The strikers' cause was also hurt when visiting A.F. of L. officials from the Sacramento Federated Trades Council took the employers' side in the dispute. When employers claimed in late December that the strike had ended, union spokesmen bravely denied it. Yet union leaders clearly recognized that the strike's collapse was imminent. Attendance at strike meetings had fallen off sharply, the flow of relief from the outside had slowed to a trickle, and the *Western Worker* reported in early January that strikers and their families were "feeling the pinch of hunger." Finally, at a meeting on January 20, CAWIU members acknowledged the obvious and voted to end their strike.[98]

The more than two months of sacrifice, suffering, and intimidation that Vacaville strikers had endured gained them nothing in the end. Farm employers were plainly in firmer control of the labor situation in the region after the strike than they had been before it began. For the CAWIU the Vacaville defeat was a serious but only temporary setback. Union leaders emerged from the long struggle with more than a few battle scars, but also considerably wiser in the ways of successful strike leadership. Although they were unwilling to say so publicly, union leaders recognized that calling the strike at a time when farm employers were not under immediate pressure to reach a settlement, as they would have been at harvesttime, was clearly a mistake, and surely an important factor in explaining its eventual collapse. It was a mistake they would not repeat. A second and equally useful lesson was that so-called home guards, those family farmworkers who lived in an agricultural region on a permanent or semipermanent basis, could, despite their reputed prudence and docility, be organized into a strong, militant strike force. Even before the Vacaville strike had ended, Communist strategists were beginning to wonder if this more sedentary class of farmworkers might not in the long run be better material from which to build a strong union than migratory workers had been, however impressive the migrants' reputation for militancy.[99]

The end of the Vacaville strike also marked the end of three years' effort by labor affiliates of the Communist Party to build a labor movement in California agriculture. On the surface, the record that the CAWIU and its predecessors had compiled was anything but notable. Each of the four strikes in which it had played a leading role since 1930 ended in defeat for the union, for the farmworkers it sought to lead, and for agricultural unionism in the state.

Yet the state of the CAWIU's health and the prospects for farm unionism in 1933 were not so poor as the record of the previous three years tended to suggest. Despite its failures, the union had demonstrated considerable staying power in an environment bitterly hostile to unionism and radicalism. It had withstood both the legal and extralegal blows rained on it by powerful antilabor forces throughout the state; had developed, under Sam Darcy's leadership, a corps of able new organizers to replace those eliminated by the 1930 criminal syndicalism prosecutions; and had slowly learned, through an often painful and costly process of trial and error, to adapt its methods to meet the special organizational problems posed by a multiracial, multilingual farmworker population that lacked a tradition of cooperative enterprise. Of still greater significance, the CAWIU had succeeded by the beginning of 1933 in gaining the attention, the respect, and the confidence of farmworkers in almost every major agricultural district of the state. Emboldened by the support it had attracted and encouraged by unmistakable signs of deepening discontent within the state's rural work force, the union resolved to make its fourth year the most momentous in the history of agricultural labor relations in California and the nation.

5

The Great Upheaval: 1933

In the history of labor relations in the United States few years can match 1933 for sheer commotion and friction. After three years of a depression more debilitating than any the nation had previously endured, and with what they initially believed was the warm support of a newly elected reform administration in Washington, workers across the country turned to unionism as a means of ameliorating their disadvantaged condition.[1]

For many of the same reasons that workers nationwide manifested an activist mentality in 1933, California farmworkers evinced unequivocal signs of militancy as the spring harvest season approached. Agricultural wages, which had steadily declined as the Depression worsened, reached their nadir early in 1933, further aggravating the suffering of an occupational group that even in times of general prosperity had little firsthand knowledge of a decent standard of living. What lent particular volatility to agricultural labor relations in California in 1933, however, was that the discontent of the state's farmworkers found in the radical Cannery and Agricultural Workers Industrial Union a willing and eager institutional outlet. With the constituency it had long sought finally resigned to the necessity of organization and economic struggle, the CAWIU promptly set off a series of explosions that shook California's industrialized agriculture to its foundations.[2]

In seeking to give direction to the latent energy that farmworker dissatisfaction represented, the CAWIU's Communist organizers were under restraints imposed by the extreme present-mindedness of the agricultural work force. The ideological content of their appeal was kept at a minimum, and for a good reason. Most farmworkers were unschooled, and simply too engrossed in a daily struggle for survival to derive much inspiration or comfort from the utopian prospects offered by communism. While CAWIU organizers were able to arouse farmworkers to militant words and actions, and thus to radicalize their behavior, they did not achieve a political radicalization of the agricultural proletariat. For the vast majority of California farmworkers who joined the union in 1933, membership signified neither an understanding nor an endorsement of communism; it seems to have meant only that they accepted the idea of collective action as the most promising means of solving the economic problems which oppressed agricultural workers in the state. If Communists distant from the fields and orchards of California misunderstood or chose to ignore the true nature of the CAWIU's appeal, those party members who actually carried out the difficult work of organizing agricultural labor did not. The CAWIU's power to attract members in 1933 existed in exact proportion to its organizers' success in convincing farmworkers that the union could assist them in bettering their wages, working conditions, and standard of living. Whether they liked it or not, CAWIU organizers understood this simple equation and conducted themselves accordingly.

The CAWIU's 1933 organizational drive began early in the year, while the memory of the Vacaville struggle was still fresh and before the spring harvest season had arrived. Union organizers, usually unpaid and forced to travel by any means they could find, fanned out into almost every important farming region of the state between January and March. Once in the target areas, organizers typically employed a method of organization that was simple but effective. After locating the main concentration of farmworkers in the region and establishing friendly contacts, union organizers interviewed individuals and groups of laborers informally to learn their principal grievances. As soon as they discovered which concerns were foremost in the workers' minds, organizers tailored their appeals correspondingly. To assist them in their work, organizers quickly recruited the most militant farmworkers in the region into the CAWIU. Members of this hastily marshaled cadre generally became the nucleus for a new CAWIU local, and used their familiarity with other workers in the area to attract further support for the union. As the harvest period drew near, the local CAWIU unit usually called a public meeting to which all agricultural workers in the vicinity were invited. At such a meeting, normally controlled without much difficulty by CAWIU members, workers were encouraged to formulate a list of specific demands for the coming season, and asked to give their advance approval to a strike to be called if employers failed to meet those demands. When union organizers received the strike authorization they sought, the list of demands was widely publicized among the remainder of the farm-labor force in the area. If organizers had done their work with proper attention to detail, they found themselves on the eve of the harvest season in a position to issue a strike call that was likely to attract the immediate support of enough workers to halt or seriously disrupt work in the target fields.[3]

The vigor with which the CAWIU pursued its organizational campaign during the early months of 1933 quickly became a matter of considerable concern to agricultural interests in California. Early in February, Captain William Hynes of the Los Angeles Police Department's "Red Squad" wrote to Imperial County District Attorney Elmer Heald, advising him that CAWIU organizers had quietly entered the valley for the purpose of initiating a "campaign of agitation" among the region's farmworkers. Hynes warned that valley authorities should be on the lookout for Pat Chambers, a veteran Communist recruited by Sam Darcy and the union's leadership to direct the organizational drive. "If it is your desire to stop this agitation and organizational work at its inception, would suggest you don't delay getting him out of the valley too long as he is of the persistent and agressive [*sic*] type, a typical soap-box orator and active at all times."[4] In response to Hynes's warning, Judge Von Thompson, the man who had presided at the 1930 criminal syndicalism trial, wrote that Imperial Valley law-enforcement officials were conferring "for the purpose of meeting the proposed activities and taking care of Mr. Pat Chambers in the proper way."[5]

In other areas of the state where the CAWIU was active, farm employers' concerns prompted more overt counteractions by sympathetic public authorities. In Gonzales, a small town in the Salinas Valley, the activities of militant Mexican unionists were met with harassment at first by local authorities and later by federal immigration officials, who deported seven of the most effective CAWIU members in the area.[6] Not far away, in the coastal town of Castroville, police and immigration officers invaded a CAWIU meeting on March 21 on the pretext of checking the citizenship status of those present. The actual purpose of the raid became obvious, however, when the authorities confiscated and burned union literature and the membership books of those Mexican workers attending the meeting. Several workers were detained for a time, and released only after being threatened with deportation unless they immediately forswore further involvement in union activities.[7]

The harassing tactics of farmers and law-enforcement agencies notwithstanding, the CAWIU agitation produced its first important results in mid-April, when 2,000 pea pickers in Alameda and Santa Clara counties struck for higher wages and improved conditions. The decision to promote a strike among pea pickers was made by CAWIU leaders meeting in Stockton on March 12. As in every dispute in which the CAWIU participated, the issue of poor wages was exploited by union organizers in order to attract workers' support. Weeks in advance of the pea harvest, organizers began encouraging workers in the vicinity of Hayward to demand a picking wage of 32 cents per hamper or 35 cents per hour, an amount nearly double the prevailing rate.[8] To enhance the CAWIU's influence among the region's farmworkers, organizers recruited cadres in each of the farm-labor camps in the harvest area. A strike committee composed of fifteen workers was formed at each of the camps, and given the responsibility of directing the activities of camp inhabitants during the anticipated strike. In addition, each of the camp committees of fifteen was instructed to select a representative who would serve on a general strike committee working out of the CAWIU's district headquarters in San Jose. This committee was invested with the overall responsibility of coordinating the strike and negotiating with employers.[9]

On April 12 an estimated 185 delegates representing pea pickers throughout the two-county area met to complete strike plans. The final demands adopted by the delegates were for a wage of 30 cents per hamper or 35 cents per hour, and for a closed-shop arrangement that guaranteed that all hiring would be done through union committees rather than labor contractors. Delegates voted to strike on April 14 if local growers failed to accede to the workers' demands. When pea farmers reiterated their intention to pay pickers only 17 cents per hamper, 2,000 Mexican, Filipino, and white workers walked off their jobs in various parts of the harvest region.[10]

During the two weeks that the dispute lasted, strikers saw several strikebreaking tactics employed against them. Growers made an immediate effort to recruit scab labor from outside the region, and also from nearby towns and cities. Welfare authorities in Alameda County cooperated by forcing hundreds of unemployed workers off the relief rolls and then directing them to seek work in the struck pea fields. Support of a more direct kind was provided to farmers by local police agencies, state highway patrolmen, and dozens of special deputies drawn from the ranks of the American Legion and other patriotic groups. Armed with a variety of weapons, these forces assisted farmers in dispersing picket lines, breaking up strike meetings, evicting strikers from various labor camps, and generally intimidating workers to the point of forcing them either to return to their jobs or to leave the region. The major clash between authorities and strikers came on April 15 near the small town of Decoto, when a force of lawmen invaded a large labor camp serving as the headquarters for a particularly militant group of strikers. Using clubs and tear gas, authorities succeeded in routing the camp's entire population after a few minutes of fighting. Commenting on the attack some months later, the sheriff who led the assault noted with considerable pride that there were "quite a number of sore heads" around when he and his men had completed their work. When a Communist official later demanded that the sheriff protect the strikers' constitutional right of assembly, the apparently bemused lawman allegedly replied, "Between you and me, what the hell is the Constitution?"[11]

In light of the intimidation, violence, and other strikebreaking tactics to which they were subjected, striking pea pickers were remarkably successful in tying up the pea harvest during the first few days of the strike. The strike committees established before the walkout generally functioned well in the beginning, coordinating the mass picketing that was the CAWIU's primary weapon and overseeing relief and other activities in the workers' camps. Following the violent assault at the Decoto camp, however, the strike slowly but steadily lost its effectiveness. Beyond the third or fourth day of the strike, each succeeding day saw ever larger numbers of scabs working in the struck pea fields under armed guards. Unable to maintain its picket lines in the face of intense police pressures, the CAWIU was helpless to stop the flow of replacement labor into the fields. In addition, union leaders found themselves increasingly unable to keep strikers from returning to work, especially after a rumor began to circulate through the camps that some small farmers in the area had rasied wages slightly. Finally on April 30 the CAWIU called off the strike, in recognition, its leaders said, of the slight wage increases reported in some parts of the harvest area. In reality, the strike was ended because CAWIU leaders knew it was on the verge of collapse, and felt that the union's image would be less damaged if they called an end to the walkout than if they simply allowed it to fizzle out. When the remaining strikers finally straggled back to work, they did so without having realized any of their demands. Despite the union's claim that the strike had advanced wages by a few cents in some fields, the general wage rate of 17 cents per hamper that prevailed at the beginning of the walkout remained in force throughout most of the region.[12]

During most of May the CAWIU continued its organizational work but was involved in little strike activity. The union did seek to gain influence among Filipino lettuce workers in the Salinas and Pajaro valleys when they struck for higher wages early in the month. Several CAWIU organizers in the vicinity of Watsonville worked particularly hard to gain the allegiance of striking Filipino workers, but the strike ended in failure before they could achieve their goal. Nevertheless, CAWIU spokesmen claimed, with little apparent justification, that "great prestige and influence" had been realized by the union as a result of its activities during the dispute.[13]

Most CAWIU strategists spent May analyzing the failure of the pea strike and trying to determine what steps might be taken "to tighten the organization."[14] Union leaders tended to agree that "tremendous prestige" had been gained among workers during the strike despite its failure. At the same time, though, they were aware that several organizational and tactical weaknesses that had become evident as the strike wore on needed to be acknowledged and corrected. District party officials suggested that strike leaders at every level had been derelict in establishing and maintaining close contacts with the rank and file, and that the top union leadership had been unresponsive to the widespread feeling among strikers that their wage demands were unrealistically high. Party spokesmen also suggested that CAWIU leaders had failed to inculcate in the workers a militancy equal to the challenge that a strike in agriculture posed. To remedy this last deficiency, district party officials advised the union's leaders to begin publication, in both English and Spanish, of a periodical bulletin that could serve as a medium for exercising the "ideological control" over farmworkers necessary to successful strike action.[15]

Party strategists did not have to wait long to see how effectively the CAWIU would implement the reforms that their study of the pea strike had indicated were in order. In June the union initiated two major agricultural strikes, one among berry pickers around the town of El Monte, in the San Gabriel Valley, the other involving cherry pickers in the northern portion of the Santa Clara Valley.

The El Monte strike was undoubtedly the most confused and confusing dispute in which the CAWIU was involved during its 1933 campaign. It began on June 2 after several weeks of preparatory agitation by Communist organizers among the large population of Mexican farmworkers in the area. The employers in this case were Japanese berry growers farming roughly 700 acres of land leased from various white landowners east of Los Angeles in the San Gabriel Valley.[16]

The dispute was almost entirely centered on the issue of wages, although the CAWIU also made its usual demands for recognition and hiring through the union. Late in May mass meetings called by the CAWIU attracted several hundred Mexican farmworkers. The purpose of the meetings was to discuss prevailing conditions, especially wages, in the berry fields, and to gain support for a strike call. At a final meeting on June 1, an estimated 500 to 600 workers voted to strike under CAWIU leadership on the following day unless employers raised pickers' wages from 15 cents to 25 cents per hour, or from 35 cents to 65 cents per crate if a piece rate was in effect. When Japanese employers announced on June 2 that they would not accede to the union's demands, approximately 1,500 Mexican berry pickers went on strike.[17]

Although affected growers immediately sought to bring scab labor into their fields, they also showed an early willingness to negotiate an end to the dispute. Only three days into the strike a representative of organized Japanese growers in the region approached union leaders with a proposed settlement calling for a piece rate of 40 cents per crate. The union strike committee, consisting mainly of young Mexican workers, refused the offer, stating that the strikers' minimum requirements for a settlement were 25 cents per hour or 50 cents per crate. Two days later growers made still another offer, this one providing for 20 cents an hour or 45 cents per crate and official recognition of the CAWIU. Intoxicated by the extremely high strike spirit pervading the workers' camps and convinced that complete victory was close at hand, strike committee members haughtily rejected the growers' second offer without really having given it serious consideration.

For the CAWIU, which had done its utmost to create the highest possible strike feeling among local workers, the extreme militancy that Mexican berry pickers displayed proved to have decidedly detrimental side effects. From the earliest days of their agitation among the farm labor force around El Monte, CAWIU organizers had been regarded as outsiders by Mexican workers. When the workers agreed to strike under the union's auspices, their action did not represent an endorsement of the CAWIU or signify their approval of Communist organizers. It probably indicated only that they were extremely dissatisfied with existing wages and willing to strike once they had been convinced that such an action could materially benefit them. Even after the strike had begun, fewer than 10 percent of the original 1,500 strikers appear to have joined the CAWIU.[18]

As the Mexicans gained confidence in their own ability to direct the course of the strike, the CAWIU and its organizers became expendable. Shortly after the second of the growers' offers had been rejected by the strike committee, a small group of noncommunist Mexican committee members, motivated by a militant ethnic consciousness, openly challenged CAWIU organizers for control of the strike. In mounting their challenge the insurgents successfully enlisted the aid of the Mexican government. Armando Flores, the leader of the insurgents, contacted

Mexican labor minister Luis Morones in Mexico City during early June, and advised him that the Mexican government might be able to bolster its sagging support within the Mexican labor movement at home by openly championing the efforts of exploited Mexican farmworkers in Southern California to form a union and strike for better conditions. Recognizing that domestic political advantages might well be realized from such a policy, Mexican officials quickly responded to Flores's appeal for assistance. Ricardo Hill, the Mexican vice-consul at Los Angeles, was instructed by his government to assist berry pickers at El Monte in gaining a favorable settlement of their strike and was authorized to provide some relief funds. Against the wishes of the CAWIU's leadership, Hill was invited by Armando Flores to a strikers' meeting held about June 8. Hill's purpose was to undermine the CAWIU and to encourage support for the exclusively Mexican leadership offered by the Flores faction. Hill denounced the CAWIU as a Communist union controlled entirely by outsiders, and warned workers of the potential dangers facing them because of their association with a red organization. Couching his appeal in language calculated to excite ethnic pride, Hill advised strikers that their interests would be better served through an all-Mexican union, which, he guaranteed, would have the wholehearted support of the Mexican government. Not having felt much allegiance to the CAWIU in the first place, the mass of Mexican strikers were easily persuaded to switch their support to Flores.[19]

With the help of a small group of militant Mexican youths who had been formed into a section of the Young Communist League early in the strike, CAWIU leaders made a determined effort to win back the workers' support that Flores and Hill had lured away. For a brief time the CAWIU counterattack against its "fake liberal" rivals was sufficiently effective to create considerable doubt among workers as to which faction was in control of the strike situation. The CAWIU was soon eliminated from the competition for good, however, when local authorities, who had so far exercised uncharacteristic restraint, began systematically to arrest and jail the most active Communist organizers in the area.[20]

Communist spokesmen attributed the mounting arrests to a conspiracy between local authorities and the Flores-Hill faction to prevent the CAWIU from "exposing" the latter's "fakery." That local authorities were cooperating with the Mexican leaders in eliminating their Communist rivals was privately confirmed by Thomas Barker, a state mediator, in his official report to State Labor Commissioner Frank C. MacDonald. A more plausible explanation, however, is that local authorities, conditioned by long-prevailing racist attitudes, seized the opportunity to remove Communist organizers from the scene in order to permit full control of the strike to fall to presumably less clever and more malleable Mexican leaders.[21]

If in fact growers and authorities around El Monte believed that passage of strike control from the CAWIU to Mexican leaders would ensure an early settlement, they were badly mistaken. Rather than seeking an end to the berry pickers' dispute, Mexican leaders sought to expand the strike to include thousands of additional Mexican workers employed in various types of agriculture throughout Los Angeles County and adjacent areas. With the help of Mexican consular officials, strikers formed the Confederación de Uniones de Campesinos y Obreros Mexicanos (CUCOM) and entered into negotiations with the Japanese berry growers' association. Encouraged by the widespread support their new union had received, strike leaders at first refused to compromise on wage demands. Flores and his associates believed that they had Japanese growers on the run, and thus refused to accept employers' wage concessions even in the face of great pressure from state mediators and representatives of the agricultural department of the Los Angeles Chamber of Commerce. Not until mid-July did CUCOM leaders finally come to terms with growers and call an end to the berry pickers' strike. The settlement provided for a standard wage of $2 per nine-hour day, with a minimum hourly wage of 25 cents for men and 20 cents for women. Despite the wage increases, however, large numbers of strikers failed to benefit from the settlement. Because scabs had picked much of the berry crop during the six-week strike, relatively little work remained to be done. And in violation of the terms of their agreement with the CUCOM, Japanese growers refused to discharge scabs and permit former strikers to have their jobs. Thus, while the berry pickers' strike demonstrated the potential power of ethnic unionism, it probably increased rather than lessened the economic suffering of most of the Mexican farmworkers who took part in it.[22]

From the point of view of the CAWIU, the El Monte strike was not only a failure but an acute embarrassment. It is likely, however, that the El Monte debacle would have done even more damage to the Communists' reputation had the CAWIU's nearly simultaneous strike action among Santa Clara Valley cherry pickers not succeeded.

Although the farm-labor force in the Santa Clara Valley, as in the San Gabriel Valley, was composed mainly of Mexicans, the work of CAWIU organizers in early June produced strong support for the union. Organizers centered their agitation on the wage issue, pointing out that while the rate of 20 cents an hour established by growers represented a decline of 33 percent from the previous year's rate, the price that farmers were receiving for their crop had increased by one-third. Easily persuaded that something must be done to guarantee them a fair wage for the 1933 season, several hundred cherry pickers met under CAWIU auspices in San Jose on June 13 to formulate a plan of action. The rather familiar plan proposed by CAWIU leaders and enthusiastically endorsed by the assembled workers called for a strike beginning the next day unless area cherry growers agreed to a standard wage of 30 cents per hour, an eight-hour day, and union recognition.[23]

The immediate response of several of the smaller cherry growers in the valley was to accept the union's terms. The largest growers, however, ignored the ultimatum, and in response about 500 cherry pickers struck twelve of the area's biggest orchards on June 14. In keeping with its earlier strike policy, the union's leadership employed mass picketing as the strikers' main weapon. Having determined that most of the growers in the region would follow the lead of the largest employers, strike leaders selected the valley's biggest cherry orchards as concentration points for picketing.[24]

In choosing to confront the most powerful growers in the area, the CAWIU exposed itself to an all-out antiunion assault. Encouraged by aroused employers, local authorities, augmented by dozens of special deputies and a contingent of state highway patrolmen, took aggressive steps to break the strike. When pickets massed at target orchards, local lawmen dispersed them with pickax handles and tear gas. Generally the strikebreaking tactics employed by the authorities were simple and direct, but they demonstrated on at least one occasion during the strike that they were capable of bringing a little imagination to their work. On June 16 at the Spaulding ranch, the largest in the area, strike leaders were assaulted in a fashion that would have strained the genius of a Hollywood scriptwriter. As Pat Callahan, the strike's principal leader, was walking a picket line with several other strikers, the ranch foreman advanced upon the group and invited Callahan to come into the orchard to discuss a possible settlement. The moment Callahan accepted the invitation, the foreman gave a prearranged signal and a squad of deputy sheriffs who were hidden in nearby trees leaped to the ground and set upon the unsuspecting strike leader, now an obvious trespasser. The first deputy to reach Callahan struck him in the face with the butt of a shotgun, knocking him to the ground. His jaw broken, Callahan struggled to his feet, only to be attacked by other deputies and knocked to the ground again. When several of his fellow strikers rushed to his aid, they too were attacked by deputies. Following the assault, the battered strikers were arrested for resisting an officer. The next day, scores of club-swinging deputies and highway patrolmen using less imaginative tactics charged into a picket line of about 250 strikers, a large number of whom were women. Nearly thirty pickets were arrested and more than twice that number were beaten. Bail for those arrested was set at prohibitively high levels in order that they might be kept out of action until after the cherry-picking season had passed.[25]

While the violent methods of local authorities were intended to break the strike by demoralizing the workers who had joined it, just the opposite result was actually produced. Workers already on strike became even more militant in the face of police terror, while hundreds of additional cherry pickers were persuaded to join the walkout as a result of the well-publicized attacks. By June 18, nearly 1,000 cherry pickers were on strike at twenty ranches in the northern Santa Clara Valley.[26]

When it finally became apparent to the region's major growers that the strike could not be broken and that their crop was in danger of being lost, they grudgingly raised the picker's wage to 30 cents an hour. Although a few growers continued to pay only 20 cents an hour and the CAWIU had not gained formal recognition from employers, the union's strike committee decided on June 24 to end the walkout, since the workers' principal demand had been won.[27]

The success of the Santa Clara Valley strike, coming as it did while the memory of the union's humiliating setback at El Monte was still fresh, not only buoyed the deflated hopes of CAWIU leaders, but provided a dramatic and long-awaited confirmation of their assumption that California farmworkers, despite the tradition of powerlessness that they had endured for generations, were capable of empowering themselves through organization and collective action. For cherry growers in the Santa Clara Valley, who had employed every strikebreaking tool at their disposal to no avail, the besting they experienced not only introduced them to the bitter taste of defeat, but impressed upon them in ways too graphic and painful to soon be forgotten that because of the perishable nature of their products they were more vulnerable to organized workers than any other group of employers in the state.

In combination, the El Monte and Santa Clara strikes produced a disquietude that quickly rippled through farm employers' circles throughout the state. Especially disconcerting to employers, who had chosen to regard earlier labor disputes as localized outbreaks, was the fact that the outlines of a wider movement were discernible in the June strikes. J. M. Fallin, an official of the U.S. Farm Labor Service, warned San Joaquin Valley farm employers in July that the rise of unionism among farmworkers was not a local phenomenon, but a movement "in various stages of development throughout the agricultural areas of both California and Arizona."[28] With the harvest season only a few weeks away, fruit growers throughout the northern and central parts of the state were easily persuaded that the danger that Fallin and others described was real. Yet when employers began to consider precautions they could take against possible labor problems during the fruit harvest, they neglected the conciliatory measures that might have eased the threat of trouble in favor of perfecting their strikebreaking capabilities. While they recognized the obvious connection between extremely low wages and the rising militancy of farm labor, most employers seemed determined to derive the fullest possible personal benefit from the higher prices their crops were commanding in 1933 by keeping wages as near as possible to the 1932 rate of from 12½ to 15 cents an hour. When directors of the Agricultural Labor Bureau of the San Joaquin Valley met in advance of the harvest season to fix the wage rate for fruit picking, they heard Frank Palomares, the bureau's manager, warn that there was "agitation by Communists throughout the district in the matter of wages and intended strikes and that the agitators were creating discontentment among peaceable laborers." Apparently finding it more congenial economically to view the threat confronting them as a product of "Communist agitation" rather than genuine worker discontent, the bureau's directors stuck by their low-wage policy, establishing a rate of only 15 to 17½ cents an hour for the 1933 season.[29]

Just a week before the bureau acted, Joseph DiGiorgio, one of the largest farm employers in the San Joaquin Valley, had sought to counter the growing threat of labor trouble by adopting a wage rate of 25 cents an hour. Unwilling to concede the merit of DiGiorgio's strategy, a spokesman for the bureau complained that so high a wage "disrupted the labor set-up for the Valley." Officials of the agricultural department of the Los Angeles Chamber of Commerce, though unwilling to speak ill of their fellow agribusinessmen in public, privately denounced the bureau for establishing a wage rate so "ridiculously low" that it "lent encouragement" to agitators' efforts to promote strike action in the state.[30]

While the CAWIU had already committed itself to a vigorous organizing campaign during the fruit harvest, the decision of most employers to keep wages approximately the same as they had been in 1932 gave additional force to its argument that "the bosses" were trying "to shift the burden of the [Depression] crisis on the backs of the workers, especially the agricultural workers." But the argument that organizers used to the greatest advantage during July and early August was that the union had proved in the Santa Clara strike that it could lead migratory workers to better wages and conditions.[31]

While its organizers carried the union's enhanced credentials into the countryside, Communist Party leaders in the state, still not fully convinced that the CAWIU was prepared for the challenges ahead of it, subjected its performance to a probing analysis. Because it had failed so miserably, the union's strategy in the El Monte berry pickers' strike was scrutinized with particular thoroughness. The strike leaders at El Monte were chided for, among other things, their failure to conduct a careful preliminary study of economic and other conditions in the region, their failure to share control of the strike with workers, their poor judgment in allowing overly emotional workers to reject the substantial wage increases and union recognition offered by the growers in their second settlement proposal, and their failure to give Mexican workers enough "political guidance" to make them more resistant to the anticommunist cajolery of the "fake liberals" who usurped control of the strike. In the last analysis, party leaders decided, the only positive aspect of the El Monte experience was that it afforded CAWIU leaders an opportunity to profit from their several mistakes. Writing in the *Western Worker,* party spokesman Lawrence Ross noted: "The El Monte strike was a costly lesson, but highly valuable. The gravity of our mistakes there have [*sic*] impressed us with the necessity of the correct steps to be taken in future CAWIU work in the fields."[32]

Taking their cue from party officials, CAWIU leaders took immediate steps to put their house in order. On August 5, just before the state's fruit harvest got under way, twenty-nine delegates representing what the *Western Worker* claimed was a total union membership of 4,000 met in convention to discuss, among other things, the "correct steps" to organizational success to which Lawrence Ross had made an oblique reference in his El Monte analysis.[33] After the assembled delegates had raised their voices in a hearty rendition of "Hold the Fort," an appropriately stirring anthem to class struggle, they set about the task of exposing past weaknesses in order that the union's campaign during the remainder of the 1933 harvest season might proceed on a basis consistent with sound organizational and tactical principles. Using the party's now painfully familiar critique of the El Monte strike as their text, union leaders guided the delegates through a detailed retrospective of their collective ineptitude, pointing out each "error" that marred their past stewardship as well as its "correct" obverse. Their obligation of self-abasement finally discharged, the delegates adopted a lengthy resolution formally confessing the union's past failings and boldly specifying intended reforms. Cited as the union's chief deficiencies were:

1. A lack of proper preparation and good judgment in promoting and conducting strikes, especially relating to the union leadership's failure to set up the various committees necessary to a successful strike, and then to see that workers from the rank and file actively participate in every phase of the strike's governance.
2. A long-standing failure to recruit a permanent, dues-paying membership that reflected the union's true influence among agricultural workers in the district.
3. A lack of sufficient attention to worker education and training, particularly involving fundamental instruction in how to organize and conduct a strike, how to set up strike committees, and how to recruit and activize non-union workers.
4. The absence of a properly designed and functioning union apparatus which would insure smooth interaction between district committees, section committees, and the union locals.
5. The lack of any substantial influence among cannery workers, due to the failure of organizers to give proper attention to the needs and problems of women workers, who constitute a majority of the labor force in the canning industry.
6. An inadequate or nearly non-existent base of support among the youth and children employed in agriculture, even though the potential militancy of the young was clearly demonstrated in the El Monte strike.
7. A failure to expose the "misleaders" of "fake unions," and to bore from within rival unions for the purpose of giving their members the correct revolutionary leadership.

To remedy these defects, the resolution pointedly stipulated that the following steps should be taken.

1. A strong, integrated union apparatus should be established, one which provides for a network of locals in each section, with a section headquarters through which all local activities would be coordinated. To insure the greatest possible strength, the union should endeavor "to build up a section leadership of rank and file workers who are in daily contact with the workers." Union locals should be conveniently located in order that the special needs of migratory farm workers among the membership can be served.
2. A district bulletin, printed in the predominant languages, must be established to facilitate the "education" of agricultural workers. In addi-

tion, the local union should function as a point of dissemination for information and instructions relating to the proper organization and conduct of strikes, and also serve as the place "where each member is made union-conscious and class-conscious."[34]

3. The Union should aggressively work to bring women, youth, and children into its ranks, not just during periods of struggle, but on a permanent basis. To this end, each local should introduce special features into its meetings that will attract and hold these previously neglected groups of workers.

4. Each local should cultivate an awareness of "opponent organizations" working in the same territory, and seek to "penetrate" them for the purpose of substituting revolutionary leadership for that being given to workers by "fakers" and "misleaders."

5. Closer cooperation should be established between C.A.W.I.U. members and the "growing thousands of unemployed agricultural workers." Union locals should organize unemployed workers in order that a united effort could be made to secure relief for all who need it. [Another obvious, if unstated, advantage of such an alliance was that it would tend to discourage unemployed workers from scabbing on union members during strikes.]

"A clear understanding of our weaknesses and a sincere effort to correct them," the delegates solemnly declared, "blazons the way for a powerful Cannery and Agricultural Workers Industrial Union that will protect the interests of the agricultural workers."[35]

With a rapidity that surely must have surprised even the most optimistic union leaders, the militant spirit of the San Jose meeting was immediately transported into the fields and orchards of the state. Within less than a week of the convention, CAWIU organizers called the first of a long, rapid-fire sequence of strikes that were to keep the agricultural regions of California in nearly constant turmoil for almost three months.

Mexican and Filipino sugar-beet workers led off the strike campaign on August 7, when they struck several farms around the Ventura County town of Oxnard. Numbering about 1,000, the strikers demanded a minimum wage of 35 cents an hour, an eight-hour day, union recognition, and several other changes in living and working conditions. On the following day, an estimated 400 tomato pickers near San Diego also went out on strike under CAWIU leadership. They too demanded, among other things, 35 cents an hour, an eight-hour day, and union recognition.[36]

Still other farm-labor struggles were brewing to the north, among thousands of fruit pickers in the San Joaquin and Santa Clara valleys. Union organizers, under the covert personal direction of Sam Darcy and other party leaders, had been busy for several weeks in both regions, assiduously cultivating the workers' discontent over newly established wage rates that averaged between 15 and 20 cents an hour. During the second week of August, the union had gained sufficient support from pear pickers around San Jose and peach pickers on the giant Tagus Ranch near Tulare to call mass meetings at which final strike demands were formulated. On August 14 workers in each area struck when their demands were rejected.[37]

The San Jose strike, which lasted only four days, involved approximately 1,000 pear pickers. The workers' principal demands were for an increase in the hourly wage from 17½–20 cents to 30 cents, an eight-hour day, and recognition of the CAWIU. As a result of the diligent and thorough preparatory work of union organizers, the strikers, most of whom were union members, were exceptionally well disciplined throughout the brief struggle, carrying out their mass picketing duties with obvious effectiveness. In addition to the direct strikebreaking methods employed during the cherry pickers' strike, growers sought to use the power of the courts against striking workers. At the request of an attorney retained by employers, an accommodating San Jose judge issued an injunction designed to eliminate effective picketing by prohibiting strikers from interfering in any way with scabs and strikebreakers sent into the struck orchards. When strikers nevertheless continued to picket, authorities arrested six CAWIU leaders on contempt charges.[38]

Because the union had seen to it that the strike's leadership was as widely diffused as possible, the arrests neither broke nor even weakened the workers' will to continue their fight. Faced with the possible loss of their crop and under pressure from Louis Bloch of the California Bureau of Labor Statistics to accept an arbitrated settlement of the strike, growers finally decided on August 17 to compromise by increasing wages to 25–27½ cents an hour. They remained unwilling, however, to recognize the CAWIU even indirectly, as their rejection of Bloch's arbitration proposal made plain. Despite their failure to win all of their demands, strikers considered the wage increase a clear victory. On the advice of CAWIU leaders, strikers voted on August 17 to end the strike.[39]

Though similar in many ways to the San Jose dispute, the strike of 750 peach pickers on the Tagus Ranch, one of the largest and most highly industrialized agricultural operations in California, helped to stimulate a much wider strike movement that quickly spread through the fruit-growing districts of six San Joaquin Valley counties. Thoroughly organized in advance by Pat Chambers, the CAWIU's district organizer, the Tagus strikers demanded a wage increase from 15 to 35 cents per hour, a forty-hour week, union recognition, payment of wages in cash rather than company scrip, and abolition of a requirement that workers trade at a company store that charged prices 25 to 30 percent higher than those outside the ranch.

Determined to break the strike, the ranch manager secured an injunction barring picketing, and also ordered all workers who refused to work for 15 cents an hour to be evicted from company-owned housing. On the advice of the Tulare County district attorney, who doubted the legality of the antipicketing injunction, authorities made no attempts to halt the mass picketing at the Tagus Ranch. On August 15, however, several strikers and their families were evicted from ranch housing by armed company employees, one of whom menacingly waved a submachine gun apparently on loan from the Tulare Police Department. The personal belongings of the evicted families were piled onto trucks and hauled to a spot just north of Tulare, where they were unceremoniously dumped along the highway.

By refusing to negotiate with CAWIU leaders and attempting to break the strike by force, the Tagus manager caused union leaders to threaten an escalation of the struggle. Following the evictions of strikers from company housing, Pat Chambers announced that unless the union's demands were granted, a general strike would be called in orchards throughout the San Joaquin Valley. Before the union could act, however, the strike situation was altered by collateral events.

On the same day that the Tagus strike began, 2,000 peach pickers, influenced but apparently not led by the CAWIU, walked off their jobs on two Merced County fruit ranches owned by the California Packing Corporation, one of the largest of the vertically integrated companies that had come to dominate the state's industrialized agriculture by the 1930s. Faced not only with a halt in its picking operations but also with costly shutdowns of several canneries, the company was eager to settle the dispute as quickly as possible. Further impetus for an early settlement came when State Director of Industrial Relations Timothy Reardon was dispatched to the valley by Governor James Rolph to mediate the peach pickers' strikes. On August 16, Cal-Pak executives in San Francisco announced that the company had decided to increase the wages of peach pickers at its Merced County ranches from 17½ to 25 cents an hour. Although the strikers had earlier demanded 30 cents an hour, they readily accepted the company's offer.

Once Cal-Pak had announced its decision to pay 25 cents an hour, pressure mounted for the Tagus Ranch to do likewise. Both in private and through the press, state mediators endorsed the Cal-Pak settlement as fair and reasonable, and urged the Tagus management to settle on the same basis. Persuaded that its public image would be enhanced by adoption of a conciliatory posture, the CAWIU, through strike leader Pat Chambers, announced that as long as state mediation efforts continued, the union's threatened valley-wide strike would be postponed. Unwilling to risk public censure and unable to break the strike through force and intimidation, the Tagus Ranch reluctantly agreed on August 18 to increase pickers' wages to 25 cents an hour and to rehire strikers without discrimination. Chambers immediately announced the strikers' acceptance of the compromise and declared the dispute at an end.

Although the CAWIU publicly abandoned its plans for a general strike following the Tagus settlement, dozens of small strikes broke out among peach pickers throughout the San Joaquin Valley as word of the Cal-Pak and Tagus victories spread. Many were led by the CAWIU. Others were spontaneous but clearly reflected the union's spreading influence. Despite their inclination to hold out, growers quickly succumbed to the pressures exerted by state mediators and a ripening crop. One by one, each adopted the 25-cents-an-hour wage rate established in the Cal-Pak and Tagus settlements. On dozens of additional fruit ranches, strikes were made unnecessary when growers, now resigned to the inevitable, voluntarily adopted the new wage scale. On August 20, only a week after the first strikes started, the *Fresno Bee* reported that 25 cents an hour had been established as the prevailing wage in every fruit-growing district of the San Joaquin Valley. Encouraged by their success, some fruit pickers sought still larger gains. Under the leadership of the CAWIU, several hundred peach pickers near the Butte County town of Gridley struck for 30 cents an hour. After weathering a brief but violent strikebreaking campaign by growers and local authorities, the Gridley strikers won their wage demand, becoming as a result the highest paid fruit pickers in the state.[40]

For the CAWIU, August had been a month of spectacular successes. Strikes led or influenced by the union resulted in wage increases of as much as 100 percent for thousands of agricultural workers. While the general agricultural wage in California at the beginning of August had ranged from 15 to 17½ cents an hour, at month's end the prevailing hourly wage throughout most of the state was firmly fixed at 25 cents. Understandably pleased and encouraged by the CAWIU's accomplishments, Communist Party spokesmen who had been its sharpest critics only two weeks earlier were heaping lavish praise on the union. And at the same time that they savored those victories of "revolutionary unionism" that had brought workers "flocking into the CAWIU," party leaders rather smugly recalled, with obvious selectivity, the contemporary failures and deficiencies of "reformist" unions operating under the A.F. of L.'s banner. With equal ebullience an official of the Trade Union Unity League promised the state's farmworkers that the CAWIU's success in winning them higher pay was "only a start in the fight for a living wage, which the agricultural union is leading."[41]

State Labor Commissioner Frank MacDonald, who had helped to mediate many of the peach pickers' strikes during August, tended to agree that the upward movement in agricultural wages that the CAWIU had set in motion was irreversible. On August 21 he publicly warned California's farm employers that those among them still paying less than 25 cents an hour could expect serious labor problems if they persisted in their low-wage policies.[42]

Beyond the success of the August strikes, a notable feature of the struggles was that they were, with few exceptions, free of the violence that had accompanied most of the earlier farm-labor disputes involving the CAWIU. Only in the sugar-beet workers' strike at Oxnard, the one struggle that ended in defeat for the union, was extensive violence employed against strikers. The violence at Oxnard was probably due to the peculiar relationship between employers and local authorities there. The mayor of Oxnard was himself a prominent sugar-beet grower, and when strikers sought to picket his and his fellow employers' fields, he promptly invoked his police powers to break the strike by force.[43]

The comparatively low level of violence in the remainder of the August strikes was largely attributable to the orderly and nonviolent manner in which the CAWIU conducted the struggles. Union leaders consistently counseled strikers to avoid unlawful activities, and in most cases the workers complied. Law-enforcement officers, too, practiced unusual restraint, though not all did so willingly. Sheriff George Overholt of Fresno County, where much of the trouble centered, confessed to fellow law-enforcement officers at a state convention in late August that his plans to break the peach pickers' strikes by force were foiled by the strikers' strict observance of the law. In lamenting the strikers' orderliness, Overholt complained, "We are well equipped to handle riots. We are not afraid of any overt act they might commit. In fact, that is the thing that troubles us; they don't commit any overt act, don't give us a chance to help ourselves by legally getting out and getting them by the neck. They just agitate and agitate and keep the farmers unsettled."[44]

After more than three years of impotence, the CAWIU's sudden and stunning victories over farm employers who had earlier seemed indomitable produced a sense of invincibility among the union's exuberant organizers. It was a short-lived sensation. Two strikes among grape pickers in the San Joaquin Valley in early September provided brutal reminders of the inherent vulnerability of any farmworkers' union seeking to establish its power within industrialized agriculture's sphere of influence.

The first of these strikes began brewing in the vicinity of Fresno even before the last of the peach pickers' disputes had been settled. Encouraged by the gains being won by fruit pickers, grape pickers under the CAWIU's influence announced in mid-August that a general strike would ensue if vineyardists refused to increase wages to at least 25 cents an hour, about double the rate paid in 1932. Despite a warning by State Labor Commissioner MacDonald that a strike by 5,000 grape pickers was unavoidable unless wages were raised to 25 cents an hour, area vineyardists met on August 24 and adopted a piece rate that was roughly equivalent to 20 cents an hour. State mediators criticized the employers' decision as arbitrary and shortsighted, and again warned that the CAWIU would call a general strike of grape pickers if a wage of less than 25 cents an hour was offered.

Apparently convinced that grape pickers in the area had been sufficiently aroused by the fruit pickers' struggles to make any further organizational work unnecessary, CAWIU organizers around Fresno neglected the careful preparation that a successful strike demanded. Several days before the union's leadership had intended the struggle to begin, spontaneous strikes broke out among grape pickers in various parts of the lower San Joaquin Valley. A few were settled when individual employers agreed to pay 25 cents an hour. More typical, however, was the unhappy experience of 250 grape pickers at a vineyard near the Tulare County town of Visalia. As soon as the first signs of trouble appeared, local authorities acting at the employers' request crushed the strike by arresting its entire leadership.

Not until September 6 did the CAWIU issue an official strike call. By then so much confusion reigned in the strike area that it became virtually impossible to measure the degree of support that the union's announcement elicited. Hundreds and even thousands of grape pickers were reportedly on strike at various times throughout the lower valley, but they were clearly not all striking under the CAWIU's effective auspices. For the most part, growers around Fresno remained unwilling to compromise on the wage issue, and readily adopted the strategy of their Tulare County counterparts by soliciting the active assistance of local law-enforcement agencies in helping them break the strikes. Picket lines were forcibly dispersed by county authorities and deputized growers, and strike leaders were arrested on charges ranging from vagrancy to criminal syndicalism. In tribute to the special utility of the latter charge, the editor of the *Fresno Bee* wrote on September 13: "Fortunately for the best interests and welfare of the state the criminal syndicalism law still is on the statute books." Persuaded that the CAWIU was endeavoring not to win higher wages but to overthrow the American government, the editor encouraged authorities to use the law as fully as the situation demanded.

Although mediation was continually offered by state officials, neither side seemed interested in accepting it. Growers saw no reason to seek a compromise settlement as long as they were succeeding in their efforts to break the strike by force. The CAWIU refused to accept mediation as long as more than twenty of its leading members were being held in jail on "trumped up" charges. Finally, after more than a week of intimidation, physical assaults, and mounting arrests, CAWIU leaders reluctantly called off the strike. In doing so they acknowledged their own failure to make adequate preparations, but also vowed to continue their drive for higher wages.[45]

True to its leaders' vow, the CAWIU continued its agitation among the San Joaquin Valley's grape pickers despite the failure of the Fresno strike. As the grape harvest moved northward into the vicinity of Lodi, union organizers with ambitious new organizational plans moved with it. On September 13, the day before the CAWIU announced its decision to end the Fresno strike, several hundred grape pickers meeting under the union's sponsorship in Lodi voted to demand 50 cents an hour for picking the region's crop. Only a week before the workers' meeting, approximately 600 vineyardists in the Lodi area had made public their decision to adopt a piece rate equivalent to about 20 cents an hour.

After having taken their respective stands on the wage issue, workers and employers waited for nearly two weeks before reaching the point of actual conflict. Neither side was idle, however. CAWIU organizers worked to perfect strike plans and to enlist the widest possible worker support for the approaching struggle. Grape growers and local authorities used the time to devise strategies to combat the strike and ensure an unimpeded harvest. Neither side appeared especially interested in a negotiated settlement, although the wage gap separating them had been narrowed somewhat as a result of independent compromises.

On September 26 the CAWIU called a mass meeting in Lodi. Among the demands finally agreed upon were an eight-hour day, 40 cents an hour with time and a half for overtime, union recognition, hiring through the union, and no discrimination against union members. Expecting that the growers would refuse their demands, workers authorized a strike call for the following day.

With vineyardists standing firm on a final wage offer of 25 cents an hour—a rate that might have undermined the strike agitation had it been offered three weeks earlier—between 500 and 700 grape pickers walked off their jobs on September 27 at an estimated 150 vineyards in the Lodi area. Over the next few days the strikers' ranks swelled to between 3,000 and 4,000. Mindful of the difficulties experienced during the Fresno grape strike, CAWIU leaders sought to confine mass picketing to three of the largest vineyards.[46]

Growers and authorities, however, had also learned from the Fresno strike. On the day the Lodi strike began, they set in motion a carefully formulated plan to smash it. Underlying the growers' decision to break the strike by any means necessary was their belief, strongly asserted by farm employers during most agricultural labor disputes in California throughout the 1930s, that farm-labor strikes were patently irrational because they represented attempts by labor to deny the irrefutable economic logic governing farming no less than any other kind of business enterprise. Unwilling to acknowledge their own subjectivity, Lodi grape growers took the position that their final wage offer, in light of prevailing economic conditions, marked the limit of their ability to pay. When farmworkers' minds were not being poisoned by "outside" agitators, growers argued, they had little difficulty in resigning themselves to the sometimes iniquitous dictates of economic forces that buffeted the employer no less mercilessly than his employees. When farmworkers, for whatever misguided reasons, chose to strike, and thus to ignore the economic limitations under which farm employers operated, they deserved whatever methods farmers and their allies were forced to adopt in order to resist such an inherently unreasonable challenge.[47]

The methods adopted by Lodi grape employers were at once uncomplicated and effective. Scores of growers, local businessmen, and American Legionnaires were deputized as soon as the strike began and placed under the command of Colonel Walter E. Garrison, a leading farm employer and retired military man. Once this special strikebreaking force was formed, duly constituted law-enforcement officials faded into the background. Impressed with the results obtained by authorities during the Fresno strike, Garrison instructed his men to concentrate their efforts against CAWIU leaders. Although picketing was not prohibited by law, Garrison arbitrarily declared that all picketing would be considered disturbance of the peace, and ordered his charges "to arrest two or three leaders on each truckload of pickets." Local growers were instructed to sign the necessary complaints.

Beginning on September 28, the second day of the strike, special deputies began their campaign of arrests and intimidation in earnest. Picket captains were identified and arrested with mounting frequency, and in a raid on CAWIU headquarters in Lodi six strike leaders were arrested on vague charges of conspiracy to obstruct justice. Within two days some thirty strikers had been jailed for no reason other than Garrison's desire to break the strike. He also forced public and private relief agencies in the area to discontinue all aid to strikers and their families. And when strikers attempted to conduct meetings in Lodi, they were subjected to threats, intimidation, and physical assaults from authorities, employers, and local townspeople.

Despite the forces arrayed against them, strikers persisted in their efforts to halt the grape harvest. To counter the strikebreaking strategy of growers, the CAWIU adopted hit-and-run "guerrilla" picketing tactics that reduced the vulnerability of pickets to arrest. A few small growers in the Lodi area finally raised their wage offer to 40 cents an hour. The union demonstrated confidence in its ability to withstand the strikebreaking campaign of growers by resisting several determined attempts by state mediators to promote a back-to-work movement.

When the strike continued despite the energetic efforts of local authorities and special deputies to break it, the patience of employers and their supporters finally reached the breaking point. On the evening of October 2, approximately 1,500 vineyardists, businessmen, American Legionnaires, and other Lodi residents met in a local theater to decide how the strike could be ended without further delay. After much debate, a "Committee of 1500" was established to drive strikers out of the area on the following morning. At the insistence of the county sheriff, a state deputy labor commissioner, and Colonel Garrison, vigilantes reluctantly agreed to discharge their duties in an orderly and nonviolent manner as long as strikers offered no resistance. At six o'clock the following morning, several hundred vigilantes armed with a variety of clubs and firearms gathered in the center of Lodi to carry out their plan.

When about 100 strikers assembled in front of CAWIU headquarters to plan the day's picketing activities, the calm was suddenly shattered. Abandoning their pledge of nonviolence, vigilantes charged into the strikers' midst with clubs and fists flailing. As vigilantes drove the frightened and battered strikers toward the edge of town, local authorities and state highway patrolmen quietly stood by watching. Most strikers offered no resistance. When a few strikers did attempt to defend themselves against their attackers, however, the police suddenly intervened to arrest them on charges of "resisting an officer" or "rioting." Assaults continued throughout the morning as vigilantes cruised the area in automobiles, routing strikers from their camps. Later in the day, when strikers attempted to regroup, they were scattered by vigilantes and local authorities using fire hoses and tear gas.

Within a day of the vigilante attacks on strikers, Lodi growers insisted that the strike was at an end. On October 5 the *San Francisco Examiner* reported that strikers were leaving the region "in droves," and that "barely a hundred" remained in town. Immediately following the vigilante actions, district leaders of the CAWIU communicated a vigorous protest to Governor James Rolph, demanding that he take steps to protect the strikers' civil rights. This and other protests against vigilantism in Lodi failed to elicit a response from Rolph.[48]

Neither public protests nor widespread press reports of vigilante excesses did anything to moderate the attitudes or behavior of authorities in the Lodi area. Even after the strike had been broken, the bitterness it engendered remained much in evidence. On October 6 several strike leaders arrested during the Lodi conflict were arraigned before Judge J. K. Solkmore, who had been an open supporter of the vigilantes. When the strikers' attorney demanded that they be accorded the legal rights to which they were entitled, Judge Solkmore stormed, "These men are nothing but a bunch of rats, Russian anarchists, cutthroats, and sweepings of creation. This defendant [referring to one striker who had requested a jury trial] doesn't know when he's well off if he wants a jury trial. In some places they would take him and the rest of his kind out and hang them from the town hall." When the strikers' attorney interrupted to suggest that the people of Lodi surely would not countenance lynchings, Solkmore replied, "Don't you be too sure about that. This town may see a few hangings yet." When the attorney persisted in his request for a jury trial, the judge shouted, "Juries be damned. Juries are reminiscent of medievalism. They are a means of escape for guilty men. If I were innocent, I'd rather go before a judge. They usually get twelve boneheads to sit on a jury." But finally, having regained his composure and judicial equanimity, Solkmore agreed to grant the defendants a change of venue to an adjoining county and an atmosphere presumably more conducive to justice.[49]

Coming on the heels of the union's spectacular victories in August over peach and pear growers, the successive defeats suffered at the hands of vineyardists at Fresno and Lodi served to remind CAWIU leaders both of the dangers posed by their own overconfidence and of the awesome resources that employers were able to summon up when they approached the task of strikebreaking in an organized and determined way. Yet as formidable as the strikebreaking apparatus employed against it proved to be, the CAWIU might well have given a better account of itself, in the Lodi strike especially, if many of the union's ablest leaders had not been occupied a hundred miles to the south preparing for a still more important organizational venture in the cotton-growing districts of the lower San Joaquin Valley. Weeks before the Lodi strike was launched, plans for a potentially massive confrontation between cotton pickers and growers in the state's great central valley were being formulated by the union's leaders. By the first week of October it had become apparent to both the union and organized cotton growers that a struggle of extraordinary proportions lay before them. Neither workers nor farmers understood at that point, however, that they were on the verge of the greatest single strike in the history of agricultural labor relations in America. In commenting on the special significance of this collision, economists Paul Taylor and Clark Kerr wrote:

> As the faulting of the earth exposes its strata and reveals its structure, so a social disturbance throws into bold relief the structure of society, the attitudes, reactions, and interests of its groups. In the San Joaquin Valley of California the alignment of groups, their opinions and behavior under stress of an unfamiliar situation were exposed by the cotton pickers' strike of 1933, when thousands of agricultural workers, largely of alien race and under communist influence, clashed with conservative American growers. The significance of the event is far more than incidental. It exhibits in full detail the essential characteristics of numerous lesser conflicts in California agriculture both before and since, in which ardent officials and laborers each overstep the law, and citizens finally cry to the State authorities for peace, if necessary at the hands of troops.[50]

Had the cotton strike's significance derived entirely from the imposing dimensions it assumed, its importance as an episode in the labor conflict that beset California's large-scale agriculture during 1933 would still have been very great. The cotton strike became an extraordinary farm-labor dispute, however, when it was caught up in the whirlpool of reformist zeal that spread in widening spirals from Washington as ardent New Dealers pursued their singular mandate to restore vitality as well as order and system to the country's Depression-ravaged economy and failed economic institutions. And although the direct involvement of New Dealers in farm-labor relations in California was to be short-lived, their brief intervention left a residue of anti-unionism that reinforced the already powerful forces arrayed against farmworkers, and thus contributed significantly to the ultimate destruction of the agricultural labor movement in the state.

6

Agricultural Unionism and the
New Deal: The Cotton Strike

Nascent revisionism notwithstanding, it has long been an article of faith among historians of modern American life that for the labor movement in the United States, the New Deal was a watershed. And certainly a simple comparison of the labor movement before and after the New Deal era can only substantiate that judgment. On the eve of the New Deal the labor movement was emaciated and dispirited, saddled with an inept, frightened, and backward-looking leadership devoid of both ideas and ideals. Within less than a decade there was a transformation so dramatic that even the movement's oldest friends could scarcely recognize it. It had more than quadrupled in size, as well as transfigured itself, by finally acknowledging the Industrial Revolution. More important, it was not simply big, but, despite a pronounced fratricidal tendency, it was muscular, aggressive, and self-confident. Most important of all, it was possessed of new legal rights that had helped it amass power and influence great enough to ensure that whenever government or employers undertook decisions affecting labor's interests, they generally did so within the narrowed latitudes imposed by the formidable political and economic presence of organized workers.

None of the changes that marked the New Deal years was more significant or fundamental than that which occurred in the nation's industrial power relationships as a result of the emergence of a powerful labor movement whose strength was based no longer on narrow craft unions, but on new organizations representing the millions of workers in America's great mass-production industries. Ironically, however, this change, which has generally been regarded as one of the New Deal's greatest achievements, may in fact have been its most profound defeat. To the extent that the growth of broadly based and independently powerful labor unions in the 1930s acknowledged and served to institutionalize conflict as an ineradicable fact of industrial relations, it dispelled for good the progressive vision of cooperative and harmonious relations between labor and capital which lay at the heart of the original New Deal labor policies.

Despite the diversity of background and experience evident among New Deal policy makers in 1933, on the "labor question" there was a remarkable homogeneity of opinion. Whether social worker, technocrat, industrial democrat, national planner, or "enlightened" businessman, each of the New Dealers who helped to shape the initial labor policies of the Roosevelt administration regarded American workers as a dependent class. Each acknowledged and disapproved the cruel exploitation that had been the workers' lot during preceding decades, and expressed genuine sympathy for those suffering the particularly acute hardships of the Depression. And with an unquestionable sincerity of purpose, they resolved to afford wage earners a new deal.

The approach that New Deal brain trusters first chose to effect changes favorable to labor, however, reflected a fundamental antiunion bias. Theirs was clearly not the selfish and defensive antiunionism of most American employers, but an aversion based on a shared conviction that the class conflict that had necessitated unions was neither an inevitable nor a natural by-product of the capitalist system. Once capitalism had been purged of those exploitive features spawned by unconstrained economic individualism and infused with the ethic of the national welfare, the New Dealers argued, industrial conflict would disappear, and with it the need for strong unions. Franklin Roosevelt had first embraced this vision of a conflict-free capitalist economy during the Progressive era, and it remained with him as he assumed the presidency. In his clearest exposition of this theme, Roosevelt said, "There is no such thing as a struggle between labor and capital. Not only is there no struggle, but there is and has always been the heartiest cooperation for neither can capital exist without the cooperation of labor, nor labor without the cooperation of capital. Therefore, I say there is no struggle between the two, not even a dividing line."[1]

The force of this belief was apparent in the National Industrial Recovery Act (NIRA), which represented the Roosevelt administration's first and most comprehensive program for the rehabilitation of capitalism and the establishment of harmonious and cooperative relations between workers and employers. Though promoted as an emergency act whose purpose was to address the desperate economic crisis at hand, the NIRA, insofar as it addressed the problem of industrial relations, represented New Deal thought in its purest form, before it was adulterated by subsequent political imperatives.

The act represented a merging of the two most distinct and forceful motives of the first New Deal: national planning and paternalism.[2] Neither was compatible with the historic and transcendent ambition of the labor movement: the right to organize and employ collective economic power in advancing and protecting self-defined group interests. That the early New Dealers regarded unionism as no less anachronistic and potentially harmful a manisfestation of unregulated individualism than the machinations of renegade free-enterprisers was testified to by the fact that their original drafts of the labor section of the recovery bill ignored the right of organization entirely. Frances Perkins, Roosevelt's secretary of labor, recalled that the NIRA was not expanded to include the right of organization and collective bargaining until the A.F. of L.'s William Green, upon seeing the bill in what its authors regarded as near final form, told her that the inclusion of such a guarantee was a *sine qua non* for labor's political support.[3]

The guarantee of labor's right to organize and bargain collectively given in Section 7(a) was a belated political concession that contradicted the spirit and underlying paternal and collectivist philosophy of the NIRA. The intention of the first New Deal was to eliminate concentrations of independent power in the economy by substituting national planning and management for the selfish private entrepreneurship that had led the nation to the brink of ruin. The first New Dealers did not seek to erect an industrial relations system based on the idea of countervailing power. And such political concessions as those made to labor in Section 7(a) gave them, as one said, "twinges of apprehension." All were aware, as Rexford Tugwell expressed it, that "big labor and big business had always had the possibility of conspiring to further a mutual interest which would be far from coincidental with the public good."[4] Despite the contrary implications of Section 7(a), the New Dealers, inspired by a vision of the organic nation, believed in a system of industrial relations that rested on a negative balance of power, in effect a countervailing powerlessness made viable by the omnipotent paternalism of the federal government. Only by such a system could a sense of the nation's welfare be inculcated among all participants in the economic life of the country.[5]

As a result of this attitude among New Deal policy makers, especially those responsible for the administration of the NIRA, a fundamental misunderstanding arose over what the rights granted to labor in Section 7(a) actually amounted to.[6] Even as Roosevelt advised workers of their new rights, he was urging them to rely on government rather than on the power those new rights conferred to improve wages and working conditions:

While we are making this great common effort, there should be no discord and dispute. This is no time to cavil. . . . It is time for patience and understanding and cooperation. The workers of this country have rights under this law which cannot be taken from them, and nobody will be permitted to whittle them away but, on the other hand, no aggression is now necessary to attain those rights. The whole country will be united to get them for you. The principle [cooperation] that applies to the employers applies to the workers as well, and I ask you workers to cooperate in the same spirit.[7]

In the weeks and months that followed, spokesmen for the National Recovery Administration (NRA) repeatedly implored labor not to exercise the rights afforded by Section 7(a), not only because of the economic emergency at hand, but because the NIRA never contemplated and could not abide the unplanned, independent exercise of power toward the advancement of self-defined, inherently selfish group interests.[8] Perhaps the fullest and frankest expression of this attitude was provided by NRA chieftain Hugh Johnson before the annual convention of the A.F. of L. in 1933. The great challenge of the moment, and the NRA's gravest responsibility, said Johnson, was to achieve "cooperation between industry, labor and government as one great team, to preserve the economic health of the nation and [permit] the organization of both industry and labor without which such cooperation would be wholly impossible." While acknowledging that the benefits deriving from organization were very great, Johnson also warned labor of "danger signals" that it must heed:

The power of organization is immense. A fully organized and unchecked industry could exploit and dominate a whole nation. A fully organized and unchecked labor could do exactly the same. There must be responsibility in each such organization. There must be a check on these great powers. Our government is government of the whole people. Its principal excuse for existence is protection of the whole people. These vast organizations of industry and of labor must each be responsible to government and each must admit governmental participation and control. No industrial combination must be permitted to practice monopolistic oppression and exploitation. No labor combination must be permitted to paralyze a whole industry by the unchecked use of power. These three principles, then— organization—cooperation—government participation—are of the very essence of the National Recovery Act.

The NRA, Johnson continued, marked "a profound change in [the] economic policy of a great nation . . . something new under the sun."

170

But change so fundamental exacted great sacrifices of cherished traditions. While reaffirming his personal allegiance to Jefferson's dictum that the best government is that which governs least, Johnson insisted that individual (and, by implication, group) liberty must be surrendered "if we are to live in the increasing complexity of modern life."

> The old order is gone forever and by no man's designing. The roaring, clacking, soulless complex of our great industry and commerce have become a great and highly active machine of which no individual is more than an integrated part. . . . The business of industry is your business. The success or failure of industry is your success or failure. Whether or not you are so called—you are a partner with your employer. There is never a proper question of what is the most you can get out of him. The real question is what is fairly necessary to the success of your joint adventure. That also is of the very essence of the Recovery Act.

While repeatedly stressing the desirability of voluntary cooperation by organized labor, Johnson left little doubt that the Roosevelt administration felt that labor had no choice but to comply with its recovery plan. It would, he warned, be "an act of economic lunacy" for the people to permit any selfishly motivated group to interfere with the advancement of national interests. But surely, he said, gaining organized labor's cooperation with the NRA would be no problem. Never had a national administration harbored kindlier feelings toward labor or pledged itself more forthrightly to uplift the labor movement. Revealing the paternal intent of the NRA, Johnson promised trade unionists:

> In this new scheme of things labor organization has a new place that it never occupied before—new duties, new benefits, new responsibilities. In the old days of exploitation you had to form aggressive units literally to fight for the life of labor. You had to be sometimes militant and always on the alert defensive. That is no longer necessary under the Recovery Act. . . . Labor needs to use no aggression in this process and you will get . . . the maximum of what the economic situation permits, and no amount of militant pressure can change that result.

Though his listeners appear not to have grasped the central implication of Johnson's message, it was, patronizing rhetoric notwithstanding, an essentially antiunion formula. While promising better wages and working conditions, it sought to divest workers' organizations of any independent economic power they might possess. When Johnson insisted that labor "does not need to strike under the Roosevelt plan," he was in fact saying that the new deal the NIRA afforded labor could not accommodate the independent spirit that authentic unionism fostered. Nothing short of complete destruction, Johnson warned, would befall those who spurned this new order of things and persisted in regarding unionism as an instrumentality through which the collective economic power of workers was brought to bear in attaining goals that they alone had defined. Since, he argued, the federal government had pledged that "from the beginning to the end of this process [NIRA] you are given a complete and highly effective protection of your rights," labor must show its good faith by discarding the old weapons of economic warfare. To do otherwise was to invite the wrath of the whole people. Johnson concluded:

> The plain stark truth is that you cannot tolerate strikes. Public opinion is the essential power in this country. In the end it will break down and destroy every subversive influence. If now—when the whole power of this government and its people are being given in an effort to provide and maintain to the ultimate the rights of every man who works for pay—you permit or countenance this economic evil, that public confidence and opinion will turn against you, and . . . the turn will be either to the extreme right or to the extreme left and either would result in your destruction as you know better than I can tell you.[9]

Hugh Johnson's description of the place and function of labor unions within a capitalist system rehabilitated and redirected by New Dealers ought to have been a source of profound disquietude among A.F. of L. leaders. The kind of wholly dependent organization he had described bore little resemblance to the genuine trade union, but was instead the very image of the company union gone public. The function of workers' organizations envisioned by the early New Dealers was not to fulfill the historic aspirations of American unionists, but to facilitate a process of economic rationalization necessitated by the collapse of the old order. Organization was not promoted to empower workers so that they might exercise a greater measure of control over their own economic lives, but to facilitate the control and discipline of labor within industrial spheres supervised and regulated, but not controlled outright, by planners and technocrats within the federal government. Through the operation of such an industrial relations system, wrote Louis Hacker, "class antagonisms were to be charmed away." Writing only a year after the NIRA had become law, Hacker concluded, "The New Deal, to put it baldly, assumed that it was possible to establish a permanent truce on class antagonisms."[10]

Had organized labor accepted the place and function within the economy which the early New Dealers had in mind, it seems unlikely that an independent labor movement could have survived. Of course unionism and the labor movement did survive—indeed, they later prospered—but only because the labor policies embodied in the NIRA, the New Deal's most far-reaching and idealistic vision of post-Depression America, were never fully implemented. When A.F. of L. leaders finally recognized the law's antiunion implications; when they realized that their understanding of unionism and the guarantees of Section 7(a) was opposed to that of New Deal reformers; when they began to understand that the law, however benign in theory, had the practical effect of institutionalizing the powerlessness of labor, they became its implacable foes. Once this realization emerged, wrote a group of Brookings economists, "union development was . . . carried along not by faith in the rights granted by Section 7(a), but by a somewhat defiant determination to make the law, as interpreted by the A.F. of L., a reality through the force of organized and direct action."[11] In effect, the A.F. of L., after a prolonged flirtation with the grand design of the first New Deal, rejected paternalism in favor of that old-time religion, voluntarism.

Thus while the labor policy of the first New Deal might have been disastrous for the labor movement had it operated as the Rooseveltians intended, its failure prompted the development of a new labor policy based on an assumption of the inevitably conflictful nature of industrial relations under capitalism—the antithesis of the assumption that underlay the NIRA. The National Labor Relations Act, passed with the reluctant blessing of the Roosevelt administration in 1935, provided a legal and institutional framework for industrial conflict, and an environment conducive to the growth of a self-directed, independently powerful labor movement that could confront employers directly. Though the Wagner Act defined the rights of workers as they had never been defined before, it represented, as Rexford Tugwell somewhat ruefully concluded, "an about-face in policy," a "return to more traditional policies" necessitated by the refusal of both labor and management to accept "the collectivist approach to national economic problems" embodied in the NIRA.[12]

The Wagner Act marked the end of the planners' influence in shaping New Deal labor policy. The ideal of an industrial relations system rooted in economic unitarianism gave way to the more realistic industrial pluralism based on countervailing power which is generally associated with the New Deal era.

For the broad mainstream of the American labor movement, the labor policies of the first New Deal constituted little more than a brief, if disconcerting, detour on the way to winning dramatic improvements in the economic status of organized workers and a secure place in the institutional life of the country. Yet for at least one less durable and resilient branch of the labor movement the application of those policies created an antiunion momentum whose effects could not be overcome.

The spirit of organization among industrial workers weathered and was even strengthened by the antiunion impulses of the early New Deal, and after 1935 the unions they forged became the backbone of the American labor movement. The labor movement in California agriculture was more fragile. The organizational spirit among the state's farmworkers, though no less ardent than that among industrial workers, lacked the vibrancy, the stamina, and, most important, the transmutability into political power needed to resist well-intentioned New Deal reformers determined to implement their formula for rational and nonconflictive labor relations.

It is more than a little ironic that the New Deal labor policies set forth in the NIRA should have affected the agricultural labor movement at all, much less that they helped to promote its full devastation. For while the law did not expressly exempt agricultural workers from its application, within only a few weeks of its passage they were effectively excluded by administrative decree. Sensitive to the political risks that would be incurred within its rural constituencies if the apparent protections of Section 7(a) were extended to agricultural labor, the Roosevelt administration worded the President's Re-employment Agreement in such a way that the blanket wage and hour code it promulgated excluded farmworkers. Although considerable confusion attended the question of farm labor's status under the law well into 1934, especially insofar as those employed on California's industrialized farms were concerned, the administration consistently held that the provisions of Section 7(a) did not apply to agricultural workers. Using an outworn variation on trickle-down income theory, New Deal spokesmen argued that the economic interests of farmworkers, like those of sharecroppers and tenant farmers, would be protected under the Agricultural Adjustment Act, which would provide not only a greater aggregate income for the agricultural sector, but also a fair sharing of that new wealth at every level of the farming economy. This argument, based on the same paternalistic logic that underlay so many of the early New Deal policies, gave special reinforcement to the belief that unionism among agricultural workers was particularly unnecessary and undesirable.[13]

Yet the administration could hardly ignore the active and militant labor movement among California farmworkers in mid-1933, especially when it had the demonstrated ability to disrupt the state's leading industry and seriously retard recovery. The obvious remedy, believed George Creel, the federal administrator who first addressed the problem, was a liberal application of freshly compounded New Deal labor policies. The patient's only responsibility was an abiding trust in the healer's good intentions.

In George Creel the first New Deal had an emissary as devoted and faithful to its tenets as any who went out from Washington in 1933. Steeped in the same progressive faith that Roosevelt and his leading advisers confessed and sought to revive, Creel saw the 1932 election as both a long-awaited mandate for reform and a vindication of the nationalist idealism of the early twentieth century. Writing about a long interview he had had with Roosevelt just before the inauguration, Creel reported with undisguised enthusiasm that the president-elect shared his belief that the election "was not a Democratic victory but a triumph for progressivism."[14] "It is his fixed belief," Creel approvingly wrote of Roosevelt, "that America has come to the end of an era—an era of unplanned, uncontrolled and wasteful production—and that what we are now enduring is in no sense a 'slump,' but the breakdown of a system. He holds that the sole purpose of an economic order is to provide those who live under it with the necessities of life and freedom from the fears of existence. Failing, it must give way to a new and better order."[15]

The key to this "new and better order" was, of course, national planning. "That is the big idea at the back of the Roosevelt head, and not so far back either." With the reascendancy of progressivism, Creel argued, came an opportunity to introduce planning and thereby to eliminate forever the "hit-or-miss, helter-skelter, devil-take-the-hindmost system under which America has been operating." Roosevelt was aware, said Creel, that a new breed of public servant was needed to design, install, and operate this new rational state, and this "is where the technicians, scientists, engineers and economists come in. Men not primarily concerned with barter and profits, but possessing a sense of state and ability to see the whole picture."[16]

Though not a technician, scientist, engineer, or economist, Creel clearly saw himself as an agent of Roosevelt's New Deal. "I left the President-elect," he wrote, "with an enthusiasm I had not known since the days of Woodrow Wilson, and when he took office I made an instant offer of my services as a volunteer in the field." Creel's induction into the ranks of the New Deal came with the passage of the NIRA. Given the responsibility for implementing the recovery act in California, Creel, possessed of a formidable, even arrogant confidence in his progressive mission, took up his labors in August 1933. Introducing himself as "the sole source of authority" for the New Deal in California, Creel found both labor and management in the state mired in a pitiable malaise of "bewilderment and unhappiness," and "eager to adopt any suggestion or order that was put forward authoritatively."

The role of patron-savior was one for which Creel's philosophy of authoritarian progressivism provided an excellent psychological basis. Among his first official acts was the issuance of a proclamation to labor and employers. The central aim of the New Deal, he advised, was

> to bring about a co-operative order, as opposed to an unlimited competitive order, with the public interest enforced as against the selfish interests of any group. This policy applies to labor unions as well as to employers. Just as management is called upon to change their outlook, so must organized labor prepare for radical departures from old habit. . . . When employers are robbed of the power to crush workers, unions cannot expect to retain the right to bedevil industry with a babel of demands. Labor, therefore, must develop a code of collective practice which will not appear to reflect the temporary benefit of separate groups, but which will be recognized instantly as part of the more rational organization of the various forces in industry to achieve the end of greater stability, more regular employment, and the attainment of the highest possible standard of living.[17]

Creel's notion of the proper function of unions was identical to that of Roosevelt and the first New Deal brain trust. He was not opposed to worker organization. Indeed, he was to advise farm employers toward the end of 1933 that the principal failing of their industrial relations policy was that it discouraged rather than encouraged worker organization.[18] Like other devotees of economic planning, Creel felt that organization was an indispensable prerequisite to effective management and control of labor. Conversely, he tended to regard unions that were self-actuated and self-interested as unhealthy manifestations of economic individualism, and thus incompatible with the collectivist premise of the New Deal. Nowhere did this inherent antiunion bias of the first New Deal show itself more plainly and consistently than in the federal government's handling, through Creel and a succession of similarly oriented bureaucrats, of labor disputes in California agriculture, beginning with the cotton strike of 1933.

Federal intervention in the state's agricultural labor relations came at a unique moment in the history of farmworker organization in California. At the time Creel assumed his duties as director of the Western District of the NRA, the agricultural regions of California were, as a result of the CAWIU's ambitious campaign of organization and direct-action, in a state of unprecedented upheaval. The union had plainly succeeded in transforming the perennial discontent of California farmworkers into a militant force for change. The tension between union and political goals which had caused debilitating problems in other Communist unions was largely absent in the CAWIU, mainly because the extreme present-mindedness of farmworkers discouraged the natural tendency of Communists to politicize economic struggles. Having largely overcome the internal problems that had contributed to its early failures, the CAWIU was by the time of its confrontation with cotton growers a union whose reputation rested on a proven ability to win substantial wage increases, better working conditions, and de facto if not formal recognition in farming regions throughout the state.

Most farmworkers in California initially believed, as did most workers across the country, that the enactment of the NIRA represented an endorsement of unionism by the Roosevelt administration.[19] And, like workers in other industries, farmworkers showed an increased interest in organization, even though the President's Re-employment Agreement expressly excluded them from the law's application.

The extreme militancy of the CAWIU, combined with the Communist Party's official opposition to the NIRA, placed the union on a clear collision course with the New Deal labor policies that George Creel was determined to implement. While A.F. of L. unions and even a few ethnic unions in agriculture were willing to give the Roosevelt administration a chance to demonstrate its avowed friendship for labor,[20] the CAWIU's leadership almost immediately raised the suspicion that the administration's labor policies were implicitly antiunion. At the union's first annual district convention in early August, less than three months after the NIRA had become law, the membership was warned that the Roosevelt labor policy, "advertised by every agency in the country as a cure for the ills of the workers, is a snare and delusion." The administration's opposition to strikes, union leaders argued, revealed its antiunion bias, since those who had struck during the summer of 1933 were doing nothing more than "fighting for the very conditions promised by the NIRA." Reviewing their own union's brief history as well as that of the labor movement generally, CAWIU leaders reminded their listeners that any gains that workers had won were "solely due to unremitting struggle." Thus, they concluded, "the only way for workers to better their conditions is organizational struggle."[21] When compared to the docile rhetoric of many A.F. of L. unions in mid-1933, that of the CAWIU had a distinctly radical flavor. Yet farm-workers were in fact expressing their allegiance to the historic touch-stones of the A.F. of L.: pure and simple unionism and voluntarism. As one convention spokesman put it: "The bosses won't do anything for the workers and neither will 30,000 NIRA's. We got to organize. Our union is young, and the only militant one."[22]

Apparently believing that the union could not simply ignore a national labor relations policy that the government and the press had so widely and extravagantly "ballyhooed as bringing back prosperity and work," CAWIU leaders encouraged the convention to follow the example of workers in other industries by adopting a code governing conditions of employment in agriculture. Anxious that such a code not be misinterpreted by outsiders as an endorsement of NRA labor policies, union leader Jack Wright emphasized that it should not be regarded as a collection of proposals, but as "a set of demands; a declaration of war between agricultural workers and bosses."[23] In its final form, the CAWIU code, free of "legal verbiage" and encompassing "the simple minimum needs" of California's agricultural workers, demanded:

1. A minimum wage of 50¢ per hour for unskilled, and 75¢ per hour for skilled field, shed, packing house, and cannery workers.
2. A maximum eight-hour day, with time-and-a-half for overtime; and when a worker is called on the job and does not work a full day he is to be paid for not less than 6 hours.
3. Corresponding wage increases with rising cost of commodities.
4. Equal pay for equal work for men, women and young workers.
5. Abolition of child labor to the age of sixteen (16).
6. Abolition of all forms of contract system.
7. Recognition of the Cannery & Agricultural Workers Industrial Union as representatives of the agricultural workers in the State of California.
8. All negotiations between Union and growers or mediators to be finally decided upon by the workers.
9. Free sanitary housing, wood, light and water, and transportation to and from jobs at great distance; schools and nurseries for children of migratory parents.
10. Immediate cash relief for unemployed agricultural workers and Federal unemployment insurance.
11. The right of the workers to organize into the union of their choice, to strike, and to picket.

12. No discrimination on the job or in relief because of race, color or creed.[24]

In studied defiance of the NRA's repeated assertion that the road to national economic recovery lay in the direction of cooperation rather than conflict, union delegates resolved "to develop struggles in every cannery, on every ranch for compliance with this code."[25] The union's distrust of the NRA, or any other governmental program that New Dealers might have devised in the area of labor relations, was revealed in Jack Wright's emphatic declaration that "no government has ever come out with a program for the working class."[26]

The San Joaquin Valley cotton strike, which was to demonstrate the irreconcilable conflict between the CAWIU's militant unionism and the federal government's new rational and paternalistic labor policies, grew out of the same aggravated economic conditions that had produced the earlier farm-labor troubles in 1933. Unable to lower their fixed costs of production as cotton prices plummeted and squeezed by the finance and ginning companies that controlled the valley's multi-million-dollar cotton industry, growers had followed the same strategy for survival adopted by other farm employers in the state during the early years of the Depression: passing as large a share of their losses as possible on to farmworkers in the form of ever lower wages. Thus while the typical California cotton farmer's income fell considerably between 1929 and 1932, the wages of those who picked his crop declined even more sharply. In 1929 the piece rate for picking cotton in the San Joaquin Valley was $1.50 per hundred pounds. After sharp reductions in 1930 and 1931, wages hit bottom in 1932 at 40 cents per hundred, a decrease of nearly 75 percent in only three years. And while the cost of living also declined over the same period, it did so much more gradually. When combined with deteriorating working conditions and an increasingly unfavorable labor market, depressed wages created a state of mind among cotton pickers that was charged with just the kind of potential the CAWIU thrived on.[27]

As the 1933 cotton harvest approached, however, an abrupt improvement in the nation's agricultural economy reversed the pattern of the previous four years, sending commodity prices, including the price of California cotton, steadily upward. Principally as a result of the newly enacted Agricultural Adjustment Act, prices had risen rapidly enough by the fall of 1933 to increase the total value of the state's cotton crop by almost 150 percent over the previous year.[28]

In light of the industry's suddenly improved economic picture,

CAWIU organizers had little difficulty in convincing the cotton pickers amassing in the San Joaquin Valley that a substantially higher wage was in order for the 1933 season. Working out of the union's headquarters in Tulare, a small group of veteran Communists led by chief organizer Pat Chambers visited virtually every labor camp in the lower valley during September, enlisting new members in the CAWIU and promoting support for a wage demand of $1 per hundred pounds. Of the 15,000 or so farmworkers who made up the labor force for the cotton harvest, more than 75 percent were Mexicans, mainly migrant families. The remainder of the work force was composed of southern blacks and white migrants, most of whom had recently arrived in California from the drought-ravaged Southwest, and a sprinkling of Filipinos. Whatever their ethnic background or language, the workers' response to the CAWIU's appeal was uniformly enthusiastic.[29]

As early as September 12 the valley's growers were advised that a strike was likely unless the 1933 wage was raised to $1 per hundred pounds.[30] On September 19 growers belonging to the Agricultural Labor Bureau of the San Joaquin Valley met, as they had done every year since 1926, to determine the wage to be paid for cotton picking during the coming season. Although cotton growers were represented in the bureau's leadership, it was dominated by agents for finance and ginning companies in the valley, both of whom competed directly with farmworkers for a share of the growers' earnings.[31] At the request of the CAWIU, Pat Chambers was permitted to attend the meeting and to read, but not discuss, the union's demands: $1 per hundred pounds for picking, abolition of the contract labor system, hiring through the union, and a guarantee of no discrimination against union members. After listening to the demands, growers promptly agreed on a wage of 60 cents per hundred pounds.[32]

Recognizing that a confrontation of unprecedented proportions lay immediately ahead, each side sought to prepare itself. Late in September, the San Joaquin Valley Peace Officers' Association met in Fresno to discuss "ways and means of coping with agitators if a strike of cotton pickers is attempted." Invited to attend the meeting and share in the lawmen's deliberations were several of the valley's most prominent cotton growers.[33] Aware that the close association of valley law-enforcement agencies with growers made it unlikely that strikers could rely on authorities to protect their civil rights, CAWIU leaders sought the help of well-known liberals. One union organizer wrote to author Lincoln Steffens, a prominent supporter of leftist causes, asking that he seek the help of state and federal officials in protecting the cotton strikers' rights.[34] A similar letter to Rabbi Irving Reichert, a member of the State Recovery Board, prompted a highly publicized appeal to Governor James Rolph for an end to the violent strikebreaking tactics that San Joaquin Valley lawmen had employed in earlier farm-labor disputes. Referring in particular to the activities of authorities during the Fresno and Lodi grape strikes, Reichert complained: "In recent labor disputes involving . . . fruit pickers . . . , our investigations . . . established the disconcerting fact that in the great majority of clashes between the peace officers and the strikers, the former were responsible for inciting to violence." Apparently hoping to lend additional weight and urgency to his appeal, Reichert reminded Rolph: "We are passing through one of the most critical periods of the NRA program. President Roosevelt, Secretary [of Labor Frances] Perkins, and General [Hugh] Johnson are deeply concerned lest the confidence of the American worker in the New Deal be destroyed by an arbitrary use of power on the part of minor police officials."[35] More embarrassed than moved by Reichert's entreaty, Rolph chose the path of political expediency and did nothing.

Still not knowing how employers and local authorities would respond, CAWIU members voted at a mass meeting held in Tulare on October 1 to strike throughout the entire region on October 4. Almost immediately, however, hundreds of cotton pickers began walking off scattered ranches in Kern and Kings counties, where the harvest season first got under way each year. The appearance of pickets at a ranch north of Bakersfield on October 2 provoked a response that revealed in microcosm much of what was to occur on a massive scale once the cotton strike had become general. The grower in question, making no effort to explore the possibilities of a peaceful settlement, had himself sworn in as a "special deputy" by an obliging local official, armed himself, and promptly arrested thirteen pickets on unspecified charges. In hopes of further discouraging strikers, he announced his intention to import 300 scabs and strikebreakers unless pickers returned to work at once.[36]

Despite confident predictions by cotton growers in the lower valley that a general strike would not materialize, picking operations were at a virtual standstill when the CAWIU's call for a total work stoppage was issued on October 4. When the actual dimensions of the strike at last became apparent to them, the growers' early optimism quickly gave way to a common feeling that the threat to them was real. By October 5, growers and their allies were conferring throughout the strike area, hoping to devise a plan that would rapidly return cotton pickers to work at the wage of 60 cents per hundred pounds. A negotiated settlement was ruled out.

Having eliminated negotiations as a possible means of ending the strike, growers naturally gravitated toward the most obvious alternative method available: force. Between October 5 and 10, antiunion forces in the lower San Joaquin Valley employed a variety of steadily more violent strikebreaking tactics. On October 5 about seventy-five growers in the Corcoran area of Kings County began forcibly evicting strikers and their families from employer-owned labor camps. Strikers at the first camp visited by the growers were given five minutes either to resume work on the employers' terms or to vacate the premises. When the camp's inhabitants, mostly Mexican families, failed to act within the time allotted, growers loaded their belongings aboard trucks and dumped them beside a nearby highway. Unable to find other shelter on such short notice, many of the evicted families camped along the highway until local growers shut off their water supply.[37]

Similar evictions occurred throughout the strike area over the next few days. When CAWIU leaders protested that evictions without adequate notice were illegal, county law-enforcement officers imply ignored them. In discussing the evictions after the strike had ended, Kings County District Attorney Clarence Wilson freely acknowledged their illegality, but said, "The sheriff and I told the growers not to worry much about the pickers' rights anyway." The willingness of valley lawmen to acquiesce in the growers' lawlessness was a central feature of the cotton strike. For the most part, law-enforcement officials indulged the growers' excesses out of fear that to do otherwise would expose them to unacceptable political consequences. District Attorney Wilson later admitted, "The growers really were more trouble and danger than the strikers were. We could control the strikers because they didn't amount to anything and couldn't even vote, but the growers were well known and had lots of influence and we were much more afraid we couldn't control them."[38] An undersheriff in Kern County expressed the same sentiment in somewhat more positive terms when he proudly asserted, "We protect farmers out here in Kern County. They are our best people. They are always with us. They keep this country going. They put us in here and they can put us out again, so we serve them."[39] On several occasions during the cotton strike, valley lawmen not only countenanced violations of the law by growers, but actually encouraged them. While instructing growers in their rights, an assistant district attorney reportedly advised that "should any agitators present themselves at or near your ranches, get hold of them and pour a bottle of castor oil down their throats. That will cure them of agitating."[40]

Aware that valley authorities were in complete sympathy with their intention to break the strike by force, cotton growers and their allies felt free to adopt any methods they thought necessary to achieve their goal, without regard for legal conventions. Unlawful evictions of striking cotton pickers and their families were only a first step, and a comparatively temperate and peaceful one in light of subsequent events. On October 6, newspapers in the strike region reported that at the urging of finance and ginning companies, chambers of commerce, the Farm Bureau, and the area's largest growers, farmers' "protective associations" were being formed in Tulare, Kings, and Kern counties for the purpose of driving "agitators" out of the valley.[41]

From the strike's beginning, growers were most concerned and angered over the mass picketing methods used by the CAWIU. With the strike area more than 100 miles long and between 30 and 40 miles wide, the union, determined to bring cotton picking in the valley to a complete standstill, sent out large groups of pickets in car and truck caravans with instructions to stop and picket only where they found workers still on the job. As armed farmers stood by daring them to trespass, pickets swarmed about on the shoulders of county roads bordering the cotton fields, using a variety of impassioned pleas and thinly veiled threats to pull pickers off the job. Legally helpless to prevent such activity, growers seethed as the relatively few cotton pickers they had induced to remain on the job were persuaded to join the strike.[42]

With the organization of the various protective associations, a vigorous and often violent campaign to halt all picketing activities got under way. When strikers attempted on October 7 to hold a meeting in the Tulare County town of Woodville, a large force of growers appeared and ordered them to disperse. After a brief fight, in which the strikers gave a very good account of themselves, one of the growers was permitted to read aloud a "Notice to the Public at Large," in which employers declared:

We the undersigned, the agricultural producers and business men operating in the Porterville, Cutter, Woodville and Tipton sections of Tulare County, State of California, do hereby, by this agreement declare ourselves to be in a frame of mind to protect ourselves from present strike agitators and strikers, and do hereby incorporate ourselves into an agri-

183

cultural protective association with full intentions legally to disburse [*sic*] all strike agitators and strikers from our locality. Our motto: STRIKERS WORK PEACEFULLY OR LEAVE THE STATE OF CALIFORNIA.[43]

Though the Woodville skirmish had little apparent significance, it played an important part in spawning a strike leadership actually drawn from the rank and file. From their earliest involvement among California farmworkers, CAWIU organizers recognized that the racial and ethnic diversity of the state's farm-labor force greatly complicated the already difficult task of organization. And despite their best efforts, union organizers had made little headway in persuading workers to put aside their prejudices in the cause of solidarity. A related problem that had affected the leadership of earlier agricultural strikes was that white Communist organizers, while they usually did their utmost to gain acceptance among the workers they were seeking to lead, seldom succeeded in allaying completely the suspicions of nonwhite farmworkers toward outsiders, no matter how sincere their professions of friendship and selfless intention. Thus while such able Communist organizers as Pat Chambers and Pat Callahan had succeeded on many occasions in winning the confidence of farmworkers, they never ceased to be outsiders.

When Sam Darcy assumed personal responsibility for mapping the CAWIU's organizing strategy in 1933, he emphasized that the union's fortunes would depend to a large extent on its success in recruiting leaders from the several racial and ethnic groups represented in the work force. Darcy's admonition was forcefully reiterated after the union's costly mismanagement of the El Monte strike, and organizers endeavored thereafter to integrate and democratize the leadership of strikes to the fullest degree possible.

During the two months of planning that preceded the cotton strike, party and union strategists sought to assemble a leadership cadre in the valley that met the criteria established through their analyses of earlier strikes. Conceiving of such a leadership, however, proved considerably less difficult that actually fashioning it. The scale of the cotton strike, both in number of workers involved and in geographical area covered, created unprecedented problems of leadership for the union. Recalling these special problems, Sam Darcy wrote that they made the cotton strike "the toughest strike I ever knew." Not even the 1934 San Francisco general strike, he insisted, was "as tightly or as bitterly fought."[44] From the start, however, the union's ability to coordinate the strike efforts of the various groups of workers involved was limited by its inability to break down the barriers between them. The several hundred white migrants taking part in the conflict presented an especially difficult problem. Union leaders found that while the whites brought to the strike a combative disposition that made them militant and courageous fighters, they also brought racial attitudes from their southern homelands that rendered them incapable of regarding their nonwhite collaborators in the struggle as equals. When added to the antagonism that had long existed between Mexican and Filipino laborers, and the uniformly strong bias of all three groups toward the black workers taking part in the strike, the separatist mentality of white strikers presented union leaders with especially delicate problems of strike consolidation. Unable to find a ready solution to their dilemma, Darcy and his cohorts were, he later wrote, "forced to let developments take their course for we found that by common consent, Negro as well as white, Mexican as well as Filipino, accepted the idea that they must each constitute a separate group within the strike."

Yet the debilitating effects of disunity were greatly alleviated, if not eliminated entirely, as a result of the brief clash between strikers and farmer-vigilantes at Woodville. As soon as the battle broke out, the separate groups of strikers quickly put aside their differences to defend themselves and their allies against a common foe. Almost at once, Darcy recalled, the union's leaders saw that the disunity among strikers would be reduced "not by lecturing, but by using the instinct of fighters to subordinate everything to the needs of the battle." The Woodville fight also produced a rank-and-file leader who was able to command the respect and loyalty of the strike's participants without regard to race. With probable literary license, Sam Darcy described "Big Bill" Hammett as "a big Okie father with the physical appearance of John Brown." A self-educated "preacher" in his mid-fifties, Hammett and his family, which included five strapping sons, had arrived in the state from Oklahoma not long before the cotton strike began. And although Hammett had apparently been in the background during the first days of the strike, the singular ferocity with which he and his sons responded to the provocations of vigilantes at Woodville not only helped to cool the growers' ardor for further physical combat but propelled him instantly into a position of strike leadership. Greatly impressed by the prowess he had shown in battle, the other strikers, their ethnic differences notwithstanding, immediately accepted Hammett as their leader. And Darcy lost little time in taking advantage of Hammett's newly won prominence. With a flattering approach calculated to enhance the strike's effectiveness as well as to stroke Hammett's ego, Darcy suggested to him that "as a real leader of the men he needed lieutenants," and wondered if it "wouldn't be a good idea to have a lieutenant for the Negro people, one for the Mexicans, and one for the Filipinos."[45] Not averse to the idea of having his own general staff, Hammett quickly designated three subordinates acceptable to the groups of strikers they represented. Thus in the immediate aftermath of the Woodville encounter the leadership of the strike was finally constituted on an effective basis. Darcy remained the strike's dominant but secret strategist; Pat Chambers and Caroline Decker, the CAWIU's young secretary, spoke for the union; and Big Bill Hammett and his multiracial general staff served as the spokesmen for the rank and file. The strikers' tendency to segregate themselves during meals and at strike meetings continued in force, but the strike leadership, at the unwitting instigation of employers, was fully integrated and remarkably unified throughout the remainder of the strike.

And given the intensification of the employers' strikebreaking campaign as the conflict entered its second tumultuous week, the solidification of the strikers' leadership came not a moment too soon. Between October 7 and 9, valley newspapers approvingly reported that groups of armed growers were moving throughout the strike area, alternately threatening and attacking all strikers who refused either to return to work or to leave the region. Valley law-enforcement officers, assisted by special deputies drawn mainly from the growers' ranks, cooperated in this strikebreaking effort by arresting workers whom they suspected of being strike leaders.[46]

Beyond their campaign of threats and intimidation, growers also endeavored to break the strike by denying strikers and their families access to food and other essential supplies. Early in the strike growers elicited pledges from public and private relief agencies in the region that no food or other assistance would be provided to striking cotton pickers. When growers in the vicinity of Tulare learned that some small merchants who were in sympathy with the strike had donated supplies or extended credit to the strikers, they publicly threatened to boycott the "disloyal" storekeepers. In a paid advertisement in the *Tulare Advance-Register,* the newly formed Farmers' Protective Association of Tulare County warned: "We, the farmers of your Community, whom you depend upon for support, feel that you have nursed too long the Viper that is at our door. These Communist Agitators MUST be driven from town by you, and your harboring them further will prove to us your non-cooperation with us, and make it necessary for us to give our support and trade to another town that will support and cooperate with us."[47]

Rather than weakening the strike, the tactics employed by growers and local authorities during the early days of the struggle probably served to strengthen it. The forcible evictions of strikers from grower-owned housing led to the establishment of numerous makeshift strike camps throughout the lower valley. With thousands of strikers concentrated in these camps rather than scattered among the hundreds of cotton ranches in the region, the tasks of organizing picketing caravans, maintaining solidarity within the ranks, and keeping the rank and file in close contact with the strike leadership were greatly facilitated. The strike camp established by evicted workers on a barren four-acre lot on the outskirts of Corcoran became a center of especially militant strike activity. With an estimated 3,000 strikers living there and sharing not only the misery of hunger and sickness but also a curiously invigorating sense of community, the Corcoran camp, dubbed "Little Mexico City" by its inhabitants, assumed a powerful symbolic as well as practical importance in keeping the cotton strike alive.[48]

In much the same way, the growers' early lawlessness and their efforts to deny food to strikers tended to sustain rather than discourage further struggle. As armed growers and their allies acted to break the strike through threats, intimidation, and physical violence, union leaders were able to confront their followers with seemingly incontrovertible evidence that the Communist theory of class struggle stressed by the CAWIU was being validated. When valley authorities openly cooperated in the growers' attacks, the union's collateral assertion that government was inevitably a boss-controlled instrument of class oppression was also apparently confirmed.[49]

Similarly, the CAWIU's otherwise simplistic characterization of cotton growers, particularly the largest ones, as unfeeling exploiters of labor was apparently corroborated when employers publicly announced their plan to deny food and other essentials of life to strikers and their families. Upon learning of the growers' threat to boycott valley merchants who sold or gave food to hungry cotton pickers, State Labor Commissioner MacDonald denounced it as a cruel and unwarranted attempt "to starve out" strikers and their families. To the detriment of the growers' image, newspapers throughout California and the nation picked up MacDonald's statement, and public sympathy for the strikers and protests against the growers' methods increased markedly.[50]

Despite numerous physical assaults, dozens of arrests, and an almost

Strikers' camp at Corcoran during the 1933 cotton strike. At far left is the Circo Azteca, where striking workers gathered for nightly entertainment. Photo: Bancroft Library, University of California, Berkeley.

A family of Mexican migrants at "home" in Corcoran strikers' camp during the 1933 cotton strike. Photo: Bancroft Library, University of California, Berkeley.

Children at play in Corcoran strikers' camp during the 1933 cotton strike. Photo: Bancroft Library, University of California, Berkeley.

Workers gathered at makeshift CAWIU office inside Corcoran strikers' camp during the 1933 cotton strike. Note the "100%" endorsement of the NRA affixed to front post. Photo: Bancroft Library, University of California, Berkeley.

Mexican pickets calling workers out of the fields during the 1933 cotton strike.
Photo: Bancroft Library, University of California, Berkeley.

Picket caravan during the 1933 cotton strike. Photo: Bancroft Library, University of California, Berkeley.

unending string of progressively more savage threats from growers, the cotton strike had grown to unprecedented proportions by October 9. An estimated 12,000 workers were on strike in Tulare, Kings, and Kern counties, leaving millions of dollars' worth of rapidly maturing cotton in deserted fields. Yet rather than abandon the strikebreaking tactics they had used without apparent effect for over a week, growers resolved to employ still more drastic methods.

Although most valley newspapers gave editorial support and encouragement to the growers when they sought to defeat the strike through force, state officials concerned over the escalating level of violent rhetoric criticized their intransigence and increasingly lawless behavior. State officials were particularly critical of growers for their refusal even to consider mediation as a means of settling the dispute. As early as October 6 state mediators had approached both growers and the union with an offer to assist negotiations to end the strike. After some initial hesitation, the CAWIU accepted the state's offer, but the growers, speaking through the Agricultural Labor Bureau of the San Joaquin Valley, informed state mediators that they were unalterably opposed to any dealings with the union, which they denounced as a Communist organization whose purpose in forcing workers to strike against their will was manifestly subversive. More significant, however, was the growers' announcement that mediation was pointless in light of their steadfast determination to pay no more than 60 cents per hundred pounds for cotton picking.[51]

State Labor Commissioner MacDonald, the man designated by Governor Rolph to direct the state's mediation effort, responded that by refusing to negotiate growers were doing more to promote communism than the CAWIU. In a statement released to the press on October 8, MacDonald said, "I think their [the growers'] refusal to allow any officials, state or federal, to act as mediators is unjustifiable and tends to encourage communism and to precipitate . . . dangerous conditions."[52] MacDonald was joined in his condemnation of the growers' attitude by H. L. Walker, manager of the state employment office in Bakersfield. In commenting on the growers' claim that mediation would have the effect of encouraging further Communist subversion, Walker said that "radicals don't make a strike and needless to say the run of the strikers don't know the difference between Communism and somnambulism."[53]

While it, too, was critical of the growers' obstinacy, the federal government was particularly distressed by the lawless strikebreaking methods being used by growers with the open approval and assistance of valley authorities. Convinced that it was the state's responsibility to maintain order in the strike region, Rabbi Reichert wrote to Governor Rolph on behalf of the NRA, demanding that he act immediately to stem the growing tide of violence and ensure that strikers' rights were safeguarded. Reminding the governor of his earlier warning that vigorous state action was required if farm employers and local police were to be dissuaded from employing the violent strikebreaking methods they had used in previous strikes, Reichert angrily complained:

> The lawlessness which I predicted has come to pass. The high-handed and outrageous methods of the so-called Vigilantes, instead of being firmly suppressed by the civil authorities, are aided and abetted by them. Gangsterism has been substituted for law and order in the cotton areas. . . .
> There is no question but that the present lawlessness in Kern, Tulare, Kings, and Madera counties constitutes a threat against constitutional government in California.

In closing, Reichert implored Rolph to halt "this reign of terror which is causing unspeakable distress and anguish to hundreds of decent and law-abiding men, women, and children, and retarding the recovery program in California."[54] Even if Rolph had been willing to take the forceful action that Reichert demanded, and he was not, it is doubtful that he could have acted in time to halt the deadly violence that occurred on October 10. Growers, frustrated by the inefficacy of their original tactics in breaking the strike, had decided by October 9 to use any level of force required to end the conflict once and for all. The mounting impatience of cotton growers was explicitly revealed at a meeting of roughly 700 farm employers and their supporters at the Corcoran ball park on the evening of October 9. Called there by a representative of a leading cotton ginning company for the stated purpose of mapping a more "drastic" strikebreaking strategy, growers brimmed with enthusiasm when the featured speaker declared that "the time had come when the growers would have to take the law into their own hands."[55] Reviewing the strike situation on October 9, the *San Francisco Examiner* reported darkly that "the atmosphere of the valley is that of a smoldering volcano."

On the following afternoon, the violent eruption that the strikers had anticipated finally occurred.[56] At Pixley, a small town about fifteen miles south of Tulare, a large group of strikers gathered in a vacant lot across from the local CAWIU hall to protest the arrests of several pickets at a nearby ranch. As strike leader Pat Chambers was addressing the crowd, a caravan of automobiles bearing about forty armed growers arrived on the scene. Brandishing a variety of pistols, rifles, and shotguns, the growers approached the strikers' meeting, issuing loud threats as they came. Fearing violence, Chambers immediately declared the meeting at an end and instructed the men, women, and children in attendance to cross the road and enter the union headquarters. As the workers made their way toward the building, one of the growers following them discharged a rifle. When a striker approached the grower and pushed the barrel of his gun downward, another armed grower rushed forward and clubbed him to the ground. While he still lay on the ground the grower shot him to death. Immediately the rest of the growers opened fire on the fleeing strikers and their families. Amid the screams of those who lay wounded on the ground, growers continued to fire into the union hall until their ammunition was exhausted. When the last shot had been fired, the growers piled back into their cars and headed out of town. As the growers' caravan departed, a group of highway patrolmen and deputy sheriffs who had watched the attack from hiding gathered in the middle of town to try to determine what action they should take. After what one observer described as "some hemming and hawing," the lawmen set out in unenthusiastic pursuit of the growers. A few miles out of town authorities finally succeeded in stopping the growers' caravan. After collecting several firearms "still warm and strong with the odor of powder," the officers, inexplicably, allowed the growers to proceed. In the wake of the growers' attack, two Mexican strikers were dead. Eight others, including one woman, had been wounded. Miraculously, none of the many children in the strikers' midst was injured. According to a newspaper reporter who witnessed the Pixley "riot," at no point during the encounter had "so much as a water pistol appeared in the hands of the besieged strikers."[57]

At almost exactly the same time that the Pixley tragedy was unfolding, another fatal confrontation between strikers and armed growers occurred about sixty miles to the south, near the small Kern County town of Arvin. As pickets arrived at a ranch in the area during the morning, a large group of armed growers appeared and stationed themselves just inside the ranch's property line. For almost five hours the two groups faced each other across an imaginary barrier, trading threats and exchanging menacing looks. When the tension along the line reached the breaking point, a fight erupted with growers using gun

Armed farmers hiding across the street from strikers' headquarters at Pixley just before they fired on unarmed workers attending a strike rally during the 1933 cotton strike. Photo: University of California, Berkeley.

Union leader Pat Chambers addressing striking workers at Pixley headquarters moments before farmers fired into the crowd. Photo: Bancroft Library, University of California, Berkeley.

One of the many strikers wounded when armed farmers attacked a strike meeting at Pixley during the 1933 cotton strike. Photo: Bancroft Library, University of California, Berkeley.

Striking Mexican cotton pickers demanding that authorities disarm farmers follow-ing armed attacks on pickets at Pixley and Arvin during the 1933 cotton strike. Photo: Bancroft Library, University of California, Berkeley.

butts against pickets armed with wooden grape stakes. After several minutes of combat a shot rang out and one Mexican striker fell dead. Suddenly all of the growers began shooting as a deputy sheriff on the scene threw a tear-gas bomb into the group of strikers. When the shooting stopped, several strikers lay wounded, one so seriously that his arm was later amputated. Accepting without question an allegation by growers that a striker perched in a nearby tree had fired the shot that killed the Mexican picket, authorities arriving at the scene immediately arrested several strikers on murder charges and many others on rioting charges. Later, after an investigation revealed that the strikers had carried no firearms and that all of the shooting was done by growers, the murder charges were dismissed. No attempt was ever made by authorities to determine which of the growers had fired the shot that killed Pedro Subia, the Mexican picket.[58]

The killings of October 10 prompted an immediate flood of protest. Growers and valley authorities were roundly condemned for their lawlessness, as was the state for failing to protect the rights and lives of strikers. The Pixley and Arvin tragedies also brought a small army of state and federal mediators, highway patrolmen, investigators, protest delegations, and relief officials into the strike area. Also, because one of the two Mexicans killed at Pixley was the Mexican government's honorary representative in Tulare, Mexican Consul Enrique Bravo rushed to the area from Monterey to investigate the shootings.[59]

The most urgent and insistent demand of protesters was that authorities in the area immediately disarm all growers. Rather than complying with such demands, valley authorities made matters worse. The *San Francisco Chronicle* reported on October 13 that in Kern County alone authorities had issued 600 permits allowing growers and others to carry concealed weapons. When a delegation from the leftist National Committee for the Defense of Political Prisoners demanded that Tulare County growers be prohibited from carrying guns, both the sheriff and the district attorney replied that in arming themselves growers were entirely within their rights, since all possessed valid hunting licenses. In many other cases valley authorities guaranteed growers the right to bear arms legally by simply swearing them in as special deputies. But Tulare County authorities were finally forced to take action against growers implicated in the Pixley shootings. On October 11 eight growers known to have participated in the armed assault against strikers were arrested. Authorities sought to mollify employers who were angered over the arrests by arresting Pat Chambers at the same time on a charge of criminal syndicalism. In keeping with the bizarre character of justice in the region, the criminal complaint leading to Chambers' arrest was lodged by another of the growers who had taken part in the Pixley attack.[60]

Governor James Rolph, to whom many of the protests arising from the Pixley and Arvin slayings were directed, remained reluctant to exercise his police powers in the valley. When critics of law-enforcement agencies in the strike region demanded that the state assume responsibility for maintaining law and order there, Rolph replied that he saw "no cause for alarm," since duly constituted authorities in the valley seemed perfectly able to handle the situation. Rejected on similar grounds was a request to the governor by the ACLU and ILD that a special prosecutor from outside the valley be appointed to investigate the Pixley killings and other strike-related violence in Tulare County. Rolph did issue a public reminder to valley authorities that the rule of law should be upheld, and that growers carrying guns "illegally" should be disarmed. He also increased the number of state highway patrolmen in the strike region. Neither of these actions had much effect, however, since valley authorities insisted that growers were armed legally, and state highway patrolmen had tended to ignore violence against strikers, as at Pixley, and to assist growers and local law-enforcement officers in their efforts to break the cotton strike.[61]

Beyond the obvious political considerations affecting his decision against more forceful state intervention, Rolph's attitude was also probably influenced by the nature of the information he was receiving from the strike region. Reports came to the governor from only two men, Chief E. Raymond Cato of the highway patrol and Clarence S. Merrill, director of the California Bureau of Criminal Identification and Investigation. Both men were vociferous anticommunists and in the past had cooperated enthusiastically with agricultural interests in their efforts to defeat farm unionism in California. In their reports to Rolph following the events of October 10, both men emphasized in vivid detail the unruliness and Communist affiliations of strike "agitators," while playing down the vigilante mentality of growers and the violent strikebreaking activities of local lawmen.[62]

Despite the toll of dead and wounded strikers resulting from the Pixley and Arvin attacks, union leaders wasted little time in exploiting an otherwise tragic situation in ways calculated to strengthen the strike by extracting the greatest possible advantage from the sudden upsurge of public support and sympathy for the cotton workers' cause. Reinforcing the workers' morale hardly proved to be the problem union leaders expected it to be. Indeed, given the anger that surged through the strikers' ranks in the aftermath of the growers' attacks, union leaders found themselves struggling to restrain their followers rather than to excite new enthusiasm for the strike among them. The strikers' temper was revealed in an episode that occurred when the union resumed its mass picketing. Sam Darcy directed the union's Central Strike Committee to see to it that pickets were "prepared for a business-like demonstration." As Darcy later explained, he meant only that strike leaders should make plans for "an efficiently organized picket line such as would be required to handle five thousand men and women." "Early the next morning," Darcy wrote,

> as I approached the road where we were to gather I saw a line of jalopies reaching as far as the eye could see. They had been organized during the night by Bill Hammett and his field leaders. But protruding from each car was a long slim object which did not seem to be any familiar automobile accessory. These turned out to be a great variety of shotguns, rifles, and other weapons. I called Bill Hammett and demanded to know what this meant. He insisted that I had issued orders for them the day before. I was astounded until he explained that this was what they all understood by my urging them to "be prepared for a business-like demonstration." They were Oklahoma and Mexican ranchers who understood each other well but did not understand the exaggerated emphasis of language common to city people.[63]

For the most part, strike leaders succeeded in preventing armed reprisals against growers, although a few individual strikers apparently engaged in minor acts of sabotage and vandalism directed at the property of some employers who were also conspicuous vigilantes. Plainly, however, the militancy of nearly all strikers was increased as a result of the Pixley and Arvin attacks, and the cotton strike was greatly strengthened as a consequence.

In addition to toughening the strikers' resolve to continue their struggle, the growers' resort to violence tended to increase public support for the beleaguered workers and to impress upon public officials outside the valley the deadly seriousness of the strike situation. Thus, almost before the sounds of gunfire had stopped reverberating across the flat landscape of the lower valley, would-be mediators, conciliators, and arbitrators were in the strike region in greater numbers than ever, "striving frantically," noted one newspaper, to effect a settlement before more blood was shed and more lives were lost.[64] The most immediate consequence of this heightened public and official concern was a strong demand for a quick settlement of the strike. A more significant effect from the CAWIU's point of view was that the popular and official reactions to escalating strike violence tended to confer upon the union a measure of legitimacy and respectability far greater than that accorded in any of its previous strikes. The union's suddenly enhanced status was dramatically demonstrated on October 12, when Governor Rolph personally received a special strikers' delegation sent to Sacramento to demand state protection for striking cotton pickers, prosecution of growers responsible for the Pixley and Arvin killings, and immediate relief for strikers and their families. Rolph responded to the first two demands by simply repeating his earlier statement that valley authorities should uphold the law. In regard to the demand for relief, however, Rolph's response was more encouraging. Acting at the instructions of federal relief officials, Rolph advised the delegation that henceforth the State Emergency Relief Administration would provide relief to all needy workers in the valley whether or not they were on strike. For perhaps the first time in American history, the federal government had decided to feed hungry strikers, and thus to subsidize workers engaged in a labor dispute.[65]

In the end, however, the most important ramification of the Pixley and Arvin episodes was that they appeared to indicate the state's inability to cope with the cotton strike, and thus provided the justification that George Creel had sought for unrestrained federal intervention. Though the federal government, having excluded agricultural workers from the application of the NIRA, lacked any statutory authority to intervene in the cotton strike, Creel had no intention of letting technicalities stand in the way of a progressive reformation. He not only ignored the fact that the law did not apply to agricultural workers, but also ignored an administration decision in late September which transferred responsibility for the settlement of industrial disputes from the NRA to the newly created National Labor Board. Operating on the assumption that an air of authority could, be as functional as the real thing, Creel used a combination of rhetorical flimflam and sheer bravado to fashion both real and illusory powers great enough to permit him to act with a virtual free hand throughout the cotton strike. When a spokesman for farm employers wrote to him challenging his authority to intervene in a farm-labor dispute, Creel explained that "although agricultural labor comes under the Agricultural Adjustment Act, the industrial disputes in agriculture are under the jurisdiction of the National Labor Board."[66] He succeeded in cloaking himself with the authority of the National Labor Board by simply declaring publicly that he was its duly appointed representative in California and daring Senator Robert Wagner, the head of the NLB in Washington, to contradict him. Describing his machinations to an admiring colleague within the NRA, Creel wrote: "Whenever an industrial dispute has broken out I have taken charge at once as mediator, simply making the public statement that I am the representative of the National Labor Board, with full power to act. At the same time I [wire] the National Labor Board and four or five days later . . . I [receive] a telegram confirming my authority." Other committed reformers wanting to escape the constraints of jurisdiction and divided authority should, Creel added, "follow the same course."[67]

Creel's intervention in the cotton strike was initially quiet and indirect. While state mediators worked to gain a settlement in the early days of the strike, Creel's office did little more than urge Governor Rolph to control the growing lawlessness of organized employers and vigilantes in the cotton districts.[68] Once state efforts to settle the strike had failed, Creel acted more openly and aggressively. His goal was not simply to end the strike, but to demonstrate to both employers and the union that the federal government, acting on behalf of the public's interest, was assuming a definitive new role in the previously anarchic orbit of labor-management relations. In place of a settlement determined by brute strength and violence, and which reflected concern for selfish interests rather than the public welfare, Creel, his New Deal progressivism shining through, resolved to impose a settlement based on what was fair in the judgment of a disinterested, public-spirited third party. "This strike," he declared publicly, "is going to be settled in a way fair to all; but the federal government is going to insist on a settlement."[69]

To overcome the extreme intransigence of both parties to the dispute, Creel alternatively worked behind the scenes and in the open, using, always with dubious authority, every imaginable lever of federal power and influence. From the beginning he focused his attention on the employers, trying to force them to recognize the limits of their own power and to accept his and the federal government's authoritative intervention. In part, his decision to apply pressure first against the employers reflected nothing more than a realization that they were the more powerful party in the dispute, and that their strategy of breaking the strike through terror was intolerable. No less important a factor in the decision, however, was Creel's belief that the union was only a transient and irrational manifestation of the workers' discontent, and would disappear along with the "handful of tramp agitators" he believed responsible for fomenting the cotton strike once a fair settlement was imposed.[70] That the CAWIU was led by avowed Communists tended to reinforce his conviction that unionism in the cotton fields was simply an agitational ploy rather than an idea to which the mass of workers actually subscribed. His assumption, common among liberals and conservatives alike, that Communists were never true unionists, while arguable in the abstract, ignored the many pressures on the CAWIU leadership to abandon ideology and practice a rather straightforward and apolitical brand of unionism. Creel never acknowledged, as did one A.F. of L. leader in Bakersfield, that throughout the cotton strike "the Communists talked strike and not revolution."[71]

Working first through Rabbi Reichert, a member of the State Recovery Board whom he had earlier appointed director of the NRA's Bureau of Mediation and Adjustment in California, Creel advised employers that the Roosevelt administration would not countenance the crude and reckless strikebreaking methods of former times. Arguing that NRA intervention was justified "because of the economic participation of the Federal Government in our agricultural problems," Creel warned employers through Reichert that their participation in the agricultural recovery programs of the New Deal was "inferentially conditioned upon a fair deal to those who labor in the industry." It would be "unfortunate," he added, if some cotton growers lost those benefits as a result of their obstinacy in the matter of the cotton strike. Applying still another form of pressure, Creel informed employers that federal relief would be made available to all who needed it, including striking cotton pickers and their families.[72]

When employers made no immediate response to Creel's offer of mediation and vowed to increase the level of violence against strikers, an NRA spokesman publicly warned them that "the choice lies between immediate arbitration or martial law. No other course lies open."[73] Privately, however, Creel's office sought to reassure employers that the NRA's policy was not "in any sense partisan," and that in fact the government's sympathies were with the growers. In a soothing letter to the manager of the giant Tagus Ranch near Tulare, Reichert wrote, "We realize the tremendous difficulties and serious handicaps which the cotton growers are facing. We fully appreciate the terrific burdens that they are carrying. Our sentiments quite naturally are inclined toward the citizens of our own state whose industry, initiative, and resources contribute to California prosperity. At the same time, we cannot ignore the problems of the workers." As far as the CAWIU was concerned, he added, "Certainly we cannot countenance communistic and radical agitation that strikes at our democratic institutions. The

CAWIU leader Pat Chambers speaking to strikers from the steps of the courthouse in Visalia during the 1933 cotton strike. Photo: Bancroft Library, University of California, Berkeley.

Union leader Pat Chambers, at left, with his aides during the 1933 cotton strike. Photo: Bancroft Library, University of California, Berkeley.

CAWIU secretary Caroline Decker meeting with Mexican strikers at the union's headquarters in Tulare during the 1933 cotton strike. Photo: Bancroft Library, University of California, Berkeley.

State Labor Commissioner Frank C. MacDonald and Mexican consular official advising workers at Corcoran strikers' camp to return to work pending a settlement of the 1933 cotton strike. Photo: Bancroft Library, University of California, Berkeley.

Lawmen and farmers outside the entrance to Corcoran strikers' camp warning those inside that they will be evicted if no strike settlement is reached (1933). Photo: Bancroft Library, University of California, Berkeley.

NRA gives no aid or comfort to those who would destroy the foundations of American democracy."[74]

While these efforts to bring employers into line were still under way, Creel was personally pressuring Governor Rolph to support the NRA's settlement plan. If the state failed to act, Creel warned, the federal government would have no choice but to move on its own. Sensitive to the political implications of unilateral federal intervention, Rolph readily agreed to accept Creel's formula for a settlement. At Creel's direction Rolph named a three-member fact-finding commission to investigate the strike and suggest a basis for settlement.[75]

Faced with the threat of exclusion from New Deal farm programs and the prospect of unending federal relief to strikers, growers reluctantly agreed to accept Creel's fact-finding proposal.[76] They insisted, however, that they would not be bound by the commission's findings. Leaders of the CAWIU were much less hesitant to accept, partly because the commission hearings would provide a respectable forum for publicizing the pitiful conditions of life and work prevailing among farmworkers, and thus help to mold a more favorable public opinion toward the strike. More important, though, acceptance of the fact-finding proposal promised to legitimize the union's status as the representative of all strikers in the region, and perhaps to advance its central goal of formal employer recognition as well. But the union's rank and file had to be won over to the plan. An earlier proposal by the union leadership to wire President Roosevelt asking for federal intervention was overwhelmingly rejected by the strikers. As one opponent of the idea said bluntly, "The son of a bitch reads the newspapers. If he wants to act why does he need a wire?"[77] Yet when government spokesmen announced that strikers would have to agree to fact finding if they wanted the federal relief that Rolph had promised, they quickly assented. Like the employers, however, strikers declared that they would not be bound by the commission's findings.[78]

In agreeing to accept fact finding, union spokesmen emphasized that they had no intention of sending workers back to work until an acceptable strike settlement had been reached. Because Creel and his cohorts, as a means of persuading growers to accept fact finding, had assured them that strikers would immediately return to work at 60 cents per hundred, the union's refusal to suspend strike activities led state and federal officials to launch a widely publicized back-to-work movement. In deciding on such a course, Creel was motivated in part by a desire to undermine the CAWIU's leadership of the strike. He had also apparently received assurances from Mexican Consul Enrique Bravo that Mexican strikers were willing to return to work despite the opposition of union leaders. In giving such an assurance, Bravo was greatly overestimating his own influence with Mexican strikers and greatly underestimating their loyalty to strike leaders.[79]

On October 14 and 15 copies of an "Official Notice to all Cotton Growers and Striking Cotton Pickers" were distributed at strike camps throughout the valley. Carrying the appended official endorsements of Governor Rolph, George Creel, Consul Bravo, Labor Commissioner MacDonald, State Emergency Relief Administrator R. C. Branion, Commissioner of Conciliation E. H. Fitzgerald, and the San Joaquin Cotton Committee of the California Farm Bureau Federation, the notice advised strikers that in light of the agreement by both sides to cooperate with the fact-finding commission, it was now "the duty of the striking cotton pickers to proceed with the picking of California's cotton crop subject to the decision of the Federal-State Arbitration Commission's findings and decisions." Accompanying the notice was a somewhat ambiguous declaration that the federal relief promised earlier would be denied to those who failed to return to work as directed.[80]

On the morning of October 16, the date set by officials for the strikers' return to work, cotton-picking operations remained at a standstill while strikers conducted the second of two massive but solemn funeral processions for the workers killed at Pixley and Arvin. True to their leaders' words, strikers demonstrated that they had not the slightest intention of harvesting the state's cotton crop until an acceptable wage agreement had been reached.[81]

The state's plan to condition the distribution of federal relief on the strikers' return to work failed miserably. When strikers learned that strings were attached to the relief supplies offered to them, they refused to accept them. The *Fresno Bee* reported on October 16 that milk and other foodstuffs were left to spoil just outside the strikers' Corcoran camp because none of the more than 3,000 obviously hungry workers inside would accept relief if it meant abandoning the strike. Finally, when several strikers' children died from malnutrition and a public scandal seemed imminent, state officials relented and eliminated the "red tape" that they said had been the source of the strikers' anxiety concerning the acceptance of relief. By October 21 strikers were receiving relief without conditions attached.[82] The sudden shift in the state's policy prompted angry growers to complain that relief workers were now dispensing aid to strikers on condition that they remain off the job.[83]

With tension rising almost by the hour, the fact-finding commission finally opened two days of hearings in Visalia on October 19. Consisting of Catholic Archbishop Edward J. Hanna of San Francisco, a former chairman of the state Commission of Immigration and Housing; Tully C. Knoles, president of the College of the Pacific; and Ira Cross, a distinguished labor historian and member of the economics department of the University of California, the commission was under attack by growers before the hearings were an hour old. Edson Abel, the Farm Bureau attorney representing growers at the hearing, opened the employers' presentation by challenging the impartiality of commission members and declaring that growers would not compromise on the issue of wages under any circumstances. Following his constrictive preface, Abel called a series of witnesses, mainly representing finance and ginning companies, to testify in support of the employers' contention that 60 cents per hundred pounds was a fair wage that guaranteed an adequate standard of living to pickers, and all that they could afford to pay in any case.[84]

On the second day of the hearings strikers took the witness stand. Represented by Caroline Decker, who had become the union's most visible leader following the arrest of Pat Chambers, strikers offered testimony that conflicted totally with that given by the growers' spokesmen. One by one, Mexican, black, and white cotton pickers, including children as young as seven, took the stand, each describing in unaffected and irreducible terms the deprivation and misery of their lives. When Caroline Decker asked a Mexican mother of eight if she could afford to buy her children shoes out of her earnings as a cotton picker, the woman answered that her children had not worn shoes since 1930. When asked if her children worked beside her in the fields, she replied, "Yes, if they did not they would starve."[85] Every witness drawn from the strikers' ranks testified that it was impossible to maintain even a minimally decent standard of living on a wage of 60 cents per hundred pounds. Interrupting the testimony, the growers' counsel, Abel, charged that the strikers' witnesses had obviously been coached. Caroline Decker immediately offered to let him personally select all further strikers' witnesses from the group of more than 200 workers crowded into the hearing room. Abel declined the offer.[86]

When the hearings concluded at the end of the day on October 20, the positions of the contending parties, though somewhat more fully delineated as a result of the lengthy testimony presented, remained fundamentally unaltered. The hearings had, however, served to bring growers and strikers together for the first time during the strike, and provided a brief but welcome respite from the nearly constant battling that had gone on for close to three weeks. Finally, what the hearings lacked in healing powers they apparently compensated for in sheer spectacle. Socialist leader Norman Thomas, an observer at the hearings, described the confrontation between growers and cotton pickers at Visalia as "the most dramatic strike scene" he had ever witnessed.[87]

Despite repeated public assurances that he had only nonbinding fact finding in mind, Creel privately resolved from the beginning to regard the commission's effort as binding arbitration. And even as the commission was conducting its hearings, Creel was acting to influence the outcome. After consultations with officials of the Federal Intermediate Credit Bank, which was financing a part of the cotton crop, Creel privately advised the commission that in his view "75¢ per hundred pounds was all that the growers could possibly pay without loss to themselves."[88] Whether as a result of Creel's influence or their own independent assessment, on October 23 the fact finders announced their decision that 75¢ per hundred was a fair compromise.[89]

Both the strikers and the employers immediately denounced the decision, the former because it was too niggardly, the latter because it was too generous.[90] Creel ignored both and set about forcing acceptance. When employers declared they would not abide by the commission's finding, Creel once again raised the specter of their exclusion from New Deal farm programs, especially those related to crop financing. Yet while he threatened he also offered employers several important inducements. Once they agreed to 75 cents per hundred, he assured employers, all federal relief to strikers would immediately be terminated and workers returning to the fields would be given full protection from strikers. In practical terms this proposal meant that federal and state officials would no longer stand in the way of local authorities' efforts to ban all picketing and close down strikers' camps by force.[91] After bitter debate, employers announced on October 25 that they were accepting the fact finders' recommendation "in the interests of good American citizenship, law and order, and in order to forestall the spread of communism and radicalism and to protect the harvesting of other crops."[92]

Forcing the strikers to accept the compromise settlement proved a more trying task for Creel. Still seeking to undermine the CAWIU and its leaders, Creel appealed directly to the strikers, at once entreating them to return to work and warning that those who refused would no longer receive federal relief. Creel's use of relief to promote a settlement along the lines he thought proper reflected with particular clarity his

215

notion of how the federal government should function as a power broker in labor disputes. Explaining his strategy to an acquaintance, Creel wrote, "I have taken the position that Federal relief must be extended to all strikers up to the time of an adjudication and award, otherwise strikers would be starved into submission. After the Government has heard the case, however, and made an award, I have held that Federal relief should not be given to able-bodied men who have a chance to go back to work."[93]

The CAWIU countered Creel's appeal for a settlement on the basis of the fact-finding commission's recommendation with one of its own calling for a wage rate of 80 cents per hundred pounds and union recognition by employers. The demand for 80 cents was prompted not by a sinister desire on the part of "agitators" to prolong the strike, as Creel charged, but by the fact that several Kern County growers, frightened by the prospect of a total crop loss, had expressed their willingness to pay the higher rate. The demand for union recognition, which Creel opposed no less strenuously than did employers, had been the CAWIU's major goal from the beginning, and after three weeks of bloody struggle and intense suffering by thousands of strikers the union was not willing simply to forget it, as the fact-finding commission's proposal required.[94]

In attributing the workers' rejection of the fact finders' proposal to the artful manipulations of a few "lawless" and "communistic" union leaders, Creel badly misjudged the strikers' temper and underestimated the depth of their allegiance to the CAWIU. While Creel assured Senator Wagner on October 25 that at least 80 percent of the strikers were eager to return to work at 75 cents, there appears in fact to have been virtually no support for the idea among the rank and file. Decision making throughout the strike remained a remarkably democratic process, and strikers consistently and overwhelmingly voted in favor of holding out for a wage of at least 80 cents per hundred and formal union recognition by employers.[95] Even when a large body of heavily armed police and vigilantes massed outside the Corcoran camp on October 26 and announced their intention to evacuate it by force, the workers answered with defiant shouts in support of *"la huelga"* (the strike) and angry threats to resist any attack against them.[96]

The stalemate was finally broken not by strikers clamoring to return to work at 75 cents per hundred but by the union's Communist leaders, who concluded that the strike had caused enough suffering and that neither the strikers nor the union could gain anything by prolonging it further. At a meeting of the Central Strike Committee on October 26, these leaders argued successfully that the strike should be terminated and that the strikers ought to return to work at 75 cents per hundred. On the next day the strikers were persuaded by their leaders to end the strike.[97] The failure to gain union recognition was a source of bitter disappointment, and union leaders lost no time in placing blame for this defeat at the door of the federal government. In announcing an end to the strike, the Central Strike Committee stated: "The representatives of the government have made clear to us that the government does not wish to recognize our union. It is clear to the workers, that the government will not recognize any union which has a militant policy of struggle in the interests of the working class."[98]

For weeks after the strike both employers and the union laid feeble claims to victory. Employers claimed that in successfully resisting the CAWIU's demand for recognition they had triumphed over the forces of communism. The union claimed no less signal a victory by pointing to the fact that cotton pickers in the San Joaquin Valley were earning wages 25 percent higher as a result of the strike. Yet the vigor and vehemence with which both sides attacked George Creel and the federal government's role in the strike demonstrated that neither had any trouble figuring out who the real victor had been.[99]

Creel clearly was not hesitant to claim a victory for the new federal labor policies he had launched in the name of the New Deal.[100] Yet neither was he willing to rest once he felt he had both farm employers and the CAWIU on the run. Less than a week after the cotton strike ended, Creel was in contact with citrus growers in Tulare County, advising them how they might rationalize their labor policy in order to defeat unionism in the region. The cotton strike, Creel argued, "constituted an indictment of the labor policy of the growers." Had the cotton growers practiced a more enlightened policy toward their workers, he insisted, it would have been impossible for "a small group of agitators to come in from the outside and win the workers away from . . . employers."[101]

In letters to various agribusiness leaders in the state, Creel suggested what he thought an enlightened and progressive labor policy in agriculture would be. He felt that employers must finally begin to share power in the determination of wages and working conditions. Yet this sharing of power was not to be with workers and their unions, but with a third party: government. Though opposed to genuine unions, Creel did favor the organization of farmworkers by employers as a means of bringing more order to labor-management relations. Citing the cotton growers' failure in this regard, he wrote: "Where producers have made no effort to develop responsible leadership and authoritative spokesmen among workers, these communists have had things their own way. In every case, however, where the men have been dealt with through representatives, and given some understanding of the problems of the producers, the agitators have failed entirely." As Creel saw it, "the answer to industrial troubles in agricultural regions is very obvious. It consists in the promotion of some form of collective bargaining between employers and the workers, to the end that clear understandings may be reached, and some sort of contractual relation promoted."[102]

One farm employer who failed to grasp the peculiar meaning that Creel attached to the term "collective bargaining" responded with considerable agitation that "through all the years of the citrus industry in this valley we have never had collective bargaining, nor have the workers demanded or even thought of collective bargaining." The demand for collective bargaining, he continued, "comes from outside forces who are not interested at all in the welfare of the workers, in the principle of collective bargaining, or in anything but their desire to stir up agitation [that] leads to economic and agricultural discontent." There was, he reminded Creel, "a vast difference between dealing with . . . the American Federation of Labor" and dealing with the CAWIU. Leaders of the A.F. of L., he wrote, were "patriotic American citizens and, if necessary, would subordinate the rights of labor to the good of the country." As far as Creel's criticisms of the traditional labor policy of farm employers were concerned, he added, "They might not have established regular organizations of contact, but they have . . . established and maintained contacts with their men through their authoritative spokesmen, and these authoritative spokesmen are men who are devoted to both the interests of the growers and of the workers."[103]

Creel patiently replied:

> With reference to . . . your letter you say that "through all the years of the citrus industry in this valley, we have never had collective bargaining nor have the workers demanded or even thought of collective bargaining." A little further on, however, you say that the growers "have established and maintained contacts with their men through their authoritative spokesmen." This is exactly what I mean by collective bargaining, and all that I meant.[104]

In a final bit of advice to farm employers faced with future challenges from the CAWIU, Creel suggested that they should not, as growers had done during the cotton strike, resort to vigilantism and lawlessness. Instead, he proposed that the same antiunion ends could be achieved through a fuller and more effective use of the state's criminal syndicalism statute.[105]

The labor relations policy that Creel outlined to farm employers in California reflected an emphasis on both order and paternalism, and went a long way toward meeting the ideal that the Roosevelt brain trust had hoped to further through the NIRA. It was a policy that promised economic benefits to both workers and employers, but not without forcing each side to resign itself to the greatly expanded power of the federal government to act decisively in a realm in which private power had always ruled before. It was a policy that was antiunion in theory, and, to the extent that it was applied during the cotton strike, it proved antiunion in practice. Describing to President Roosevelt the satisfaction he felt as a result of his efforts on behalf of the NRA and NLB to settle the cotton strike and other labor disputes in the state, Creel wrote in early 1934:

> I want you to know that I have never been prouder of any association for I have a deep passionate belief in your Recovery Program, not merely as an emergency measure but as a lasting and integral part of our national life. I have preached it as a fundamental reorganization of our industrial structure along higher, finer lines, and it is this view, I think, that has confirmed California in its devotion to you and your ideas.[106]

As the capstone of the CAWIU's year-long campaign of farmworker organization, the cotton strike defied easy characterization. Union and Communist Party spokesmen, despite their bitterness toward Creel's heavy-handed settlement strategy, hailed the strike as "the most important victory of workers that has ever taken place in the history of agricultural struggle."[107] It was a claim not without substantial warrant. In its size, scope, and duration, and in the total value of the wage increases won—an estimated $1 million—the cotton strike dwarfed all earlier farm-labor disputes. In qualitative terms, cotton pickers had demonstrated unequaled solidarity and courage in the face of the most intensive strikebreaking pressures ever brought to bear in an agricultural strike. That workers were willing and able to endure such tremendous pressure and hardship was a tribute to the organizational skill and leadership ability of the CAWIU.[108]

As the final and most dramatic confrontation in a long series of clashes with farm employers during the 1933 harvest season, the cotton strike contributed enormously to the union's overall performance. With the conclusion of the strike, the CAWIU's record of strike activity for the year had reached impressive proportions. Of the 37 agricultural strikes reported in California during 1933, 24 were led by the CAWIU. Of the 47,575 farmworkers involved in these strikes, 37,550, or 79 percent, were under CAWIU leadership. And of the total number of workers who struck under the union's auspices, 32,800 won higher wages. Only four CAWIU strikes, affecting 4,750 workers, ended in total defeat.[109]

For all of its apparent achievement, however, the union was far from being in robust health as the 1933 harvest season drew to a close. Within a few short weeks of the end of the cotton strike, CAWIU locals in the San Joaquin Valley that had pulsated with activity at the height of the conflict had either disintegrated entirely or been reduced to skeleton organizations. Though the union had come close to achieving a major victory for the cause of farm unionism in California, its failure to win formal recognition from employers and the right to control employment through union-run hiring halls left it in organizational disarray and vulnerable to a debilitating process of erosion that its leaders were unable to arrest. The same union that had commanded the fierce loyalty of 12,000 San Joaquin Valley farmworkers in late October was, according to one of its officers, "about dead" in the region by mid-November.[110]

In looking ahead to 1934, CAWIU leaders seem to have realized that the task of sustaining a strong farm-labor movement in California would be more rather than less difficult as a result of their success during 1933.[111] The level of farmworker militancy was falling as wages moved upward. Agricultural employers and their allies were organizing statewide to destroy farm unionism. Popular antiradical feeling was increasing in intensity as newspaper reports of alleged Communist depredations grew in volume and stridency. Union leaders were experiencing new doubts about their ability to hold workers once they had organized them, and were justifiably apprehensive as they contemplated the union's future. Yet in the end, the most ominous and disquieting threat to the union's future progress was revealed in the federal government's determination to place the relations between farm employers and farmworkers on a footing that was consistent with the Roosevelt administration's still unclouded vision of a modern and socially responsible labor policy.

The cotton strike marked only the beginning of the federal government's efforts to incapacitate the CAWIU in the interests of more rational and harmonious labor relations in California agriculture. Yet it represented the zenith of the New Deal's larger program of permanently altering the economic power relationship between government and farm employers. Though federal officials continued to promote the policy that Creel had initiated in the San Joaquin Valley, farm employers never again compromised their power as they had done during the cotton strike. Once they began to realize that the government actually had no legal basis for intervention in agricultural labor disputes and that the Roosevelt administration was unwilling to take political risks on behalf of a hard-line policy, farm employers felt free to ignore federal efforts to gain voluntary compliance with farm-labor reforms.

New Dealers were amazingly slow to discern how deeply farm employers were committed to their traditional labor policies, in part because agricultural labor policy hardly enjoyed high priority within the administration, and in part because the administration was dedicated to the ideal of rational and paternalistic labor relations and reluctant to jettison an idea that was at the vortex of its vision of a new economic order. The cost of perpetuating this untenable idealism was borne with a predictably devastating result by an already weakened agricultural labor movement.

7

Agricultural Unionism and the
New Deal: The Imperial Valley

For the most part, the activities of the Cannery and Agricultural Workers Industrial Union during 1933 were centered north of the Tehachapi Mountains. As the winter season approached, however, the center of agricultural activity shifted steadily southward, and the hopes of both the CAWIU and the Communist Party followed close behind. Immediately after the cotton strike was settled, union organizers, hoping to preserve as much of the momentum of the 1933 drive as possible, made a brief effort to organize citrus workers in Tulare County. Their campaign quickly collapsed, however, because of the apparent strike-weariness of farmworkers and because growers and authorities, with the active encouragement of George Creel, had mobilized in advance to suppress any renewal of "agitation."[1]

The failure of organizers to gain influence among citrus workers in the lower San Joaquin Valley did not discourage a more ambitious organizational campaign shortly thereafter in the state's fabled citrus belt, a region of intensive orange and lemon cultivation that stretched through portions of Los Angeles, Riverside, and San Bernardino counties. At first glance, the potential for such action appeared exceptionally good. As always, wages and conditions were far from satisfactory, and the great majority of the area's citrus pickers were Mexicans, the group from which the CAWIU had received its greatest support in 1933. In addition, union organizers found that affiliates of the Confederación de Uniones de Campesinos y Obreros Mexicanos, the Los Angeles–based organization to which Communists had lost control of the El Monte berry pickers' strike six months earlier, were willing to form a "united front" with the CAWIU to fight for improved wages and working conditions.[2]

Initial impressions notwithstanding, however, conditions in the citrus belt were anything but conducive to successful organization and strike action during the winter of 1933–34. Organized citrus growers had closely followed the activities of the CAWIU during the summer and fall, and resolved to combat any attempt the union might make to invade their domain. When it became apparent at the end of the cotton strike that citrus workers were destined to become the CAWIU's next target group, growers set in motion a plan designed to impede farm-worker organization and to obstruct any strike action. Many of the steps they took—having dozens of special deputies appointed from their ranks, enlisting the support and cooperation of area law-enforcement agencies, promoting strong antiunion feelings within local business and fraternal groups—were entirely conventional. Additional measures, however, reflected the early development of a more compre-hensive and sophisticated antiunion strategy than had been used in earlier disputes. Throughout portions of the citrus belt antipicketing ordinances were enacted, as were measures prohibiting the distribution of union leaflets, circulars, and handbills. In addition, growers and their supporters contacted Catholic priests in predominantly Mexican parishes and persuaded them to warn their parishioners of the potential dangers facing citrus workers who participated in communist efforts to disrupt the harvest. Most important, growers sought to reduce the level of worker dissatisfaction in the region by bringing wages into line with the general hourly rate of about 25 cents established as a result of the farm-labor struggles during the summer and fall.[3]

In the face of so formidable a strategy, the CAWIU's organizational campaign made little headway. Even with the assistance of the CUCOM, organizers were unable to stimulate much enthusiasm for the CAWIU's standard list of demands. In mid-January, after several weeks of agita-tion, organizers did finally succeed in launching a strike involving approximately 550 orange pickers. But lacking the support of most workers, union leaders were soon forced to abandon their efforts.[4]

The CAWIU's failure to establish itself in California's largest and most important citrus-growing region was unquestionably a source of disappointment to union leaders, and tended to confirm earlier fears that 1934 was going to be a more difficult year for farm-labor organiza-tion than 1933 had been. Just how difficult it was to be did not become fully evident until the union sought to ply its organizational wares in the historically forbidding environs of the Imperial Valley.

The decision by Communist Party leaders in District 13 to return to the Imperial Valley, where the party's farm-labor movement had begun four years earlier and where it had suffered its first and more ignomin-ious defeat, was prompted less by a desire to settle old scores than by their feeling that the region was especially ripe for organization. Wages had been as low as 10 cents per hour during 1933, and working and living conditions, which had long been recognized as the worst in the state, had become unspeakable by 1933. And, the fact that many of the Mexican and Filipino workers assembling in the valley for the winter lettuce harvest were veterans of earlier CAWIU strikes helped to convince party and union leaders that the prospects for organization there had never been brighter. Curiously, however, district leaders entrusted the task to the party's Los Angeles and San Diego sections, neither of which had been involved to an important degree in the CAWIU's successful strike campaign during the fall harvest season. As a result, the two young party workers assigned the exceedingly difficult job of leading the union's organizing drive in the valley came to their work entirely lacking in relevant experience. Stanley Hancock, a twenty-five-year-old functionary from the San Diego section who had worked for a newspaper before assuming full-time party chores, apparently had no previous involvement in union organizing, much less among mainly non-English-speaking farmworkers. Similarly, Dorothy Ray, a nineteen-year-old activist in the Los Angeles section of the Young Communist League, took up the challenge armed with little more than high enthusiasm and a keen sense of revolutionary purpose.[5]

When Hancock and Ray arrived in the Imperial Valley in mid-November, they found a very militant attitude among the region's deeply discontented farmworkers. They also found, as Hancock later asserted, that workers who had been active in earlier CAWIU strikes were "ready and waiting to accept some more Communist leadership." Hancock and Ray, and the three or four party members who assisted them, found "no antagonism nor even antipathy" as a result of their "known party membership." They "were very freely and easily accepted as logical, legitimate, respectable . . . labor leaders."[6] Indeed, they found the attitude of valley workers so cheering that they tended to neglect the mundane organizational tasks that successful strike action required in favor of more exhilarating activities calculated to whet their followers' collective appetite for class struggle. Elmer Hanoff, who was second in authority only to Sam Darcy in District 13, commanded the party's secret apparatus in the valley during the early weeks of 1934, and was highly critical of the union leaders' organizational priorities. "Instead of concentrating on organization," Hanoff reported,

> they became satisfied with the militancy and the willingness of the workers for struggle, and, taking the line of least resistance, failed to carry out

plans for establishing organization in all sections of the Valley. NOT ONLY
THAT, BUT THEY AGITATED THE WORKERS FOR A STRIKE INSTEAD OF
EMPHASIZING ORGANIZATION SO AS TO PREPARE FOR A STRIKE. . . .

Some of our comrades in the fields were carried away with the enthusiasm of the workers to the extent that they wanted to call the strike even
before . . . having had any conferences with the workers, or [having]
organized the necessary committees such as a central strike committee and
local strike, defense and relief committees.[7]

Yet despite the organizational weakness that inexperience promoted,
it is unlikely that the CAWIU could have succeeded in the Imperial
Valley even if its most strike-tested organizers had been in charge and
the party's most ingenious strike strategy unstintingly followed. The
reason, quite simply, was that employers and authorities had resolved
to use whatever level of force and violence they had to in order to
smash any and every effort to organize the region's farmworkers. And
in the absence of effective constraints against them, that is precisely
what they ended up doing. As a result, the conflict that engulfed the
valley during the early months of 1934, though it began as a labor
struggle, quickly became a contest between organized farm employers
intent upon maintaining absolute control over labor relations and federal officials still hopeful of instituting reforms designed to place the
relations between employers and workers in the state's industrialized
agriculture on a more rational and socially tolerable footing. A militant
and independent farmworkers' union was an intolerable prospect under
either scheme, and both employers and the federal government acted to
eliminate the CAWIU and bona fide unionism as a first step toward
realizing their separate goals.

The antiunion campaign of Imperial Valley growers and shippers
began even before organizers had entered the region. In late October,
while the cotton strike was occupying the union's attention and resources, valley employers took steps to block the organization of their
workers by the CAWIU.[8] Their initial strategy, ironically, was to impede
authentic organization by encouraging the revival of the Unión de
Trabajadores del Valle Imperial, the short-lived Mexican union that
had been active during the 1928 cantaloupe harvest. With the cooperation of Joaquín Terrazas, the Mexican consul in the valley, employers
arranged a meeting with leaders of the newly resurrected union for the
purpose of establishing wages and working conditions for the coming
lettuce harvest. Out of the meeting, which involved no genuine bargaining, came an unwritten agreement by employers that the wage for

field labor would be increased from the prevailing level of roughly 15 cents per hour to 22.5 cents per hour, and that a minimum of five hours' pay would be guaranteed to lettuce workers whenever they were called to work. Employers further agreed that once lettuce prices were established for the 1934 harvest season, they would hold a second meeting with workers to discuss the possibility of a further increase in wages.[9]

If employers hoped that their actions would guarantee labor peace, they were soon disappointed. On November 13 lettuce workers belonging to the Mexican union staged a one-day strike to protest several growers' refusal to honor the working agreement reached only two weeks before. Protests of a less disruptive nature continued into December. In response to the workers' protests, representatives of the Western Growers Protective Association, the dominant employers' organization in the valley, acknowledged that there had been innumerable violations of the working agreement, but insisted that they were powerless to do anything about the situation.[10]

The refusal of lettuce growers to comply with the provisions of the working agreement undoubtedly facilitated the organizational drive that CAWIU organizers finally launched during the last week of November. Claiming that employers had conspired with Joaquín Terrazas to turn the Mexican union into a weak company union that could be easily manipulated, Communist organizers invited lettuce workers in the valley to join a "fighting union" that would win them higher wages and better conditions through uncompromising struggle. The response of Mexican workers was particularly strong in the vicinity of Brawley, and quickly resulted in the formation of a large and influential Communist-led opposition group within the Mexican union. During the latter part of December this group put increasing pressure on leaders of the Mexican union to demand substantially higher wages and improved working conditions before the lettuce harvest reached its peak.[11]

In keeping with the understanding they had reached with growers' representatives at the November 1 meeting, leaders of the Mexican union asked employers in late December to meet with them to negotiate a new working agreement. Somewhat reluctantly, growers agreed to a meeting on January 2. At the meeting Mexican leaders frankly advised growers' representatives that unless the wage for lettuce fieldwork was raised to 35 cents per hour, Communist agitators would capture complete control of their union's membership. Spokesmen for the growers replied that existing economic conditions would not permit a wage increase of any kind, and insisted that lettuce workers were bound by the existing agreement to work for 22.5 cents an hour. Feeling that they had lost face, leaders of the Mexican union promptly stepped aside to allow the CAWIU to become the exclusive representative of Mexican farmworkers in the valley.[12]

Communist organizers immediately seized the opportunity provided by the Mexican union's abrupt retreat. Confident that the militancy of lettuce workers guaranteed wide support for a strike, CAWIU organizers tended to neglect further organizational work in favor of strike-planning activities. Predicting that the lettuce harvest would reach its peak at the end of the first week of January, union leaders set January 8 as a tentative strike date. On January 4 a prestrike conference was held in Brawley to elect a central strike committee and to decide on a list of final demands. All those who attended the conference were supposed to be representing lettuce workers who were actually on the job, but because of a serious oversupply of farm labor in the valley, many delegates were in fact speaking and voting on behalf of unemployed laborers. The demands agreed upon were 35 cents per hour, a minimum five-hour day, free clean drinking water on the job, free transportation to and from work, union recognition, and abolition of the labor contracting system.

As the strike date approached, CAWIU leaders hurriedly distributed 10,000 strike bulletins, printed in both English and Spanish, to workers in towns throughout the valley. Union leaders also sought to organize various strike committees and to appoint picket captains in every workers' camp. Except for camps in the Brawley area, however, most of this work remained unfinished at the time the strike began because of the overconfidence that had earlier led organizers to neglect careful organizational work in favor of agitational activities.[13]

When the strike call went out on the morning of January 8, an estimated 3,000 farmworkers, many of whom were probably already unemployed, responded. On the following day another 2,000 or so workers joined the strike. Although employers' spokesmen later claimed that the strike had not affected the valley's lettuce harvest, the best available evidence belies those assertions.[14] George Swink, a prominent growers' representative, reported to a friend that when the lettuce strike began, "some operators were forced to discontinue work altogether for two days and the daily field operations were more or less curtailed for [a] week."[15] Not until January 13, Swink wrote, were growers able "to convince" workers to return to work.

The methods used to persuade workers to return to the fields con-sisted for the most part of unrestrained physical violence and arbitrary arrest. The use of violent strikebreaking tactics was common to most of the agricultural strikes in California during the early 1930s, but nowhere did farm employers and local authorities bring so much enthusiasm to their strikebreaking activities or pursue a course of violence and terror as single-mindedly and purposefully as in the Imperial Valley. The vigilantism that flourished there in 1934 was not just a strikebreaking expedient, but the highest and most graphic expression of regional and class patriotism. "Whether they intended it or not," wrote one contemporary critic, "they actually glorify Vigilantism."[16]

The special enthusiasm with which valley law-enforcement officers carried out their strikebreaking duties is partially attributable to a natural desire to serve the needs of the farm employers who controlled the economic and political life of the region. However, an investigation by Campbell MacCulloch, secretary of the Los Angeles Regional Labor Board, revealed that the attitudes of law-enforcement officials were also shaped by important personal considerations. In his official report MacCulloch wrote, "There is a face of the situation in the lower Imperial Valley that must to a considerable degree warp the unbiased judgment of those in control of the situation, and which will at least operate against unbiased treatment of the workers. It is the fact that most of the officials of the area are themselves growers." Among those identified by MacCulloch as growers and employers were both the sheriff and undersheriff of Imperial County, the police chiefs of Brawley and El Centro, the captain in charge of the state highway patrol office in the valley, and the police court judge and justice of the peace in Brawley. Referring to the dim prospects for justice in Brawley's municipal courts, MacCulloch wrote: "It is alleged that no worker can hope to get justice in . . . these courts since Judge [H. B.] Griffin is reported to be notoriously of the opinion that '$1 a day is enough for a Mexican field worker.' "[17]

In most of the agricultural strikes of 1933, mass picketing had been the most effective weapon available to the CAWIU. Authorities in the Imperial Valley demonstrated as soon as the lettuce strike began that they had no intention of allowing picketing of any kind, although they did not bother to enact an antipicketing ordinance until some time later.[18] They also made plain their intention to deny the strikers' right of assembly. On January 9, as hundreds of strikers in Brawley were forming a car and truck caravan to take them to a valley-wide strike meeting in El Centro, scores of city police, sheriff's deputies, state highway patrolmen, and American Legionnaires attacked with clubs and tear gas to prevent their departure. The Brawley police chief explained that the attack was a matter of routine law enforcement, since the assembled strikers had failed to obtain a valid parade permit from his office.[19]

As strikers persisted in their efforts to hold daily strike meetings, authorities' strikebreaking tactics became even more ferocious. On the evening of January 12 several hundred strikers and their families gathered for a meeting at Azteca Hall in Brawley, the strike headquarters. While the meeting was in progress a large force of police, deputy sheriffs, highway patrolmen, and deputized growers surrounded the hall, presumably to serve arrest warrants on several Communist organizers inside. Claiming that the large crowd of strikers was interfering with the execution of his duty, the Brawley police chief gave the signal for a barrage of tear gas to be fired into the hall. Once this had been done, authorities barred the doors from the outside, forcing the men, women, and children inside to break out every window in the building in order to escape the effects of the gas. When the hall had been cleared, authorities entered and destroyed every typewriter, duplicating machine, and other piece of equipment they could find, including appliances in a kitchen that had been used to feed strikers and their families. The arrest warrants for strike leaders, who clambered out a window to escape the choking gas along with everyone else, were not served.[20]

Following the Azteca Hall attack, the lettuce strike rapidly lost its effectiveness. Only in the vicinity of Brawley did the CAWIU attempt to sustain its strike activities, and it was there that valley authorities concentrated their strikebreaking efforts. All strike meetings were declared illegal, and any congregation of more than two workers on the streets of Brawley was considered an unlawful assembly. Hundreds of strikers were taken into custody by local authorities, but most were later released without being charged with a crime. Of the dozens who were formally arrested, most were charged with vagrancy or disturbing the peace. Bail ranged between $500 to $1,800 per person. When attorneys from the International Labor Defense entered the strike area to assist strikers who had been arrested, they too became immediate victims of what one commentator labeled "Imperial Valley justice." One luckless ILD lawyer was arrested on vagrancy charges and held for thirty-five days before being tried and acquitted.[21] Even representatives of the Los Angeles Regional Labor Board and the State Labor Commissioner were "detained" by valley authorities and subjected to hostile treatment. In reports to their superiors, the two men told of being confronted by a captain of the state highway patrol who warned in a threatening tone, "You men should get out of here. You are hurting our work. We don't want conciliation. We know how to handle these people, and where we find trouble makers we'll drive them out, if we have to 'sap' them."[22]

By January 18 the combined effects of police terror and inadequate preliminary organization had so greatly reduced the impact of the lettuce strike that CAWIU leaders were forced to call it off. In the Communist Party analysis published in the *Western Worker* a few weeks later, the strike's failure was attributed entirely to tactical mistakes and organizational weaknesses. Apparently unwilling to admit that valley authorities had defeated them, Communists tended to discount the effectiveness of police tactics in breaking the strike.[23] In the end, however, it was the authorities' determined and relentless suppression more than the CAWIU's organizational deficiencies that spelled the defeat of the lettuce strike. By returning to work once the authorities had shown their determination to break the strike at any cost, lettuce workers were acknowledging their powerlessness in the face of such unrestrained tactics, whether or not Communist strike leaders were willing to do the same. While their revolutionary faith hardly permitted Communists to admit that the success of their work in the valley, or anywhere else, depended on the observance of basic "capitalist" constitutional guarantees by "capitalist" law-enforcement officials, events during the lettuce strike revealed beyond any question that unless the workers' rights of free speech and assembly were protected, the CAWIU's efforts were doomed to failure.

To officials of the Southern California branch of the American Civil Liberties Union, who had closely monitored developments during the strike, denials of First Amendment rights by valley authorities constituted an intolerable affront to justice.[24] On January 21 A. L. Wirin, an ACLU attorney from Los Angeles who hoped to restore the workers' rights of free speech and assembly, asked the sheriff of Imperial County and the Brawley police chief if they would protect a workers' meeting at Azteca Hall on the evening of January 23. Each official refused, and warned that no such meeting would be tolerated. Determined that the basic constitutional rights of valley workers would be protected, Wirin secured from the Federal District Court in San Diego an order enjoining authorities from interfering in any manner with the scheduled meeting.[25] On the evening of January 23, shortly before the Azteca Hall meeting was to start, Wirin was abducted from the Planters Hotel in Brawley by a large group of vigilantes, one of whom, he later claimed, was a uniformed state highway patrolman. After being beaten, terrorized, and robbed of his personal belongings, Wirin was left barefoot in the desert about eleven miles from the small valley town of Calipatria. When he finally made his way back to his hotel in El Centro, Wirin was confronted by a mob of 300 armed vigilantes threatening more drastic action against him unless he got out of the valley for good. Advised by sheriff's deputies that they would provide him with protection only if he accepted the vigilantes' terms, Wirin quickly agreed to be escorted out of the valley. As a result of Wirin's abduction, the Azteca Hall meeting had been canceled, and the status of civil liberties in the Imperial Valley appeared more precarious than ever.[26]

The violent strikebreaking methods employed earlier to crush the lettuce strike had prompted demands for federal intervention;[27] now the kidnapping and assault of Wirin, in apparent violation of a federal court order, created a storm of protest in liberal and radical circles. Demands that the federal government intervene to restore "the rule of law" in the Imperial Valley mounted so rapidly that action of some kind became unavoidable.[28] The problem for federal officials was to respond in a way that would satisfy insistent liberals, be in general conformity with the reformist goals of the Roosevelt administration's industrial relations policy, and at the same time avoid the political risk of further alienating the agribusiness establishment in the state.

From the point of view of the ACLU, which took the lead in demanding governmental action, the situation in the valley required nothing less than a show of rigid federal backbone. Specifically, the ACLU hoped that the government would dispatch a sufficient number of federal marshals to the region to ensure that the injunction prohibiting interference with workers' meetings was enforced. And although in time the idea was endorsed by the Regional Labor Board in Los Angeles,[29] the Department of Justice steadfastly, and with rather strained legal reasoning, held that the use of federal marshals was unjustified because, technically, the injunction had not been violated. Pierson Hall, the United States attorney in Los Angeles, informed Attorney General Homer Cummings that the injunction prohibited interference by valley authorities with the workers' meeting scheduled for January 23. And while the abduction of Wirin, the meeting's scheduled speaker, was, Hall observed, a "deplorable" act, it did not constitute actual interference with the meeting, which those in attendance remained free to conduct in Wirin's absence.[30] When Cummings and his subordinates embraced Hall's line of argument, one scandalized civil libertarian, denouncing it as "a rather unskillful dodge," replied, "Suppose, Mr. Attorney General, you were the chief speaker at a large meeting in

Washington and you were kidnapped on your way to the assemblage. Would your office then insist that there had been no interference with the meeting in question? On this basis to kidnap a bridegroom as he was about to enter the church would not constitute any interference with the wedding."[31] Though Cummings did give indications of being somewhat uncomfortable with Hall's interpretation, the Department of Justice stuck by it and declined to accede to the ACLU's demands.[32]

While the liberals' appeals for federal action failed in the end to elicit a positive response from the Department of Justice, they did help to convince the National Labor Board that the time was now propitious for the investigation of agricultural labor relations that had been recommended less than a week before by Campbell MacCulloch, whose report on behalf of the Los Angeles Regional Labor Board emphasized that "relationships between employers and employees in the Imperial Valley will be unsatisfactory, and continue to produce strife at more or less regular intervals, until some permanent form of adjustment of disputes is provided in the valley itself, and which will have sufficient authority—voluntary or otherwise—to render decisions and have them obeyed." MacCulloch's own "experimental solution" to the valley's labor problems called for the establishment of a three-person "adjustment committee" empowered to conduct binding arbitrations of labor disputes, a constant monitoring of the farm-labor market in order to keep supply and demand in reasonable balance, and a joint effort by state and federal labor officials to develop guidelines for the "adjustment committee" to follow in determining future labor conditions in the region.[33]

Though Senator Robert Wagner made no mention of the MacCulloch report when he announced on January 26 that the National Labor Board was launching an inquiry into the Imperial Valley situation, he was undoubtedly influenced by it. Wagner indicated that a special three-man commission was being appointed to conduct an investigation for the somewhat vaguely stated purpose of recommending a "permanent adjustment of [the] agricultural labor situation" in the valley. The men he named to the commission were among the most knowledgeable in the state. The chairman, J. L. Leonard, was a professor of economics at the University of Southern California and chairman of the Los Angeles Regional Labor Board. Will J. French was a former director of the California Department of Industrial Relations. The final member, Simon J. Lubin, was the director of the California Bureau of Commerce in 1934, but twenty years before had, as chairman of the Commission of Immigration and Housing, headed the progressives' campaign to destroy the IWW's influence among California's farmworkers by improving working and living conditions in agriculture. Each man was an unreconstructed progressive and eager to improve the conditions affecting farmworkers in the Imperial Valley. Yet they embarked on their investigation without specific instructions and with no clear idea of what the federal government hoped to accomplish.[34]

The commission was in the valley by January 30, and on February 11, after little more than a week of hearings, interviews, and personal tours of area labor camps, it submitted its report and recommendations. Though the report included brief descriptions of the nature and structure of industrialized agriculture in the valley and acknowledged the difficult economic conditions that confronted the region's growers, its most notable and provocative sections dealt with the unsettled labor situation in the area. The report emphasized in particular the pitiful living and working conditions that valley farmworkers were forced to endure, the circumstances that combined to thwart workers' efforts to organize, and the brutal and lawless methods that growers and authorities had used to break the lettuce strike.[35]

Convinced that the extraordinary range and severity of problems affecting agricultural labor relations in the valley demanded equally extreme remedies, the commission submitted a list of recommendations designed to reform and restructure the region's employment relations in fundamental ways. The first recommendation was that state and federal authorities take immediate action to safeguard the civil liberties of the valley's workers and their supporters. Insofar as the living standards of workers were concerned, the commission suggested not only that state and federal authorities cooperate in the establishment of health, educational, and housing programs to benefit agricultural laborers, but also that they "establish subsistence farms or gardens, to enable the workers to tide over periods of unemployment characteristic of Imperial Valley." To correct what they regarded as a serious disequilibrium in the valley's labor market, the commissioners recommended two solutions. The first required the appointment of a federal "labor coordinator" who would act "to equalize and balance the labor supply," apparently by controlling hiring through some unspecified mechanism. The second and less sophisticated remedy provided for both voluntary and forced repatriation of excess Mexican labor in the region.[36]

The commission's final and most controversial recommendations went to the heart of the problem in the valley, and in industrialized agricultural in California generally: the total imbalance of power between employers and workers. Persuaded that nothing short of a drastic reordering of the existing industrial relations scheme would alleviate so complete an imbalance, the commission recommended

> that the Federal Government encourage the organization of workers, in order that collective bargaining may be effective in matters of wages and conditions, both working and living, and that the right to strike and peacefully to picket shall be maintained.
>
> Specifically do we recommend that the United States Department of Labor send representatives who can speak Spanish to aid Mexican and Filipino groups, and others, to organize for the purpose of collective bargaining.

Because their foremost desire was to rationalize and tranquilize labor relations in the valley, however, rather than simply to empower the region's farmworkers, the commissioners expressed an equally strong opinion that employers also required more effective organization. Accordingly, they recommended "that both State and Federal Governments encourage the growers and shippers to organize, that they may handle intelligently the various problems relating to the successful conduct of their business." Finally, the commission recommended that labor relations be kept in equilibrium by a federally appointed "permanent board or impartial administrator" empowered "to act in matters of dispute" regarding wages and working conditions. Such an entity was necessary, the commission concluded, because there were "no [NRA] codes for the protection of agricultural employees."[37]

The recommendations of Leonard, French, and Lubin demonstrated their own still ardent loyalty to the reformist labor-relations policy that New Dealers had hoped to establish through the National Industrial Recovery Act. Their recommendations to the National Labor Board betrayed a distinctly paternalistic orientation, as well as a strong desire to bring order, efficiency, and a sense of social purposefulness to a labor-relations system that they regarded as notoriously wasteful and disorderly, and selfishly antisocial. When agribusiness interests in the Imperial Valley and elsewhere denounced the commission's report as blatantly pro-union, they missed its essential point.[38] For while the report explicitly endorsed the idea that farmworker organization ought to be promoted so that collective bargaining might displace the economic dictatorship of farm employers, it was even more emphatic in suggesting numerous mechanisms through which the federal government could exercise ultimate control over industrial relations in the valley. Had the commission simply been pro-union, it would have taken the position that workers should be free to join the organization of their choice. Rather, it ignored entirely the obvious support that the CAWIU enjoyed among the region's workers and recommended, in effect, that the federal government become the organizational instrument of agricultural labor in the valley.

That the commission wanted to promote a farmworkers' union that was manageable rather than militant was a view readily subscribed to by Communist leaders in the state, who denounced its report and recommendations as a clumsy attempt by bourgeois liberals to destroy the CAWIU so as to clear the way for what amounted to a company union.[39] The Communists' claim that the commission was opposed to the development of a strong and independent union among Imperial Valley farmworkers was essentially correct. The commission's apparent conception of the principal function of organization was expressed by Simon Lubin, who insisted that "the thorough organization of labor and the thorough organization of business management" were necessary in order "that each may work upon its own peculiar problems, and that both might cooperate to a common end—service to the entire community."[40]

While farm employers and Communist labor organizers angrily denounced the commission's report and recommendations, the ACLU initially praised its findings as "an amazingly good job of analysis and action!" The ACLU also confidently expressed the opinion that the commission's recommendations would "be followed up without any prodding from outside."[41] In fact, when the commission's report and recommendations reached Washington and were digested by administration officials at the National Labor Board and elsewhere, no amount of prodding could persuade them that the federal government ought to involve itself in the Imperial Valley situation in the ways and to the degree urged by Leonard, French, and Lubin. Aside from the question of whether the federal government had the legal authority to intervene on such a large scale, there were, according to one administration official, "many points in the report in which neither the National Labor Board nor the Executive Departments of the Federal Government concurred." Specifically, he noted, it "seemed doubtful whether the Government ought to lend its efforts directly to the organization of labor unions."[42]

In the end, however, the administration's major objection to the commission's plan was probably rooted in political considerations. California agricultural interests were politically powerful and they had not hesitated to use their influence in Washington. In the wake of federal intervention in the San Joaquin Valley cotton strike, they had registered vigorous protests against any further meddling by New Deal agencies in their labor situation. The early confusion regarding the applicability of the NIRA's labor provisions to agriculture had been completely dispelled by early 1934, and agribusiness interests emphatically rejected any suggestion that either the National Recovery Administration or the National Labor Board had jurisdiction over agricultural labor relations. Farmworkers, of course, had no political influence, and it is unreasonable to think that the sensitive political analysts in the Roosevelt administration failed to make the point that it was exceedingly poor politics, especially in a critically important election year, to risk alienating powerful agricultural interests.

The administration's unwillingness to implement the commission's suggestions was indicated almost at once. Senator Wagner expressed his appreciation to Leonard, French, and Lubin for their "valuable report" on February 15, but at the same time advised them that he was asking George Creel to handle further labor difficulties in the Imperial Valley. A little over a week later the National Labor Board informed the three that federal action was unnecessary since "it is apparent that the State of California is so organized as to take every important action recommended by you without the assistance of the Federal Government."[43] Thoroughly bewildered, the commission members were left to wonder just what unknown forces had been at work in Washington to produce what J. L. Leonard described as the "double crossing" of which they suddenly appeared to be the victims.[44]

Though it announced on February 15 that George Creel was being sent to mediate the continuing labor troubles in the Imperial Valley, the National Labor Board was apparently determined to end its involvement in the region at the earliest opportunity. And when Creel's brief mediation effort failed, as Los Angeles Regional Labor Board officials knew it would, the national board quietly retired from the valley for good.[45]

If growers and authorities had any fear of forceful federal intervention, it was not reflected in their behavior. On the contrary, the vigilantism and antiunion violence that had drawn the federal government's attention to the valley in the first place actually intensified following the National Labor Board's investigation. In mid-February, when approximately 3,500 pea pickers struck near Calipatria, employers and authorities resorted to the heavy-handed strikebreaking tactics they knew best. With the assistance of the Imperial County Board of Supervisors, which hastily enacted an antipicketing ordinance, and county health officials, who obligingly condemned strikers' camps because of alleged health-code violations, employers moved quickly to break the strike while insisting all the while that no strike existed. After arresting suspected strike leaders on a variety of manufactured charges, deputized employers and their allies destroyed strike camps and forcibly dispersed their inhabitants. By February 20, less than a week after it had begun, the pea pickers' strike was completely broken.[46]

The vigor and alacrity with which employers and authorities responded to the pea strike indicated that they had not relaxed in the least their determination to crush all efforts to organize the valley's farmworkers. And even as they were breaking the pea strike, employers were making plans that they hoped would eliminate the possibility of labor troubles during the much more important spring cantaloupe harvest. As their predecessors had done four years earlier, Communist organizers had announced at the conclusion of the ill-fated lettuce strike that the CAWIU intended to organize workers in anticipation of a strike in early May against area melon growers. With most of its leaders in jail and the rest subject to arrest or physical attack the moment their organizing activities came to light, however, the CAWIU found it impossible to make good on its promise to hold organizational meetings throughout the valley during March.[47]

The continuing denial of workers' civil liberties caused sympathetic liberals and radicals outside the valley to renew their agitation for federal intervention. Lawyers for the ACLU had earlier won an extension of the court order prohibiting interference with workers' meetings, but understood only too well that it was, as one admitted, "but a scrap of paper" as long as it remained unenforced.[48] Repeated ACLU requests for federal marshals continued to be denied. Federal authorities, while acknowledging "that the presence of federal officials . . . would be salutary," still maintained that lawlessness in the valley was a "matter for state authorities."[49]

By the middle of March, violations of workers' rights had become so flagrant and numerous that the Southern California branch of the ACLU again sent its representatives into the valley to support the CAWIU's efforts to conduct organizational meetings and to provide legal aid to jailed union leaders.[50] Still certain that the ACLU's presence posed a threat to them, growers and valley authorities encouraged and abetted a resurgence of vigilantism during the latter part of March. Workers, union organizers, ACLU representatives, and members of various liberal groups investigating conditions in the valley were all victims of vigilante assaults during this period. Surely the most open and outrageous of these attacks was directed at attorney Grover Johnson on March 28. As he was leaving the county courthouse in El Centro after having gained the release of two CAWIU organizers, Johnson was attacked in broad daylight by a group of men that included a county supervisor and the administrator of the county hospital. Although the sheriff and several of his deputies observed the assault, they made no effort to stop it. When the battered attorney finally found sanctuary inside the courthouse, he demanded to know why the sheriff and his men had not acted to protect him. One deputy explained that since the county supervisor who had taken part in the assault was in charge of hiring and firing the personnel of the sheriff's office, it would have been impolitic for the sheriff's men to intervene. Johnson's demands that the sheriff arrest those who had attacked him and disperse an unruly mob called to the courthouse by vigilante leaders were refused.[51]

While they plainly considered vigilantism the most direct and emotionally satisfying way of combatting efforts by the CAWIU and its sympathizers to organize the valley's farmworkers, growers and their supporters also introduced in March several more sophisticated and respectable methods of accomplishing their goal. On March 14 growers and shippers met at the American Legion hall in El Centro and formed the Imperial Valley Growers and Shippers Protective Association. The purpose of the association, which functioned as a subunit of the Western Growers Protective Association, was to coordinate farm employers' efforts to defeat the CAWIU. The association sought to project the image of a completely independent local farmers' group dedicated to the protection of the valley's yeomanry from Communist diabolism. Although the association presumed to speak for all growers and shippers in the valley, it was controlled from the beginning by a very small group of men representing the largest and most powerful agricultural concerns in the region.[52]

Formed at the same time, and designed to function in close cooperation with the growers' protective association, was the Imperial Valley Anti-Communist Association. Jointly controlled by leading county officials and farm employers, the Anti-Communist Association was described by its founders as a "citizens'" group established to promote "Americanism" by fighting communism. In fact, the Anti-Communist Association's exclusive function was to assist valley farm employers in their campaign to smash the CAWIU. On March 21, a joint meeting of the directors of the Anti-Communist Association and the growers' protective association met "to co-ordinate their plans in opposing the Reds."[53] Among the duties taken on by the Anti-Communist Association was the recruitment and assignment of labor spies to keep CAWIU activities under close surveillance. Operating on the coercive principle that anyone not willing to join the association was probably a Communist or communist sympathizer, the group's leaders were able to report that within little more than a week of its founding the association had between 7,000 and 10,000 members.[54]

The final and most important step taken by growers and their supporters involved the establishment of what amounted to an employer-dominated closed shop in the valley. Immediately following the collapse of the pea strike in February, Mexican consul Joaquín Terrazas, with the support and encouragement of valley farm employers, initiated a plan to organize another exclusively Mexican farmworkers' union. Finally established as the Mexican Association of the Imperial Valley, the organization was at once embraced by the region's growers and shippers as the only "legitimate" farmworkers' group in the valley. By mid-March Mexican farmworkers were being advised that membership in the association was an absolute prerequisite to employment in the region's agricultural industry. On March 27 the relationship between farm employers and the Mexican association was formalized with the signing of a working agreement for the approaching melon harvest. Included in the agreement, which was unilaterally dictated by farm employers, were provisions for an hourly wage of 25 cents, a piece rate of 13 cents per crate, work for association members only, armed guards in the fields to protect against "communist elements," a commission of four growers to settle all workers' grievances, and official grower recognition of the Mexican association.[55] While Mexican workers objected to the transparently coercive strategy that underlay the association's appeal and resented its obvious subservience to the valley's farm employers, most finally joined when it became apparent that to do otherwise meant being blacklisted.[56]

Though federal authorities had hoped that the state government would act to restore order in the valley, and thus spare them a hard political decision, the unabated vigilantism and lawlessness in the region during February and March generated such strong and insistent protests that federal action of some kind again became unavoidable. Liberals demanded, in particular, to know why the government had failed to respond to the recommendations set forth in the National Labor Board's report, especially in light of the fact that subsequent events appeared to confirm the special commission's conclusion that nothing short of large-scale federal intervention could remedy the desperate situation in the valley, and the ACLU resumed its agitation for federal marshals.[57] Even the Los Angeles Regional Labor Board made a special point of informing Washington in early March that the situation demanded forceful federal action, suggesting that perhaps the Agricultural Adjustment Administration use its considerable leverage to force growers to moderate their reckless behavior.[58]

When federal officials had finally resigned themselves to the necessity for some action, they sought a means of intervention that would expose the administration to the smallest possible political risk. As a result they ruled out both the use of federal marshals and any serious attempt to implement the recommendations embodied in the National Labor Board's report. In short, administration officials ruled out any action forceful enough to compel valley farm employers to abandon their misanthropic labor policies. To the extent that order and system were introduced into the labor policies followed by Imperial Valley growers, administration officials were determined that it must be through a voluntary program that kept political costs to a minimum.

Rather than permit the somewhat too independent and politically unruly National Labor Board to reinvolve itself in the region, the Roosevelt administration entrusted the task of defusing the labor situation in the valley to the Department of Labor. From the beginning the Labor Department took the position that the troubles in the Imperial Valley would be solved as soon as employers agreed to treat their employees more fairly. The department's leaders, including Secretary of Labor Frances Perkins, further believed that the unionization of farmworkers was more likely to retard than to advance efforts to persuade employers to adopt a less exploitive attitude toward workers. As a result, the department's approach to conciliation in the region was, from beginning to end, founded on the assumption that before progress could be made toward placing agricultural labor relations on a stable and non-conflictful footing the disruptive and misguided drive by Communists and others to establish a farmworkers' union had to be halted.[59]

In seeking an emissary with the special qualifications she believed the situation required, Secretary Perkins was guided by her social-worker instincts. After studying the turbulent pattern of labor relations in the valley, Miss Perkins concluded "that it was the instability of the situation that was so tragic, that these people [farm employers and farmworkers] were too nervous, too overwrought and too highstrung. They couldn't settle down." Recalling her reaction to the challenge confronting her, Perkins said:

> I got this brainstorm and said to myself, "What kind of people are they? They're like children and children take comfort in authority. When chil-

dren are having a tantrum when grandma, or old Aunt Susan, who is a person of authority comes in, they calm right down, because Aunt Susan knows where she's going and what she intends to have. There isn't any of this fluttering like dear, kind, sweet mama who doesn't seem to know what it is one's aiming at, trying to obey all the rules of child guidance and rearing."[60]

The person selected by Miss Perkins to be the Labor Department's "old Aunt Susan" in the Imperial Valley was Brigadier General Pelham D. Glassford, U.S. Army, Retired. No stranger to strife or controversy, Glassford was the superintendent of metropolitan police in Washington, D.C., during the Bonus March in 1932, and had resigned the post after a bitter dispute with his superiors over the violent methods they adopted to drive veterans from their capitol encampment.[61] It was, in fact, Glassford's military background and his behavior during the Bonus March that persuaded Miss Perkins that he was just the sort of man who could project the image of benevolent authoritarianism she believed the Imperial Valley situation required. Glassford impressed Perkins as "a man of humanitarian impulses, but not at all silly"; someone possessing "that curious ability for prompt action and a kind of orderly, patterned, completely conventional action that army training gives a man. You don't do anything new and experimental and imaginative, but you do something very practical and do it quick." Describing Glassford's demeanor, she later said:

> He was bluff, but not blustery, plain spoken, very quick, very competent, very alert, very straight and erect. He was a very military looking person, although he had been retired for a long time. But he had that quick alert look, as though he were going somewhere. He moved himself around the office just as though he had a purpose to his movements. There was no lolling around.
>
> I gathered that he would be a humanitarian in the situation, but I also gathered that he knew that these poor, idle, mistreated fellows were also perfect bums, that they would get the best of you if they could. You had to keep your eye out and expect that. He wouldn't be broken-hearted if they were. He was a practical person. He knew you couldn't give them the millennium, but that you could see that they had a place to sleep, and so forth and so on.[62]

When on March 27 the Department of Labor formally announced Glassford's appointment as special "labor conciliator" for the Imperial Valley, the public was informed that the government was acting in accordance with the recommendations made nearly six weeks earlier by the Leonard-French-Lubin commission.[63] In truth, Glassford's appointment represented a studied effort to avoid acting on the National Labor Board report. When Congresswoman Isabella Greenway of Arizona first advised Glassford of the Labor Department's intention to appoint him, she emphasized that the action was being taken because of a widespread feeling in Washington that the National Labor Board report had "not been satisfactory."[64] Charles E. Wyzanski, Jr., solicitor of the Department of Labor, emphasized the same point on March 27 when he gave Glassford his formal instructions.[65]

While the CAWIU and its liberal supporters welcomed Glassford's appointment because it appeared to signal the federal government's intention to act at long last on the National Labor Board's report,[66] growers and their allies bitterly assailed what they feared would be an effort to stir up the labor situation in the valley just as they were on the verge of wiping out the last vestiges of worker resistance to their absolute authority and control.[67]

Having spent much of his retirement in the Salt River Valley of Arizona, an area whose agriculture closely resembled that of the Imperial Valley, Glassford brought to his new assignment a fairly solid knowledge of industrialized farming. He also brought a fundamental opposition to agricultural unionism, an openly disdainful attitude toward Mexican farmworkers, and a strong, if not particularly vehement, animus toward Communists.

Though Glassford's long-range goal was to effect a "permanent economic and social adjustment" of labor relations in the valley, his immediate objective, as outlined for him by Charles Wyzanski, was to ensure that the spring cantaloupe harvest was completed without interruption, and that the violence and vigilantism that had flourished in the region since early January was somehow halted.[68] Even before he arrived in the valley in early April, Glassford was apparently convinced that neither his immediate nor his long-range goal could be achieved as long as the CAWIU maintained an active presence in the region. And this belief was immediately confirmed when he held his first meetings with growers and local authorities. Glassford further determined that if he was to have the opportunity to reform the labor-relations system in the valley, it would be only after he gained the confidence and cooperation of the region's dominant farm employers. Anything that he and the federal government tried to do to remedy the valley's labor problems, Glassford decided, would have to reflect an awareness and acceptance of "the unalterable fact that the officials, shippers and growers, and a large proportion of the white population are determined to keep out the outside organizers of the Cannery and Agricultural Workers Industrial Union, no matter at what cost."[69]

The policy that Glassford resolved to implement was essentially the same one that George Creel had followed during the cotton strike. The difference was that while Creel appeared to have the power to compel farm employers to cooperate with the government's efforts to establish a rational and socially viable labor-relations system, Glassford was empowered to do nothing more than undertake "some impartial intervention in a friendly fashion," and employers knew it.[70] Persuaded that employers could be won over to a program of voluntary cooperation with the government's plan to reform agricultural labor policies only if the threat of unionism were eliminated, the general gave his full support to growers' efforts to smash what remained of the CAWIU in the region. Thus throughout April, Glassford's time in the valley was spent in the company of employers and local authorities, and his frequent public pronouncements were calculated to establish his sympathy for the growers' cause and his animosity toward the CAWIU. When anti-union forces promoted a frenzied red scare as the cantaloupe harvest approached, Glassford lent his enthusiastic support, repeatedly denouncing the CAWIU as a "communistic" front whose "only objective is to create dissension, destroy private property and foment a strike," and warning workers of the violent consequences if they followed "the red banner of outside agitators . . . being assisted by a few professional Mexican trouble-makers."[71] So enthusiastic was Glassford in his effort to win the employers' confidence that Charles Wyzanski finally had to advise him against further anticommunist tirades because they were proving an embarrassment to certain federal officials, especially Emergency Relief Administrator Harry Hopkins, who had "the function of feeding a considerable number of alleged 'reds' "in the Imperial Valley.[72]

Yet if Glassford's blasts against communism became a source of mild consternation in Washington, they tended to delight and mollify agricultural interests in the valley. The *Imperial Valley Press* reported shortly after the first of the general's anticommunist statements that the initially strong grower opposition to him was rapidly lessening.[73] Equally pleasing to employers was Glassford's decision to regard the grower-backed Mexican Association of the Imperial Valley, which he privately referred to as a "company union,"[74] as the only legitimate representative of farmworkers in the region.[75]

Though he opposed agricultural unionism as a matter of policy,[76] the public enthusiasm that Glassford brought to the task in the Imperial Valley was largely for the benefit of employers. As he explained to his superiors in Washington: "It is absolutely essential at the present time that they believe me to be entirely under their control."[77] After having helped them to destroy the CAWIU, he thought, the employers, convinced of his and the federal government's good faith, would agree not only to improvements in wages and conditions for their workers, but to reforms that would give the government a permanent role in balancing labor relations in the valley in the best interests of workers, growers, and the public.[78] As evidence that his strategy was beginning to pay dividends, Glassford confidently informed Secretary Perkins in mid-April that he had persuaded the Imperial County Board of Supervisors that instead of resorting to vigilantism they should seek an "injunction against agitators continuing their veiled malicious activities."[79]

In choosing a course of action that placed him firmly on the side of growers and in opposition to the CAWIU and the right of valley farmworkers to organize, Glassford greatly disappointed and angered leaders of the ACLU, who had welcomed his appointment as evidence of the federal government's commitment to a restoration of civil liberties in the region. When Glassford failed to condemn the lawlessness of growers and authorities and instead blamed the unrest in the region on Communist agitators, he precipitated a long and at times caustic debate with various ACLU spokesmen.[80]

Glassford's difficulties with the ACLU ultimately centered around a proposal that an election be held to determine the preferences of valley farmworkers insofar as union representation was concerned, and around the Southern California branch's insistence on conducting a "goodwill" tour through the region to test the status of civil liberties there. The idea for a farmworkers' representation election was first suggested by CAWIU organizer S. C. Alexander, who proposed to Glassford on April 3 that a vote be taken to determine which union, the CAWIU or the Mexican Association of the Imperial Valley, was supported by a majority of the valley's agricultural labor force.[81] It was the ACLU, however, that pushed the idea.

From the beginning, Glassford opposed the election proposal. His principal reason was that he felt such a plan would antagonize growers, and thus "jeopardize [his] own plans for a solution to Imperial Valley difficulties."[82] To supporters of the election proposal, Glassford reiterated his argument that the uncompromising opposition of employers to the CAWIU made it impossible for the union to have any future role in the valley.[83] At the same time, he privately complained to Wyzanski that the ACLU recognized that he had the "situation quite well in hand insofar as the melon crop is concerned," and by pressing the idea of a workers' election was "doing everything in its power to foment trouble, and to aggravate the citizens of Imperial Valley."[84] Before rejecting the idea of an election completely, however, Glassford asked various other federal officials for their opinions. In every case, they advised against an election. Beyond the question of whether or not the federal government had the authority to sponsor such an election, most of the officials with whom Glassford consulted declared the proposal both impractical and politically unwise.[85] Of course, even if an election had been held, the region's growers, who vehemently opposed the idea, would not have been bound in any legal sense by its outcome. It is interesting to note, however, that Glassford privately felt as of mid-April that had an election like that contemplated by the ACLU been held, the CAWIU would probably have won, despite the many months of suppression it had endured.[86]

While Glassford's differences with the ACLU over the advisability of a farmworkers' election were deep, they did not produce the depth of ill feeling that ultimately resulted from the general's unsuccessful attempts to keep the ACLU's Southern California branch from baiting vigilantes in the Imperial Valley. The dispute was rooted in the ACLU's persistent demand that the federal government take action to halt vigilantism and official lawlessness and to restore the civil liberties of workers and CAWIU organizers in the valley. With Glassford's appointment, ACLU officials hoped that the action they had long demanded was finally close at hand. Because Glassford was himself determined to see the CAWIU eliminated as a force in the valley, however, he showed no interest in upholding the rights of Communist organizers and union members. And on more than one occasion the general expressed sympathy for growers who resorted to extralegal methods to protect their crops from those seeking to foment a strike.[87]

In spite of his lack of concern for the rights of CAWIU organizers and members, Glassford was hopeful that he could halt vigilante attacks against representatives of the ACLU and other liberal and radical groups. He found himself in a nearly impossible predicament, however. When he asked the Department of Labor to specify his powers regarding the maintenance of law in the valley, he was informed that he had no "actual police authority," and was encouraged to rely on the force of his personality to dissuade the region's residents from engaging in further lawless acts.[88] Since he lacked any real power, a fact that growers and local authorities fully appreciated, Glassford's only potential weapon in combatting vigilantism consisted of strong public condemnations of those responsible for its perpetuation. Had he resorted to such a tactic, however, his rapprochement with growers would have been immediately destroyed, along with his long-range plan of winning better wages and conditions for farmworkers through voluntary concessions. Unwilling to jeopardize his ultimate goals, Glassford refused to condemn the lawlessness of local authorities and, as he privately described them, the "obstinate and arrogant officials and leaders of the Imperial Valley Shippers and Growers Protective Association."[89]

In light of Glassford's refusal to condemn those responsible for the lawlessness that pervaded the Imperial Valley, ACLU leaders decided that it had again become necessary to provide some dramatic demonstration of the disorderly conditions in the region in order to generate public demand for more forceful action by state and federal authorities. The means they chose was a widely publicized "goodwill" tour of the valley by twenty or so representatives of various liberal groups. Certain that their presence would provoke a lawless response from vigilantes, ACLU spokesmen openly advised Glassford that their intention was to "demonstrate [the] breakdown of local [and] state law enforcement" in the region.[90] After feverish efforts to stop the tour, which he considered an irresponsible and provocative act, Glassford did his best to secure police protection for the group. Having promised protection, however, he was unable to persuade either county or state authorities to provide it.[91] As a result, when the tour group came into the valley on May 5, it was met in Brawley by vigilantes who roughed up its members and forced them at gunpoint to return to San Diego. Feeling that they had been betrayed by Glassford, ACLU leaders finally took the action they had been heading toward for weeks. On May 13 the ACLU's national office sent telegrams to President Roosevelt, Secretary Perkins, and other administration officials, demanding Glassford's immediate recall on the grounds that he had failed to protect civil liberties in the valley and had taken the side of growers against workers and the CAWIU in clear violation of both the letter and the spirit of his appointment as an "impartial" conciliator. ACLU leaders also renewed their demand for federal marshals to restore civil liberties and the rule of law.[92]

From the ACLU's often myopic point of view, the Glassford mission had failed miserably. In response to the charges against him, Glassford insisted that the "goodwill" tour had "completely destroyed" his efforts to restore freedom of speech and assembly in the valley. Emphasizing his strong opposition to the provocative methods of the ACLU, Glassford wrote: "I am convinced that the Imperial Valley situation cannot be corrected through sudden and drastic measures, but that the cure must be accomplished through evolution, in which education gradually will bring about a change in local public opinion. I am glad to say that I see the beginning of such an evolution, and I would appreciate the cooperation (instead of the antagonism) of the A.C.L.U."[93]

Though the agitation for Glassford's ouster continued for weeks, administration officials, who were generally well satisfied with his performance in the valley, remained largely impervious to ACLU complaints. Among his ACLU critics, there was little disposition to regard Glassford's influence on labor relations in the valley as other than disastrous.[94] Only Helen Marston, a young civil libertarian from San Diego who had joined several of the liberal forays into the region, appears to have guessed that Glassford's conspicuously energetic cooperation with employers' efforts to destroy the CAWIU was part of a larger strategy designed to increase their amenability to subsequent proposals for voluntary reform of labor relations in the valley. As she informed Secretary Perkins, however, Glassford's credibility among the region's farmworkers was irretrievably lost.[95]

Glassford contentedly reported toward the middle of May that the CAWIU was "whipped so far as the Imperial Valley is concerned," and that the melon harvest was proceeding without the threat of a strike.[96] Having accomplished the initial phase of his strategy for reform, he confidently turned to the next phase. Yet when he tried to implement the second half of his plan, to collect the debts he felt the employers now owed him, he soon discovered that he had badly misjudged the valley's growers, who had no more intention of sharing their power over labor matters with the federal government than with the CAWIU. All of his suggestions for reform were summarily rejected.[97] In the same report to Washington in which he described the complete elimination of legitimate unionism in the valley, Glassford advised Secretary Perkins that farm employers had become so secure in their power that they would no longer deal with even their own company union.[98] At the end of May, Glassford wrote, "I have my back to the wall so far as they are concerned." In a letter to Wyzanski he reported that employers were determined to run the valley "as they see fit," and that responsibility for any future labor troubles in the region "can be placed squarely on the shoulders of the growers and shippers."[99]

Finally convinced of the employers' bad faith and of the impossibility of instituting the reforms he had in mind, Glassford decided to break with the valley's controlling elements.[100] For about three weeks the general sought an opportunity to launch his attack on growers and valley authorities. Such an opportunity came unexpectedly on June 8, when Ernest Besig, an ACLU attorney in the valley under Glassford's guarantee of protection, was brutally assaulted as he sat on a railway platform in the small valley town of Niland.[101] Beyond denouncing the attack and demanding immediate action to bring Besig's assailants to justice, Glassford began to compose a wider indictment of growers and authorities in the Imperial Valley. On June 13 he issued his first blast at the valley's bosses. After briefly reviewing the lawless tactics they had used to suppress workers and others in the region, Glassford concluded: "The valley is governed and controlled by a small group which in advertising a war against communism, is spreading terrorism, intimidation, and injustice." Included in this small group, he charged, were "some of the leading officials in Imperial County."[102]

Quickly warming to his task, Glassford resumed his verbal assault on the following day:

> Apparently a small group of growers and shippers who have set themselves up to rule Imperial Valley desire only to fog the issue with their doctrines of violence, intimidation, and suppression of the workers. Instead of setting an example of law, order, sanity, and reform, they are breeding violence and discontent among the workers. They are placing themselves in the position of being the most dangerous "reds" ever to come to Imperial Valley. . . .
>
> Satisfied that there is little danger of a disturbance during the present melon season, the big growers and shippers apparently are content to do little or nothing toward ameliorating conditions of the workers.
>
> The feeling of security is enhanced by the fact that the principal labor agitators have been incarcerated. It is unfortunate that our courts of justice should be used as a means for eliminating the agitators from the situation, on what are apparently trumped up charges.[103]

On June 15 Glassford further announced that his experience in the region had convinced him that the critical analysis of Imperial Valley conditions contained in the much maligned National Labor Board report was "substantially correct."[104]

Glassford's final and most damning indictment of valley growers and authorities came on June 23, when he submitted a list of recommendations to the Board of Supervisors of Imperial County. In recommending a special state-supervised grand jury investigation of lawlessness in the valley, Glassford reported:

> After more than two months of observation and investigation in Imperial Valley, it is my conviction that a group of growers have exploited a "communist" hysteria for the advancement of their own interests; that they have welcomed labor agitation, which they could brand as "Red," as a

means of sustaining supremacy by mob rule, thereby preserving what is so essential to their profits—*Cheap labor*; that they have succeeded in drawing into their conspiracy certain county officials who have become the principal tools of their machine.[105]

Following this salvo, Glassford left the Imperial Valley, hoping his work there would produce some good but convinced that conditions were not likely to change for a long time to come.[106] Though his dramatic break with growers and their allies was a source of considerable satisfaction to his former ACLU critics,[107] the inescapable irony of the situation was that Glassford and the federal government had willingly participated in or condoned nearly every union-busting activity for which the general so indignantly called employers to account after his strategy for voluntary reform had failed. If, as the general charged, the employers' behavior had consistently revealed a lawless and cynical disregard for workers' rights, his and the federal government's record on the same score was only slightly less discreditable.

Glassford's unfulfilled plan for valley farmworkers, which conformed in every way to the labor-relations formula outlined in the NIRA, would have provided, he later said, for "a regimentation by the Government," an organizing of farmworkers into what "you might call . . . a Government or a Federal labor union."[108] Because farm employers would not voluntarily accept that kind of government intervention in the industry's labor relations, and the Roosevelt administration would not accept the political costs that would have been incurred by compelling their acceptance, the new economic order that Glassford, and Creel before him, visualized was never fully transformed from inspiration to practice. Yet the aborted effort to effect that transformation had, as the Imperial Valley experience abundantly demonstrated, served to promote the destruction of the CAWIU, which represented the most vigorous and promising movement to bring about farmworker organization that California, or the nation, had seen.

For the CAWIU, which had entered the Imperial Valley intent upon proving its organizational vitality, the successive defeats suffered at the hands of growers, vigilantes, and antiunion reformers not only left it in a shambles there, but greatly reduced the union's capacity to carry on its organizing activities among farmworkers elsewhere in the state. Union organizers had been active in other agricultural districts, however, and a few strikes had resulted, although none was to assume particular importance. In January the CAWIU was responsible for a strike among several hundred Filipino vegetable workers in San Mateo County. Despite strenuous efforts by authorities to break the strike, it apparently ended with a compromise settlement providing for slightly improved wages and partial union recognition.[109] Another minor victory was won by the union in Sacramento County in April, when between 500 and 700 Mexican and Filipino strawberry pickers successfully struck for a 25 percent wage increase and union recognition.[110] In a number of smaller strikes, workers led by the CAWIU forced farm employers to grant modest increases in wages and improvements in conditions.[111]

In late April, while the union's last feeble efforts to salvage its reputation among Imperial Valley farmworkers were still under way, the second, and last, annual convention of the CAWIU met in Sacramento. With apparently undiminished enthusiasm, the delegates planned an ambitious new organizational campaign for the 1934 summer and fall harvest seasons. Declaring that the CAWIU had "become the pass-word for working class struggle among the agricultural workers of the entire West Coast," convention leaders reported that during the preceding year the union had "led 50,000 workers in militant strikes."

> These strikes have encouraged thousands more workers to spontaneous action against their intolerable living and working conditions. The majority of strikes have resulted in real gains for the workers, either complete or partial victories; and the influence of the Union among the workers, and the fear of the Union among the bosses, caused wages to be raised in many sections without strikes. Our record is one of having put millions of dollars into the pockets of the workers, thereby enabling them to buy back more of the products they have produced.

Though the delegates heard the CAWIU characterized as a "revolutionary union" consecrated to "militant" and "uncompromising struggle" on behalf of "agricultural workers . . . the most exploited section of the working class," the convention was remarkably short on blustery political rhetoric and long on nuts-and-bolts unionism. Emphasizing the dominant theme of the convention, union leaders noted that while their organization's ability to fight "the boss-class" had been "tested and proven" in innumerable strikes, insufficient attention had been given to its long-run institutional development. The truth of their allegation was revealed, they claimed, in the fact that while the CAWIU had "issued twenty-one thousand membership books," its negligible dues-paying constituency revealed that "these thousands of members are only *card members*" who "have not yet been welded into a strong, solid mass union." To remedy that situation, the convention endorsed a variety of union-building programs, including membership drives, the establishment of a network of permanent locals staffed by "home-guard workers," new campaigns of organization among the state's mainly nonmigratory packing-shed and cannery workers, an expanded union bulletin through which members could gain information and express their opinions, and the development of "interesting special activities" designed both to enrich the lives of the membership and to foster a stronger sense of solidarity and union community. As a means of fulfilling this final goal, union leaders suggested activities ranging from baseball teams to "defense classes, socials, open forums and debates." Once invested with the institutional vitality that these changes were supposed to confer, the CAWIU would, its leaders pledged, truly become "the strongest weapon of the agricultural workers in their battle for existence."[112]

Despite their enthusiasm, convention delegates could not have been more mistaken in their forecast of the CAWIU's future. A far better indication of what lay ahead for the union was provided a few weeks later when it launched a strike of about a thousand workers against fruit growers near the Contra Costa County town of Brentwood and suffered a humiliating defeat. Before the Brentwood conflict had run its calamitous course, the CAWIU not only had absorbed a brutal battering by state and local lawmen and highly organized employers, but had also lost control of the strike to the newly formed Cannery Workers Union No. 18893, an A.F. of L. affiliate whose apparent organizational strategy was to capitalize on its relative "respectability" in comparison to the "red" CAWIU.[113] In the end, however, the most ominous aspect of the Brentwood debacle, as far as the CAWIU was concerned, was that it marked the first direct involvement of the Associated Farmers of California in an agricultural labor dispute.

The campaign by industrialized farming interests to develop a coordinated, statewide union-busting apparatus began in earnest following the CAWIU's spectacular strike victories in the fall of 1933. While the trauma of the cotton strike was still reverberating in farming circles, leaders of the Agricultural Committee of the State Chamber of Commerce and the California Farm Bureau Federation were enlisting farm employers from every important agricultural county of the state in a crusade to combat and ultimately destroy the CAWIU. In March 1934 the Associated Farmers of California, Inc., was formed. While the organization's activities were directed by representatives of the largest agricultural interests in the state, they were financed almost entirely by railroads, utilities, banks, oil companies, and other industrial interests that were convinced that the defeat of farm unionism would in time retard the urban labor movement in the state.[114]

At no time did the Associated Farmers demonstrate an interest in combatting the CAWIU by improving the deplorable working and living conditions that fostered the discontent and desperation that Communist organizers had become so expert at exploiting. The methods adopted by the Associated Farmers consisted of a statewide anticommunist propaganda campaign to arouse public feeling against the union; political agitation to deny federal relief to striking or voluntarily unemployed farmworkers; a drive to enact antipicketing and other legislation in agricultural counties as a means of breaking farm strikes; and a scheme to eliminate the union leadership through the use of the state's criminal syndicalism law.[115]

Of the several methods, greatest emphasis was placed on the last. To gather the evidence required to support charges of criminal syndicalism, the Associated Farmers hired several private investigators and at least one labor spy who successfully infiltrated the Communist Party and gained the confidence of CAWIU leaders.[116] In addition, leaders of the Associated Farmers were in frequent contact with law-enforcement agencies and state officials for the purpose of gaining their cooperation in the organization's anti-CAWIU strategy. Finally, the Associated Farmers made a special effort during June and early July to exploit the antiradical feeling generated in the state by the highly publicized San Francisco general strike for its own more narrow purpose.[117]

On July 20 the arrests that the Associated Farmers had sought took place. In a raid on the CAWIU headquarters in Sacramento, which coincided with a statewide crackdown on radicals by local, state, and federal authorities,[118] police rounded up seventeen men and women involved in various facets of the union's activities. Included in this group were Pat Chambers and Caroline Decker, perhaps the CAWIU's most effective and visible leaders. In time, each of the seventeen was charged with multiple violations of the state's criminal syndicalism law.[119]

From the moment the arrests were made, officials of the Associated Farmers worked in close cooperation with the Sacramento County district attorney to ensure that the cases were vigorously prosecuted. Investigators and special secretarial help were provided to the prosecutor at the Associated Farmers' expense in order to facilitate the gathering and organizing of evidence, and the organization's antiradical propaganda campaign was intensified to create a public mood conducive to a legal crusade against communist "subversion." Determined to spare no effort or expense in achieving the results it desired, the Associated Farmers even went so far as to hire District Attorney Elmer Heald of Imperial County to prepare the criminal syndicalism indictments for his Sacramento County counterpart, who lacked experience in such cases. Guernsey Frazer, the executive secretary of the Associated Farmers, personally supervised the organization's activities in regard to the case, meeting on several occasions with the prosecutor to plan strategy and discuss evidence. In all, the Associated Farmers incurred expenses of $13,780.59 in advancing the Sacramento criminal syndicalism cases. For the services he rendered to the prosecutor as an "expert" adviser on communism, the Los Angeles Police Department's indefatigable Captain Hynes alone received payments in excess of $6,000 directly from the Associated Farmers.[120] So helpful were the Associated Farmers, in fact, that the cases might never have come to trial without the organization's assistance. In a letter to George P. Clements of the Los Angeles Chamber of Commerce on the eve of the trial, Guernsey Frazer wrote:

> It is a rather maddening situation in which we find ourselves. The trial of the seventeen Communists in Sacramento begins Tuesday. The only organization that has done one single solitary thing in this case has been our organization [Associated Farmers]. This is stated by the District Attorney and his assistants, and they have further stated that without the help and assistance which we have given them in the case that it would have been a hopeless proposition. By reason of our contacts and knowledge of the situation we have been able to shape that case, compile the evidence and even assist in the rounding up of material witnesses, and we have had to bear the entire expense ourselves out of our budget, which should be used to keep the organization going.[121]

After many weeks of delay, the trial that the Associated Farmers had courted bankruptcy to bring about finally began in mid-January 1935. As the prosecutor remarked at the outset, it was the Communist Party, rather than the individual defendants, that was actually on trial. Beyond the testimony of informants who had successfully infiltrated the party and the CAWIU, the prosecution's case was founded on the assumption that the party's teachings were patently unlawful under the criminal syndicalism act, and that as admitted Communists the defendants shared in the party's guilt. Beyond denials by the individual defendants that they had in any way violated the criminal syndicalism law, the defense's case was highlighted by Communist Party District Organizer

Sam Darcy's testimony that the hundreds of revolutionary tracts introduced into evidence by the prosecution to prove the party's unlawful advocacy of violent class rebellion could not be taken literally. The substance of Darcy's testimony was that the Communist Party was, its inflammatory rhetoric notwithstanding, devoted to democratic principles and practices, and that it shunned force and violence as a means of realizing its revolutionary ambitions. On March 29, after one of the longest and most highly publicized trials in California's history, the Sacramento criminal syndicalism cases went to the jury. On April 1, after 66 hours of deliberation and 118 ballots, the jury returned to court to announce that eight of the defendants, including Chambers and Decker, had been found guilty as charged on two of six counts, but that the remaining defendants had been found innocent of all the charges against them. Conviction on each count of violating the criminal syndicalism law carried a sentence of from one to fourteen years, and those found guilty began serving their sentences in various California prisons. The cases were immediately appealed, and in 1937 the State Court of Appeals reversed the Sacramento verdicts, freeing those CAWIU officials still in prison.[122]

The Associated Farmers had delivered to the CAWIU, and to agricultural unionism in California, a stunning and debilitating blow, but not a fatal one. That was left for the Comintern to deliver. Early in 1934, the message began to filter out from Moscow that the growing threat of fascism in the world dictated that each national Communist Party forsake its independent revolutionary policies in favor of a "popular front" with other antifascist forces. Insofar as Communist trade-union policy was concerned, the new party line required the abandonment of independent labor movements in favor of a return to the policy of "boring from within" the established nonrevolutionary trade unions.[123]

Throughout 1934, Communist leaders in the United States worked to bring the American party's trade-union policies into line with the Comintern's new directives. Since there were no well-established nonrevolutionary trade unions in agriculture to infiltrate, the popular-front policy required, in effect, that the Communist Party dissolve the CAWIU and largely abandon its efforts to build a labor movement in American agriculture. With the robot-like fidelity that characterized the American party's relationship with the Comintern, the Trade Union Unity League was officially laid to rest in March 1935. Among the offspring that accompanied it to the grave was the Cannery and Agricultural Workers Industrial Union.[124] Inasmuch as it was a change in the Communist

Party's line that brought the CAWIU and the radical farm-labor movement in California into being in the first place, it was perhaps fitting that another change in international party policy, rather than the efforts of antiunion agricultural interests and their allies, should have dictated their ultimate demise.

During the four years of the CAWIU's existence, it led tens of thousands of California farmworkers in the largest agricultural strikes in the history of the United States. Together these strikes not only produced higher wages for nearly all farmworkers in the state, but also helped to focus public attention on the generally abysmal living standards that agricultural laborers and their families were forced to endure. The CAWIU also brought California farmworkers closer to escaping the chronic powerlessness that attended their lives than they had ever come before. Ironically, however, it was in the end the powerlessness of farmworkers, especially the lack of a political dimension to their lives, that caused the party, after four years of organizational endeavor, to abandon the California countryside in favor of more fertile organizational ground.

Throughout the period of the union's activity among farmworkers, farm employers constantly lodged the charge that its Communist leaders were primarily interested in advancing the fortunes of the Communist Party rather than those of agricultural workers, whom the employers consciously misrepresented as guileless dupes of sinister radical manipulators. In suggesting that the motives of Communist farm-labor organizers encompassed more than simply winning higher wages and better conditions, employers were essentially correct. When the American Communist Party began its campaign to build an independent labor movement in 1929, it did so for the basic purpose of advancing its revolutionary aims. And while party leaders plainly recognized that winning higher wages and better working conditions was an indispensable first step in gaining the confidence and allegiance of workers, they also believed that achieving such improvements could never be an end in itself. It was probably this belief, more than any other, that differentiated Communist trade unionists from their "reformist" counterparts, who, like Samuel Gompers, were true believers only in the idea of "more."

Because the ultimate objective of the Communist labor movement was to promote the collapse of capitalism in America, the party sought to concentrate its organizational efforts among those workers who derived the least economic benefit from the capitalist system. The Communists' guiding assumption, and it was not an altogether unreasonable one, was that their greatest hope of success in building a revolutionary consciousness in America rested with those groups of workers who, because of their disadvantaged economic status, were likely to have the weakest attachment to the prevailing capitalist order. And it was only natural that Communists considered the rural proletariat in California an especially vulnerable group. Farm laborers were, beyond any question, among the most disadvantaged workers in the United States. They spent their lives in a maze of abject poverty seemingly without avenues of escape. In the eyes of society, they were at once indispensable and despised. They were the essential reason for the prosperity of California's industrialized agriculture but were the state's least prosperous workers. Yet in indulging the impression that California farmworkers were, because of their demeaned status, likely to be amenable to anti-capitalist political remedies, Communist planners fell victim to their own intellectual myopia. For unlike Communists, who necessarily looked to a fixed ideology to make sense of the volatile economic conditions of the early 1930s, farmworkers seeking to identify the principal cause of their economic suffering did not conclude that capitalism had failed them. Most farmworkers, using a brand of logic as primitive as it was sensible in their experience, concluded that they were desperately poor because they did not receive enough money for their labor. And, in the absence of a political consciousness that might have afforded them a less provincial understanding of their plight, the solution that suggested itself to California farmworkers was not the disestablishment of capitalism, but higher wages.

Though they would surely have preferred to employ their considerable organizational skills among workers with a keener appreciation of the political implications of industrialized farming, both CAWIU organizers and district party leaders were forced to accept the fact that if agricultural unionism was to succeed in California, it would have to be on the workers' terms. As a result, the vigorous labor movement that the CAWIU led in 1933 was, despite the revolutionary clichés in which its appeals were sometimes couched, a remarkably conventional enterprise. The demands the union fought for were indistinguishable from those on which the conservative trade-union movement was built, and CAWIU leaders consistently resisted pressures exerted by party functionaries outside District 13 to force changes in the union's policy. It was not that CAWIU leaders were less devoted to Marxist tenets than their party critics, but rather that they had firsthand knowledge of the way farmworkers responded to political tutelage that they regarded as irrelevant to their lives. Whenever party members impatient with the union's conventional bread-and-butter orientation had endeavored to transform it into a more forceful political instrument, the workers, according to CAWIU secretary Caroline Decker, had simply "packed up and walked out."[125]

By 1934 CAWIU leaders found themselves caught between workers whose allegiance was conditioned upon the union's continued devotion to immediate economic goals and party officials, mainly in the East, who insisted that the union discharge its revolutionary obligations by giving proper emphasis to the previously neglected political aspects of its work.[126] In reviewing the most successful strikes led by the CAWIU during 1933, a leading architect of the Communist Party's agrarian program noted that while it was all well and good that higher wages had been won for thousands of farmworkers, the struggles must in the end be regarded as failures because they lacked true revolutionary significance. The essential function of the CAWIU was not to win strikes, but to politicize them "by teaching the workers . . . that it is not possible under capitalism to achieve any lasting improvement of their conditions."[127]

When the adoption of a new "line" caused the party to abandon its organizational work among farmworkers, the tension resulting from the conflicting demands made of the CAWIU was relieved in perhaps the only way it could have been. In the last analysis, it seems unlikely that the Communist Party, for all its fugitive success among California's agricultural proletariat, could ever have satisfied its own institutional desires through a liaison with workers so completely lacking in political rights and so thoroughly innocent of political instincts. While farmworkers had demonstrated an almost heroic capacity for economic struggle, given the enormous power arrayed against them, they were powerless to convert their economic gains into the political currency that was the preeminent medium of exchange in the New Deal era.

8

Passage to No Man's Land

From the middle of the nineteenth century, when the pattern of industrialized agriculture in California first began to take shape, until the mid-1930s, when the New Deal began to give programmatic expression to the reformist impulses of modern American liberalism, the predominating constant in the lives of those who worked for wages on the state's large-scale farms was their individual and collective powerlessness. Though it cannot have been much comfort to them, farmworkers were hardly alone in lacking control over their working lives. For millions of workers employed in the great mass-production industries that evolved as the nation rushed toward modernity, the ambience and physical setting of powerlessness were distinct from those familiar to California farmworkers, but no less real and compelling.

With the enactment of the National Industrial Recovery Act in 1933 and the exclusion of agricultural labor from the benefits it appeared to bestow, the long-standing community of powerlessness between farmworkers and industrial workers began to dissolve. Yet because the labor provisions embodied in Section 7(a) failed, for the most part, to confer effective rights of organization and collective bargaining, improvements in the status of industrial workers were more illusory than real.

In 1935, however, the previously parallel traditions of the country's rural and urban proletariats reached a point of abrupt divergence with the passage of the National Labor Relations Act. By enacting the NLRA the Democrat-controlled Seventy-fourth Congress not only acknowledged the failure of Section 7(a) to invest labor with effective rights, but also revealed a growing appreciation of both the actual and potential political power of industrial workers. The Congress was equally attuned to the prevailing political exigencies when it decreed that the body of workers who gained the protections and rights the new law provided "shall not include any individual employed as an agricultural laborer."

The decision to exclude farmworkers from the benefits of the NLRA was made behind closed doors and without a single voice having been raised in their defense. Significantly, when Senator Robert Wagner first introduced his labor bill early in 1934, its provisions extended to all private-sector wage earners. According to its preamble, the bill was prompted by a recognition of the fact that "the tendency of modern economic life toward integration and centralized control has long since destroyed the balance of bargaining power between the individual employer and the individual employee, and has rendered the individual, unorganized worker helpless to exercise actual liberty of contract, to secure a just reward for his services, and to preserve a decent standard of living, with consequent detriment to the general welfare and the free flow of commerce." The bill's goal was to remedy this imbalance of power in the workplace "by removing the obstacles which prevent the organization of labor for the purpose of cooperative action in maintaining its standard of living, by encouraging the equalization of the bargaining power of employers and employees, and by providing agencies for the peaceful settlement of disputes."[1]

That workers employed in industrialized agriculture suffered the effects of this imbalance of power, and thus were deserving of the protection and benefits the bill was to afford workers generally, was emphasized by William Leiserson, a labor-relations expert who testified in support of the proposed legislation during Senate hearings in March 1934. When asked if the legislation should apply to all employers, regardless of the number of workers employed, Leiserson replied, "You might want to except a small farmer with a few employees, but you certainly would not want to except him in a situation like the one you have out in the Imperial Valley now, with a great number of people working in agricultural employment."[2]

Though neither organization sent a representative to the Senate hearings to state its position openly, both the American Farm Bureau Federation and the National Grange filed statements with the Committee on Education and Labor in opposition to the inclusion of farmworkers under the Wagner Bill. The Farm Bureau, which emerged during the New Deal as the most powerful representative of the country's agricultural interests, took the position that it was "obviously not the intent of the sponsors of this legislation to have it apply to farm laborers, or to farm employers." And in what Chester Gray, the organization's chief lobbyist, portrayed as a friendly effort "to make more vivid the seeming intent of the measure," the Farm Bureau offered several "clarifying amendments" designed to transform its self-serving assumption into explicitly stated exclusions of farmworkers and farm employers from the bill's application. Apparently hoping to convince the committee of the Farm Bureau's helpful intentions, Gray wrote, "These amendments are presented not in the least to obstruct favorable consideration of the measure, and have no purpose to delay its consideration."[3]

The Grange, which represented family farmers rather than the labor-intensive agricultural enterprises that tended to support the Farm Bureau, argued that neither farm employers nor farmworkers could reasonably be compared to their industrial counterparts, and thus should be excluded from the purview of the proposed legislation. Couching its position in language distinctly less diplomatic than that of the Farm Bureau, the Grange, through its legislative representative, Fred Brenckman, asserted that it was "manifestly . . . absurd to place hired farm labor in the same category with the industrial labor, and to give the proposed national labor board jurisdiction over the farmer's hired help." Suggesting that the Grange had no fundamental objection to the bill's larger purposes once its own interests were safeguarded, Brenckman advised Senator David Walsh, "It is our conviction that the workability of the Wagner bill would be greatly improved if it were amended so as to exempt farm labor." Whatever concerns the public might have regarding the well-being of farmworkers, Brenckman insisted, could be alleviated if people kept in mind the timeless fact that the farm employer was ever "guided by the spirit of the Golden Rule in his dealings with those whom he employs."[4]

In the absence of political pressures to counter those exerted by organized farmers, the Wagner Bill was redrafted in committee to exclude agricultural workers.[5] And although the 1934 bill was ultimately sidetracked by the opposition of both business interests and the Roosevelt administration, the fate of farmworkers was sealed insofar as subsequent labor-relations legislation was concerned. When the Wagner Bill was reintroduced early in 1935, agricultural workers were excluded. When the Senate Committee on Education and Labor issued its report on the bill on May 1, it offered no explanation of the decision to exclude farmworkers other than a brief statement that for "administrative reasons" the committee had "deemed it wise" to pursue such a course.[6] The only opposition to the exclusion was voiced by Congressman Vito Marcantonio of New York, who argued eloquently in the minority report of the House Committee on Labor that it made no sense to deny farmworkers the benefits of the bill, since it was "a matter of plain fact that the worst conditions in the United States are the conditions among the agricultural workers." Reminding his colleagues of the "complete denial of civil liberty and the reign of terror in the Imperial Valley," Marcantonio stated that there was "not a single solitary reason why agricultural workers should not be included under the provisions of this bill. The same reasons urged for the adoption of this bill in behalf of the industrial workers are equally applicable in the case of the agricultural workers, in fact more so as their plight calls for immediate and prompt action."[7]

During the House debates that followed, Marcantonio reiterated his arguments and offered an amendment designed to include farmworkers. Representative William Connery, the chief sponsor of the bill in the House, noted that "the committee discussed this matter carefully in executive session and decided not to include agricultural workers." Assuring Marcantonio that the exclusion need not be regarded as permanent, Connery declared: "We hope that the agricultural workers eventually will be taken care of. I might say to my friend from New York at this point, certainly I am in favor of giving the agricultural workers every protection, but just now I believe in biting off one mouthful at a time. If we can get this bill through and working properly, there will be opportunity, and I hope soon, to take care of the agricultural workers."[8] Marcantonio's amendment was rejected on a voice vote, and the exclusion of farmworkers remained a feature of the National Labor Relations Act when it was signed into law by President Roosevelt on July 5, 1935.

In denying agricultural labor the same rights and protections extended to industrial workers under the NLRA, the Seventy-fourth Congress, which was to establish a reputation as perhaps the most liberal-minded in American history, began a process that transformed farmworkers in California, and in other states where labor-intensive farming flourished, into what was for all practical purposes a rural caste. For while the disadvantaged status of agricultural wage earners in the state was well established long before the New Deal's legislative program took shape, it was a product of irrational social and economic forces rather than a function of reasoned public policy. With the exclusion of agricultural workers from the NLRA and the subsequent explicit denials of equal protection to them under both the Social Security Act and the Fair Labor Standards Act, New Deal lawmakers effectively codified the traditional powerlessness of farm laborers.[9] And whether they intended to do so or not, they also legitimized a notion of agricultural exceptionalism that would serve for decades thereafter as an ideological rationale for denying farmworkers the rights afforded other workers and exempting farm employers from the responsibilities and constraints imposed on their industrial counterparts.

To the extent that the New Deal's legislative program was designed to rehabilitate and reform the economy by involving the federal government to an immensely greater degree in its future operation, the economic life of the country was necessarily politicized. For workers and farmers, two economic groups that had exercised disproportionately small degrees of political influence at the national level as long as business and industry were secure in their enormous economic power, the disintegration of the old order and the ascendancy of a reform administration acutely interested in fashioning a mass constituency created special opportunities to acquire the power that had previously eluded them. With an obvious premium on organization, each group endeavored, by consolidating and concentrating its existing political power, to develop its potential influence in Washington in order to advance special economic interests that had been little more than distant hopes before the New Deal era. And if the nationalist idealism that the Roosevelt administration embraced in 1933 was largely negated as organized farmers and workers successfully pursued the politics of self-interest, the changes in economic power relationships that their activism promoted represented a signal advance in the development of democratic pluralism in the United States.

Yet while the politicization of the economy proved advantageous to those groups capable of organization, and thus of commanding the attention of a politically sensitive federal government, it tended to exacerbate the plight of groups that lacked an equal capacity to advance and protect their interests through the same process of political brokerage. Certainly the situation of California farmworkers was aggravated rather than improved as the Roosevelt administration gravitated toward a policy of distributing the benefits of economic reform on the basis of an interest group's ability to command favorable consideration by applying political leverage. Completely incapable of amassing the political influence necessary to counter the pressures exerted by agricultural interests and isolated from the urban labor movement, agricultural workers were vulnerable not only to the private power that had always oppressed them, but now also to the public power that the federal government indirectly placed at the disposal of their economic antagonists by denying farmworkers equal protection under the NLRA and other labor legislation.

The special irony of the situation was that while the Roosevelt admin-

An example of the kind of migrant camp that the State Emergency Relief Administration found throughout the San Joaquin Valley during the 1935 harvest season. Photo: Bancroft Library, University of California, Berkeley.

A tattered tent and an old Ford: symbols of the migrants' existence within California's agribusiness economy (San Joaquin Valley, 1935). Photo: Bancroft Library, University of California, Berkeley.

A small community of migrants camping in the San Joaquin Valley during the 1935 harvest season. Photo: Bancroft Library, University of California, Berkeley.

A migrant family making do in industrialized agriculture (San Joaquin Valley, 1935). Photo: Bancroft Library, University of California, Berkeley.

Dust Bowl migrants at home in the San Joaquin Valley (1935). Photo: Bancroft Library, University of California, Berkeley.

Cardboard and mud structure housing a migrant family in the San Joaquin Valley during the 1935 harvest season. Photo: Bancroft Library, University of California, Berkeley.

Dust Bowl migrants enjoying a baseball game at the Farm Security Administration's model camp at Tulare (1940). Photo: Bancroft Library, University of California, Berkeley.

istration's legislative record suggested a nearly complete lack of concern for agricultural workers' well-being, there was in fact fairly widespread sympathy for farmworkers within the ranks of New Dealers. The constant dilemma confronting those in the administration who were eager to help farmworkers was to figure out how to render assistance without offending the political sensibilities of powerful agricultural interests. And no matter how ardent their desire to improve the miserable conditions under which they knew farmworkers lived and worked, even the most sympathetic New Dealers were usually constrained by the knowledge that it was, as one discouraged official noted, "politically fatal to take up the question of these workers in the fields."[10]

To the extent that such federal agencies as the Resettlement Administration and later the Farm Security Administration did seek to assist agricultural wage earners between 1935 and the beginning of World War II, it was to relieve the most visible symptoms of their powerlessness rather than to alter the one-sided relationship between them and their employers. The federal labor-camp program designed to provide housing for the tens of thousands of Dust Bowl migrants who entered California during the latter half of the 1930s typified the Roosevelt administration's essentially conservative approach to the problems of agricultural labor in the state. While they largely ignored the equally desperate living conditions of the nonwhite workers who had long constituted a majority of the state's farm-labor force, and who continued to provide much, if not most, of the labor power on which industrialized agriculture depended throughout the late 1930s, the well-intentioned officials responsible for launching the modest camp program were motivated by a sincere desire to afford recent migrants minimally decent housing conditions.[11] Despite their great popularity among the migrant families who inhabited them,[12] however, the dozen or so labor camps being operated by the Farm Security Administration by 1941 actually represented an indirect subsidy to farm employers, whose responsibility to provide either decent housing or wages high enough to support a decent living standard was relieved as long as the federal government was willing to foot the bill for housing thousands of farmworkers in leading agricultural districts throughout the state.[13]

Yet if the labor-camp program tended to aid industrialized agriculture as much as migratory workers, there is no evidence to suggest that federal authorities intended such an effect. In contrast, an equal degree of inadvertence cannot be attributed to other important federal programs that served the interests of farm employers at a high cost to farmworkers. The U.S. Farm Placement Service, an agency of the Department of Labor, functioned as a virtual adjunct of such powerful employer organizations as the Agricultural Labor Bureau of the San Joaquin Valley and the Associated Farmers. W. V. Allen, the Farm Placement Service's director in California, had personal financial ties to industrialized agriculture, and consistently managed his agency in ways calculated to keep wages low by ensuring that the supply of agricultural labor was always well in excess of demand. And though organizations friendly to farmworkers regularly demanded that the Department of Labor force the Farm Placement Service to abandon its blatantly pro-employer policies, the operative argument that it was "politically fatal" to act on behalf of farmworkers' interests was apparently sufficient to dissuade Labor Department officials from introducing reforms.[14]

The political faintheartedness of New Dealers revealed itself with even more hurtful consequences to agricultural workers when it came to the administration of federal relief policies in the state. No policy of the Roosevelt administration in 1933 had generated greater resentment among California farm employers than that governing the distribution of federal relief. Under the supervision of Harry Hopkins, the Federal Emergency Relief Administration recognized need as the essential determinant of eligibility. Almost immediately farm employers objected that federal relief payments were so generous and readily provided that they were undermining both the wage structure and the labor-market conditions on which industrialized agriculture depended. Even more galling to employers was the FERA's reluctance to force workers off the relief rolls at harvesttime as long as agricultural wages in the state were maintained at the same levels that prevailed in 1932. It was the government's decision to extend relief to strikers during the cotton strike, however, that prompted outraged agricultural interests to launch an all-out political agitation against FERA policies.[15]

As local officials assumed an increasingly important role in the administration of federal relief during 1934, farm employers were able to exercise considerable influence on behalf of their own interests in those counties dominated by large-scale agriculture.[16] When the FERA transferred responsibility for the handling of direct relief to the State Emergency Relief Administration in 1935, the Associated Farmers quickly persuaded compliant state officials to adopt relief guidelines that buttressed the wage and employment policies of industrialized agriculture.[17] Yet with the creation of the Works Progress Administration and the emergence of work relief as the principal form of federal assistance to needy workers, farm employers were immediately faced with a new political challenge. As they soon discovered, however, the Roosevelt administration was by 1935 much less reluctant to compromise its relief policies than it had been two years earlier. Agribusinessmen found WPA administrators in the state very sympathetic to the needs of farm employers, and entirely willing, as an intermediary informed the Los Angeles Chamber of Commerce late in 1935, to make "a definite ruling that workers are to be released [from work relief] when needed for private employment, regardless of the probable lower wage scale on the farm."[18] As a result of this policy, which remained in force throughout the late 1930s, farmworkers were regularly forced off federal work relief projects that afforded them relatively high, if still inadequate, wages in order to satisfy the seasonal labor requirements of the state's farm employers. The WPA's accommodating disposition proved beneficial to both farm employers and the Roosevelt administration. The former were able to maintain their low-wage structure, and the latter was able to avoid accumulating an added political liability. Not surprisingly, the only losers turned out to be politically powerless California farmworkers, who were, as a confidential report by the Farm Security Administration noted, often forced to accept farm wages that were "so low that it was almost criminal to send the men out."[19]

If farmworkers in California had ever embraced the faith spread far and wide by New Deal apostles that the Roosevelt administration was a government for the "little man" and the "underdog," the mistreatment and neglect they suffered at the hands of politically motivated federal officials throughout the late 1930s plainly did more to promote apostasy and cynicism in their ranks than to sustain and fortify whatever devotion they had earlier professed. Yet perhaps the most compelling evidence that farmworkers were a forsaken class derived from the ultimate disinclination of the industrial labor movement, which was rising to unprecedented heights of power in the late 1930s, to regard the organization of agricultural labor as an important objective.

Had the urban labor movement made an all-out effort to organize farmworkers, it is by no means certain that its exertions would have produced positive results. Indeed, the problems associated with farmworker organization in California were probably greater after 1935 than they had been earlier. With the emergence of the Associated Farmers, agricultural interests were better equipped to resist unionism, and the entry of tens of thousands of Dust Bowl migrants into the farm-labor force not only created new racial barriers to solidarity, but also greatly aggravated the special organizational problems resulting from surplus labor-market conditions. Finally, the exclusion of agricultural workers from the provisions of the NLRA enabled farm employers to use union-busting tactics that the law expressly banned in other industries.

In the end, however, the question of the labor movement's ability to meet the exceedingly difficult challenge of farmworker organization in California remained unresolved for the simple reason that it was never seriously addressed. When the beleaguered Cannery and Agricultural Workers Industrial Union abandoned its independent organizational efforts in 1934, its Communist leaders sought to implement the "popular front" mandate of the Communist International by organizing agricultural labor under the auspices of the American Federation of Labor. Between 1935 and 1937, the A.F. of L. issued several federal charters to small unions claiming to represent agricultural workers. While some of those unions actually had small memberships, many others were paper organizations created by Communists in the hope of establishing footholds in the federation. The larger goal of Communist organizers was to enlist the support of the California State Federation of Labor in a campaign to establish a statewide industrial union whose jurisdiction would extend to cannery and packing-shed labor as well as to farmworkers. This goal was consistent with the strategy of the Communist Party nationally, which revealed itself in repeated attempts between 1934 and 1936 to persuade the A.F. of L. to issue an international charter providing organizational jurisdiction over agricultural, cannery, and packing-shed workers.[20]

The party's efforts at the national level got them nowhere. The conservative, craft-oriented leaders of the A.F. of L. were engaged in a bitter struggle to hold back the rising tide of industrial unionism during the mid-1930s, and they looked no more favorably on a vertically organized union in agriculture than on one in steel or autos.[21] In California Communists experienced little trouble in selling the idea of a statewide agricultural, cannery, and packing-shed workers' union at the grass-roots level, even among those laborers organized in such ethnic unions as the Confederación de Uniones de Campesinos y Obreros Mexicanos. But persuading the conservative leadership of the State Federation of Labor to support the idea proved impossible.

Both Edward Vandeleur, secretary of the state federation, and Paul Scharrenberg, its former secretary, strongly opposed farmworker organization because they believed that unions of migratory workers could not be established on a permanent and financially self-sufficient basis and because they had no desire to jeopardize the generally amicable relations that existed between organized labor and agricultural interests in the state. Each man gave private assurances to leaders of the Associated Farmers that the A.F. of L. had no interest in organizing farm-workers, and pledged the federation's cooperation with farm employers in their drive to combat those whose ambition to build rural unions defined them as "radicals" in the minds of conservative craft unionists and agribusinessmen alike. In mid-1934, when a delegation from the Associated Farmers called on Paul Scharrenberg to ask where the A.F. of L. stood on the question of farmworker organization, he reportedly replied:

> The American Federation of Labor has spent a considerable sum of money during the past years in attempting to organize agricultural laborers. In my opinion, it cannot be successfully done. May I offer you the full cooperation of the American Federation of Labor in opposition to the subversive wave that is sweeping over California? For the first time in the history of labor in California farmers have come to us with a clean bill of health and have laid their cards on the table. I appreciate tremendously your coming and I want to have you know that you have our full cooperation in your opposition to this situation which is becoming so dangerous in California.[22]

The depth of Scharrenberg's personal antipathy toward agricultural unionism was even more emphatically revealed in his offhand statement to a newspaper reporter in 1935: "Only fanatics are willing to live in shacks or tents and get their heads broken in the interest of migratory labor."[23]

Despite their personal opposition to the state federation's involvement in a campaign to build a statewide agricultural, cannery, and packing-shed workers' union, Vandeleur, Scharrenberg, and other hidebound craft unionists were finally forced to make a number of concessions to the loose coalition of Communists, Socialists, and liberals who were championing the idea. When representatives of several A.F. of L. and independent ethnic unions met in June 1936 to discuss the formation of a vertically structured union that could serve the organizational needs of workers in agriculture and allied industries, Vandeleur reluctantly endorsed the endeavor.[24] But he gave private assurances to anxious leaders of the Associated Farmers that the State Federation of Labor would not lend its resources and energies to the advancement of the conference's impelling purpose.[25]

The June conference, which took place in Stockton in an atmosphere charged with enthusiasm and punctuated by militant professions of organizational intent, gave its unequivocal endorsement to the proposition that an industrial union with statewide jurisdiction offered the only certain means of remedying the collective powerlessness of agricultural, cannery, and packing-shed workers. "The organization of agricultural workers," the convention report declared,

> shall be state-wide in character, comprising all workers in the cannery and agricultural industry, based on the principles enunciated by the A.F. of L. The ultimate object is declared to be to get all the affiliated unions into the ranks of the American Federation of Labor. As soon as feasible, a convention of all agricultural workers locals in the country shall be called, which convention shall make application to the A.F. of L. for an international charter.[26]

Though Vandeleur refused to take part in its deliberations, he made a curt opening statement that left little doubt as to where the leadership of the state federation stood in regard to the convention's essential aim. Having earlier promised leaders of the Associated Farmers that he "would talk 'right' "[27] when he addressed the conference, Vandeleur bluntly stated:

> I want to call your attention to the position of the American Federation of Labor. It is our belief and desire that the agricultural workers should be organized, but I mean into *bona fide* labor unions under the banners of the American Federation of Labor and the California State Federation of Labor. The A.F. of L. and the State Federation of Labor will not for one moment tolerate any other type of organization. With the desire to better the conditions of the workers, you will find us with you, but if it comes to a question of a few who are not satisfied and expect the Federation of Labor to follow them, you are going to be mistaken.[28]

Less than three weeks after the close of the conference Vandeleur gave a further indication of the state federation's hostility toward an activist farm-labor movement by demanding the resignation of Julius Nathan, a militant but noncommunist A.F. of L. organizer for whom farm employers had developed an especially deep enmity. Apparently aware of the employers' intense dislike for Nathan, Vandeleur reportedly informed a representative of the Associated Farmers, "You need not fear Nathan any more. We have asked him to resign, not because he had anything to resign from because we never invited him to get into this movement. But he has been told to quit his activities. We don't want him with us."[29]

With radical activists determined to establish a statewide union that

275

would provide a strong organizational link between farm labor and those workers employed in canneries and packing sheds, and conservative A.F. of L. leaders just as determined to uphold the rigid craft principles on which the federation was founded, a break became unavoidable. It came in the spring of 1937, when the leadership of the state federation flatly rejected a widely supported plan calling for a statewide organizing drive by an integrated agricultural and cannery workers' union.[30] Encouraged by Harry Bridges, whose militantly left-wing International Longshoremen and Warehousemen's Union (ILWU) was itself locked in a bitter struggle with state A.F. of L. leaders over the issue of industrial unionism, disgruntled radical activists representing federation locals and independent ethnic unions met in April to found the California Federation of Agricultural and Cannery Unions. This organization, dominated by veterans of the CAWIU and other Communist-led unions, immediately pledged itself to undertake the comprehensive organizing campaign that the state federation had rejected.[31]

While the insurgents had originally hoped to circumvent the State Federation of Labor and appeal for recognition and financial support directly to the national leadership of the A.F. of L., they quickly opted for a complete break with the federation when the rival Committee for Industrial Organization announced in the spring of 1937 that it intended to sponsor a nationwide organizing campaign among workers in agriculture and allied industries. The CIO's decision to expand its operation from the mass-production industries, where it had just achieved stunning victories in steel and autos, was apparently made as a result of Harry Bridges's success in persuading CIO chief John L. Lewis that agricultural and cannery workers in California were ripe for organization.[32]

In championing the organization of agricultural and cannery workers, Bridges was simply widening the battle front of a bitter jurisdictional war that had begun in 1936 when the ILWU proposed an ambitious "march inland" to organize all workers who contributed their labor to the production, processing, packaging, handling, and transporting of the products that moved across the docks of the state's unionized ports. Since agricultural products were among California's leading exports, Bridges's plan projected the organization of a chain of workers stretching all the way from inland warehouses, canneries, and packing sheds to the fields and orchards of the state's industrialized farms. Given the already deep division between left-wing and conservative factions within the State Federation of Labor, the ILWU's proposed drive inland elicited a predictably hostile reaction from those

A.F. of L. officials who had grown increasingly distrustful of Bridges as his pro-CIO sympathies became more overt. And when leaders of the International Brotherhood of Teamsters claimed that the new jurisdiction that Bridges was trying to carve out for his Maritime Federation of the Pacific was rightfully theirs, the A.F. of L. executive council promptly awarded them the exclusive right to organize warehouses in the state's interior.[33] Committed to industrial unionism and ideologically estranged from the conservative mainstream of the A.F. of L., Bridges led the unions comprising the Maritime Federation of the Pacific out of the A.F. of L. in 1937 and affiliated with the burgeoning CIO. Not surprisingly, the generally radical leaders of the agricultural labor movement in the state immediately followed suit.[34]

The new organization that became the steward of CIO efforts in California to organize workers in agriculture and allied industries was the United Cannery, Agricultural, Packing and Allied Workers of America (UCAPAWA), founded in July 1937 at a national convention of agricultural and cannery workers held in Denver.[35] With the movement of the CIO into agriculture, the likelihood of successful farmworker organization in California appeared greater than it ever had before. So quickly had the CIO's reputation for organizational accomplishment grown during the early months of 1937 that even before the UCAPAWA was officially chartered, some observers were forecasting the thorough organization of workers employed in industrialized agriculture. In apparent anticipation of the CIO's success on the farm, Secretary of Agriculture Henry Wallace sought in June 1937 to develop a plan to minimize the conflict that an activist agricultural labor movement was likely to generate. In a letter to Secretary of Labor Frances Perkins, Wallace wrote: "It would be highly desirable if the incipient new development in labor organization among farm workers could profit by the experiences of the past so that it would not be necessary to go through many of the mistakes and many of the time-consuming conflicts and controversies that have characterized the development of organizations among industrial employees."[36] Some officials of the U.S. Conciliation Service appear to have shared Wallace's view that the CIO was destined to achieve unprecedented organizational success among farmworkers, and thus to escalate the level of economic conflict affecting labor relations in agriculture. One Conciliation Service field investigator advised John Steelman, its director, that there was an urgent need to make "preparations . . . in order more completely to meet the conciliation problems which circumstances may thrust on us soon."[37]

In California, where the conflict between A.F. of L. and CIO factions in agriculture was well advanced by the time of the UCAPAWA's founding, farm unionists and agribusinessmen alike expressed the belief that an organizing campaign of unparalleled intensity was on the horizon.[38] The Associated Farmers warned its members in August 1937 that the CIO was "rapidly expanding its organizational campaign," and that "agricultural labor is being organized faster than it ever has been." Betraying a distinct note of anxiety, the organization's secretary advised farm employers throughout the state that the CIO posed an extreme danger to their continued control of labor relations. "We state without fear of honest contradiction," he wrote, "that the situation is serious—more serious than is realized. WE MUST ACT—AND ACT QUICKLY. All of California agriculture must be effectively organized to combat this Communist menace."[39] In a subsequent warning, the Associated Farmers nervously declared: "The watch-ward now is: 'Look out for the C.I.O.' so far as field labor is concerned. We find the C.I.O. very active all over California, in fact there is more agitation by them now than there ever has been by any organization at any time in the fields and orchards of the state."[40] Blaming the new CIO "menace" in agriculture on Harry Bridges, whom he described as "the worst enemy California has had in modern times," Colonel Walter Garrison, president of the Associated Farmers, assured Frances Perkins, "Farmers of California will never surrender to the organization of their workers under the dictation of this communistic alien." Secretary Perkins should, Garrison advised, order the "immediate deportation of this communistic disrupter."[41]

In view of the conspicuous presence of UCAPAWA organizers in the principal farming districts of the state during the latter half of 1937, and the verbal zealousness that infused their organizational activities, the concern that farm employers expressed was understandable. In fact, they had much less cause for concern than immediate circumstances suggested. While the idea of one all-encompassing union of agricultural, cannery, and packing-shed workers plainly had much to commend it as an organizational paradigm, the practical consequence of lumping farmworkers together with cannery and packing-shed workers was to ensure that the former, whose organization posed enormous challenges, would be neglected in favor of the latter, whose unionization, though by no means an easy task, was a less formidable undertaking.

The leadership of the UCAPAWA, which was dominated by Communists who were intimately familiar with the earlier organizational tribulations of the CAWIU, was inclined from the first to concentrate the union's organizing efforts among cannery and packing-shed workers, who, unlike farmworkers, were overwhelmingly nonmigratory, able to afford modest union dues, and eligible to claim the rights and protections afforded by the National Labor Relations Act. The UCAPAWA's unlikely president, Donald Henderson, an unfrocked economics lecturer at Columbia University whose grasp of the farm-labor situation tended to be more intellectual than experiential, had expressed the view in 1936 that cannery and packing-shed workers were clearly superior to farmworkers as organizing material. Writing in the *Rural Worker,* a publication he edited, Henderson argued that the inability of the CAWIU "to develop a stable organization" was due to its preoccupation with "migratory field workers" and its resultant failure "to concentrate sufficiently on the more regularly employed and higher-paid workers who would have supplied a more stable group for permanent organization."[42] Reflecting Henderson's orientation, the UCAPAWA immediately assigned the organization of farmworkers a lower priority than the organization of workers employed in canneries, packing-sheds, and other industries allied to agriculture.[43]

In California the shift away from farmworkers and toward cannery and packing-shed labor was evident in the organizational agenda of radical unionists well before the UCAPAWA emerged to give its formal endorsement to the strategy. And as the emphasis and focus changed, conservative A.F. of L. loyalists who had disdained farmworker organization quickly acted to protect their largely unexercised jurisdictional claims over cannery and packing-shed workers.[44] The A.F. of L.'s most important allies in its jurisdictional contest with pro-CIO insurgents during the spring of 1937 were employers in the canning and packing industries, many of whom had resigned themselves to the unionization of their employees and believed that the federation was the lesser of two evils. The cooperative nature of the relationship that blossomed between A.F. of L. conservatives and cannery owners was revealed with particular clarity during a strike launched by radicals operating under a federation charter against several major canneries in Stockton in April 1937. With the assistance of several hundred vigilantes provided by the Associated Farmers, the affected employers initially adopted a variety of violent tactics to break the strike. Their strategy changed abruptly, however, when the State Federation of Labor suddenly declared the strike illegal. At once employers who had earlier pledged their allegiance to the principle of the open shop entered into negotiations with Edward Vandeleur to fashion a "master contract" that recognized the State Federation of Labor as the exclusive bargaining agent for their employees.[45] Eager to press their advantage following the Stockton victory, A.F. of L. conservatives began an all-out assault on radical-controlled agricultural and cannery workers' locals, while simultaneously entering into new working agreements with cannery owners throughout Northern California. By the fall of 1937, newly chartered A.F. of L. locals, which were little more than company unions, had bargaining rights covering approximately 60,000 cannery workers. Though vilified by their critics as "sell-out" artists and "labor fakirs," Vandeleur and his followers were nevertheless firmly entrenched in the state's canning industry. And with employers determined to maintain their "most favored union" policy, a successful challenge to the A.F. of L.'s control became a virtual impossibility.[46]

Despite the heavy odds against them, UCAPAWA organizers in District 2, which included California, tried during the summer and fall of 1937 to gain the foothold among cannery workers which union strategists had decided was the key to organizing the entire agribusiness complex in the state. With few exceptions their efforts failed miserably. To the extent that cannery and packing-shed employees were working under union contracts at the end of 1937, they were represented almost exclusively by A.F. of L. unions. And though the UCAPAWA stubbornly persisted in its organizing efforts during 1938 and 1939, its position remained conspicuously precarious while that of the A.F. of L. grew more secure.[47]

Rather than convincing UCAPAWA leaders that the energy and resources expended in the drive to organize cannery workers might be more profitably employed in the cause of farmworker organization, a field in which competition from the A.F. of L. was virtually nonexistent, the failure of their organizational strategy tended to reduce their already less than ardent interest in agricultural labor to a level approaching indifference. For the most part, the union's involvement among the state's farmworkers between 1937 and 1940 went no further than what was required to lend a minimal degree of credibility to its activist rhetoric. To the degree that the UCAPAWA took part in the many strikes that the state's farmworkers were involved in during the late 1930s, it was usually in response to pleas for assistance from unorganized workers who had struck spontaneously out of sheer desperation.[48] Most such strikes ended in total defeat, although even when they resulted in slight improvements in wages or conditions, they produced nothing in the way of an organizational legacy.[49] Union leaders seem to have concluded by the end of 1938 that even this modest involvement might be too much. In November the leadership of District 2 decreed that the UCAPAWA would avoid further involvement in spontaneous strikes unless an investigation by union officials disclosed that the potential organizational benefits of intervention were great enough to justify the probable costs.[50] In the absence of a policy that established farmworker organization as its foremost objective, the practical effect of the union's decision was to isolate agricultural wage earners even further from the CIO and the broadening mainstream of the American labor movement.

For all its success in stirring up the state's agribusiness community and fueling the reactionary machinations of the Associated Farmers, the UCAPAWA, when it quietly took leave of California's fields and orchards in 1940, left farmworkers as powerless as it had found them. From time to time the union had assisted thousands of unorganized workers to prosecute spontaneous strikes, but its membership figures documented a pathetically weak organizational record. At the end of 1937 the Farm Security Administration estimated that about 3,000 farmworkers in California held membership in UCAPAWA locals.[51] Toward the end of 1939 the union officially estimated that in California and Arizona combined its total farmworker membership amounted to no more than 2,500 to 3,000.[52]

Despite repeated assertions to the contrary, the CIO appears to have shared the opinion of the A.F. of L. that trying to organize California farmworkers was simply more trouble than it was worth. No matter how emphatically and regularly CIO leaders reiterated their conviction that in the long run farmworkers would enjoy an equal place in the organization's councils, their neglect of agricultural labor in the short run virtually guaranteed that there would never be a long run.

In the end, the CIO adopted the view, long held by the A.F. of L., that agricultural workers did not constitute a labor problem as much as a social problem.[53] As UCAPAWA president Donald Henderson suggested to delegates attending the 1939 convention of the CIO in San Francisco, the disadvantaged status of those employed on California's industrialized farms had to be recognized as more than "just a trade-union organizational problem." The powerlessness and degradation that attended the lives of the state's farmworkers were symptomatic, he said, of "a fundamental, deep-lying, widespread social problem, that goes right to the roots of our whole social system here."[54] Consistent with that emphasis, the resolution on agricultural labor adopted by the convention consigned responsibility for dealing with the farmworker "problem" not to union organizers, but to the federal government and the "public conscience."[55]

Had an awareness of the agricultural labor "problem" and a sense of moral obligation been the only absolute prerequisites to federal action, important steps might well have been taken during the late 1930s to alleviate the chronic powerlessness of farmworkers in California, and in the nation generally. The disadvantaged condition of agricultural workers had prompted sincere expressions of concern in various precincts throughout the federal bureaucracy. And in a few New Deal agencies, most notably the Farm Security Administration, that concern manifested itself in modest efforts to relieve some of the most visible symptoms of distress among farmworkers.

For the most part, however, an impenetrable political force field kept New Dealers sympathetic to the plight of farm labor from acting on their concerns. When a group of middle-level officials scattered throughout the Agriculture and Labor departments joined forces following the 1936 election to explore ways in which the federal government might bring greater equality to bargaining relationships in industrialized agriculture, they found that translating their intentions into policy was a politically impossible enterprise.[56] After nearly three years of discussion, this group, frustrated by the Roosevelt administration's studied neglect of agricultural labor, declared that "it was time to stop talking and do things." Convinced that the Department of Agriculture, which had nominal authority over farm-labor policy, was unlikely ever to act because of a well-conditioned fear of "stepping on the toes of its clients—the farmers, the entrepreneurs," the group agreed that needed reforms would not be achieved until a successful effort was made to "dramatize the plight of the agricultural laborer." Concluding that the "arousal of public concern is a necessary prelude to action," they expressed the hope that something would happen to bring "the agricultural laborer . . . into the limelight."[57]

The notion that the powerlessness and misery of agricultural workers would somehow be ameliorated once the American people understood that there was a degraded and mistreated class in their midst expressed an abiding faith in the common man's sense of justice. Yet while it was a hopeful idea, it was wrong. The powerlessness of agricultural wage earners was not a product of public ignorance, but of the political and economic power of organized agribusiness interests. Had public awareness of the California farmworker's plight been enough to spur a serious reform movement, labor relations in the state's industrialized agriculture ought to have experienced a full-scale reformation by the end of the 1930s. For while agricultural wage earners and their collective plight were indeed virtually invisible to the public eye before the

1930s, they achieved enough visibility during the New Deal era to put them in the line of sight of all Americans except those determined not to see the less happy and egalitarian facets of the national estate.

In addition to the visibility conferred on the farmworker's plight as a result of the unprecedented conflict that attended agricultural labor relations in California from 1933 to the end of the decade, several other developments focused attention on the disadvantaged condition of farm laborers. The entry of tens of thousands of white migrants into California's farm-labor force during the Dust Bowl years led to exposures of working and living conditions that genuinely shocked and dismayed a public that had been largely indifferent to the suffering of brown, yellow, and black farmworkers caught in the same web of misfortune. With the publication in 1939 of *The Grapes of Wrath,* John Steinbeck's all too realistic novel of human erosion, Americans were confronted not only with a disturbing chronicle of the white migrant's Depression odyssey, but with a damning indictment of the abusive labor policies that prevailed in California's industrialized agriculture.[58] And though it enjoyed a smaller readership than *The Grapes of Wrath,* Carey McWilliams's *Factories in the Field,* also published in 1939, provided conclusive evidence that California's industrialized agriculture bore only a superficial resemblance to the family farming with which most Americans were familiar. Finally, the plight of agricultural labor in California was widely publicized throughout the nation as a result of extensive public hearings conducted at the end of 1939 by Senator Robert La Follette's subcommittee of the Senate Committee on Education and Labor. Authorized to investigate violations of labor's civil and constitutional rights, the La Follette Committee discovered a veritable mother lode of abuses when it inquired into the labor practices of the state's leading farm employers.[59] Drawing the only conclusion possible from the extraordinary picture that emerged from its hearings and investigations, the committee reported that "the economic and social plight of California's agricultural labor is miserable beyond belief."[60]

Yet as successful as these and other efforts were in bringing the disadvantaged status of agricultural workers to the attention of the American people, they failed to stimulate a public clamor for governmental actions that might have introduced more equity into the relationship between farmworkers and their employers. To illuminate social and economic injustice was not to redress it, and the power of agribusiness in California was in little danger of being diminished as a consequence of simply having been brought to the public's attention. Lecturing the ardent young reformers who comprised the staff of the La

Follette Committee on the limitations of moral outrage as a force for change, Senator Elbert Thomas expressed the unhappy truth that the agribusiness complex in California was an "empire" whose "impregnability" was not fully appreciated by those who believed that public exposure of the human degradation in which it trafficked would somehow guarantee reform. "It is traditional in the West," Thomas said, "and is so much an ingrained habit that nothing this committee could say would even scratch that empire."[61]

Certainly there was little in the experience of California farmworkers during the New Deal era to suggest that Thomas's pessimism was unwarranted. Whatever the advantages that ultimately accrued to the majority of American workers as a result of the legislative accomplishments of New Deal liberalism, the spirit of reform left little in the way of a positive imprint on the lives of those who worked for wages in agriculture. Farmworkers in California were poor, uprooted, and powerless people long before Franklin Roosevelt's voice crackled over the radio imploring middle America to have courage in the face of depression and promising a new order of prosperity and economic justice in the days and years ahead. And they were no less poor, uprooted, and powerless after the reformist enthusiasm of the New Deal had waned and the attention of the nation had shifted from domestic to foreign affairs.

Because the Roosevelt administration found it politically expedient to embrace the fiction urged upon it by agribusiness interests that farm employers were not really employers in the industrial sense, the New Deal era witnessed the exile of farmworkers to what Secretary of Agriculture Henry Wallace described in 1936 as a "no man's land."[62] It was a special category whose convenience was appreciated by those organized groups that profited by rationalizing the continuing powerlessness of agricultural labor. For reasons pertinent to the maintenance of their own power, agribusiness, the Roosevelt administration, and the labor movement each saw special advantages in defining the status of agricultural wage earners in a way that denied them their rightful place as full-fledged members of the working class. The effect of adding this new dimension to the powerlessness of farmworkers was not immediately clear. Not until a generation later, when agricultural laborers in California once again took up the struggle against their powerlessness, would it become apparent that reclaiming their collective identity as authentic workers was at once their most urgent challenge and their brightest hope for the future.

In the end, the triumph or failure of the liberal reform movement that manifested itself in the ideas and actions of progressives and New Dealers cannot be judged by its impact or lack of impact on California farmworkers. Plainly, criteria more general and central to the national experience must be used in judging so large and complex an undertaking. What can be fairly said of a political movement that conditioned reform on the power of an aggrieved class to compel ameliorative action is that it was inherently incapable of responding to the distress of a group whose powerlessness was so profound and engulfing as to have become at once the cause and effect of its wretchedness.

Notes

1. *The Erosion of Agrarian Idealism*

1. Adrienne Koch and William Peden, eds., *The Life and Selected Writings of Thomas Jefferson* (New York: Modern Library, 1944), p. 280.

2. Adrienne Koch, *Jefferson and Madison: The Great Collaboration* (New York: Alfred A. Knopf, 1950), pp. 132–33. See also A. Whitney Griswold, *Farming and Democracy* (New Haven: Yale University Press, 1952), pp. 18–46, and "The Agrarian Democracy of Thomas Jefferson," *American Political Science Review* 11 (August 1946):657–81; John M. Brewster, "Perpetuating the Agrarian Dream," in *Land Use Policy and Problems,* ed. Howard W. Ottoson (Lincoln: University of Nebraska Press, 1963), pp. 86–92.

3. Thomas Jefferson to John Jay, August 23, 1785; Jefferson to James Madison, December 20, 1787; Jefferson to Jean Baptiste Say, February 1, 1804, all in *Life and Selected Writings,* ed. Koch and Peden, pp. 377–78, 436–41, 574–75; Carl Becker, "What Is Still Living in the Political Philosophy of Thomas Jefferson?," *Proceedings of the American Philosophical Society* 87 (1944):201–10; Koch, *Jefferson and Madison,* p. 133. See also Regional Oral History Office, "Paul Schuster Taylor: California Social Scientist," Earl Warren Oral History Project, Bancroft Library, University of California (Berkeley, 1975), 2:69–70 (hereafter cited as Taylor interview).

4. Quoted in testimony of Paul S. Taylor in U.S. Congress, Senate, Subcommittee of the Committee on Education and Labor, *Hearings on S. Res. 266, Violations of Free Speech and Rights of Labor,* 74th Cong., 2d sess. (Washington, D.C.: Government Printing Office, 1939), pt. 47, p. 17280 (hereafter cited as La Follette Committee, *Hearings*).

5. Gilbert C. Fite, *The Farmers' Frontier, 1865–1900* (New York: Holt, Rinehart & Winston, 1966), pp. 15–21.

6. *Report of the Commission on Country Life* (New York: Sturgis & Walton, 1917), pp. 91–92.

7. Ibid., pp. 59–62.

8. California State Agricultural Society, *Transactions, 1888* (Sacramento, 1889), p. 449 (hereafter cited as CSAS, *Transactions,* followed by the date).

9. Taylor interview, 1:58. See also Paul W. Gates, "The Homestead Law in an Incongruous Land System," *American Historical Review* 41 (July 1936): 652–81.

10. Hubert Howe Bancroft, *History of California* (San Francisco: History Company, 1890), 7:5.

11. Ibid.

12. M. R. Benedict, "The Economic and Social Structure of California Agriculture," in *California Agriculture*, ed. Claude B. Hutchison (Berkeley: University of California Press, 1946), p. 397.

13. CSAS, *Transactions, 1864–1865*, pp. 184–85.

14. Ibid., p. 185.

15. CSAS, *Transactions, 1868–1869*, p. 161.

16. Warren P. Tufts and others, "The Rich Pattern of California Crops," in *California Agriculture*, ed. Hutchison, p. 114.

17. CSAS, *Transactions, 1888*, p. 451. See also Rodman W. Paul, "The Great California Grain War: The Grangers Challenge the Wheat King," *Pacific Historical Review* 27 (November 1958): 331–49.

18. CSAS, *Transactions, 1886*, p. 194.

19. CSAS, *Transactions, 1880*, p. 231.

20. Ibid.

21. CSAS, *Transactions, 1886*, p. 189. Also see *Transactions, 1870–1871*, 82–85.

22. CSAS, *Transactions, 1874*, p. 201.

23. CSAS, *Transactions, 1886*, pp. 193–94. For an earlier expression of the same sentiment, see *Transactions, 1870–1871*, pp. 84–85.

24. CSAS, *Transactions, 1886*, p. 194.

25. CSAS, *Transactions, 1887*, p. 738. See also John Lee Coulter, "Agricultural Laborers in the United States," *Annals of the American Academy of Political and Social Science* 40 (March 1912):43–44.

26. CSAS, *Transactions, 1880*, p. 230.

27. CSAS, *Transactions, 1886*, p. 201.

28. Frank Adams, "The Historical Background of California Agriculture," in *California Agriculture*, ed. Hutchinson, pp. 41–42.

29. Varden Fuller, "The Supply of Agricultural Labor as a Factor in the Evolution of Farm Organization in California," reprinted in La Follette Committee, *Hearings*, pt. 54, pp. 19792–94. See also Paul S. Taylor, "Foundations of California Rural Society," *California Historical Society Quarterly* 24 (September 1945): 193–228.

30. William C. Blackwood, "A Consideration of the Labor Problem," *Overland Monthly* 3 (May 1884):454. The attitudes of California's farm employers toward labor, and particularly the idea of racial suitability for farmwork, are also revealed in CSAS, *Transactions, 1887*, pp. 97–107; *Pacific Rural Press*, November 3, 1883, pp. 378–79; and Luther W. Spoehr, "Sambo and the Heathen Chinee: California's Racial Stereotypes in the Late 1870s," *Pacific Historical Review* 42 (May 1973): 185–204.

31. *California Farmer*, May 25, 1854, p. 164.

32. Blackwood, "Consideration of the Labor Problem," p. 458.

33. Ibid.

34. Ibid., pp. 455–56.

35. *Ninth Census of the United States* (1870), 1:722. See also "How Our Chinamen Are Employed," *Overland Monthly* 2 (March 1869):231–40.

36. For a broad treatment of the status of Chinese labor in California during this period, see Mary Roberts Coolidge, *Chinese Immigration* (New York: Henry Holt, 1908), pp. 337–56. A more recent scholarly treatment is Ping Chiu, *Chinese Labor*

in California, 1850–1880: An Economic Study (Madison: University of Wisconsin Press, 1963), chap. 5.

37. CSAS, *Transactions, 1870–1871*, p. 87.

38. Ibid., pp. 88–89. On the anti-Chinese agitation in general, see Elmer C. Sandmeyer, *The Anti-Chinese Movement in California* (Urbana: University of Illinois Press, 1939).

39. CSAS, *Transactions, 1880*, p. 229.

40. CSAS, *Transactions, 1879*, p. 300.

41. CSAS, *Transactions, 1880*, p. 231.

42. CSAS, *Transactions, 1881*, p. 395.

43. CSAS, *Transactions, 1880*, p. 231.

44. CSAS, *Transactions, 1882*, pp. 29–30.

45. For typical expressions of this point of view, see CSAS, *Transactions, 1876*, pp. 74, 82; *Transactions, 1884*, pp. 280–85; and *Transactions, 1883*, p. 131.

46. *Pacific Rural Press*, November 3, 1883, pp. 378–79, and February 2, 1888, p. 116.

47. *Report of the State Board of Agriculture*, February 1, 1888, in CSAS, *Transactions, 1887*, pp. 12–13.

48. Ibid., p. 233.

49. Paul S. Taylor and Tom Vasey, "Historical Background of California Farm Labor," *Rural Sociology* 1 (September 1936):286.

50. CSAS, *Transactions, 1890*, pp. 202–3.

51. Ibid., pp. 195–97.

52. Ibid., p. 190. See also Richard J. Orsi, "The Octopus Reconsidered: The Southern Pacific and Agricultural Modernization in California, 1865–1915," *California Historical Quarterly* 54 (Fall 1975):197–220.

53. CSAS, *Transactions, 1885*, p. 200.

54. CSAS, *Transactions, 1888*, p. 456.

55. J. W. Jeffrey, "The Orange in Southern California," in Twenty-sixth Fruit Growers' Convention, *Proceedings* (1901), p. 128. See also Tufts and others, "Rich Pattern of California Crops," pp. 217–19.

56. CSAS, *Transactions, 1891*, p. 98. See also *California Fruit Grower*, March 2, 1889, p. 5.

57. On this point see Rex Burns, *Success in America: The Yeoman Dream and the Industrial Revolution* (Amherst: University of Massachusetts Press, 1976); Richard Hofstadter, *The Age of Reform* (New York: Vintage Books, 1955), pp. 23–59; and Henry Nash Smith, *Virgin Land: The American West as Symbol and Myth* (New York: Vintage Books, 1950), pp. 138–305. For background on the general economic development of California, see Walton Bean, *California: An Interpretive History*, 3d ed. (New York: McGraw-Hill, 1978), pp. 161–94, 226–38.

2. *In Search of a Peasantry*

1. For a typical example of this new agricultural archetype, see "A California Fruit Crop," in California State Agricultural Society, *Transactions, 1890* (Sacramento, 1891), pp. 235–37 (hereafter cited as CSAS, *Transactions*, followed by the date).

2. CSAS, *Transactions, 1889,* pp. 914–15.

3. Ibid., pp. 532–38.

4. Warren P. Tufts and others, "The Rich Pattern of California Crops," in *California Agriculture,* ed. Claude B. Hutchison (Berkeley: University of California Press, 1946), p. 166.

5. "Report of the California Fruit Union for 1889," in CSAS, *Transactions, 1889,* pp. 313–18.

6. For the development of these organizations, particularly among citrus growers, see Rahno Mabel MacCurdy, *The History of the California Fruit Growers' Exchange* (Los Angeles, 1925); W. W. Cumberland, *Cooperative Marketing: Its Advantages as Exemplified in the California Fruit Growers Exchange* (Princeton, 1917); Charles C. Teague, *Fifty Years a Rancher* (Los Angeles, 1944); H. Clark Powell, *The Organization of a Great Industry: The Success of the California Fruit-Growers Exchange,* Transvaal University College Bulletin no. 6 (Pretoria, 1925); E. O. Kraemer and H. E. Erdman, *History of Cooperation in the Marketing of California Fresh Deciduous Fruits,* University of California Agricultural Experiment Station Bulletin no. 557 (Berkeley, 1933); H. E. Erdman, "The Development and Significance of California Cooperatives, 1900–1915," *Agricultural History* 32 (July 1958):179–84; A. J. Schoendorf, *Beginnings of Cooperation in the Marketing of California Fresh Deciduous Fruits and History of the California Fruit Exchange* (Sacramento, 1947); Josephine K. Jacobs, "Sunkist Advertising," Ph.D. dissertation, University of California, Los Angeles, 1966; Albert J. Meyer, Jr., "History of the California Fruit Growers Exchange, 1893–1920," Ph.D. dissertation, Johns Hopkins University, 1952.

7. Thirty-sixth Fruit-Growers' Convention, *Proceedings* (Watsonville, Calif., December 7–10, 1909), pp. 14–15.

8. Tufts and others, "Rich Pattern of California Crops," pp. 166–70.

9. California State Commissioner of Horticulture, *Third Biennial Report, 1907–1908* (Sacramento, 1909), p. 37.

10. The nature, structure, and growth of industrialized agriculture are described in illuminating detail in Taylor and Vasey, "Historical Background of California Farm Labor," *Rural Sociology* 1 (September 1936):281–95; Paul S. Taylor and Tom Vasey, "Contemporary Background of California Farm Labor," *Rural Sociology* 1 (December 1936):401–19; State Relief Administration of California, Division of Special Surveys and Studies, *Migratory Labor in California* (San Francisco, 1936), pp. 3–15; Carey McWilliams, *Factories in the Field* (Boston: Little, Brown, 1939), pp. 48–65, 81–102; Edward J. Rowell, "Index to a Report on the Background and Problems Affecting Farm Labor in California," Work Projects Administration, Federal Writers Project (Oakland, 1938), pp. 1–36; Clarke A. Chambers, *California Farm Organizations: A Historical Study of the Grange, the Farm Bureau, and the Associated Farmers, 1929–1949* (Berkeley: University of California Press, 1952), pp. 1–8; Lloyd H. Fisher, *The Harvest Labor Market in California* (Cambridge: Harvard University Press, 1953), pp. 1–2. See also the following materials in U.S. Congress, Senate, Subcommittee of the Committee on Education and Labor, *Hearings on S. Res. 266, Violations of Free Speech and Rights of Labor,* 74th Cong., 2d sess. (Washington, D.C.: Government Printing Office, 1939): testimony of Paul S. Taylor, pt. 47, pp. 17216–28, 17239–41, 17266–86; testimony of James E. Wood, pt. 47, pp. 17297–306; and "Selected Large-Scale Farming Enterprises in California," in pt. 62, exhibit 9587, pp.

22773–800 (hereafter cited as La Follette Committee, *Hearings*). See also U.S. Congress, Senate, Subcommittee of the Committee on Education and Labor, *Report, Violations of Free Speech and Rights of Labor*, report no. 1150. 77th Cong., 2d sess. (Washington, D.C.: Government Printing Office, 1942), pt. 3, pp. 161–69 (hereafter cited as La Follette Committee, *Report*).

11. Taylor and Vasey, "Historical Background of California Farm Labor," p. 283; CSAS, *Transactions, 1890*, pp. 189, 199.

12. CSAS, *Transactions, 1889*, pp. 738–39.

13. CSAS, *Transactions, 1890*, p. 200. See also California State Bureau of Labor Statistics, *First Biennial Report, 1883–1884* (Sacramento, 1885), pp. 10–11.

14. William C. Blackwood, "A Consideration of the Labor Problem," *Overland Monthly* 3 (May 1884):451.

15. Ibid., p. 455; M. R. Benedict, "The Economic and Social Structure of California Agriculture," in *California Agriculture*, ed. Hutchison, pp. 400, 404; CSAS, *Transactions, 1890*, pp. 204–7; *California Fruit Grower*, June 2, 1888, p. 9.

16. CSAS, *Transactions, 1882*, p. 18.

17. A summary of farm employers' attitudes toward the employment of Chinese labor, undertaken in 1886 by John S. Enos, commissioner of the California Bureau of Labor Statistics, revealed a distinct willingness to forgo continued use of Chinese farmworkers. In a resolution sent to Enos by the State Horticultural Society, fruit growers asserted that they were "already convinced of the advantage of substituting other labor for the Chinese." See John Summerfield Enos to California State Horticultural Society, April 30, 1886, in California State Bureau of Labor Statistics, *Second Biennial Report, 1885–1886* (Sacramento, 1887), pp. 44–66.

18. CSAS, *Transactions, 1882*, p. 19.

19. *Pacific Rural Press*, February 11, 1889, p. 116.

20. CSAS, *Transactions, 1882*, p. 19; *Pacific Rural Press*, April 28, 1888, p. 376; *California Fruit Grower*, July 21, 1888, p. 7; Varden Fuller, "The Supply of Agricultural Labor as a Factor in the Evolution of Farm Organization in California," reprinted in La Follette Committee, *Hearings*, pt. 54, pp. 19816–17.

21. Chief Executive Viticultural Officer, *Second Annual Report to the Board of State Viticultural Commissioners, 1882–1884* (Sacramento, 1884), p. 28–29.

22. CSAS, *Transactions, 1885*, pp. 200–201; *Transactions, 1886*, p. 201; *Transactions, 1894*, p. 96; *Pacific Rural Press*, February 11, 1888, p. 116; California State Bureau of Labor Statistics, *First Biennial Report, 1883–1884*, pp. 10–11.

23. Blackwood, "Consideration of the Labor Problem," pp. 454–55.

24. Fuller, "Supply of Agricultural Labor," p. 19818.

25. Twenty-fifth State Fruit-Growers' Convention, *Transactions* (San Francisco, December 4–7, 1900), pp. 168 and 191.

26. Ibid., pp. 151–52.

27. Twenty-sixth Fruit-Growers' Convention, *Official Report* (San Francisco, December 3–6, 1901), p. 76.

28. H. P. Stabler, "The California Fruit-Grower, and the Labor Supply," in California State Board of Horticulture, *Eighth Biennial Report, 1901–1902* (Sacramento, 1902), pp. 268–72.

29. California State Board of Horticulture, *Eighth Biennial Report, 1901–1902*, pp. 272–81.

30. Ibid., pp. 395–98. Regarding the reputation of Japanese labor among farm employers, see also California State Bureau of Labor Statistics, *Twelfth Biennial*

Report, 1905–1906 (Sacramento, 1906), pp. 67–71; and Chester H. Rowell, "Chinese and Japanese Immigrants—A Comparison," *Annals of the American Academy of Political and Social Science* 34 (September 1909):4–6.

31. California State Board of Horticulture, *Eighth Biennial Report, 1901–1902,* p. 415.

32. "Report of Committee on Farm Labor," in Twenty-eighth Fruit-Growers' Convention, *Official Report* (Los Angeles, May 5–8, 1903), pp. 89–93.

33. "Report of the Committee on Labor," in Twenty-ninth Fruit-Growers' Convention, *Official Report* (Fresno, December 8–11, 1903), pp. 217–21.

34. "Report of the California Employment Committee," in California Commissioner of Horticulture, *First Biennial Report, 1903–1904* (Sacramento, 1905), pp. 387–388.

35. California Commissioner of Horticulture, *Second Biennial Report, 1905–1906* (Sacramento, 1907), pp. 423–24.

36. Ibid., pp. 464–68.

37. At the 1907 Fruit-Growers' Convention, delegates voted with only one member dissenting to send to the Congress a memorial requesting that the Exclusion Act be amended to permit a restricted flow of Chinese farmworkers into the country. See Thirty-third Fruit-Growers' Convention, *Official Report* (December 1907), pp. 65–66.

38. Thirty-sixth Fruit-Growers' Convention, *Proceedings,* p. 13. See also G. H. Hecke, "The Pacific Coast Labor Question from the Standpoint of a Horticulturalist," and John P. Irish, "Labor in the Rural Industries of California," both in Thirty-third Fruit-Growers' Convention, *Proceedings* (December 1907), pp. 67–72 and 54–66.

39. Thirty-sixth Fruit-Growers' Convention, *Proceedings,* pp. 13–14. Also see the summary of a special report on Japanese labor in California in the *Pacific Rural Press,* June 11, 1910, p. 468.

40. Commissioner Jeffrey's views on the symbiotic relationship between progressivism and large-scale agriculture in California are expressed in California Commissioner of Horticulture, *Third Biennial Report, 1907–1908* (Sacramento, 1909), pp. 36–39.

41. *Report of the Commission on Country Life* (New York: Sturgis & Walton, 1917), pp. 91–92, 97–99.

42. California State Agricultural Society, *Report, 1910* (Sacramento, 1911), pp. 35–38.

43. Hecke, "Pacific Coast Labor Question," pp. 67–72; U.S. Immigration Commission, *Reports of Immigrants in Industries,* pt. 25: "Japanese and Other Immigrant Races in the Pacific Coast and Rocky Mountain States," vol. 24 (Washington, D.C.: Government Printing Office, 1911), p. 25 and 44. For a broader treatment of this subject, see Roger Daniels and Harry H. L. Kitano, *American Racism* (Englewood Cliffs, N.J.: Prentice-Hall, 1970).

44. Sidney G. P. Coryn, "The Japanese Problem in California," *Annals of the American Academy of Political and Social Science* 34 (September 1909):48. It is interesting to note that only a few years earlier, when farm employers in the state were in the midst of their eastern recruitment campaign, the majority view in agribusiness circles was that white farmworkers were superior to nonwhites because of a greater natural affinity for agricultural tasks. On this point see U.S.

Industrial Commission, *Reports,* vol. 11 (Washington, D.C.: Government Printing Office, 1901), pp. 108–10.

45. For typical characterizations of white "bindle stiffs" by farm employers, see California State Board of Horticulture, *Eighth Biennial Report, 1901–1902,* pp. 270, 274, 276–77, 395–97; and M. F. Tarpey, "Some Possibilities of the Development of New Labor during the War," in Fiftieth State Fruit-Growers' Convention, *Proceedings* (Sacramento, November 21–23, 1917), pp. 74–79. A very useful scholarly treatise on the character of white labor in large-scale agriculture is Carleton Parker's classic study, *The Casual Laborer and Other Essays* (New York: Harcourt, Brace & Howe, 1920), pp. 61–165.

46. For thoughtful analyses of the relationship of hired labor to large-scale farming in California from the agribusinessman's point of view, see George P. Clements, "California Casual Labor Demands," paper presented at the Annual Conference of Friends of the Mexicans, Pomona College, Claremont, Calif., November 13, 1926, reprinted in La Follette Committee, *Hearings,* pt. 53, Exhibit 8742, pp. 19669–73; and, by the same author, "A Commentary on California Agricultural Labor," August 10, 1937, in ibid., Exhibit 8744, pp. 19677–80. See also testimony of Howard A. Miller in ibid., pp. 19430–68.

47. Thirty-eighth Fruit-Growers' Convention, *Proceedings,* p. 150. See also Spencer C. Olin, Jr., "European Immigrant and Oriental Alien: Acceptance and Rejection by the California Legislature of 1913," *Pacific Historical Review* 35 (August 1966):303–16.

48. On this point see Mansel G. Blackford, *The Politics of Business in California, 1890–1920* (Columbus: Ohio State University Press, 1977), pp. 13–39.

49. Fiftieth State Fruit-Growers' Convention, *Proceedings* (Sacramento, November 21–23, 1917), pp. 70–89, 102–9. See also Mark Reisler, *By the Sweat of Their Brow: Mexican Immigrant Labor in the United States* (Westport, Conn.: Greenwood Press, 1976), pp. 24–48; and Otey Scruggs, "The First Farm Labor Program, 1917–1921," *Arizona and the West* 2 (1960):319–26.

50. The California State Bureau of Labor Statistics estimated in 1926 that 75 percent of the Mexicans in California were illegal immigrants. See Louis Bloch, "Report on the Mexican Labor Situation in the Imperial Valley," in California State Bureau of Labor Statistics, *Twenty-second Biennial Report, 1925–1926* (Sacramento, 1926), p. 121.

51. George P. Clements, "Mexican Immigration and Its Bearing on California's Agriculture," *California Citrograph* 15 (November 1929):3, 28–29, 31. See also Ricardo Romo, "Responses to Mexican Immigration, 1910–1930," *Aztlán* 6 (Summer 1975):173–91; Victor S. Clark, *Mexican Labor in the United States,* U.S. Bureau of Labor Bulletin no. 78 (September 1908), pp. 482–85, 496–513.

52. "Labor Needs in California Crop Production with Particular Reference to the Mexican," in *Report of Governor C. C. Young's Fact-Finding Committee: Mexicans in California* (San Francisco, 1930), pp. 153–71. The relative importance of Mexicans within the total agricultural labor supply of California as of 1930 is examined in George M. Peterson, "Composition and Characteristics of the Agricultural Population in California," University of California College of Agriculture, *Agricultural Experiment Station Bulletin No. 630* (Berkeley, June 1939), pp. 15–22, 25–39, 47.

53. For a full scholarly discussion and analysis of Mexican immigration and the

debate it excited, see Reisler, *By the Sweat of Their Brow,* pp. 49–76, 151–226, 265–67. For farm employers' attitudes toward restriction, see the following hearings in U.S. Congress, House, Committee on Immigration and Naturalization: *Seasonal Agricultural Laborers from Mexico: Hearings on H.R. 6741, H.R. 7559, and H.R. 9036,* 69th Cong., 1st sess. (Washington, D.C.: Government Printing Office, 1926), pp. 4–23, 128–37; *Immigration from Countries of the Western Hemisphere: Hearings on H.R. 6464, H.R. 7358, H.R. 10955, and H.R. 11687,* 70th Cong., 1st sess. (Washington, D.C.: Government Printing Office, 1928), pp. 153–76, 225, 264, 295–329; and *Western Hemisphere Immigration: Hearings on H.R. 8523, H.R. 8530, and H.R. 8702,* 71st Cong., 2d sess. (Washington, D.C.: Government Printing Office, 1930), pp. 59–83, 139–45, 147–54, 263–64; also U.S. Congress, Senate, Committee on Immigration, *Restriction of Western Hemisphere Immigration: Hearings on S. 1296, S. 1437, and S. 3019,* 70th Cong., 1st sess. (Washington, D.C.: Government Printing Office, 1928), pp. 26–83; *Mexicans in California,* pp. 158–71; Clements, "Mexican Immigration," pp. 3, 28–29; Parker Frisselle, "The Agricultural Labor Situation," Sixtieth Convention of California Fruit Growers and Farmers, *Proceedings* (Stockton, November 16–17, 1927), pp. 74–80; Charles C. Teague, "A Statement on Mexican Immigration," *Saturday Evening Post* 200 (March 10, 1928):169–70; *Pacific Rural Press,* January 28, 1928, p. 115. The California State Federation of Labor's prorestriction policy is stated in Twenty-eighth Annual Convention of the California State Federation of Labor, *Proceedings* (1927), pp. 26, 61, 63, 79–80. See also La Follette Committee, *Report,* pt. 3, pp. 255–60. The social consequences of federal immigration policies toward Mexico are examined in Paul S. Taylor, *Mexican Labor in the United States: Migration Statistics IV,* University of California Publications in Economics, vol. 12, no. 3 (Berkeley: University of California Press, 1934), pp. 23–49; Emory S. Bogardus, *The Mexican in the United States,* University of Southern California Social Science Series no. 8 (Los Angeles: University of Southern California Press, 1934), pp. 18–58, 68–98; *Mexicans in California,* pp. 2–21, 175–214; Robert N. McLean, "Mexican Workers in the United States," in National Conference of Social Work, *Proceedings* (1929), pp. 531–38; J. B. Gwin, "Social Problems of Our Mexican Population," in National Conference of Social Work, *Proceedings* (1926), pp. 327–32; George P. Clements to W. Frank Persons, October 16, 1935, in La Follette Committee, *Hearings,* pt. 53, Exhibit 8750, pp. 19691–93; Helen W. Walker, "Mexican Immigrants as Laborers," *Sociology and Social Research* 13 (September–October 1928):55–62; Don D. Lescohier, "The Vital Problem in Mexican Immigration," in National Conference of Social Work, *Proceedings* (1927), pp. 547–554; Louise F. Shields, "Mexican Ambassadors of Good Will," *World Tomorrow* 11 (February 1928):81–82; Paul S. Taylor, "More Bars against Mexicans?," *Survey* 64 (April 1930):26–27; R. N. McLean, "Tightening the Mexican Border," *Survey* 64 (April 1930):28–29, 54–56; Carey McWilliams, "Getting Rid of the Mexicans," *American Mercury* 28 (March 1933):322–24; R. N. McLean, "The Mexican Return," *Nation* 135 (August 24, 1932):165–66; W. V. Woehlke, "Don't Drive Out the Mexicans," *Review of Reviews* 81 (May 1930):66–68; Abraham Hoffman, *Unwanted Mexican Americans in the Great Depression: Repatriation Pressures, 1929–1939* (Tucson: University of Arizona Press, 1974); Carey McWilliams, *North from Mexico: The Spanish-Speaking People of the United States* (Philadelphia: Lippincott, 1949); John R. Martinez, "Mexican

Emigration to the United States, 1910–1930," Ph.D. dissertation, University of California, Berkeley, 1957.

54. *Western Grower and Shipper*, July 1930, p. 16.
55. Quoted in Fuller, "Supply of Agricultural Labor," p. 19865.
56. Teague, *Fifty Years a Rancher*, p. 150.

3. *Organization and Reform: The Progressive Era*

1. The patterns and quality of work and life for migratory farm laborers on California's industrialized farms are usefully described in U.S. Immigration Commission, *Reports of Immigrants in Industries*, pt. 25: "Japanese and Other Immigrant Races in the Pacific Coast and Rocky Mountain States," vol. 24 (Washington, D.C.: Government Printing Office, 1911), pp. 3–281 (hereafter cited as Dillingham Commission, *Reports*); U.S. Congress, Senate, Subcommittee of the Committee on Education and Labor, *Report, Violations of Free Speech and Rights of Labor*, report no. 1150, 77th Cong., 2d sess. (Washington, D.C.: Government Printing Office, 1942), pt. 3, pp. 161–405 (hereafter cited as La Follette Commiteee, *Report*); Lloyd H. Fisher, *The Harvest Labor Market in California* (Cambridge: Harvard University Press, 1953), pp. 1–113; U.S. Commission on Industrial Relations, *Final Report and Testimony*, vol. 5 (Washington, D.C.: Government Printing Office, 1916), pp. 4913–72; U.S. Industrial Commission, *Report*, vol. 11 (Washington, D.C.: Government Printing Office, 1901), pp. 77–132.

2. La Follette Committee, *Report*, pt. 3, pp. 238–54; Stuart Jamieson, *Labor Unionism in American Agriculture*, U.S. Bureau of Labor Statistics Bulletin no. 836 (Washington, D.C.: Government Printing Office, 1945), pp. 43–46; California State Relief Administration, *Migratory Labor in California* (San Francisco, 1936), p. 55.

3. La Follette Committee, *Report*, pt. 3, p. 238; Jamieson, *Labor Unionism*, pp. 43–44.

4. On Chinese labor in California agriculture see Mary Roberts Coolidge, *Chinese Immigration* (New York: Henry Holt, 1908), pp. 337–56; Carey McWilliams, *Factories in the Field* (Boston: Little, Brown, 1939), pp. 66–80; *Migratory Labor in California*, pp. 16–18; Carl C. Plehn, "Labor in California," *Yale Review* (February 1896):409–25; Varden Fuller, "The Supply of Agricultural Labor as a Factor in the Evolution of Farm Organization in California," reprinted in La Follette Committee, *Hearings*, pt. 54, pp. 19809–26; Dillingham Commission, *Reports*, pt. 25, vol. 24, pp. 3–281; California State Bureau of Labor Statistics, *Thirteenth Biennial Report, 1907–1908* (Sacramento, 1908), pp. 117–47; "Chinese and Japanese in America," *Annals of the American Academy of Political and Social Science* 34 (September 1909):3–36, 120–30; Ira B. Cross, *A History of the Labor Movement in California* (Berkeley: University of California Press, 1935), pp. 73–129; Isabella Black, "American Labor and Chinese Immigration," *Past and Present* 25 (1963):59–76; Ping Chiu, *Chinese Labor in California, 1850–1880: An Economic Study* (Madison: University of Wisconsin Press, 1963), chap. 5.

5. Carleton H. Parker, *The Casual Laborer and Other Essays* (New York: Harcourt, Brace & Howe, 1920), p. 76.

6. Ibid., pp. 61–89.

7. On Japanese labor see Dillingham Commission, *Reports,* pt. 25, vol. 24, pp. 3–281, 298–457, 565–668; California State Board of Control, *California and the Oriental* (Sacramento: California State Printing Office, 1920); McWilliams, *Factories in the Field,* pp. 104–16; *Migratory Labor in California,* pp. 19–24; Fuller, "Supply of Agricultural Labor," pp. 19827–41; "Chinese and Japanese in America," *Annals,* pp. 3–48, 74–79, 157–67; "Present-Day Immigration with Special Reference to the Japanese," *Annals of the American Academy of Political and Social Science* 93 (January 1921):16–120; H. R. Millis, "Some Economic Aspects of Japanese Immigration," *American Economic Review* 5 (December 1915):787–804; Raymond Leslie Buell, "Anti-Japanese Agitation in the United States," *Political Science Quarterly* 37 (December 1922):605–38.

8. California State Bureau of Labor Statistics, *Twelfth Biennial Report, 1905–1906* (Sacramento, 1906), pp. 67–71; Chester H. Rowell, "Chinese and Japanese Immigrants—A Comparison," *Annals of the American Academy of Political and Social Science* 34 (September 1909):4–6; W. Flanders Setchel to Frank L. Lathrop, April 6, 1920, in *California and the Oriental,* pp. 106–7. Typical examples of strike techniques employed by Japanese farmworkers may be found in *Pacific Rural Press,* August 15, 1903, p. 103, and *California Fruit Grower,* April 18, 1903, p. 4. The labor "associations" effected among Japanese laborers are usefully described in Yamoto Ichihashi, *Japanese in the United States* (London: Oxford University Press, 1932), pp. 172–74.

9. Thirty-second Convention of California Fruit Growers, *Official Report* (Sacramento, 1907), p. 69. Also see Governor William D. Stephens to Secretary of State Bainbridge Colby, June 19, 1920, in *California and the Oriental,* pp. 7–15; and the statement, testimony, and exhibits submitted by V. S. McClatchy in U.S. Congress, House, Committee on Immigration and Naturalization, *Hearings, Percentage Plans for Restriction of Immigration,* 66th Cong., 1st sess. (Washington, D.C.: Government Printing Office, 1919), pp. 237–96.

10. Jamieson, *Labor Unionism,* pp. 50–54; McWilliams, *Factories in the Field,* pp. 111–14; *California and the Oriental,* pp. 101–8; Paul S. Taylor, *Mexican Labor in the United States: Imperial Valley,* University of California Publications in Economics, vol. 6, no. 1 (Berkeley: University of California Press, 1928), pp. 5–6; Kiyoski K. Kawakami, *Asia at the Door* (New York: Fleming H. Revell, 1914), pp. 110–15; Fuller, "Supply of Agricultural Labor," pp. 19834–37; California State Bureau of Labor Statistics, *Twelfth Biennial Report, 1905–1906,* pp. 67–71. For two very interesting statements of self-defense by the Japanese, see Japanese Association of America, *Memorial Presented to the President of the United States while at San Francisco on September 19, 1919,* and Toyoji Chiba, "Truth of the Japanese Farming in California," Japanese Association of California (n.d.), both in *California and the Oriental,* pp. 203–28. See also Thomas A. Bailey, "California, Japan, and the Alien Land Legislation of 1913," *Pacific Historical Review* 1 (March 1932):36–59; Masakazu Iwata, "The Japanese Immigrants in California Agriculture," *Agricultural History* 36 (January 1962):25–37; Roger Daniels, *The Politics of Prejudice* (Berkeley: University of California Press, 1962), p. 89; Ivan H. Light, *Ethnic Enterprise in America* (Berkeley: University of California Press, 1972), pp. 72–78; Herbert P. LePore, "Prelude to Prejudice: Hiram Johnson, Woodrow Wilson, and the California Land Law Controversy," *Southern California Quarterly* 61 (Spring 1979):99–110.

11. Fuller, "Supply of Agricultural Labor," pp. 19842-49; California State Bureau of Labor Statistics, *Fifteenth Biennial Report, 1911–1912* (Sacramento, 1912), pp. 47–50; La Follette Committee, *Report*, pt. 3, p. 241.

12. Jamieson, *Labor Unionism*, pp. 43–69; La Follette Committee, *Report*, pt. 3, pp. 238–54; *Migratory Labor in California*, pp. 67–71; A. ("Shorty") Alston, "A Brief History of the Fruit and Vegetable Industry on the West Coast," unpublished manuscript in Simon J. Lubin Society Papers, Bancroft Library, University of California, Berkeley; Fuller, "Supply of Agricultural Labor," pp. 19842–49.

13. Gerald N. Grob, *Workers and Utopia: A Study of Ideological Conflict in the American Labor Movement, 1865–1900* (Evanston, Ill.: Northwestern University Press, 1961), p. 167; Samuel Gompers, "Organized Labor in the Campaign," *North American Review* 155 (July 1892):93.

14. *Oakland Tribune*, April 21, 1903; "The Migratory Agricultural Worker and the American Federation of Labor," Work Projects Administration, Federal Writers Project (Oakland, 1939), p. 3.

15. Twenty-eighth Annual Convention of the American Federation of Labor, *Report of Proceedings* (Denver, 1908), pp. 150–239; Jamieson, *Labor Unionism*, p. 57; Lewis L. Lorwin, *The American Federation of Labor: History, Policies, and Prospects* (Washington, D.C.: Brookings Institution, 1933), p. 110; *American Federationist* 15 (July 1908):546.

16. Forty-third Annual Convention of the American Federation of Labor, *Report of Proceedings* (Portland, Ore., 1923), pp. 333–38; Hyman Weintraub, *Andrew Furuseth: Emancipator of the Seamen*, Institute of Industrial Relations (Los Angeles: University of California Press, 1959), pp. 104–5, 218n71; *San Francisco Bulletin*, February 7, 1914. IWW spokesmen in California appear to have been convinced that the A.F. of L.'s sole motive in approaching migratory farmworkers was to thwart the Wobbly campaign. On this point see George Speed, "52 Years of Seeking One Big Union," *Industrial Worker*, July 16, 1924, p. 3; Austin Lewis, "The Drift in California," *International Socialist Review* 12 (November 1911):272–74; and Frank Little to Editor, *Industrial Worker*, July 30, 1910, p. 4.

17. See the *Report of Proceedings* of the following annual conventions of the American Federation of Labor: Twenty-ninth (Toronto, 1909), pp. 229–31; Thirtieth (St. Louis, 1910), pp. 243–44; Thirty-first (Atlanta, 1911), pp. 69–71, 276, 305; and Thirty-second (Seattle, 1913), pp. 88–89, 196, 346–47, 377; Lorwin, *American Federation of Labor*, pp. 110–11; statement of Edward Vandeleur, in U.S. Congress, Senate, Subcommittee of the Committee on Education and Labor, *Hearings on S. Res. 266, Violations of Free Speech and Rights of Labor*, 74th Cong., 2d sess. (Washington, D.C.: Government Printing Office, 1939), pt. 60, p. 22055 (hereafter cited as La Follette Committee, *Hearings*); Twelfth Annual Convention of the California State Federation of Labor, *Proceedings* (1911), p. 67.

18. Vandeleur statement, in La Follette Committee, *Hearings*, pt. 60, p. 22055; Tenth Annual Convention of the California State Federation of Labor, *Proceedings* (1909), pp. 45–46; *Migratory Labor in California*, pp. 68–69; "Migratory Agricultural Worker and the American Federation of Labor," p. 2; Edward J. Rowell, "Index to a Report on the Background and Problems Affecting Farm Labor in California," Work Projects Administration, Federal Writers Project (Oakland, 1938), pp. 110–11.

19. Testimony of J. B. Dale, in U.S. Commission on Industrial Relations, *Final Report and Testimony*, vol. 5, pp. 4978–79.

20. Ibid., pp. 4972–79; Fourteenth Annual Convention of the California State Federation of Labor, *Proceedings* (1913), pp. 77–78; *Migratory Labor in California,* pp. 68–69; McWilliams, *Factories in the Field,* p. 212.

21. Paul Scharrenberg, *Minority Report,* Wheatland Hop-Fields Riot Investigation of the California Commission of Immigration and Housing (1914), in Austin Lewis Collection, Bancroft Library, University of California, Berkeley; Samuel Gompers, "Labor Camp Life—Its Evils," *American Federationist* 21 (July 1914):566–70; testimony of Paul Scharrenberg, in U.S. Commission on Industrial Relations, *Final Report and Testimony,* vol. 5, pp. 5040–52; Paul Scharrenberg, "Sanitary Conditions in Labor Camps," *American Federationist* 25 (October 1918):891–93; Vandeleur statement, La Follette Committee, *Hearings,* pt. 60, pp. 22060–62.

22. For an analysis of the composition and psychological orientation of the migratory labor force in California during the period of the IWW's greatest activity in the state, see testimony of Carleton H. Parker, in U.S. Commission on Industrial Relations, *Final Report and Testimony,* vol. 5, pp. 4932–36. See also Parker, *Casual Laborer,* pp. 61–124.

23. *Industrial Worker,* May 20, 1909, p. 2.

24. Testimony of George H. Speed, in U.S. Commission on Industrial Relations, *Final Report and Testimony,* vol. 5, pp. 4941, 4947–48.

25. *Industrial Worker,* May 18, 1911, p. 3.

26. Jay Fox, "The Jap Question Not Yet Solved," *The Syndicalist,* June 1, 1913, p. 1.

27. Carleton H. Parker, "The I.W.W.," *Atlantic Monthly* 20 (November 1917): 662. The lifestyle and mentality of migratory farmworkers during the early twentieth century are analyzed in Parker, *Casual Laborer,* pp. 61-89; Nels Anderson, *The Hobo: The Sociology of the Homeless Man* (Chicago: University of Chicago Press, 1923); Harold Lord Varney, "The Story of the I.W.W.," chap. 7, *One Big Union Monthly* 1 (September 1919):43–45; and *World Tomorrow* 6 (September 1923): *passim.*

28. Parker, "I.W.W.," p. 654.

29. Charles Ashleigh, "The Floater," *International Socialist Review* 15 (July 1914):37.

30. *Industrial Worker,* June 4, 1910, p. 2. See also Frank Thorpe, "The Harvest Isn't Over Yet," *Industrial Pioneer* 4 (September 1926):5; Varney, "Story of the I.W.W.," pp. 43–45.

31. Edward Townsend Booth, "The Wild West," *Atlantic Monthly* 126 (December 1920):786.

32. *Proceedings of the Second Annual Convention of the I.W.W.* (Chicago, 1906), p. 309.

33. Ibid., pp. 65–66.

34. *Industrial Worker,* April 22, 1909, p. 3; June 19, 1909, p. 3; November 10, 1909, p. 4.

35. For detailed accounts of the Fresno free-speech fight, see Cletus E. Daniel, "Labor Radicalism in Pacific Coast Agriculture," Ph.D. dissertation, University of Washington, 1972, pp. 47–54; Melvyn Dubofsky, *We Shall Be All: A History of the I.W.W.* (Chicago: Quadrangle Books, 1969), pp. 184–89; "Solidarity Wins in Fresno," *International Socialist Review* 2 (April 1911):634–36; "Solidarity Won in Fresno," *The Agitator,* March 15, 1911, p. 4; Fred Moe, "The Fresno Mob," *The*

Agitator, January 1, 1911, p. 4; Roger N. Baldwin, "Free Speech Fights of the I.W.W.," in *Twenty-five Years of Industrial Unionism* (Chicago: Industrial Workers of the World, 1930), pp. 15–16, 20; Hyman Weintraub, "The I.W.W. in California, 1905–1931," M.A. thesis, University of California, Los Angeles, 1947, pp. 30–31. An interesting and illuminating sidelight to the Fresno fight is provided in Charles P. LeWarne, "On the Wobbly Train to Fresno," *Labor History* 14 (Spring 1973):264–89.

36. *Industrial Worker,* March 9, 1911, p. 1.

37. For a Wobbly expression of a similar sentiment, see M.G.R., "Reflections of an Organizer," *Solidarity,* February 6, 1915, p. 2.

38. *San Francisco Chronicle,* March 4, 1911, p. 3; Weintraub, "I.W.W. in California," p. 32; *Industrial Worker,* March 16, 1911, p. 1.

39. For a description and analysis of the enervating effects of the Wheatland episode on the IWW's organization of farmworkers, see Cletus E. Daniel, "In Defense of the Wheatland Wobblies: A Critical Analysis of the I.W.W. in California," *Labor History* 19 (Fall 1978):485–509.

40. This period of the IWW's activity among farmworkers in California is discussed in detail in Daniel, "Labor Radicalism," pp. 54–73.

41. Statement of George L. Bell on Behalf of Western Governors to Council of National Defense, July 18, 1917, pp. 2, 9. A typewritten copy of the statement is in the Simon J. Lubin Papers, Bancroft Library, University of California, Berkeley. See also Harvey Duff, *The Silent Defenders: Courts and Capitalism in California* (Chicago: Industrial Workers of the World, n.d.), p. 67. The many free-speech fights of the IWW also tended to convince the public that Wobblies espoused and practiced violence, although the organization pursued a policy of passive resistance in nearly all of its free-speech struggles. See Baldwin, "Free Speech Fights," p. 15. The California Wobblies' seeming circumspection regarding sabotage is discussed in C. L. Lambert to W. D. Haywood, June 10, 1915, quoted in Philip S. Foner, *History of the Labor Movement in the United States,* vol. 4: *The Industrial Workers of the World, 1905–1917* (New York: International Publishers, 1965), p. 275.

42. *Solidarity,* October 30, 1915, p. 5; Paul F. Brissenden, *The I.W.W.: A Study of American Syndicalism* (New York: Columbia University Press, 1919), p. 337; "The I.W.W. in California Agriculture," Work Projects Administration, Federal Writers Project (Oakland, 1938), p. 45 (unpublished manuscript in Bancroft Library, University of California, Berkeley); E. Workman, *History of "400" Agricultural Workers' Organization* (New York: One Big Union Club, 1939), p. 17; *Solidarity,* November 20 and December 25, 1915, and January 29, 1916; *Report of the General Secretary-Treasurer to the Tenth Convention of the I.W.W.* (Chicago, 1916), pp. 43, 69–112. The basic elements of the internal debate over AWO affiliation within the IWW in California are revealed in numerous reports emanating from the state in early 1916. See *Solidarity,* January 1, January 8, January 29, February 5, March 4, April 8, August 26, September 2, and December 2, 1916; and Weintraub, "I.W.W. in California," p. 89. For an evaluation of the IWW's strength in rural California during early 1917, see J. Vance Thompson, "Report on I.W.W. in California," May 30, 1917, in Lubin Papers. The IWW's plans for farmworker organization in California in 1917 are discussed in *Solidarity,* April 14, 1917, p. 3.

43. The IWW's decline in California is discussed in some depth in Daniel, "Labor Radicalism," pp. 82–93. See also John S. Gambs, *The Decline of the*

I.W.W. (New York: Columbia University Press, 1932), pp. 180–82. The decline of the IWW nationally is superbly treated in Dubofsky, *We Shall Be All*, pp. 445–68. The IWW press also provides indispensable insights into the organization's rapid degeneration, especially after 1924.

44. La Follette Committee, *Report*, pt. 3, p. 255; McWilliams, *Factories in the Field*, pp. 188–89.

45. La Follette Committee, *Report*, pt. 3, p. 254.

46. George E. Mowry, *The California Progressives* (Berkeley: University of California Press, 1951), p. 143. For an analysis of the progressive mentality in California see ibid., pp. 86–104, and Spencer C. Olin, Jr., *California's Prodigal Sons: Hiram Johnson and the Progressives, 1911–1917* (Berkeley: University of California Press, 1968).

47. On this point see Mowry, *California Progressives*, pp. 143–57; La Follette Committee, *Report*, pt. 3, pp. 247–54.

48. Fuller, "Supply of Agricultural Labor," pp. 19845–46.

49. Report of Carey McWilliams, chief, State Division of Immigration and Housing, before the Subcommittee of the United States Senate Committee on Education and Labor at San Francisco, California, January 25, 1940, in La Follette Committee, *Hearings*, pt. 59, Exhibit 9371, p. 21887. See also *Migratory Labor in California*, pp. 72–73.

50. California Commission of Immigration and Housing, *Ninth Annual Report* (Sacramento, January 9, 1923), p. 21.

51. The unspeakable conditions prevailing on the Durst ranch at the time of the Wheatland incident are described in a detailed report submitted by Carleton Parker to California Governor Hiram Johnson and the U.S. Commission on Industrial Relations. See *A Report to His Excellency Hiram W. Johnson, Governor of California, by the Commission of Immigration and Housing of California on the Causes and All Matters Pertaining to the So-Called Wheatland Hop Fields' Riot and Killing of August 3, 1913, and Containing Certain Recommendations as a Solution for the Problems Disclosed*, in Parker, *Casual Laborer*, pp. 171–99. Also of interest is a report made by state labor official Harry Gorman to the California State Board of Health, reprinted in *Plotting to Convict Wheatland Hop Pickers* (Oakland: International Press, 1914), pp. 11–12. In an effort to counter Parker's report, the Yuba County Board of Supervisors, with the cooperation of the Durst brothers, prepared a report asserting that conditions on the Durst ranch were generally good and not a factor in bringing about the Wheatland strike. See *Report of Commission Investigating Conditions in Hop Fields*, August 1913, submitted to the Yuba County Board of Supervisors, July 22, 1914, in the Documents Division, California State Library, Sacramento; and R. H. Durst to Simon J. Lubin, June 23, 1914, in Lubin Papers.

52. Detailed descriptions of the Wheatland "riot" are available in abundance. In addition to Carleton Parker's official report, see George L. Bell, "The Wheatland Hop-Fields' Riot," *Outlook* 107 (May 16, 1914):118–23; George L. Bell, "A California Labor Tragedy," *Literary Digest* 48 (May 23, 1914):1239–40; *The Story of the Ford Case* (New York: American Civil Liberties Union, December 1925), pp. 3–6; *Plotting to Convict Wheatland Hop Pickers*, pp. 25–28; Mortimer Downing, "The Case of the Hop Pickers," *International Socialist Review* 14 (October 1913):210–13; A Spectator, "Justice Triumphant," *Industrial Pioneer* 3 (March 1926):7–8; Ed Delaney, "Wheatland: The Bloody Hop Field," *Industrial Pioneer* 2

(February 1925):34–36; Mortimer Downing, "California Agriculture Demands Industrial Tactics," *Industrial Pioneer* 1 (August 1921):28–30; Woodrow C. Whitten, "The Wheatland Episode," *Pacific Historical Review* 27 (February 1948):37–42; testimony of Austin Lewis, in U.S. Commission on Industrial Relations, *Final Report and Testimony,* vol. 5, pp. 4999–5000; McWilliams, *Factories in the Field,* pp. 158–61. Numerous unpublished accounts are also available. Among them are "I.W.W. in California Agriculture," pp. 15–34; Douglas M. Clark, "Wheatland Hop Field Riot," M.A. thesis, Chico State College, 1963; Ione Elizabeth Wilson, "The I.W.W. in California, with Special Reference to Migratory Labor (1910–1913)," M.A. thesis, University of California, Berkeley, 1941, pp. 44–54; and Weintraub, "I.W.W. in California," pp. 68–76.

53. *Sacramento Union,* August 5, 1913, p. 1.

54. People of the State of California, Respondent, v. Richard Ford and H. D. Suhr, Appellants, Superior Court of the State of California in and for the County of Yuba, 1914, pp. 20–21. A copy of the trial transcript is in the Austin Lewis Collection, Bancroft Library, University of California, Berkeley. See also *Sacramento Bee,* August 8, 1913, p. 1.

55. The mistreatment suffered by suspects during the roundup following the Wheatland riot is described in the following material in U.S. Commission on Industrial Relations, *Final Report and Testimony,* vol. 5: testimony of George L. Bell, pp. 4979–82, 4992–94; testimony of W. H. Carlin, pp. 4994–99; testimony of Austin Lewis, pp. 5000–5003; testimony of Robert M. Royce, pp. 5010–11, 5019–24; testimony of William A. Mundell, pp. 5011–18; and statement of Edward B. Stanwood, pp. 5025–26. See also "I.W.W. in California Agriculture," pp. 35–38; Bell, "Wheatland Hop-Fields' Riot," pp. 121–22; Downing, "Case of the Hop Pickers," p. 213; "Prosecution or Persecution" (San Francisco: California Branch, General Defense Committee, 1925), pp. 3–4; McWilliams, *Factories in the Field,* pp. 161–62; *Oakland World,* October 18 and November 22, 1913, and January 3, 1914; *Plotting to Convict Wheatland Hop Pickers,* pp. 3–10, 13–25; *The Public* 16 (October 31, 1913):1043, and 17 (September 11, 1914):878–79.

56. Austin Lewis, "Solidarity—Merely a Word?," *New Review* 3 (July 15, 1915):127; Inez Haynes Gillmore, "The Marysville Trial," *Harper's Weekly,* April 4, 1914, reprinted in *Solidarity,* May 2, 1914, p. 3; People v. Ford, pp. 32–49, 1422–27.

57. McWilliams, *Factories in the Field,* p. 162.

58. McWilliams Report, in La Follette Committee, *Hearings,* pt. 59, p. 21887; *Migratory Labor in California,* pp. 72–73.

59. Parker, *Casual Laborer,* pp. 196–99; California Commission of Immigration and Housing, *First Annual Report* (Sacramento, January 2, 1915), pp. 7–10, 15–18.

60. The origins of the commission and the political backgrounds of Lubin and his fellow commissioners are described in Samuel E. Wood, "California State Commission of Immigration and Housing," Ph.D. dissertation, University of California, Berkeley, 1942. See also Simon J. Lubin, "Can Radicals Capture the Farms of California?," paper presented before the Commonwealth Club of California, March 23, 1934, pp. 7–8, in Lubin Society Papers; and Commission of Immigration and Housing, *Ninth Annual Report,* pp. 12–14.

61. Mowry, *California Progressives,* pp. 93–94, 143.

62. Carleton Parker's background and social philosophy are revealed in Cornelia

Stratton Parker, *An American Idyll: The Life of Carleton H. Parker* (Boston: Atlantic Monthly Press, 1919), and Parker, *Casual Laborer*. See also Harold Hyman, *Soldiers and Spruce* (Los Angeles: Institute of Industrial Relations, University of California, 1963).

63. Parker's theory of labor discontent is discussed in Mark Perlman, *Labor Union Theories in America* (Evanston, Ill.: Row, Peterson, 1958), pp. 123–28. See also Parker, *Casual Laborer,* especially pp. 27–59, 125–65.

64. Parker, *Casual Laborer,* pp. 107, 163.

65. Ibid., p. 53.

66. Ibid., p. 52.

67. Ibid., p. 156.

68. Ibid., pp. 88, 89.

69. Ibid., p. 164.

70. Ibid., p. 54.

71. Ibid., p. 112.

72. Ibid., p. 165.

73. Ibid., p. 59.

74. Commission of Immigration and Housing, *First Annual Report,* p. 22.

75. Ibid., p. 19.

76. Commission of Immigration and Housing, *Ninth Annual Report,* p. 28.

77. Ibid.

78. Commission of Immigration and Housing, *Second Annual Report* (Sacramento, January 2, 1916), pp. 18–21.

79. Commission of Immigration and Housing, *First Annual Report,* p. 50.

80. Commission of Immigration and Housing, *Ninth Annual Report,* pp. 28–29, 36–44. See also Wood, "California State Commission of Immigration and Housing," pp. 166–254.

81. Lubin, "Can Radicals Capture the Farms of California?," p. 9; Commission of Immigration and Housing, *Annual Report* (Sacramento, January 1927), pp. 17–20; Report of Carey McWilliams, in LaFollette Committee, *Hearings,* pt. 59, pp. 21887–89; *Migratory Labor in California,* pp. 79–80; California State Bureau of Labor Statistics, *Twenty-third Biennial Report, 1927–1928* (Sacramento, 1929), p. 19.

82. Mowry argues persuasively that the California progressives' "bias against labor was always greater than against the large corporation," and that they consistently embraced an anti-union philosophy. See Mowry, *California Progressives,* pp. 92–96, 102–4, 143–44, 153.

83. Dubofsky, *We Shall Be All,* pp. 298–300.

84. William Kent to George W. Douglas, November 15, 1910, quoted in Mowry, *California Progressives,* p. 92.

85. Mowry, *California Progressives,* pp. 102, 153.

86. Carleton H. Parker to Honorable Hiram W. Johnson, February 10, 1914, in Lubin Papers.

87. Parker, *Casual Laborer,* pp. 89, 18.

88. Parker to Lubin, July 7, 1914, and n.d. (probably July 8–12, 1914), both in Lubin Papers.

89. The intelligence reports gathered during 1915 are in the E. Clemens Horst Investigation file in the Hiram W. Johnson Papers, Bancroft Library, University of

California, Berkeley. See also the "I.W.W. Investigations" file in the Lubin Papers.

90. Hiram W. Johnson to Governor Ernest Lister, September 28, 1915, and to President Woodrow Wilson, November 12, 1915, both in Johnson Papers; Statement of George L. Bell on Behalf of Western Governors to Council of National Defense, July 18, 1917, pp. 2, 9, in Lubin Papers; Report of Carey McWilliams, in La Follette Committee, *Hearings,* pt. 59, p. 21887; Lubin, "Can Radicals Capture the Farms of California?," p. 8; Dubofsky, *We Shall Be All,* p. 300; William Preston, Jr., *Aliens and Dissenters: Federal Suppression of Radicals, 1903–1933* (New York: Harper & Row, 1966), pp. 59–61; Foner, *History of the Labor Movement,* pp. 277–78; Duff, *Silent Defenders,* p. 67.

91. *Report of the Commission on Land Colonization and Rural Credits of the State of California* (Sacramento, 1916), p. 78. See also Elwood Mead to F. L. Lathrope, February 26, 1920, in *California and the Oriental,* pp. 123–25; Grace H. Larsen, "A Progressive in Agriculture: Harris Weinstock," *Agricultural History* 32 (July 1958):187–93; Miles C. Everett, "Chester Harvey Rowell, Pragmatic Humanist and California Progressive," Ph.D. dissertation, University of California, Berkeley, 1965.

92. McWilliams, *Factories in the Field,* p. 205.

93. For details of the Durham and Delhi settlement projects, see Elwood Mead, *Helping Men Own Farms* (New York, 1920) and *How California Is Helping People Own Farms and Rural Homes,* University of California Agricultural Experiment Station Circular no. 221 (Berkeley, 1920); Elwood Mead and others, *Colonization and Rural Development in California,* University of California Agricultural Experiment Station Circular no. 247 (Berkeley, 1922); Roy J. Smith, "An Economic Analysis of the California State Land Settlements at Durham and Delhi," Ph.D. dissertation, University of California, Berkeley, 1938; McWilliams, *Factories in the Field,* pp. 200–210; testimony of Walter E. Packard, in La Follette Committee, *Hearings,* pt. 59, p. 21754.

94. Commission of Immigration and Housing, *Annual Report* (Sacramento, January 1919), pp. 33–34. See also California Commission of Immigration and Housing, *A Report on Large Landholdings in Southern California* (Sacramento, 1919).

95. Commission of Immigration and Housing, *Annual Report* (Sacramento, January 1927), pp. 9–14, 17–20; *Migratory Labor in California* p. 80.

96. Edward J. Hanna to California Congressional Delegation, February 24, 1926, in Industrial Relations–Labor Law Enforcement File, California State Archives, Sacramento.

97. Paul S. Taylor and Tom Vasey, "Historical Background of California Farm Labor," *Rural Sociology* 1 (September 1936):281–95; Paul S. Taylor and Tom Vasey, "Contemporary Background of California Farm Labor," *Rural Sociology* 1 (December 1936):401–19; testimony of Paul S. Taylor, in La Follette Committee, *Hearings,* pt. 47, pp. 17220–28.

98. La Follette Committee, *Report,* pt. 3, pp. 262–96, 383–93. See also *Western Grower and Shipper,* July 1930, p. 16.

99. The purposes of the bureau are detailed in *The Agricultural Labor Bureau of the San Joaquin Valley: Its Aims and Responses,* an eight-page brochure in the Industrial Relations–Labor Law Enforcement File, California State Archives. See

also testimony of Frank J. Palomares, in La Follette Committee, *Hearings*, pt. 51, pp. 18583–604.

100. Detailed descriptions and analyses of the origins, structures, and functions of the several farm employers' associations that came into being during the 1920s are available in La Follette Committee, *Report*, pt. 4, pp. 407–522, 648–64; McWilliams, *Factories in the Field*, pp. 189–93, 199; Jamieson, *Labor Unionism*, p. 72. For information relating to the labor-recruitment practices typically employed by farm employers' cooperatives, see "Report on the Mexican Labor Situation in the Imperial Valley," April 2, 1926, in California State Bureau of Labor Statistics, *Twenty-second Biennial Report, 1925–1926* (Sacramento, 1926), pp. 113–27. See also transcript of Wofford B. Camp interview, pp. 206–8, in Bancroft Library, University of California, Berkeley.

101. Louis Bloch, *Facts about Filipino Immigration into California*, California State Department of Industrial Relations Special Bulletin no. 3 (San Francisco, 1930), p. 12.

102. One of the rare experiments in rural welfare capitalism in California is discussed in Howard F. Pressey, "The Housing and Handling of Mexican Labor at Rancho Sespe," *California Citrograph*, December 1929, pp. 51, 72.

103. A very full and lively account of the disadvantaged condition of the industrial worker during the 1920s may be found in Irving Bernstein, *The Lean Years: A History of the American Worker, 1920–1933* (Boston: Houghton Mifflin, 1960).

4. Communists on the Farm

1. U.S. Congress, House, Committee on Immigration and Naturalization, *Western Hemisphere Immigration: Hearings on H.R. 8523, H.R. 8530, and H.R. 8702*, 71st Cong., 2d sess. (Washington, D.C.: Government Printing Office, 1930), p. 437.

2. Ibid. Analyses of why farm employers in California tended to consider Mexican agricultural workers especially docile, and therefore a prized labor force, are available in R. L. Adams, "Labor Needs in California Crop Production with Particular Reference to the Mexican," February 1930, in the Industrial Relations–Labor Law Enforcement File, California State Archives, Sacramento (reprinted in *Report of Governor C. C. Young's Fact-Finding Committee: Mexicans in California* (San Francisco, 1930), pp. 151–71; Paul S. Taylor, *Mexican Labor in the United States: Imperial Valley*, University of California Publications in Economics, vol. 6, no. 1 (Berkeley: University of California Press, 1928), pp. 40–41. See also Louis Bloch to R. L. Adams, February 1, 1930, in Industrial Relations–Labor Law Enforcement File; Ralph H. Taylor, "Brief in Opposition to Application of Quota to Mexico," in *Hearings on Western Hemisphere Immigration*, pp. 227–39; Ricardo Romo, "Responses to Mexican Immigration, 1910–1930," *Aztlán* 6 (Summer 1975):175; Mark Reisler, "Always the Laborer, Never the Citizen: Anglo Perceptions of Mexican Immigration during the 1920s," *Pacific Historical Review* 45 (May 1976):231–54.

3. *Mexicans in California*, p. 123.

4. Ibid., pp. 123–33. See also Juan Gómez-Quiñones, "The First Steps: Chicano Labor Conflict and Organizing, 1900–1920," *Aztlán* 3 (Spring 1973):13–45.

5. *Mexicans in California*, p. 129. See also Manuel Gamio, *Mexican Immigra-*

tion to the United States (Chicago: University of Chicago Press, 1930), pp. 134–36.

6. U.S. Congress, Senate, Subcommittee of the Committee on Education and Labor, *Hearings on S. Res. 266, Violations of Free Speech and Rights of Labor,* 74th Cong., 2d sess. (Washington, D.C.: Government Printing Office, 1939), pt. 55, pp. 20124–35 (hereafter cited as La Follette Committee, *Hearings*); Taylor, *Mexican Labor,* pp. 29–40; U.S. Congress, Senate, Subcommittee of the Committee on Education and Labor, *Report, Violations of Free Speech and Rights of Labor,* report no. 1150, 77th Cong., 2d sess. (Washington, D.C.: Government Printing Office, 1942), pt. 4, pp. 435–43 (hereafter cited as La Follette Committee, *Report*); statement of W. O. Blair, in *Hearings on Western Hemisphere Immigration,* pp. 139–45.

7. The State Commission of Immigration and Housing regarded labor-camp conditions in the Imperial Valley as being among the worst in the state, and farm employers in the region to be among the most resistant to its recommendations for improvement. See Commission of Immigration and Housing, *Ninth Annual Report* (Sacramento, January 9, 1923), pp. 38–39, and *Annual Report* (Sacramento, January 1927), pp. 17–20.

8. Taylor, *Mexican Labor,* p. 53.

9. The union subsequently changed its name to the Mexican Mutual Aid Society of the Imperial Valley in an apparent effort to improve the organization's image in a region notoriously antagonistic toward farmworkers' unions. See Louis Bloch, "The Strike of Mexican Cantaloupe Pickers," in *Mexicans in California,* p. 150.

10. Details of the strike are contained in Bloch, "Strike of Mexican Cantaloupe Pickers," pp. 135–50; Taylor, *Mexican Labor,* pp. 40–54; Charles Wollenberg, "Huelga, 1928 Style: The Imperial Valley Cantaloupe Workers' Strike," *Pacific Historical Review* 38 (February 1969):45–58; and "Organization Efforts of Mexican Agricultural Workers," Work Projects Administration, Federal Writers Project (Oakland, 1938), pp. 16–19.

11. For popular attitudes toward Filipino farmworkers, see statements of Fred J. Hart and Chester B. Moore, in *Hearings on Western Hemisphere Immigration,* pp. 192–211 and 239–251. See also *Pacific Rural Press,* January 19, 1929, p. 72; April 13, 1929, pp. 476–77; and February 15, 1930, p. 209. For additional information relating to the special problems encountered by Filipino farmworkers in California, see Louis Bloch, *Facts about Filipino Immigration into California,* California State Department of Industrial Relations, Special Bulletin no. 3 (San Francisco, 1930), pp. 2, 13, 37, 73–76; Sonia Emily Wallovits, "The Filipinos in California," M.A. thesis, University of Southern California, 1966, pp. 1–3, 42–127; Donald E. Anthony, "Filipino Labor in Central California," *Sociology and Social Research* 16 (September–October 1931):149–56; Emory S. Bogardus, "American Attitudes toward Filipinos," *Sociology and Social Research* 13 (September–October 1928):472–79, and *Anti-Filipino Race Riots* (Los Angeles: University of Southern California, 1930); Carey McWilliams, *Factories in the Field* (Boston: Little, Brown, 1939), pp. 130–33, 137–45; Cletus Edward Daniel, "Organized Anti-unionism in Triumph: The 1936 Salinas Lettuce Packers' Strike," M.A. thesis, San Jose State College, 1969, pp. 39–48; Commonwealth Club of California, "Filipino Immigration," *Transactions* 24, no. 7 (November 1929): 307–78; Varden Fuller, "The Supply of Agricultural Labor as a Factor in the Evolution of Farm Organization in California," reprinted in La Follette Committee,

Notes

Hearings, pt. 54, p. 19880. For an overview of the Filipino immigration experience, see Bruno Lasker, *Filipino Immigration to Continental United States and to Hawaii* (Chicago: University of Chicago Press, 1931), especially pp. 358–68, and H. Brett Melendy, *Asians in America* (Boston: Twayne Publishers, 1977), pp. 17–110.

12. The policy of dual unionism was not new to Communist trade unionists in the United States. Between 1919 and 1921, before the infant Communist movement in the country had undergone "bolshevization" and before its trade-union policy had been brought under the control of the Red International of Labor Unions (Profintern), Communist trade unions in America pursued a policy of revolutionary dual unionism which they hoped would weaken and in time destroy the influence of the "reactionary" American Federation of Labor within the nation's working class. See Theodore Draper, *American Communism and Soviet Russia* (New York: Viking Press, 1960), pp. 215–16, and William Z. Foster, *From Bryan to Stalin* (New York: International Publishers, 1937), pp. 133–42.

13. A. Lozovsky, "Problems of Strike Strategy," *Communist International* 5 (March 1, 1928):17, and "Results and Prospects of the United Front," ibid. (March 15, 1928):142–48; Foster, *From Bryan to Stalin,* pp. 213–15; Draper, *American Communism and Soviet Russia,* pp. 284–90; J. Ballam, "The Cleveland Convention—Building a New Trade Union Center," *Communist* 8 (April 1929):163–71; *The Trade Union Unity League: Its Program Structure, Methods, and History* (New York: Trade Union Unity League, 1929), pp. 20–30.

14. "Thesis on the Agrarian Question," adopted by the Second Congress of the Communist International, July 17–August 7, 1920, reprinted in *Communist* 10 (December 1931):1046.

15. Ibid., pp. 1047, 1053. See also *The Second Year of the Workers (Communist) Party of America: Report of the Central Executive Committee to the Third National Convention: Theses, Program, Resolution,* December 30, 1923–January 2, 1924 (Chicago: Workers Party of America, 1924), pp. 120–22; and Workers (Communist) Party of America, *Fourth National Convention,* August 21–30, 1925 (Chicago: Daily Worker Publishing Company, 1925), pp. 109–15.

16. The inefficacy of the TUEL during the 1920s is clear even from the generous analysis of its founder, William Z. Foster. See Foster, *From Bryan to Stalin,* pp. 164–215, and "The Party Trade Union Work during Ten Years," pt. 1, *Communist* 8 (September 1929):488–93, and pt. 2, ibid. (November 1929):609–18. American Communists did acknowledge the disadvantaged status of agricultural workers during the 1920s, and argued both for their right to organize and for their protection under federal labor laws. The party did not, however, show any strong interest in assuming the task of farmworker organization itself. See "Workers Party Draft Platform of Class Struggle," *Daily Worker,* May 26, 1928, p. 6.

17. Foster, " Party Trade Union Work," pt. 2, p. 616. The split that the adoption of dual unionism prompted within the ranks of the American Communist party is described in Draper, *American Communism and Soviet Russia,* pp. 282–314, 377–441. See also Irving Howe and Lewis Coser, *The American Communist Party: A Critical History (1919–1957)* (Boston: Beacon Press, 1957), pp. 175–272.

18. Foster, *From Bryan to Stalin,* pp. 216–17, 241; *American Labor Year Book: 1930* (New York: Rand School of Social Science, 1930), pp. 95–103; William Z. Foster, "The T.U.U.L. Convention," *Communist* 8 (September 1929):528–33; *Trade Union Unity League,* p. 20.

19. "Building the Trade Union Unity League," *Party Organizer* 3 (May 1930):10–11. Communists on the Pacific coast, where the movement to organize agricultural labor was ultimately centered, had by the end of 1929 became conscious of the multiplying signs of discontent among farmworkers in California, but continued to focus their attention and interest on urban industrial workers. See "Draft Resolution of the District No. 13 Plenum on the Political and Economic Situation in the District," December 7–8, 1929, in U.S. Congress, House, Special Committee to Investigate Communist Activities in the United States, *Hearings on H. Res. 220: An Investigation of Communist Propaganda in the United States,* 71st Cong., 2d sess., pt. 5, vol. 4 (Washington, D.C.: Government Printing Office, 1930), pp. 226–34 (hereafter cited as Fish Committee, *Hearings*).

20. Edmundo L. Aragón to Manager of Vegetable Growers of the Valley, January 3, 1930, Industrial Relations–Labor Law Enforcement File.

21. Interestingly, when the 1930 lettuce workers' strike began, those who had been vigorously fighting for restrictions on Mexican immigration throughout the late 1920s argued that such labor difficulties could be reduced or eliminated by a more restrictive immigration policy. Imperial Valley farm employers vehemently disagreed. While they encouraged federal immigration officials to deport any Mexican identified with unionism, they opposed any restriction of the flow of cheap labor from Mexico. See *Los Angeles Times,* January 7, 1930, p. 1.

22. "The Imperial Valley Strikes of January and February, 1930," transcript of an interview with H. Harvey, January 18, 1938, p. 1, Federal Writers Project Collection, Bancroft Library, University of California, Berkeley.

23. Ibid., pp. 1–2, 6; testimony of Elmer W. Heald, in Fish Committee, *Hearings,* pt. 5, vol. 3, pp. 258–59; *Western Worker,* July 15, 1932, p. 2; American Civil Liberties Union, Press Bulletin no. 423, September 9, 1930, in Papers of the American Civil Liberties Union, vol. 404, Princeton University Library (hereafter cited as ACLU Papers). See also R. W. Henderson to Roger N. Baldwin, March 9, 1931, in ACLU Papers, vol. 417.

24. Harvey interview, pp. 4–5. See also *Daily Worker,* January 23, 1930, p. 1; Frank Spector, *Story of the Imperial Valley* (New York: International Labor Defense, n.d.), p. 18.

25. *Calexico Chronicle,* January 14, 1930, p. 1; Spector, *Story of the Imperial Valley,* p. 18; *Daily Worker,* January 7, 1930, p. 1; Harvey interview, pp. 2–5.

26. Quoted in *Calexico Chronicle,* January 14, 1930, p. 1.

27. Harvey interview, pp. 2–4; Spector, *Story of the Imperial Valley,* pp. 18–19; *El Centro Press,* January 10, 1930, p. 1.

28. *Brawley News,* January 13 and January 28, 1930; *El Centro Press,* January 10, 1930; Harvey interview, p. 3; Conrad Seiler, "Cantaloupes and Communists," *Nation* 131 (September 3, 1930):244: "No Civil Liberties for Farm Workers in Valley," *Open Forum,* January 18, 1930.

29. Harvey interview, pp. 5–6; *Brawley News,* January 13, 1930; *El Centro Press,* January 10, 1930; "No Civil Liberties," p. 1; Spector, *Story of the Imperial Valley,* p. 18.

30. "Summary of Facts Concerning the Invasion of Civil Rights of Strikers in Imperial Valley, California," n.d., typescript in ACLU Papers, vol. 417. See also ACLU, Press Bulletin no. 392, February 21, 1930, in ibid., vol. 404; *Open Forum,* January 25, 1930; *Daily Worker,* January 13 and January 14, 1930.

31. *Daily Worker,* January 14, January 17, and January 18, 1930; Harvey

interview, p. 13; "Spector, from San Quentin Prison Cell, Tells the Story of the Imperial Valley Fight," *Labor Defender* 5 (December 1930):254–56.

32. Harvey interview, pp. 2–4, 6–7; Spector, *Story of the Imperial Valley,* p. 19.

33. *Daily Worker,* January 18, 1930, p. 7; Harvey interview, p. 7.

34. *Daily Worker,* January 13, January 18, and January 23, 1930; Spector, *Story of the Imperial Valley,* pp. 18–19; *Los Angeles Times,* January 16, 1930; Frank Spector, "Imperial Valley Fights," *Labor Defender* 5 (July 1930):136–37; Harvey interview, p. 13, See also Charles T. Connell to H. L. Kerwin, January 17, 1930, in Records of the U.S. Conciliation Service, Record Group 13, National Archives, File no. 170-5463 (hereafter cited as RG 13, uscs).

35. *Daily Worker,* January 23, 1930, pp. 1–2.

36. Ibid., January 30, February 13, February 22, and March 1, 1930; Spector, *Story of the Imperial Valley,* pp. 22–23; Stuart Jamieson, *Labor Unionism in American Agriculture,* U.S. Bureau of Labor Statistics Bulletin no. 836 (Washington, D.C.: Government Printing Office, 1945), p. 83; testimony of Elmer Heald, in Fish Committee, *Hearings,* pt. 5, vol. 3, pp. 258–65.

37. *Daily Worker,* January 23, 1930, p. 2; Spector, *Story of the Imperial Valley,* p. 18; testimony of Elmer Heald, in Fish Committee, *Hearings,* pt. 5, vol. 3, p. 258; "Frank Spector . . . Tells the Story," pp. 254–56; Clinton J. Taft, "The Lowest-Down Sheriff's Office in the World," n.d., typescript in aclu Papers, vol. 417.

38. *Daily Worker,* February 13, 1930; *Brawley News,* February 12, 1930; Harvey interview, p. 8; Jamieson, *Labor Unionism,* p. 82. The designation of Mexicans as "nonwhites," rather than reflecting a legitimate scientific scheme of racial classification, reflects instead what was in California and the Southwest the popular contemporary belief subscribed to by most "whites." Though most Mexican farmworkers were of native American descent, the Census Bureau, owing in part to the insistence of Mexican Americans, classified all people of Mexican heritage as whites. That there was considerable confusion attending this matter of racial classification is indicated by the fact that in the 1930 census Mexicans were officially counted as a separate "race," only to be regarded once again as "whites" in 1940. Whatever the preferences of anthropologists and census takers, however, the popular perception of Mexicans as nonwhite had the practical effect of consigning them to a racial status that subjected them to pervasive discrimination. On this point see Fernando Peñalosa, "Toward an Operational Definition of the Mexican American," *Aztlán* 1 (Spring 1970):1–13; Gamio, *Mexican Immigration,* p. 53.

39. Harvey interview, pp. 8–11; *Brawley News,* February 18, 1930. See also R. W. Henderson to Roger N. Baldwin, June 6, 1930, in aclu Papers, vol. 417.

40. Charles T. Connell to H. R. Kerwin, January 17 and February 19, 1930; A. N. Jack to Connell, January 22, 1930; all in File no. 170-5463, RG 13, uscs. See also *Eighteenth Annual Report of the Secretary of Labor* (Washington, D.C.: Government Printing Office, 1930), p. 48.

41. *Brawley News,* March 1, 1930; *Daily Worker,* March 1, 1930; *Monthly Labor Review* 30 (April 1930):124.

42. *Daily Worker,* March 25, 1930.

43. Bruce Bliven to Roger Baldwin, March 4, 1930, in aclu Papers, vol. 417.

44. *Brawley News,* March 15, 1930.

45. Ibid., January 28, 1930. See also Connell to Kerwin, May 8, 1930, File no. 170-5463, RG13, uscs.

46. Testimony of Elmer Heald, in Fish Committee, *Hearings,* pt. 5, vol. 3, pp. 257–59; Spector, "Imperial Valley Fights," pp. 136–37; Spector, *Story of the Imperial Valley,* pp. 5–6; Seiler, "Cantaloupes and Communists," and the following letters in File no. 170-5463, RG 13, USCS: p. 244; Connell to Kerwin, January 17 and February 19, 1930; A. N. Jack to Connell, April 18, 1930, and Connell to Jack, April 24, 1930. On the earlier use of the state's criminal syndicalism law against radicals, see Woodrow C. Whitten, *Criminal Syndicalism and the Law in California: 1919–1927* (Philadelphia: American Philosophical Society, 1969).

47. Copies of the various circulars and leaflets through which the AWIL sought to politicize the melon strike are in File no. 170-5463, RG 13, USCS. See also Howe and Coser, *American Communist Party,* p. 193.

48. Henderson to Baldwin, May 19, 1930, in ACLU Papers, vol. 417. See also Connell to Kerwin, April 24, 1930, and Jack to Connell, April 18, 1930, both in File no. 170-5463, RG 13, USCS. Commissioner Charles T. Connell of the Los Angeles office of the U.S. Conciliation Service was so convinced of the noneconomic origins of labor conflict in the Imperial Valley that his official report to Washington listed "agitation by Communist leaders" as the only cause of unrest in the region. See "Summary of Final Report of Commissioner of Conciliation," June 13, 1930, File no. 170-5463, RG 13, USCS.

49. *Daily Worker,* March 25, 1930, p. 3.

50. *Brawley News,* April 15, 1930; *El Centro Press,* April 15, 1930; *Los Angeles Times,* April 15, 1930; *Daily Worker,* April 16, April 19, and April 24, 1930; Spector, *Story of the Imperial Valley,* pp. 5–6; Spector, "Imperial Valley Fights," pp. 136–37; Seiler, "Cantaloupes and Communists," p. 244; Henderson to Baldwin, May 4, 1930, in ACLU Papers, vol. 417; ACLU, Press Bulletin no. 402, April 30, 1930, and Press Bulletin no. 405, May 21, 1930, in ACLU Papers, vols. 404 and 391, respectively.

51. Testimony of Elmer Heald, in Fish Committee, *Hearings,* pt. 5, vol. 3, pp. 258–63; Spector, *Story of the Imperial Valley,* p. 26; *Daily Worker,* April 28, 1930; *Brawley News,* May 1, 1930; *El Centro Press,* May 1, 1930; Seiler, "Cantaloupes and Communists," p. 244. The role of the Southern California branch of the American Civil Liberties Union in the Imperial Valley's labor troubles is described in James Gray, "The American Civil Liberties Union of Southern California and Imperial Valley Agricultural Labor Disturbances: 1930, 1934," Ph.D. dissertation, University of California, Los Angeles, 1966, chap. 2.

52. Agricultural Workers Industrial League to All Agricultural Workers in Imperial Valley, n.d. [May 1930], reprinted in Fish Committee, *Hearings,* pt. 5, vol. 4, 1458–60.

53. In explaining the AWIL's decision to abandon plans for the cantaloupe workers' strike, the *Daily Worker* commented editorially that it could not have been won after the mass arrests of union leaders in mid-April, and thus to have attempted to pursue it would have "proved a disastrous move for the T.U.U.L. and the Party." See "The Imperial Valley Case," *Daily Worker,* June 27, 1930, p. 2. See also Connell to Kerwin, May 8, 1930, File no. 170-5463, RG 13, USCS.

54. *Daily Worker,* May 15, May 17, May 22, June 5, and June 9, 1930; testimony of Elmer Heald and Hon. Von H. Thompson, in Fish Committee, *Hearings,* pt. 5, vol. 3, pp. 263–64 and 268–69; Gray, "American Civil Liberties Union," pp. 34–38.

55. *Open Forum,* June 7, 1930; Esther Lowell, "Erickson Speaks from Prison,"

Labor Defender 5 (September 1930):180; *Daily Worker,* May 28 and May 31, 1930.

56. People v. Horiuchi et al., 114 Cal. App. 415, 300 Pac. 457 (1931). Trial arguments are repeated and summarized in a number of sources. In addition to daily accounts of the trial's progress in the *Brawley News, El Centro Press, Calexico Chronicle, Los Angeles Times,* and other Southern California newspapers between May 31 and June 13, 1930, see *Open Forum,* June 7, June 14, and June 21, 1930; *Daily Worker,* June 2, June 4, June 5, June 7, and June 11, 1930; William Simons, "Imperial Valley Criminal Syndicalism Case," *Daily Worker,* June 12, 1930, p. 6; Spector, *Story of the Imperial Valley,* pp. 6–17; Lowell, "Erickson Speaks from Prison," p. 180; "Frank Spector . . . Tells the Story," pp. 254–56; Seiler, "Cantaloupes and Communists," p. 244; testimony of Elmer Heald, in Fish Committee, *Hearings,* pt. 5, vol. 3, pp. 258–65; ACLU, Press Bulletin no. 409, June 9, 1930, and International Labor Defense press release, June 14, 1930, both in ACLU Papers, vols. 404 and 417, respectively.

57. AWIL organizers claimed at the close of the El Centro trial that Heald had approached them after their arrests in mid-April with a deal: the criminal syndicalism indictments against them would be quashed if they agreed to accept five-month vagrancy sentences without appeal. Heald's intention, the organizers claimed, was to see that they were safely locked away during the cantaloupe harvest, and thus unable to provide leadership for a strike that could not have succeeded without them. See *Daily Worker,* June 16, 1930; Henderson to Baldwin, May 4, 1930, in ACLU Papers, vol. 417; Connell to Kerwin, May 8, 1930, File no. 170-5463, RG 13, USCS.

58. *Los Angeles Times,* April 30, 1930; testimony of Elmer Heald, in Fish Committee, *Hearings,* pt. 5, vol. 3, pp. 258–61; *Open Forum,* June 7, 1930; *Daily Worker,* June 14, 1930. Heald, Judge Thompson, and Sheriff Gillett were all running for reelection in 1930, and thus especially eager to remain on the best possible terms with the powerful farm employers who controlled the economic and political life of the Imperial Valley.

59. Henderson to Baldwin, June 6, 1930, in ACLU Papers, vol. 417. See also Henderson to International Labor Defense, n.d., in ibid.

60. Testimony of Elmer Heald, in Fish Committee, *Hearings,* pt. 5, vol. 3, p. 265.

61. Ibid., p. 262; testimony of Hon. Von H. Thompson, in ibid., p. 269; *Brawley News,* June 14, 1930; *El Centro Press,* June 14, June 16, and June 17, 1930; *Daily Worker,* June 14, June 16, and June 17, 1930; *Open Forum,* June 21, 1930; Seiler, "Cantaloupes and Communists," p. 243; Spector, "Imperial Valley Fights," pp. 136–37; Lowell, "Erickson Speaks from Prison," p. 180.

62. George H. Shoat, "Imperial Valley Outrage," *Open Forum,* June 5, 1930; *Daily Worker,* June 23 and June 24, 1930; *Open Forum,* June 21, 1930. For samples of Communist propaganda generated by the Imperial Valley convictions, see Fish Committee, *Hearings,* pt. 5, vol. 4, pp. 1517–26.

63. *Daily Worker,* June 18, 1930; *Open Forum,* June 21 and June 28, 1930. In its annual review the ACLU cited the Imperial Valley convictions as the most important denials of civil liberties anywhere in the United States during 1930. See *A Strike Is Criminal Syndicalism—in California* (New York: American Civil Liberties Union, March 1931), p. 3; ACLU, Press Bulletin no. 413, July 16, 1930, and

Clinton J. Taft to Baldwin, May 5, 1930, both in ACLU Papers, vols. 404 and 417, respectively.

64. Baldwin to Taft, June 6, 1930, in ACLU Papers, vol. 417.

65. Sam Darcy to Baldwin, July 11, 1930; Baldwin to Darcy, July 9 and July 30, 1930; all in ACLU Papers, vol. 417.

66. Baldwin to Felix Frankfurter, July 30, 1930; Frankfurter to Baldwin, August 5, 1930; Alfred Bettman to Baldwin, August 27, 1930; Baldwin to Bettman, August 29, 1930; Forrest Bailey to Taft, November 19, 1930; all in ibid.

67. Henderson to International Labor Defense and ACLU, May 28, 1931, in ACLU Papers, vol. 478; People v. Horiuchi et al., 114 Cal. App. 415, 300 Pac. 457 (1931); *Daily Worker,* March 12 and June 6, 1931; *Open Forum,* June 6, June 13, June 20, July 4, July 25, and November 7, 1931; Frank Spector, "The Status of the Imperial Valley Case," *Western Worker,* May 1, 1932, p. 6; *Western Worker,* September 1, 1932, and February 20 and March 6, 1933; Joseph Pass, "42 Years?," *Labor Defender* 6 (June 1931):107; Frank Spector, "California's Parole Racket," *Labor Defender* 8 (November 1932):172–73; P.F., "One More to Free," *Labor Defender* 8 (November 1932):213–14; *American Labor Year Book: 1932* (New York: Rand School of Social Science, 1932), p. 159; International Labor Defense, *Free the Imperial Valley Prisoners* (New York: Workers Library Publishers, 1932).

On the internal ideological conflicts involved in the case, see Henderson to Forrest Bailey, June 8, 1931; Baldwin to Henderson, July 23, 1931; Henderson to Baldwin, July 28, 1931; Baldwin to Henderson, August 8, 1931; Henderson to George Maurer, August 19, 1931; Bailey to Henderson, September 1, 1931; and Henderson to Ida Rothstein, November 18, 1931; all in ACLU Papers, vol. 478.

On the campaign to win paroles for the imprisoned organizers, see Harry F. Ward to Raymond A. Leonard, August 31, 1931; Ward to C. L. Neumiller, August 13, 1931; Ward to Ed H. Whyte, August 13, 1931; Mark E. Noon to C. M. Ripley, November 4, 1931; ACLU press bulletin, December 1, 1931, all in ACLU Papers, vol. 478; Spector to Baldwin, March 23, 1932; Baldwin to Spector, March 26, 1932; International Labor Defense press release, July 29, 1932; Baldwin to Secretary of Labor William N. Doak, July 29, 1932; and Harry E. Hull to Baldwin, August 8, 1932, all in ACLU Papers, vol. 559.

68. "Imperial Valley Criminal Syndicalism Case," p. 6; *Daily Worker,* May 22, 1930, p. 4. See also ACLU, Press Bulletin no. 409, June 19, 1930, ACLU Papers, vol. 404.

69. "Some Historical Aspects of the Criminal Syndicalism Law in California: With Special Reference to the California State Federation of Labor," typescript in Federal Writers Project Collection, n.d., pp. 23–29.

70. *Daily Worker,* June 18, 1930; Reggie Carson, "Significance of the Imperial Valley Case," ibid., June 27, 1930; William Schneiderman, "Reign of Terror in Southern California," ibid., June 30, 1930, p. 4; "Frank Spector . . . Tells the Story," pp. 254–56; Pass, "42 Years?," p. 107; Spector, "Status of the Imperial Valley Case," p. 6, and "California's Parole Racket," pp. 172–73; *Open Forum,* June 21, June 28, and July 25, 1931; *A Strike Is Criminal Syndicalism,* pp. 8–11; "Draft Thesis for the District Convention, District No. 13, Communist Party of the United States" [May 1930], in Fish Committee, *Hearings,* pt. 5, vol. 3, pp. 54–58; "Minutes of the Pacific Coast Conference of the International Labor Defense," July

27, 1930, in Fish Committee, *Hearings,* pt. 5, vol. 3, pp. 58–70; *Western Worker,* February 15, 1932, pp. 1–2. For copies of various ILD circulars calling for repeal of the criminal syndicalism law, see Fish Committee, *Hearings,* pt. 5, vol. 4, pp. 1519–25.

71. *Daily Worker,* May 22, 1930, p. 4; Simons, "Imperial Valley Criminal Syndicalism Case," p. 6; Eva Shafran, "Imperial Valley—Another Gastonia," *Daily Worker,* May 23, 1930, p. 4; Irving Kreitzberg and Jose Arispe, "The Mexican Workers and the Communist Party," *Daily Worker,* May 28, 1930, p. 4; "Imperial Valley Case," p. 4; Carson, "Significance of the Imperial Valley Case," p. 4; S. Mingulin, "The Crisis in the United States and the Problems of the Communist Party," *Communist* 9 (June 1930):505, 507; William Weinstone, "The Economic Crisis in the United States and the Tasks of the Communist Party," *Communist International* 6, no. 31 (1930):1230; and the following material in Fish committee, *Hearings,* pt. 5: "Draft Thesis for the Seventh Convention of the Communist Party, U.S.A.," adopted by the Central Committee Plenum, April 3, 1930, vol. 4, p. 398; "Draft Thesis for the District Convention, District No. 13, Communist Party of the United States" [May 1930], vol. 3, pp. 55–58; and "Draft Resolution of the Economic and Political Situation in the Los Angeles Section and the Tasks Confronting the Party" [May 1930], vol. 4, pp. 234–39.

72. For an "official" Communist analysis of the AWIL's failure to bring off the cantaloupe workers' strike, see "Imperial Valley Case," *Daily Worker,* June 27, 1930, p. 4.

73. Stuart Jamieson has argued that the work that Communists did among the unemployed during 1931 and 1932 facilitated the organizing of agricultural workers in 1933. See Jamieson, *Labor Unionism,* p. 83.

74. *Daily Worker,* August 1, August 3, August 8, and August 15, 1931; *San Jose Mercury-Herald,* July 31, August 1, August 2, and August 3, 1931; Jamieson, *Labor Unionism,* pp. 84–85. See also E. P. Marsh to H. L. Kerwin, August 4, 1931, File no. 170-6504, RG 13, USCS.

75. *Western Worker,* March 1, 1932, p. 6; Jack Stachel, "Coming Struggles and Lessons in Strike Strategy," *Communist* 10 (March 1931):207; Dick Durant, "Building Cannery and Agricultural Workers Industrial League in San Jose Section," *Western Worker,* July 1, 1932, p. 6.

76. Marsh to Kerwin, August 4, 1931, File no. 170-6504, RG 13, USCS.

77. *Western Worker,* June 15, 1932, p. 5; Jamieson, *Labor Unionism,* p. 85.

78. Harrison George, "Causes and Meaning of the Farmers' Strike and Our Tasks as Communists," *Communist* 11 (October 1932):921–22; Stachel, "Coming Struggles," pp. 205, 207.

79. *Western Worker,* May 15, 1932, p. 2. It should probably be noted that the CAWIU's failures during this period reflected the overall failure of the TUUL to accomplish the party's work among the unorganized. The leadership of the Red International of Labor Unions remarked in 1931: "The fundamental weakness of the Trade Union Unity League is the fact that at a time so favorable for revolutionary work it is still failing to organize workers in struggle for their daily demands and needs" (*American Labor Year Book: 1932,* p. 74).

80. Orrick Johns, *Time of Our Lives* (New York: Stackpole, 1937), pp. 324–25.

81. Interview with Sam Darcy, November 22, 1974.

82. Howe and Coser, *American Communist Party,* pp. 144–74. See also Industrial Association of San Francisco, *Who Are These Communists?,* Special Bulletin

C-27, May 8, 1935, in Paul Scharrenberg Papers, Bancroft Library, University of California, Berkeley.

83. For an example of the personal publicity that Darcy gained as a result of the March 6 demonstration, see *New York Times,* March 5, 1930, p. 2.

84. Darcy interview.

85. Ibid.; Sam Darcy, "Autobiography," unpublished manuscript in Mr. Darcy's possession, pp. 15–16. Earl Browder, following his expulsion from the American Communist Party in 1945, wrote that Darcy, along with William Z. Foster, constituted his "permanent (but usually secret) opposition in America." See Earl Browder, "The American Communist Party in the Thirties," in *As We Saw the Thirties: Essays on Social and Political Movements of a Decade,* ed. Rita James Simon (Urbana: University of Illinois Press, 1967), p. 234.

86. Darcy, "Autobiography," pp. 16–33; Darcy interview.

87. Durant, "Building Cannery and Agricultural Workers Industrial League," p. 6; [Sam Darcy], "Not Reliance on Spontaneity but Organization Is Needed," *Party Organizer* 4 (September-October 1931):82–83.

88. "Draft Resolution of the District 13 Convention of the Communist Party, U.S.A.," July 1932, *Western Worker,* August 1, 1932.

89. *Western Worker,* August 15, 1932.

90. Ibid., August 15, September 1, October 1, and November 28, 1932.

91. Ibid., November 28, 1932; Bebel Alonzo, "Frank H. Buck Brings Prosperity," ibid., p. 4; Johns, *Time of Our Lives,* pp. 329–30.

92. Alonzo, "Frank H. Buck," p. 4; Jamieson, *Labor Unionism,* pp. 85–86; *Western Worker,* December 5, 1932.

93. *Western Worker,* November 28, 1932; Alonzo, "Frank H. Buck," p. 4; *Sacramento Union,* November 15 and November 16, 1932.

94. *Western Worker,* November 18 and December 5, 1932; *Sacramento Union,* November 22, 1932. For a sympathetic explanation of the employers' motives in trying to break the strike, see Andrew Ham to Lucille B. Milner, n.d., in ACLU Papers, vol. 559.

95. *Western Worker,* December 5 and December 12, 1932; *Sacramento Union,* December 3, 1932.

96. *Western Worker,* December 12 and December 19, 1932; *San Francisco Examiner,* December 5 and December 6, 1932; *San Francisco Chronicle,* December 6, 1932; *Sacramento Bee,* December 6, 1932; *Sacramento Union,* December 6, 1932; *Northern California Political Prisoners Bulletin* 1 (Summer 1933):1. See also Orrick Johns to "Friends," n.d.; Roger Baldwin to William L. Patterson, December 12, 1932; ACLU to Chief of Police O. E. Alley, December 6, 1932; Alley to ACLU, December 8, 1932; Baldwin to Alley, December 9, 1932; International Labor Defense press release, December 10, 1932; affidavit of Orrick Johns, January 5, 1933; affidavit of Anita Whitney, January 10, 1933; Austin Lewis to Lucille B. Milner, January 3, 1933; Baldwin to Lewis, January 9, 1933; Johns to Baldwin, January 9, 1933; William A. Smith to Johns, December 30, 1932; all in ACLU Papers, vol. 559.

97. *Western Worker,* December 5, 1932, p. 2; Orrick Johns, "Vacaville Fights!," ibid., January 16, 1933, p. 2.

98. *Western Worker,* December 19 and December 26, 1932, and January 2, January 9, and February 6, 1933. For examples of the special abuses experienced by Filipino workers in California during the early 1930s, see Melendy, *Asians in*

America, pp. 17–110; Howard A. DeWitt, "The Watsonville Anti-Filipino Riot of 1930: A Case Study of the Great Depression and Ethnic Conflict in California," *Southern California Quarterly* 61 (Fall 1979):291–302.

99. *Western Worker,* December 5, 1932, p. 4.

5. *The Great Upheaval: 1933*

1. For an interesting and instructive treatment of labor's rise during 1933, see Irving Bernstein, *Turbulent Years: A History of the American Worker, 1933–1941* (Boston: Houghton Mifflin, 1970), especially chaps. 1–3.

2. Stuart Jamieson, *Labor Unionism in American Agriculture,* U.S. Bureau of Labor Statistics Bulletin no. 836 (Washington, D.C.: Government Printing Office, 1945), pp. 8–21, 30–42; Daniel J. Ahearn, Jr., *Wages and Farm and Factory Laborers, 1914–1944* (New York: Columbia University Press, 1945), pp. 143–79; Sidney C. Sufrin, "Labor Organization in Agricultural America, 1930–35," *American Journal of Sociology* 43 (January 1938):549–53; Carey McWilliams, *Factories in the Field* (Boston: Little, Brown, 1939), p. 211; Josiah C. Folsom, "Farm Laborers in the United States Turn to Collective Action," U.S. Department of Agriculture, *Yearbook of Agriculture, 1935* (Washington, D.C., 1935), pp. 188–91; Paul S. Taylor and Clark Kerr, "Uprisings on the Farms," *Survey Graphic* 24 (January 1935):19–22, 44; U.S. Congress, Senate, Subcommittee of the Committee on Education and Labor, *Report, Violations of Free Speech and Rights of Labor,* report no. 1150, 77th Cong., 2d sess. (Washington, D.C.: Government Printing Office, 1942), pt. 3, pp. 332–43 (hereafter cited as La Follette Committee, *Report*), and *Hearings on S. Res. 266, Violations of Free Speech and Rights of Labor,* 74th Cong., 2d sess. (Washington, D.C.: Government Printing Office, 1939), pt. 62, Exhibits 9574 and 9575, pp. 22515–31 (hereafter cited as La Follette Committee, *Hearings*). See also Report of Thomas A. Reardon to Governor's Council, April 1933, in Records of the California Department of Industrial Relations, Division of Immigration and Housing, Bancroft Library, University of California, Berkeley (hereafter cited as DIR Records).

3. District Committee of the Cannery and Agricultural Workers Industrial Union, "Strike Strategy in the Agricultural Fields" (n.p., 1933), a circular in the Paul S. Taylor Collection, Bancroft Library, University of California, Berkeley; Jamieson, *Labor Unionism,* pp. 87–88; transcript of an interview with H. Harvey, January 18, 1938, p. 14, in Federal Writers Project Collection, Bancroft Library; *Western Worker,* April 3, 1933, p. 1.

4. William F. Hynes to Elmer Heald, February 11, 1933, in La Follette Committee, *Hearings,* pt. 64, Exhibit 10410, p. 23640.

5. V. N. Thompson to Captain William F. Hynes, February 15, 1933, in ibid., Exhibit 10411, pp. 23640–41.

6. *Western Worker,* March 27, 1933, p. 1.

7. Ibid., April 10, 1933, p. 3.

8. Ibid., April 3 and May 29, 1933.

9. Ibid., April 24, 1933, p. 1.

10. Ibid., pp. 1 and 4, and ibid., May 29, p. 3.

11. Thirteenth Annual Convention of the California Peace Officers' Association, *Proceedings* (August 1933), pp. 116–17; *Western Worker,* April 24, May 1, and

May 29, 1933; Ronald R. Cooley, "Peas Are Cheap," *Western Worker,* May 3, 1933, p. 4; *Oakland Tribune,* April 14, April 15, April 16, and April 17, 1933; *San Jose Mercury-Herald,* April 16, 1933; Orrick Johns, *Time of Our Lives* (New York: Stackpole, 1937), pp. 332–33.

12. *Western Worker,* April 24, May 1, May 8, and May 29, 1933; Jamieson, *Labor Unionism,* p. 89; Thirteenth Annual Convention of the California Peace Officers' Association, *Proceedings,* pp. 116–17. See also Report of Thomas A. Reardon to Governor's Council, June 1933, in DIR Records.

13. *Western Worker,* May 15, May 22, and May 29, 1933; La Follette Committee, *Report,* pt. 4, p. 478; La Follette Committee, *Hearings,* pt. 73, Exhibit 13712, p. 27036.

14. *Western Worker,* May 8, 1933, p. 1.

15. Ibid., May 29, 1933, p. 3.

16. "Berry Pickers' Strike," report of Ross H. Gast to Dr. George P. Clements, Agricultural Department, Los Angeles Chamber of Commerce, June 27, 1933, in La Follette Committee, *Hearings,* pt. 53, Exhibit 8751, p. 19693. See also Ronald W. Lopez, "The El Monte Berry Strike of 1933," *Aztlán* 1 (Spring 1970):101–13.

17. *Western Worker,* June 5 and June 12, 1933; Lawrence Ross, "Lessons from the Southern California Strike," ibid., August 7, 1933, p. 3; *Los Angeles Times,* June 2 and June 3, 1933; Thomas Barker to Frank C. MacDonald, July 3, 1933, in File no. 170-8083, Records of the U.S. Conciliation Service, Record Group 13, National Archives (hereafter cited as USCS).

18. *Western Worker,* June 12, 1933, p. 1; Gene Gordon, "Impressions of the Strike in San Gabriel Valley," ibid., June 19, 1933, p. 2; Ross, "Lessons," p. 3; Charles B. Spaulding, "The Mexican Strike at El Monte, California," *Sociology and Social Research* 18 (July–August 1934):573–76; Theodore Rodriguez and W. G. Fennell to Editors, August 16, 1933, *Nation* 137 (September 6, 1933):272; First Annual District Convention of the Cannery and Agricultural Workers Industrial Union, *Minutes* (San Jose, August 5, 1933), pp. 6–7, in Federal Writers Project Collection, Bancroft Library.

19. "Berry Pickers' Strike," in La Follette Committee, *Hearings,* pt. 53, p. 19694; *Western Worker,* June 19, 1933; Ross, "Lessons," p. 3; Spaulding, "Mexican Strike," pp. 573–74; First Annual CAWIU Convention, *Minutes,* p. 7; Rodriguez and Fennell to Editors, *Nation,* p. 272; Barker to MacDonald, July 3, 1933, File no. 170-8083, RG 13, USCS; *La Opinión* (Los Angeles), June 21 and June 22, 1933.

20. Barker to MacDonald, July 3, 1933, File no. 170-8083, RG 13, USCS.

21. *Western Worker,* June 19 and June 26, 1933; Ross, "Lessons," p. 3; Spaulding, "Mexican Strike," pp. 574, 576. Spaulding insists that until the summer of 1933, "Mexican workers had been regarded [by whites generally] as having little inclination or ability for organization" (p. 571). See also R. A. Wellpott to Captain William F. Hynes, June 7, 1933, in La Follette Committee, *Hearings,* pt. 64, Exhibit 10392, pp. 23628–29.

22. "Berry Pickers' Strike," in La Follette Committee, *Hearings,* pt. 53, pp. 19693–95; Spaulding, "Mexican Strike," pp. 574–80; Jamieson, *Labor Unionism,* pp. 428–29; Rodriguez and Fennell to Editors, *Nation,* p. 272; *Western Worker,* July 17 and July 31, 1933; Ross, "Lessons," p. 3; International Labor Defense, "Report of Arrests for the Month of June, 1933," in Papers of the American Civil Liberties Union, vol. 618, Princeton University Library (hereafter cited as ACLU

Papers); and the following letters in File no. 170-8083, RG 13, USCS; Barker to MacDonald, July 6, 1933; Barker to E. A. Fitzgerald, July 18, 1933; and J. M. Fallin to F. A. Stewart, July 20, 1933.

23. *Western Worker,* June 19 and June 26, 1933; "Pick Ax Handles and Fair Wages: The Story of the San Jose Cherry Pickers," *Northern California Political Prisoners Bulletin* (Summer 1933):2.

24. *San Jose Mercury-Herald,* June 15, 1933, p. 1; "Pick Ax Handles," p. 2; First Annual CAWIU Convention, *Minutes,* pp. 7–8; *Western Worker,* June 26, 1933, p. 1.

25. *San Jose Mercury-Herald,* June 16, June 17, and June 18, 1933; *San Francisco Chronicle,* June 18, 1933; *San Francisco Examiner,* June 18, 1933; *Western Worker,* June 26 and July 3, 1933; Ella Winter, "'For the Duration of the Crop,'" *Nation* 76 (October 25, 1933):304–5; "Pick Ax Handles," p. 2; testimony of Caroline Decker, in People v. Chambers, 22 Cal. App. (2d) 687, 72 Pac. (2d) 746 (1937); International Labor Defense, "Report of Arrests for the Month of June, 1933," ACLU Papers, vol. 618.

26. First Annual CAWIU Convention, *Minutes,* p. 8; *Western Worker,* June 26, 1933, pp. 1, 3; "The Case of Mrs. Minton," *Northern California Political Prisoners Bulletin* 1 (Summer 1933):3.

27. *Western Worker,* July 3, 1933, pp. 1, 3.

28. Fallin to Stewart, July 20, 1933, File no. 170-8083, RG 13, USCS. For additional expressions of concern among farm employers, see O. D. Miller to C. B. Moore, July 5, 1933, in La Follette Committee, *Hearings,* pt. 71, Exhibit 12915, p. 26150; "Berry Pickers' Strike," in La Follette Committee, *Hearings,* pt. 53, p. 19695.

29. Meeting of the Board of Directors of the Agricultural Labor Bureau of the San Joaquin Valley, Inc., *Minutes,* August 7, 1933, in La Follette Committee, *Hearings,* pt. 72, Exhibit 13273, p. 26526. See also F. J. Palomares to Leonard E. Wood, July 9, 1934, in ibid., pt. 72, Ehxibit 13295, pp. 26552–53.

30. Palomares to Charles L. Pioda, August 8, 1933, in ibid., pt. 72, Exhibit 13275, p. 26538; Meeting of the Board of Directors of the Los Angeles Chamber of Commerce, *Minutes,* September 14, 1933, in ibid., pt. 63, Exhibit 9598, p. 22937. See also John A. Dennis to Associated Farmers of California, July 30, 1934, in ibid., pt. 53, Exhibit 8760, pp. 19699–700.

31. First Annual CAWIU Convention, *Minutes,* p. 1; Cannery and Agricultural Workers Industrial Union, "Resolution of District Committee," August 5, 1933, p. 1, Federal Writers Project Collection.

32. Ross, "Lessons," p. 3.

33. *Western Worker,* August 14, 1933, p. 3. The *Western Worker*'s estimate that the CAWIU had a membership of 4,000 in California at the time of the San Jose convention is undoubtedly much too high. Only two weeks earlier, another article in the same paper reported that the CAWIU's membership in Northern California, where virtually all of the union's influence was centered, was only 2,000. Moreover, since the union had been consistently lax in retaining its members following strikes, it is likely that its effective membership was well below the 2,000 mark. Included in the resolution adopted during the San Jose convention was an unhappy admission that the CAWIU's membership was "negligible." See "The Agricultural Workers in the United States," *Western Worker,* July 24, 1933, p. 4; CAWIU, "Resolution of District Committee," p. 2.

34. On a more practical level, convention delegates were issued a four-page

leaflet that outlined basic strategy pertaining to the organization and conduct of CAWIU strikes. Three means of strike agitation were described: an "open method," which relied on mass meetings to build strike support; a "quiet method," by which preliminary organizational work was carried on in secret among a select group of influential workers, who would later become the principal strike leaders and promoters; and a "combination method," which included the most advantageous features of both the open and quiet approaches. Other instructions contained in the leaflet had to do with the actual conduct of strikes, including advice on such topics as strike committees, relief, publicity, picketing, recruiting, and defense. See District Committee of the CAWIU, "Strike Strategy," pp. 1–4.

35. CAWIU, "Resolution of District Commiteee," pp. 2–7.

36. *Western Worker,* August 7 and August 21, 1933; *Oxnard Daily Courier,* August 7 and August 8, 1933.

37. *Western Worker,* August 14 and August 21, 1933; *San Jose Mercury-Herald,* August 15, 1933; *Tulare Advance-Register,* August 15, 1933; interview with Sam Darcy, November 22, 1974; Sam Darcy, "Autobiography" (unpublished manuscript in Mr. Darcy's possession), pp. 31–32, 103–4.

38. *Western Worker,* August 21 and 28, 1933; *San Jose Mercury-Herald,* August 15, August 16, and August 17, 1933; Caroline Decker to T. J. O'Donnell, August 18, 1933, in Federal Writers Project Collection, Bancroft Library; "The Peach Strike," *Northern California Political Prisoners Bulletin* 1 (Summer 1933):4.

39. Decker to O'Donnell, August 18, 1933, in Federal Writers Project Collection, Bancroft Library; *Western Worker,* August 28, 1933; *San Jose Mercury-Herald,* August 18, 1933; *Fresno Bee,* August 18, 1933.

40. *Western Worker,* August 14, August 21, August 28, and September 4, 1933; *Tulare Advance-Register,* August 15, August 16, August 18, and August 19, 1933; *Hanford Journal,* August 15, 1933; *Fresno Bee,* August 14, August 15, August 16, August 17, August 18, August 19, August 20, and August 23, 1933; Darcy interview; Darcy, "Autobiography," pp. 103–4; "Peach Strike," p. 4; *Merced Sun-Star,* August 14, August 15, and August 16, 1933; Report of Thomas A. Reardon to Governor's Council, August 1933, in DIR Records; *Sutter County Farmer,* August 24, 1933; McWilliams, *Factories in the Field,* p. 219.

41. *Western Worker,* August 28 and September 4, 1933; Sam Darcy, "Agricultural Strikes," *Party Organizer* 6 (August–September 1933):82–83.

42. *Fresno Bee,* August 21, 1933.

43. *Western Worker,* August 28, 1933; *Oxnard Daily Courier,* August 18, 1933; Fitzgerald to Kerwin, August 12, September 13, and September 18, 1933, all in File nos. 170-9201 and 176-413, RG 13, USCS; and the following letters in ACLU papers, vol. 649: ACLU to Hon. Frances Perkins and Senator Robert Wagner, August 28, 1933; Lucille B. Milner to A. L. Wirin, September 26, 1933; and Wirin to Milner, October 11, 1933.

44. Thirteenth Convention of California Peace Officers' Association, *Proceedings,* p. 118; "Peach Strike," p. 4.

45. *Western Worker,* August 28, September 4, September 11, September 18, and September 25, 1933; *Fresno Bee,* August 21, August 25, September 3, September 4, September 6, September 8, September 9, September 10, September 11, September 13, and September 14, 1933; *San Francisco Examiner,* September 9, September 10, September 11, September 12, September 13, and September 14, 1933.

46. "Chronological Summary of Grape Strikes in California," in U.S. Congress,

House, Committee on Labor, *Hearings on H.R. 6288, Labor Disputes Act,* 74th Cong., 2d sess. (Washington, D.C.: Government Printing Office, 1935), pp. 360–63; *Western Worker,* September 25 and October 2, 1933; *San Francisco Chronicle,* September 28, 1933; *Stockton Record,* September 28, 1933; *San Francisco Examiner,* September 29, 1933; *Lodi Sentinel,* September 28, 1933.

47. For an expression of this feeling during the Lodi strike, see the statement of Colonel Walter E. Garrison in *San Francisco Examiner,* October 4, 1933, p. 9.

48. *Stockton Record,* September 28, September 30, October 1, October 2, October 3, and October 4, 1933; *Lodi Sentinel,* September 28, September 29, September 30, and October 1, 1933; *Sacramento Bee,* October 2 and October 3, 1933; *San Francisco Examiner,* September 29, September 30, October 1, October 4, and October 5, 1933; *Western Worker,* October 9, 1933; *Modesto Bee,* September 29, 1933; *Oakland Tribune,* October 3, 1933; *San Francisco Chronicle,* October 4, 1933; *Fresno Bee,* October 3 and October 4, 1933; La Follette Committee, *Hearings,* pt. 72, Exhibits 13389–92; "Fascism in Lodi," *Northern California Political Prisoners Bulletin* 1 (Fall 1933):4. See also Rabbi Irving F. Reichert to James Rolph, Jr., October 3, 1933, in Letter File of Rabbi Irving F. Reichert, Federal Writers Project Collection, Bancroft Library.

49. "Chronological Summary of Grape Strikes," pp. 364–65; *San Francisco Examiner,* October 6 and October 7, 1933; *Stockton Record,* October 7, 1933; *San Francisco Chronicle,* October 7, 1933. See also "Fascism in Lodi," p. 4; Ella Winter, "California's Little Hitlers," *New Republic* 77 (December 27, 1933):188–90.

50. Paul S. Taylor and Clark Kerr, "Documentary History of the Strike of the Cotton Pickers in California, 1933," in La Follette Committee, *Hearings,* pt. 54, Exhibit 8764, p. 19947. See also Porter M. Chaffee, "A History of the Cannery and Agricultural Workers Industrial Union," vol. 2, Work Projects Administration, Federal Writers Project (Oakland, 1938), pp. 1–61.

6. *Agricultural Unionism and the New Deal: The Cotton Strike*

1. Quoted in Daniel R. Fusfeld, *The Economic Thought of Franklin D. Roosevelt and the Origins of the New Deal* (New York: Columbia University Press, 1956), p. 50. See also Arthur M. Schlesinger, Jr., *The Age of Roosevelt,* vol. 2, *The Coming of the New Deal* (Boston: Houghton Mifflin, 1958), p. 184. Frank Freidel argues that Roosevelt's devotion to national economic planning was of long standing, and that FDR, as "an imaginative idealist," viewed the initial legislation of the New Deal as the first stage in the development of comprehensive national planning. See Frank Freidel, *Franklin D. Roosevelt,* vol. 4, *Launching the New Deal* (Boston: Little, Brown, 1973), pp. 78–80.

2. On this point see Benjamin S. Kirsh, *The National Industrial Recovery Act: An Analysis* (New York: Central Book Company, 1933), pp. 11–25; Leverett S. Lyon and others, *The National Recovery Administration: An Analysis and Appraisal* (Washington, D.C.: Brookings Institution, 1935), pp. 3–14; Matthew Woll and William English Walling, *Our Next Step—A National Economic Policy* (New York: Harper, 1934), pp. 68–82; *New York Times,* June 17, June 18, June 25, July 8, and July 26, 1933. Also interesting is Mark Sullivan's interpretation of New Deal motives in the *New York Herald Tribune,* August 21, 1933.

3. Frances Perkins, *The Roosevelt I Knew* (New York: Viking Press, 1946), pp.

199–200. It is hardly surprising that New Dealers did not look upon the labor movement in 1933 as a force for progressive change, especially in light of its uninspiring and even reactionary responses to the challenges of the 1920s and the early Depression years.

4. Rexford G. Tugwell, *The Democratic Roosevelt* (Garden City, N.Y.: Doubleday, 1957), p. 286. See also Freidel, *Launching the New Deal,* p. 429.

5. For an informative discussion of this nationalist mentality during the early New Deal, see Schlesinger, *Coming of the New Deal,* pp. 87–94, 108–10, 179–84.

6. Woll and Walling, *Our Next Step,* pp. 116–26; Lyon and others, *National Recovery Administration,* pp. 461–66; *New York Times,* August 30, 1933; *Kansas City Labor Herald,* August 18, 1933; A. J. Muste and others to Franklin D. Roosevelt, September 19, 1933, and Mary Van Kleeck to Roosevelt, December 20, 1933, both in Papers of the American Civil Liberties Union, vols. 609 and 613, respectively, Princeton University Library (hereafter cited as ACLU Papers). For additional sources pertaining to this point, see ACLU Papers, vol. 607.

7. "Radio Appeal for the NRA," July 24, 1933, in *Nothing to Fear: The Selected Addresses of Franklin Delano Roosevelt, 1932–1945,* ed. B. D. Zevin (Boston: Houghton Mifflin, 1946), pp. 29–30.

8. For examples of such statements by New Deal spokesmen, see *New York Times,* June 25, June 28, July 8, July 26, August 27, August 30, September 11, September 15, September 19, October 5, October 10, and October 22, 1933.

9. Address of General Hugh S. Johnson before the Fifty-third Annual Convention of the American Federation of Labor, Washington, D.C., October 10, 1933, in *Report of Proceedings* (1933), pp. 355–61. See also Woll and Walling, *Our Next Step,* pp. 116–26.

10. Louis M. Hacker, *A Short History of the New Deal* (New York: F. S. Croft, 1934), pp. 27–28.

11. Lyon and others, *National Recovery Administration,* p. 491. For a detailed and very instructive analysis of the labor policies of the first New Deal as embodied in the NIRA, see also ibid., pp. 413–548. The evolution of early labor policies under the NIRA is also treated at length in Irving Bernstein, *The New Deal Collective Bargaining Policy* (Los Angeles: Institute of Industrial Relations, University of California Press, 1950), pp. 29–39. See also Raymond S. Rubinow, "Section 7(a): Its History, Interpretation and Administration," Work Materials no. 45, Labor Studies Section, Division of Review, National Recovery Administration (March 1936); Woll and Walling, *Our Next Step,* pp. 116–26; and Lorena A. Hickok to Aubrey Williams, August 15, 1934, in California Field Reports, 1933–35, Harry L. Hopkins Papers, Franklin D. Roosevelt Library, Hyde Park, N.Y.

12. Rexford G. Tugwell, *F.D.R.: Architect of an Era* (New York: Macmillan, 1967), p. 123.

13. For good analyses of the status of agricultural labor under Section 7(a) of the NIRA and the arguments that the administration used in defining that status, see Robert M. Woodbury, "Limits of Coverage of Labor in Industries Closely Allied to Agriculture under Codes of Fair Competition under NIRA," Work Materials no. 45A, Labor Studies Section, Division of Review, National Recovery Administration (March 1936); and Austin P. Morris, "Agricultural Labor and National Labor Legislation," *California Law Review* 54 (December 1966):1939–51.

14. George Creel, "What Roosevelt Intends to Do," *Collier's,* March 11, 1933, p. 8.

15. Ibid., p. 7.

16. Ibid., p. 36.

17. George Creel, *Rebel at Large: Recollections of Fifty Crowded Years* (New York: G. P. Putnam's Sons, 1947), pp. 274–76.

18. George Creel to S. P. Frisselle, November 7, 1933, in Records of National Labor Board, Region IX, Record Group 25, National Archives (hereafter cited as NLB).

19. Sidney C. Sufrin, "Labor Organization in Agricultural America, 1930–35," *American Journal of Sociology* 43 (January 1938):554.

20. For example, see Pascual S. Rodrigues to Campbell MacCulloch, October 12, 1933, in NLB.

21. First Annual CAWIU Convention, *Minutes,* p. 2, in Federal Writers Project Collection, Bancroft Library, University of California, Berkeley.

22. Ibid., p. 5.

23. Ibid., pp. 1–2.

24. Ibid., pp. 13–15; "Code Adopted by Cannery and Agricultural Workers Industrial Union," August 5, 1933, in Federal Writers Project Collection.

25. CAWIU, "Resolution of District Committee," August 5, 1933, p. 7, in Federal Writers Project Collection.

26. First Annual CAWIU Convention, *Minutes,* pp. 1–2.

27. U.S. Congress, House, Committee on Labor, *Hearings on H.R. 6288, Labor Disputes Act,* 74th Cong., 2d sess. (Washington, D.C.: Government Printing Office, 1935), pp. 345–52; Clark Kerr, "Industrial Relations in Large-Scale Cotton Farming," Nineteenth Annual Conference of the Pacific Coast Economic Association, *Proceedings* (Palo Alto, 1940), pp. 62–69; Sufrin, "Labor Organization in Agricultural America," pp. 550–53; Daniel J. Ahearn, Jr., *Wages and Farm and Factory Laborers, 1914–1944* (New York: Columbia University Press, 1945), pp. 171–72.

28. "The Effect of the Depression on Agricultural Income in California," in House Committee on Labor, *Hearings on Labor Disputes Act,* pp. 348–52.

29. Paul S. Taylor and Clark Kerr, "Documentary History of the Cotton Strike," in U.S. Congress, Senate, Subcommittee of the Committee on Education and Labor, *Hearings on S. Res. 266, Violations of Free Speech and Rights of Labor,* 74th Cong., 2d sess. (Washington, D.C.: Government Printing Office, 1939), pt. 54, pp. 19947–48, 19954–56 (hereafter cited as La Follette Committee, *Hearings*); Stuart Jamieson, *Labor Unionism in American Agriculture,* U.S. Bureau of Labor Statistics Bulletin no. 836 (Washington, D.C.: Government Printing Office, 1945), pp. 100–101; U.S. Congress, Senate, Subcommittee of the Committee on Education and Labor, *Report, Violations of Free Speech and Rights of Labor,* report no. 1150, 77th Cong., 2d sess. (Washington, D.C.: Government Printing Office, 1942), pt. 4, pp. 505–6 (hereafter cited as La Follette Committee, *Report*).

30. *Fresno Bee,* September 12, 1933; *Western Worker,* September 18 and September 25, 1933.

31. La Follette Committee, *Report,* pt. 4, pp. 503–7.

32. *Fresno Bee,* September 20, 1933; *Western Worker,* September 25, 1933.

33. *Fresno Bee,* September 29 and September 30, 1933.

34. Anonymous CAWIU organizer to Lincoln Steffens, September 27, 1933, in Letter File of Rabbi Irving F. Reichert, Federal Writers Project Collection.

35. Caroline Decker to Rabbi Irving F. Reichert, August 16, 1933, and Reichert to James Rolph, Jr., October 3, 1933, both in Reichert Letter File. See also

Caroline Decker, "Organizational Letter to All Locals and Sections," September 19, 1933, in Lubin Society Papers, Bancroft Library, University of California, Berkeley.

36. *Fresno Bee,* October 2 and October 3, 1933; *Bakersfield Californian,* October 2 and October 3, 1933; *Western Worker,* October 9, 1933; Sam Darcy, "Autobiography," unpublished manuscript in Mr. Darcy's possession, pp. 107–8.

37. *Tulare Advance-Register,* October 4 and October 5, 1933; *Fresno Bee,* October 4 and October 5, 1933; *Hanford Journal,* October 4, October 5, and October 7, 1933; *Bakersfield Californian,* October 4, 1933; *Corcoran News,* October 6, 1933.

38. "Interview with Clarence H. Wilson, District Attorney of Kings County," December 22, 1933, in Paul S. Taylor Collection, Bancroft Library, University of California, Berkeley.

39. "Interview with Tom Carter, Under-Sheriff of Kern County," November 17, 1933, in Taylor Collection.

40. *San Francisco Examiner,* October 9, 1933.

41. *Fresno Bee,* October 6, 1933; *Hanford Journal,* October 6, 1933; *Visalia Times-Delta,* October 6, 1933.

42. Taylor and Kerr, "Documentary History," pp. 19959–61; interview with Sam Darcy, November 22, 1974.

43. *Report of State Labor Commissioner Frank C. MacDonald to Governor James Rolph, Jr., on San Joaquin Valley Cotton Strike, September–October, 1933,* November 3, 1933, in La Follette Committee, *Hearings,* pt. 54, Exhibit 8762-B, pp. 19899–900 (hereafter cited as *MacDonald Report*); *Tulare Advance-Register,* October 8, 1933; *Fresno Bee,* October 8, 1933. The best available evidence suggests that the word "legally" was inserted in the growers' proclamation after it was read to the strikers. See Taylor and Kerr, "Documentary History," p. 19966.

44. Darcy, "Autobiography," p. 103.

45. Ibid., p. 110. Big Bill Hammett was probably the person after whom John Steinbeck modeled the rank and file strike leader in his novel *In Dubious Battle,* which deals with an agricultural workers' strike in California during the early 1930s. Describing the strikers' leader, a character named London, Steinbeck wrote: "His shoulders were immense. Stiff dark hair grew in a tonsure, leaving the top of the head perfectly bald. His face was corded with muscular wrinkles and his dark eyes were as fierce and red as those of a gorilla. A power of authority was about the man. It could be felt that he led men as naturally as he breathed" (p. 38).

46. *Fresno Bee,* October 7, October 8, and October 9, 1933; *Bakersfield Californian,* October 8 and October 9, 1933; *Hanford Journal,* October 8, 1933; *Visalia Times-Delta,* October 9, 1933; *Tulare Times,* October 10, 1933; *Tulare Advance-Register,* October 9 and October 10, 1933; *Western Worker,* October 16, 1933; Wilson interview. The charges on which strike leaders were arrested were invariably vague. Early in the strike Sheriff Buckner of Kings County went so far as to arrest one Mexican leader for "agitating" in Spanish rather than in "American." See *Fresno Bee,* October 5, 1933.

47. *Tulare Advance-Register,* October 9, 1933.

48. Ed Royce, "A Scene from the Cotton Strike," *Western Worker,* October 30, 1933, p. 2; Taylor and Kerr, "Documentary History," p. 19975; Wilson interview; Darcy, "Autobiography," pp. 108–10; L. D. Ellett to President Franklin D. Roosevelt, October 21, 1933, File no. 176-635, RG 13, USCS; Fred Maloy, "Diary

of the Cotton Strike, October 23–27, 1933," in Bancroft Library, University of California, Berkeley.

49. Taylor and Kerr, "Documentary History," pp. 19957–58.

50. *San Francisco Chronicle,* October 10 and October 13, 1933; *San Francisco Examiner,* October 10, 1933; "Interview with H. B. Walker, Socialist City Councilman of Tulare," December 24, 1933, and "Interview with Sam White, Kern County Labor Journal," November 17, 1933, both in Taylor Collection.

51. *Fresno Bee,* October 8, October 9, and October 10, 1933; *Visalia Times-Delta,* October 9, 1933; *Bakersfield Californian,* October 9, 1933; *Tulare Times,* October 10, 1933; *MacDonald Report,* p.19899; *San Francisco Examiner,* October 9, 1933; *Hanford Journal,* October 8, 1933.

52. *Fresno Bee,* October 8, 1933.

53. Ibid., October 10, 1933.

54. Rabbi Irving F. Reichert to Governor James Rolph, Jr., October 9, 1933, in Reichert Letter File.

55. Testimony of M. B. Kearney, in *Hearings on the Cotton Strike in San Joaquin Valley by the Fact Finding Commission Appointed by James Rolph, Jr., Governor of the State of California, Held in Visalia, California, October 19 and 20, 1933,* in La Follette Committee, *Hearings,* pt. 54, Exhibit 8763, p. 19935.

56. On October 9 and 10 strike leaders demanded that state and federal law-enforcement officers protect strikers from the violence that growers had openly threatened. See *Fresno Bee,* October 10, 1933; Frances Perkins to Hon. James Rolph, Jr., October 9, 1933, Box 10, Official File 407-B, Franklin D. Roosevelt Papers, FDR Library (hereafter cited as OF, FDR Papers).

57. *San Francisco News,* October 11, 1933; *San Francisco Examiner,* October 11, 1933; *San Francisco Chronicle,* October 11, 1933; *Fresno Bee,* October 11, 1933; *Hearings of the Governor's Fact Finding Commission,* pp. 19928–29; Taylor and Kerr, "Documentary History," pp. 19988–90; Miriam Allen deFord, "Blood-Stained Cotton in California," *Nation* 137 (December 20, 1933):705; *New Republic* 76 (October 25, 1933):291; "The Committee and the Cotton Strike," *Northern California Political Prisoners Bulletin* 1 (Fall 1933):1; "Outrages Committed on Striking Workers by Armed Vigilantes," *Labor Clarion,* October 13, 1933, p. 1; *Western Worker,* October 16 and October 23, 1933; *New York Times,* October 22, 1933, p. 1-E. See also A. L. Wirin, "Never Mind the Constitution," n.d., unpublished manuscript in ACLU Papers, vol. 648.

58. *Fresno Bee,* October 11, 1933; *San Francisco Examiner,* October 11, 1933; *San Francisco Chronicle,* October 11, 1933; *Bakersfield Californian,* October 11, October 15, and October 19, 1933; Taylor and Kerr, "Documentary History," pp. 19990–91; *Western Worker,* October 16 and October 23, 1933; Carter interview.

59. *Fresno Bee,* October 11 and October 12, 1933; "Committee and the Cotton Strike," p. 1.

60. "'For a Purpose,'" *Northern California Political Prisoners Bulletin* 1 (Fall 1933):4; *San Francisco Examiner,* October 11 and October 12, 1933; La Follette Committee, *Report,* pt. 4, pp. 512–13; *Western Worker,* October 23, 1933; *Fresno Bee,* October 12, 1933; Royce, "Scene From the Cotton Strike," p. 2; Wilson interview; "Interview with District Attorney Walter C. Haight, Tulare County," December 21, 1933, in Taylor Collection; Regional Oral History Office, "Paul Schuster Taylor: California Social Scientist," Earl Warren Oral History Project, Bancroft Library, University of California (Berkeley, 1975)2:12 (hereafter cited as

Taylor interview). The case against Chambers, which was tried in Visalia during late November and early December, proved to be so weak that even with a jury decidedly hostile to the defendant, a conviction could not be gained. On December 6 the jury reported that it was deadlocked 6 to 6 and a new trial was ordered. See *Western Worker,* November 27, December 4, December 11, and December 18, 1933; *Visalia Times-Delta,* November 22–December 6, 1933; *Agricultural Worker,* December 20, 1933; Wilson interview; Haight interview; Wirin, "Never Mind the Constitution." The murder trial of the eight growers accused of the Pixley killings was not held until January 1934—delayed, according to the prosecuting attorney, because he was busy with the Chambers case. The eight growers, tried before a jury that was openly friendly to them and by a prosecuting attorney who was unwilling to introduce evidence that would have established their guilt, were promptly acquitted. Pat Chambers was then released without being tried a second time. See *Visalia Times-Delta,* February 1, 1934; *Western Worker,* January 5, January 12, January 22, January 29, February 5, and February 12, 1934; *Agricultural Worker,* February 20, 1934; Carey McWilliams, *Factories in the Field* (Boston: Little, Brown, 1939), pp. 221–22.

61. *San Francisco Examiner,* October 11 and October 12, 1933; *Fresno Bee,* October 11, October 12, and October 14, 1933; "Committee and the Cotton Strike," p. 1; Ira B. Cross to E. Raymond Cato, February 20, 1934, in Taylor Collection; *Western Worker,* October 16 and October 23, 1933.

62. Fourteenth Annual Convention of the California Peace Officers' Association, *Proceedings* (October 4–6, 1934), pp. 51–52; California State Sheriffs' Association Convention, *Proceedings* (March 22–24, 1934), pp. 19–20, 23, 65–66; *San Francisco Examiner,* October 12, 1933; *Fresno Bee,* October 12 and October 19, 1933. As the cotton strike was drawing to a close in late October, Chief Cato publicly charged that writer Lincoln Steffens was the "brains behind the strike." Bemused by Cato's allegation, Steffens advised Rolph that "the only man I have tried to agitate is the Governor of California." See *Fresno Bee,* October 26, 1933; "Agitation," *Northern California Political Prisoners Bulletin* 1 (Fall 1933):3.

63. Darcy, "Autobiography," pp. 111–12.

64. *Fresno Bee,* October 11, 1933; *San Francisco Examiner,* October 12, 1933; *MacDonald Report,* p. 19990. See also Kerwin to Fitzgerald, October 11, 1933, File no. 176-635, RG 13, USCS.

65. *Fresno Bee,* October 10, October 11, October 12, and October 14, 1933; *San Francisco Examiner,* October 13, 1933; *San Francisco Chronicle,* October 13, 1933; Reichert to Lloyd Frick, October 10, 1933, in Reichert Letter File; "Statement of R. C. Branion, Federal-State Emergency Relief Administration of California," appended to *MacDonald Report,* p. 19908; William Green to Paul S. Taylor, February 9, 1934, in Taylor Collection. For statements of the Federal Emergency Relief Adminsitration's policy toward relief for striking workers, see Harry L. Hopkins to All State Emergency Relief Administrations, October 5, 1933, and Hopkins to The President, August 29, 1934, both in Box 10, OF 407-B, FDR Papers. See also Pierce Williams to Langdon W. Post, July 11, 1933, California Field Reports, 1933–35, in Hopkins Papers.

66. Creel to Frisselle, November 7, 1933, NLB.

67. Creel to Frank Messenger, October 19, 1933, NLB. See also Creel, *Rebel at Large,* pp. 277–78; and Creel to Al Cohn, n.d., reprinted in *Minutes* of the meeting of the California State Recovery Board of the National Recovery Administration,

September 6, 1933, Records of National Recovery Administration, Region IX, Record Group 25, National Archives (hereafter cited as NRA). When the NRA's authority to intervene in industrial disputes was transferred to the National Labor Board, Creel, bitter at having his personal power reduced, resigned. At the same time, he set in motion a carefully orchestrated lobbying effort to force President Roosevelt to restore his full authority to handle labor disputes in the Western District of the NRA. Backed in Washington by Donald Richberg and in California by both business groups and the A.F. of L., Creel had his authority restored just as he took command of efforts to settle the cotton strike. See Creel to Roosevelt, September 23, 1933, and Roosevelt to Creel, October 12, 1933, both in President's Personal File no. 2346, FDR Papers (hereafter cited as PPF, FDR Papers). On Creel's campaign to regain his authority, see correspondence in Box 1, Folder 466, OF, FDR Papers, especially Creel to Stephen Early, October 14, 1933. See also Creel to Campbell MacCulloch, October 12, 1933, and Robert F. Wagner to Creel, October 22, 1933, both in NLB.

68. Reichert to Rolph, October 9, 1933, in Reichert Letter File.

69. *Visalia Times-Delta,* October 18, 1933.

70. Creel to Frisselle, November 7, 1933, NLB.

71. White interview. Sam Darcy insisted that no attempt was made to politicize the cotton strike because the workers simply had no interest in the revolutionary "message" of the party. See also Caroline Decker, "Why the Cry—'Keep the Party Out?'—How to Work in Mass Organizations," *Western Worker,* April 9, 1934.

72. Reichert to Frick, October 10, 1933, in Reichert Letter File.

73. Statement to the press by Irving F. Reichert, October 11, 1933, in Reichert Letter File.

74. Reichert to H. C. Merritt, Jr., October 13, 1933, in Reichert Letter File.

75. *Fresno Bee,* October 13 and October 14, 1933; In the Matter of the Cotton Growers of the San Joaquin Valley vs. The Cannery and Agricultural Workers Union, San Francisco Regional Labor Board, Case no. 3, October 23, 1933, and George Creel, "Memo on Strike of Cotton Pickers in San Joaquin Valley," November 10, 1933, both in NLB. See also Taylor interview, vol. 2, p. 1.

76. Frank J. Palomares to Rolph, October 13, 1933, in La Follette Committee, *Hearings,* pt. 72, Exhibit 13290-B, pp. 26549–50; Taylor and Kerr, "Documentary History," pp. 19998–99; *Fresno Bee,* October 14 and October 15, 1933; *MacDonald Report,* p. 19901.

77. Darcy, "Autobiography," p. 116. See also C. H. Earnest to Reichert, October 12, 1933, in Reichert Letter File.

78. *MacDonald Report,* p. 19901; Earnest to Reichert, October 12, 1933, in Reichert Letter File; *Western Worker,* October 23, 1933; *Fresno Bee,* October 14, 1933; *Hanford Journal,* October 15, 1933.

79. *Fresno Bee,* October 14 and October 15, 1933; *Western Worker,* October 23, 1933; Salvador Olmedo to Editor, December 4, 1933, *Agricultural Worker,* December 20, 1933, p. 3, in Lubin Society Papers.

80. Copies of the back-to-work notice are in File no. 176-635, RG 13, USCS. A copy is also appended to the *MacDonald Report,* pp. 19906–8.

81. *Fresno Bee,* October 16, 1933; *Visalia Times-Delta,* October 16, 1933; *Hanford Journal,* October 17, 1933; *Western Worker,* October 23, 1933.

82. *Fresno Bee,* October 15, October 16, October 18, October 19, and October 21, 1933; *Hanford Journal,* October 22, 1933; testimony of Caroline Decker, in

People v. Chambers, 22 Cal. App. (2d) 687, 72 Pac. (2d) 746 (1937), vol. 13, pp. 5893–94; Taylor and Kerr, "Documentary History," pp. 19976–77; *Western Worker,* October 23, 1933; Wilson interview; E. H. Fitzgerald to H. L. Kerwin, October 30, 1933, File no. 176-635, RG 13, USCS. On the susceptibility of federal relief to political manipulation during this period, see Bonnie Fox Schwartz, "Social Workers and New Deal Politicians in Conflict: California's Branion-Williams Case, 1933–1934," *Pacific Historical Review* 42 (February 1973):53–73.

83. Ellett to Creel, October 21, 1933, and Creel to Ira B. Cross, October 21, 1933, both in Taylor Collection; *Hanford Journal,* October 21, 1933; *Bakersfield Californian,* October 21, 1933.

84. *Hearings of the Governor's Fact Finding Commission,* in La Follette Committee, *Hearings,* pt. 54, pp. 19913–44.

85. Testimony of Mrs. Pauline Dominguez in ibid., p. 19932; "Committee and the Cotton Strike," p. 1; Darcy, "Autobiography," p. 123.

86. *Western Worker,* October 30, 1933; Taylor and Kerr, "Documentary History," p. 20001; Darcy interview.

87. Paul S. Taylor to Provost Monroe E. Deutsch, October 27, 1933, in Taylor Collection.

88. Creel, "Memo on Strike." See also Taylor interview, vol. 2, p. 2.

89. *Report of Governor's Fact Finding Commission to George Creel and James Rolph, Jr., October 23, 1933,* in Taylor Collection. The report is also reprinted in the *MacDonald Report,* p. 19902.

90. *Bulletin of the Central Strike Committee of the CAWIU,* October 24, 1933, Federal Writers Project Collection; *MacDonald Report,* p. 19902; *Western Worker,* October 30, 1933; *Fresno Bee,* October 23 and October 24, 1933; *Visalia Times-Delta,* October 23 and October 24, 1933; *Hanford Journal,* October 24, 1933; *San Francisco Examiner,* October 23, 1933; *San Francisco Chronicle,* October 23, 1933; Taylor and Kerr, "Documentary History," pp. 20006–20010; Wilson interview; Haight interview; "Interview with Sheriff R. L. Hill, Tulare County," December 21, 1933, in Taylor Collection; "Interview with Sheriff Van Buckner, Kings County," December 20, 1933, in Taylor Collection; "Interview with George Aydelotte, NRA Director for Kings County," December 22, 1933, in Taylor Collection.

91. Creel, "Memo on Strike." See also Creel to Wagner, October 25, 1933, NLB; *Fresno Bee,* October 23, October 24, and October 25, 1933; *San Francisco Chronicle,* October 25, 1933; *Tulare Times,* October 25, 1933; *Bakersfield Californian,* October 25, 1933.

92. *Visalia Times-Delta,* October 25, 1933.

93. Creel to Frank P. Walsh, October 30, 1933, and Creel to Frick, November 6, 1933, both in NLB. See also Creel, "Memo on Strike."

94. *Bulletin of the Central Strike Committee,* October 24 and October 27, 1933; Creel to Wagner, October 25, 1933, and Creel to Walsh, October 30, 1933, NLB; Taylor and Kerr, "Documentary History," p. 20007; Darcy, "Autobiography," pp. 123–25; *Western Worker,* October 30, 1933.

95. Maloy, "Diary of the Cotton Strike"; Creel to Wagner, October 25, 1933, NLB; Taylor and Kerr, "Documentary History," p. 20007; Darcy interview.

96. Maloy, "Diary of the Cotton Strike"; *MacDonald Report,* pp. 19899–905.

97. Darcy, "Autobiography," p. 125; Darcy interview; Maloy, "Diary of the Cotton Strike"; *MacDonald Report,* pp. 19903–4; *Bulletin of the Central Strike*

Committee, October 27, 1933; *Fresno Bee,* October 26 and October 27, 1933; *San Francisco Chronicle,* October 27, 1933; *San Francisco Examiner,* October 27, 1933; *Western Worker,* October 30 and November 6, 1933.

98. "Statement of the Cotton Strike Central Strike Committee, October 26, 1933," reprinted in *MacDonald Report,* p. 19909.

99. For the union's attacks on Creel, see *Western Worker,* November 6, November 13, November 20, and November 27, 1933; *Bulletin of the Central Strike Committee,* October 27, 1933; *Agricultural Worker,* December 20, 1933, and February 20 and April 10, 1934, in Lubin Society Papers; Cannery and Agricultural Workers Industrial Union, *1934: More Profits for Bosses—Lynchings for Workers* (January 1934), p. 1, Federal Writers Project Collection; "Labor and the N.R.A.," *New Republic* 77 (November 22, 1933):48; Darcy interview. For employers' attacks, see Taylor and Kerr, "Documentary History," pp. 20010–28; J. J. Neilsen to Dr. Tully Knoles, November 10, 1933, in Taylor Collection; Edson Abel to Knoles, November 4, 1933, in Taylor Collection; Edson Abel, "The Communist Menace to Agriculture," *Pacific Rural Press,* February 3, 1934, pp. 88–89; Wilson interview; Buckner interview; Hill interview; Haight interview; Aydelotte interview; Carter interview.

100. Creel, "Memo on Strike" and *Rebel at Large,* p. 278.

101. Creel to John E. Pickett, January 17, 1934, NLB. See also Taylor and Kerr, "Documentary History," pp. 20011–12.

102. Creel to Frisselle, November 7, 1933, NLB. See also Creel to R. E. Stark, October 30, 1933; Floyd Byrnes to Creel, November 1, 1933; Stark to Creel, October 31, 1933; all in NLB. For additional insights into Creel's antiunion strategy, see Creel to R. H. Chamberlain, February 28, 1934, NLB.

103. Stark to Creel, November 13, NLB.

104. Creel to Stark, November 16, 1933, NLB.

105. Creel to Frick, November 6, 1933, and Stark to Creel, November 13, 1933, NLB.

106. Creel to the President, April 25, 1934, PPF 2346, FDR Papers.

107. *Bulletin of the Central Strike Committee,* October 27, 1933.

108. Jamieson, *Labor Unionism,* p. 100; LaFollette Committee, *Report,* pt. 4, p. 505.

109. "Agricultural Strikes in 1933," in U.S. Congress, House, Committee on Labor, *Hearings on H.R. 6288, Labor Disputes Act,* 71st Cong., 2d sess. (Washington, D.C.: Government Printing Office, 1935), pp. 342–45.

110. "Interview with C. H. Earnest, Secretary of the MacFarland Local, C.A.W.I.U.," November 18, 1933, in Taylor Collection. See also Caroline Decker, "Consolidate the Battlefront in the San Joaquin Valley," *Western Worker,* December 11, 1933, p. 2; Taylor and Kerr, "Documentary History," pp. 20013-14.

111. *1934: More Profits for Bosses—Lynchings for Workers,* pp. 4–9; *Western Worker,* December 25, 1933; Jamieson, *Labor Unionism,* pp. 105–6.

7. *Agricultural Unionism and the New Deal: The Imperial Valley*

1. *Visalia Times-Delta,* November 18, 1933; *Western Worker,* December 4, 1933.

2. *Western Worker,* December 4, December 11, December 18, and December 25, 1933, and February 5, 1934; Stuart Jamieson, *Labor Unionism in American Agriculture,* U.S. Bureau of Labor Statistics Bulletin no. 836 (Washington, D.C.: Government Printing Office, 1945), p. 123; E. H. Fitzgerald to H. L. Kerwin, January 26, 1934, File no. 170-7205, Records of U.S. Conciliation Service, Record Group 13, National Archives (hereafter cited as USCS).

3. Meeting of the Farm-Labor Committee of the California State Chamber of Commerce, *Minutes,* January 25, 1934, in U.S. Congress, Senate, Subcommittee of the Committee on Education and Labor, *Hearings on S. Res. 266, Violations of Free Speech and Rights of Labor,* 74th Cong., 2d sess. (Washington, D.C.: Government Printing Office, 1939), pt. 67, Exhibit 11327-D, pp. 22798–99 (hereafter cited as La Follette Committee, *Hearings*); F. J. Palomares to C. L. Pioda, January 22, 1934, in ibid., pt. 72, Exhibit 13292, p. 26551; *Western Worker,* December 18, 1933.

4. *Western Worker,* February 5, 1934.

5. E. H., "Lessons of the Imperial Valley Strike," *Western Worker,* February 19, 1934, p. 4; testimony of Stanley B. Hancock, in U.S. Congress, House, Committee on Un-American Activities, *Hearings, Investigation of Communist Activities in the State of California,* pt. 2, 83rd Cong., 2d sess. (Washington, D.C.: Government Printing Office, 1954), pp. 4565–67 (hereafter cited as HUAC, *California Hearings*).

6. Testimony of Stanley Hancock, in HUAC, *California Hearings,* pt. 1, pt. 4573.

7. E. H., "Lessons," p. 4.

8. Thirty-seventh Regular Meeting of the Board of Directors, Western Growers Protective Association, *Minutes,* October 27, 1933, in La Follette Committee, *Hearings,* pt. 71, Exhibit 12913, p. 26132.

9. George Swink to C. M. Brown, February 22, 1934, in La Follette Committee, *Hearings,* pt. 71, Exhibit 12916, pp. 26150–51; Campbell MacCulloch, "Labor Conditions in Imperial Valley," January 19, 1934, Records of the National Labor Relations Board, Region IX, Record Group 25, National Archives (hereafter cited as NLB) also reprinted in La Follette Committee, *Hearings,* pt. 54, Exhibit 8765, pp. 20037–41); *Report to the National Labor Board by Special Commission consisting of J. L. Leonard, Will J. French, and Simon J. Lubin,* February 11, 1934, reprinted in La Follette Committee, *Hearings,* pt. 54, Exhibit 8766, p. 20043 (hereafter cited as *NLB Report*).

10. MacCulloch, "Labor Conditions," pp. 2–3; *NLB Report,* p. 20043; Campbell MacCulloch to Senator Robert F. Wagner, November 22, 1933, NLB.

11. E. H., "Lessons," p. 4; Swink to Brown, February 22, 1934, in La Follette Committee, *Hearings,* pt. 61, p. 26151.

12. *NLB Report,* pp. 20043–44; Swink to Brown, February 22, 1934, in La Follette Committee, *Hearings,* pt. 71, p. 26151; C. B. Moore, *A Reply to the Report on the Record of Investigation Made by Dr. J. L. Leonard, Simon J. Lubin, and Will J. French, Dated February 11, 1934, Covering Conditions of Field Labor and Other Underlying Conditions in the Imperial Valley, State of California,* n.d. [March 1934], p. 2, in Claude B. Hutchison Papers, Bancroft Library, University of California, Berkeley (hereafter cited as Moore, *Reply to NLB Report*).

13. E. H., "Lessons," p. 4.

14. Ibid.; *Brawley News,* January 9 and January 10, 1934; *Calexico Chronicle,*

January 9, 1934; *Los Angeles Times,* January 9, 1934; *San Diego Union,* January 9, 1934; Moore, *Reply to NLB Report,* pp. 7–8.

15. Swink to Brown, February 22, 1934, in La Follette Committee, *Hearings,* pt. 71, p. 26151.

16. Simon J. Lubin, "Can the Radicals Capture the Farms of California?," paper presented before Commonwealth Club of California, March 23, 1934, p. 4, in Simon J. Lubin Society Papers, Bancroft Library, University of California, Berkeley.

17. MacCulloch, "Labor Conditions," pp. 5–6.

18. U.S. Congress, Senate, Subcommittee of the Committee on Education and Labor, *Report, Violations of Free Speech and Rights of Labor,* report no. 1150, 77th Cong., 2d sess. (Washington, D.C.: Government Printing Office, 1942), pt. 9, p. 1651 (hereafter cited as La Follette Committee, *Report*).

19. *Brawley News,* January 10, 1934; *Western Worker,* January 15, 1934; *NLB Report,* p. 20044; Moore, *Reply to NLB Report,* p. 2.

20. *Brawley News,* January 13, 1934; *San Diego Union,* January 13, 1934; *San Diego Sun,* January 13, 1934; *Los Angeles Times,* January 13, 1934; *Western Worker,* January 22, 1934; *NLB Report,* p. 20044; MacCulloch, "Labor Conditions," pp. 3–4; Moore, *Reply to NLB Report,* p. 3; E. H., "Lessons," p. 4; "The Imperial Valley Farm Labor Situation," *Report of the Investigating Committee sent to the Imperial Valley April, 1934, by the co-ordinating committee representing the California State Board of Agriculture, the California Farm Bureau Federation and the Agricultural Department of the California State Chamber of Commerce,* April 16, 1934, reprinted in La Follette Committee, *Hearings,* pt. 54, Exhibit 8767-A, pp. 20058–20059 (hereafter cited as *Phillips Committee Report*); testimony of Stanley Hancock, in HUAC, *California Hearings,* pt. 2, p. 4567.

21. *NLB Report,* pp. 20049–50; MacCulloch, "Labor Conditions," p. 4; George H. Shoaf, "California's Reign of Terror," *Christian Century* 51 (February 28, 1934):283; American Civil Liberties Union Emergency Committee on Imperial Valley, "Stop Imperial Valley Terror," *Bulletin No. 1,* n.d. [April 1934], p. 3.

22. MacCulloch, "Labor Conditions," p. 5.

23. E. H., "Lessons," p. 4.

24. A. L. Wirin, "'Direct Action' in Imperial Valley," *Open Forum,* January 27, 1934, p. 1.

25. A copy of the injunction is in File no. 95-12-14, Record Group 60, Records of the U.S. Department of Justice, National Archives (hereafter cited as RG 60, DJ).

26. "Affidavit of A. L. Wirin Pertaining to the Imperial Valley Situation," n.d. [February 1934], Federal Writers Project Collection, Bancroft Library, University of California, Berkeley; Wirin to Ira B. Cross, February 13, 1934, Paul S. Taylor Collection, Bancroft Library, University of California, Berkeley; testimony of General Pelham D. Glassford, in La Follette Committee, *Hearings,* pt. 55, p. 20140; testimony of Elmer E. Heald, in La Follette Committee, pp. 20172–76; Chester Williams, "Imperial Valley Mob," *New Republic* 78 (February 21, 1934):39–41; Beverly L. Oaten, "The Appeal to Reason—or What?," *Congregationalist,* February 15, 1934, p. 111; Shoaf, "California's Reign of Terror," pp. 283–84; *Open Forum,* February 3, 1934, p. 1; *Brawley News,* January 24, 1934; *Calexico Chronicle,* January 24, 1934; *Los Angeles Times,* January 24, 1934; *San Diego Union,* January 24, 1934; *San Diego Sun,* January 1, 1934; *Western Worker,*

February 5, 1934; Roy T. Layton, "Imperial Valley and Liberal Illusions," *Western Worker,* February 12, 1934, p. 6; *NLB Report,* p. 20044.

27. Strike Committee to President Roosevelt, January 12, 1934, Official File 407-B, Box 10, Franklin D. Roosevelt Papers, FDR Library, Hyde Park, N.Y.

28. For examples of the protests generated by the Wirin kidnapping, see American Civil Liberties Union to Hugh S. Johnson, January 25, 1934, and Roger N. Baldwin to Clinton J. Taft, January 25, 1934, both in Papers of the American Civil Liberties Union, vol. 738, Princeton University Library (hereafter cited as ACLU Papers); Chester S. Williams and others to President Franklin D. Roosevelt, January 25, 1934, and Charles E. Wyzanski, Jr., to Williams, February 1, 1934, both in File no. 170-7205, RG 13, USCS; E. H. Dowell to Roosevelt, January 29, 1934, and Grover C. Johnson to Senator Burton K. Wheeler, January 25, 1934, both in file no. 95-12-14, RG 60, DJ.

29. MacCulloch to National Labor Board, February 15, 1934, NLB.

30. Pierson Hall to Attorney General, March 29, 1934, File no. 95-12-14, RG 60, DJ. See also Wirin to Baldwin, January 28, 1934, in ACLU Papers, vol. 738.

31. Corliss Lamont to Attorney General Homer S. Cummings, May 2, 1934, File no. 95-12-14, RG 60, DJ.

32. The flurry of correspondence provoked by this controversy is available in File no. 95-12-14, RG 60, DJ, and ACLU Papers, vols. 736 and 738.

33. MacCulloch, "Labor Conditions," pp. 2, 9.

34. J. L. Leonard, Will J. French, and Simon J. Lubin to Senator Robert F. Wagner, March 6, 1934, NLB; *NLB Report,* p. 20043.

35. *NLB Report,* pp. 20043–51. A copy of the transcript of the commission's hearings in the Imperial Valley is in the Pelham D. Glassford Papers, Graduate Research Library, University of California, Los Angeles.

36. *NLB Report,* p. 20052.

37. Ibid.

38. For the agribusiness community's reaction to the commission's report, see Moore, *Reply to NLB Report; Phillips Committee Report;* "Resolution of Associated Chambers of Commerce of Imperial Valley," March 29, 1934, in Federal Writers Project Collection; Swink to Brown, February 22, 1934, in La Follette Committee, *Hearings,* pt. 71, p. 26152; *Calexico Chronicle,* March 3, 1934; Ralph H. Taylor, "California's Embattled Farmers," address before the Commonwealth Club of California, San Francisco, June 8, 1934, pp. 14–18, typescript in Hutchison Papers; "Remarks by S. P. Frisselle, Chairman, Statewide Agricultural Committee, California State Chamber of Commerce, before the California State Board of Agriculture at March 9, 1934, Meeting, Sacramento," in Records of the California State Board of Agriculture, California State Archives, Sacramento; John Phillips, "Agriculture Meets the Issue," speech before the Twelve High Club, Stockton, Calif., May 14, 1934, transcript in Hutchison Papers; C. B. Moore, "Will Communists Run the Vegetable Industry?," *Western Grower and Shipper* 5 (March 1934):10–11, 13–14.

39. *Western Worker,* March 26, 1934, p. 6. See also *Main Resolution of the 2nd Annual Convention of the Cannery and Agricultural Workers Industrial Union* (Sacramento, April 29–30, 1934), p. 2, Federal Writers Project Collection; and American League against War and Facism, *California's Brown Book* (Los Angeles, n.d.), p. 12, copy in ACLU Papers, vol. 735.

40. Simon J. Lubin, "The Imperial Valley Situation," speech before the Twelve

High Club, Stockton, Calif., April 16, 1934, p. 5, transcript in Federal Writers Project Collection.

41. Baldwin to Heber Blankenhorn, March 2, 1934, in ACLU Papers, vol. 736. See also ACLU Emergency Committee, "Stop Imperial Valley Terror," pp. 2, 4.

42. Wyzanski to Pelham D. Glassford, March 27, 1934, in Glassford Papers.

43. Leonard, French, and Lubin to Wagner, March 6, 1934, NLB.

44. Leonard to L. C. Marshall, March 9, 1934, NLB.

45. National Labor Board, Press Release no. 3311, February 15, 1934; MacCulloch to George Creel, February 16, 1934; MacCulloch to National Labor Board, March 6, 1934; all in NLB.

46. Memorandum on the Imperial Valley Pea Strike by Charles I. Schottland, assistant administrator of the California State Relief Administration, February 17–20, 1934, pp. 1–3, in Lubin Society Papers (hereafter cited as Schottland Memorandum); *Los Angeles Times* February 14 and February 20, 1934; *San Diego Union,* February 14, 1934; *Imperial Valley Press,* February 14, February 17, and February 20, 1934; *Brawley News,* February 14 and February 20, 1934; *San Diego Sun,* February 16 and February 21, 1934; *Phillips Committee Report,* p. 20060; testimony of Charles Everett Nice, in La Follette Committee, *Hearings,* pt. 55, pp. 20182–83; Moore, "Will Communists Run the Vegetable Industry?," pp. 9–10; *Los Angeles News,* February 20, 1934; *Western Worker,* February 26 and March 5, 1934; Swink to Brown, in La Follette Committee, *Hearings,* pt. 71, p. 26152; *Open Forum,* February 24, 1934. See also Cannery and Agricultural Workers Industrial Union, *Imperial Valley Strike Bulletin,* no. 1 and no. 2 (February 1934), both in Glassford Papers.

47. *Western Worker,* January 29, 1934; "How Imperial Valley Was Opened to Organization," ibid., February 5, 1934, p. 2; E. H., "Lessons," p. 4; Schottland Memorandum, p. 4; Cannery and Agricultural Workers Industrial Union, *Imperial Valley Strike Bulletin,* no. 3 (February 1934), in Glassford Papers.

48. Wirin to Cross, February 13, 1934, in Taylor Collection. See also "Affidavit of A. L. Wirin Pertaining to the Imperial Valley Situation," n.d., in Federal Writers Project Collection.

49. Frank H. Kerrigan to Wirin, February 17, 1934, in Federal Writers Project Collection.

50. "A.C.L.U. 'Invades' Imperial Valley," *Open Forum,* March 24, 1934; ACLU Emergency Committee, "Stop Imperial Valley Terror," pp. 1–4; *Imperial Valley Press,* March 18, 1934; *Brawley News,* March 18, 1934; *Los Angeles Times,* March 20, 1934; A. N. Jack to Moore, March 18, 1934, in La Follette Committee, *Hearings,* pt. 71, Exhibit 12932, p. 26160. To allay the fears of Imperial Valley citizens regarding their purpose in the region, ACLU representatives made a radio broadcast in El Centro on March 17, explaining that they were not in the valley to foster the spread of communism, but only to see that the constitutional rights of workers were upheld. See transcript of ACLU radio broadcast over Station KOX in El Centro, March 17, 1934, in Federal Writers Project Collection.

51. Grover C. Johnson to Glassford, June 22, 1934, in Glassford Papers; testimony of Pelham Glassford, Chancellor Livingston, and Grover C. Johnson, in La Follette Committee, *Hearings,* pt. 55, pp. 20140–46, 20153–62. Regarding other vigilante assaults during March, see "Terror in the Imperial Valley," *New Masses* 11 (April 10, 1934):6, 8; *New Republic* 78 (April 11, 1934):226–27; Ellis O. Jones, "Kidnap Valley, California," *Nation* 138 (April 25, 1934):468–70; ACLU

Emergency Committee, "Stop Imperial Valley Terror," pp. 2–3; "Brief to Support Charges of Violations of Constitutional and Other Legal Rights in Imperial Valley," submitted by Ernest Besig to General Pelham Glassford, April 17, 1934, in Glassford Papers; "Trials Following Trouble in Imperial Valley, 1934," pp. 12–13, in Federal Writers Project Collection; *Open Forum,* March 31 and April 7, 1934.

52. Jack to Moore, March 18, 1934, in La Follette Committee, *Hearings,* pt. 55, pp. 26159–60; Moore to Jack, March 29, 1934, in ibid., Exhibit 12933, pp. 26160–61; Swink to Board of Directors, Western Growers Protective Association, May 1, 1934, in ibid., Exhibit 12934, p. 26161; Moore to A. D. McDonald, April 20, 1934, in ibid., Exhibit 12940, pp. 26164–65; La Follette Committee, *Report,* pt. 4, pp. 457–58; Jack to Members and Prospective Members of the Imperial Valley Growers and Shippers Protective Association, March 23, 1934, in Glassford Papers.

53. *Los Angeles Times,* March 20, 1934.

54. La Follette Committee, *Report,* pt. 4, pp. 458–60; testimony of Hugh T. Osborne and Charles Nice, in La Follette Committee, *Hearings,* pt. 55, pp. 20162–71, 20179–94; J. T. Saunders to A. D. McDonald, May 28, 1934, in La Follette Committee, *Hearings,* pt. 49, Exhibit 8158, p. 17922; "Notes on Vigilante Groups, Membership and Activities," n.d., Section D: "Anti-Communist League of Imperial County," typescript in Lubin Society Papers; *Brawley News,* March 15, 1934; *Calipatria Herald,* March 15, 1934.

55. *Boletín de la Asociación Mexicana del Valle Imperial,* March 28, 1934, in Glassford Papers.

56. Testimony of Pelham Glassford, in La Follette Committee, *Hearings,* pt. 55, pp. 20150–51; Glassford to Secretary of Labor, April 14, 1934, in Glassford Papers. For information regarding the origins and structure of the Mexican Association of the Imperial Valley, as well as its relationship to valley growers, see Chester S. Williams, "Imperial Valley Prepares for War," *World Tomorrow* 17 (April 26, 1934):199–201; *Phillips Committee Report,* p. 20061; Helen Marston, "A Case Study in Social Conflict: Land, Labor, and Liberty in the Imperial Valley," *Advance* 126 (June 21, 1934):236; *Los Angeles Times,* March 20, 1934; "A.C.L.U. 'Invades' Imperial Valley," p. 1; Cannery and Agricultural Workers Industrial Union, *Workman's Bulletin of Imperial Valley,* April 2, 1934, in Glassford Papers; O. C. Heitman to Glassford, April 9, 1934, and Glassford to Wyzanski, May 27, 1934, both in Glassford Papers; *Western Worker,* March 5, March 19, March 26, and April 9, 1934; Williams to Baldwin, March 20, 1934, in ACLU Papers, vol. 736.

57. Baldwin to Heber Blankenhorn, March 29, 1934; Clinton J. Taft to Wirin, March 19, 1934; Taft to Baldwin, February 21 and March 9, 1934; Baldwin to Edmund C. Campbell, February 27, 1934; Williams to Baldwin, March 20, 1934; "Statement to the Press of A. L. Wirin," n.d. [March 1934]; Baldwin to Homer Cummings, March 26, 1934; and Baldwin to Joseph B. Keenan, March 28, 1934; all in ACLU Papers, vol. 736. See also copies of protests in File no. 170-7205, RG 13, USCS, and File no. 95-12-14, RG 60, DJ.

58. MacCulloch to National Labor Board, March 6, 1934, NLB.

59. The attitudes that guided the Labor Department's efforts in the Imperial Valley are revealed in *The Reminiscences of Frances Perkins,* Oral History Research Office (New York: Columbia University, 1976), bk. 4, pp. 400–38 (hereafter cited as *Perkins Reminiscences*).

60. Ibid., pp. 405–6.

61. A brief but illuminating biographical sketch of Glassford is available in Irving Bernstein, *The Lean Years: A History of the American Worker, 1920–1933* (Boston: Houghton Mifflin, 1960), pp. 411–43. For a superb description of Glassford's involvement in the Bonus March controversy, see Roger Daniels, *The Bonus March: An Episode of the Great Depression* (Westport, Conn.: Greenwood Press, 1972).

62. *Perkins Reminiscences,* bk. 4, pp. 406, 410–11.

63. U.S. Department of Labor, press release, March 27, 1934, and Wyzanski to Glassford, March 27, 1934, both in Glassford Papers.

64. Isabella Greenway to Glassford, March 22, 1934, in Glassford Papers.

65. Wyzanski to Glassford, March 27, 1934, in Glassford Papers.

66. S. C. Alexander to Glassford, April 3, 1934; Jack Hardy to Glassford, April 12, 1934; Helen D. Marston to Glassford, April 8, 1934; Williams to Glassford, April 11, 1934; Taft to Glassford, April 9, 1934; all in Glassford Papers; Harry F. Ward, Roger N. Baldwin, and Arthur Garfield Hays to Senator Robert F. Wagner, April 24, 1934, in ACLU Papers, vol. 738.

67. Richard L. Adams to Claude B. Hutchison, n.d. [March–April 1934], and Los Angeles Chamber of Commerce to Hon. John F. Dockweiler, M.C., March 28, 1934, both in Hutchison Papers; B. M. Graham to Glassford, March 28, 1934, in Glassford Papers; *Morning Valley Farmer,* March 28, 1934; *Imperial Valley Press,* March 28, 1934; *Brawley News,* March 29, 1934.

68. Transcript of telephone conversation between Wyzanski and Glassford, April 16, 1934, in Glassford Papers.

69. Glassford to Marston, April 17, 1934, in ibid. See also Glassford to Wyzanski, April 28, 1934; Glassford to Secretary of Labor, April 12 and April 14, 1934; transcript of telephone conversation between Wyzanski and Glassford, April 16, 1934; all in ibid.

70. Wyzanski to Glassford, April 16, 1934, in ibid. See also Wyzanski to Glassford, May 10, 1934, in ibid.; Moore, "Labor Tie-up in Imperial Cantaloupe Deal Fizzes Out," *Western Grower and Shipper* (June 1934):7.

71. Glassford to All Workers in the Imperial Valley, April 30, 1934, in Glassford Papers. See also Williams to Wirin, May 1, 1934, in ACLU Papers, vol. 738.

72. Transcript of telephone conversation between Wyzanski and Glassford, April 16, 1934, in Glassford Papers.

73. *Imperial Valley Press,* April 4, 1934. See also *Brawley News,* April 7, 1934; Moore to Jack, April 15, 1934, in La Follette Committee, *Hearings,* pt. 71, Exhibit 12918, p. 26153; MacCulloch to Glassford, April 16, 1934, and Circular to Members of the Imperial Valley Growers and Shippers Protective Association, May 1, 1934, both in Glassford Papers.

74. Glassford to Secretary of Labor, April 14, 1934, and Glassford to Wyzanski, May 21, 1934, both in Glassford Papers.

75. Glassford to Secretary of Labor, April 14, 1934, and Glassford to Imperial Valley Growers and Shippers Protective Association, May 23, 1934, both in ibid.

76. Glassford to Pierson M. Hall, May 23, 1934, in ibid.; testimony of General Pelham D. Glassford, in La Follette Committee, *Hearings,* pt. 55, p. 20136.

77. Glassford to Wyzanski, April 28, 1934, in Glassford Papers.

78. Ibid.; Glassford to Marston, April 17, 1934, and Glassford to Wirin, May 30, 1934, both in Glassford Papers.

79. Glassford to Secretary of Labor, April 12, 1934, in Glassford Papers.

80. *Open Forum*, April 14, 1934; the following letters in Glassford Papers: Williams to Glassford, April 20 and May 1, 1934; Taft to Glassford, April 11, 1934; Marston to Glassford, April 14, 1934; and the following letters in ACLU Papers, vol. 738: Taft to Wirin, April 17, 1934; Ward, Baldwin, and Hays to Wagner, April 24, 1934; Taft to Wirin, April 25, 1934; Williams to Wirin, May 1, 1934. See also Unión Industrial de Obreros de Agricultura y Canerías, *Boletín Obrero del Valle Imperial*, April 27, 1934, in Glassford Papers.

81. S. C. Alexander to Glassford, April 3, 1934, in Glassford Papers; *Western Worker*, April 9, 1934. See also Williams to Baldwin, March 20, 1934, in ACLU Papers, vol. 736; transcript of telephone conversation between Wyzanski and Glassford, April 16, 1934, in Glassford Papers; Williams to Jack, April 28, 1934, in ACLU Papers, vol. 738.

82. Glassford to Williams, April 30, 1934, and Glassford to Wyzanski, April 24, 1934, in Glassford Papers.

83. Glassford to Williams, April 30, 1934, in ibid.

84. Glassford to Wyzanski, April 30, 1934, in ibid.

85. Wyzanski to Glassford, April 16, 1934; Glassford to Fallin, April 18 and April 28, 1934; Fallin to Glassford, April 21, 1934; Wyzanski to Williams, April 28, 1934; all in ibid.

86. Glassford to Secretary of Labor, April 14, 1934, in ibid.

87. Glassford to Taft, April 17, 1934, and Glassford to Elmer Heald, June 19, 1934, in ibid. On at least two occasions Glassford went beyond simply sympathizing with extralegal methods and actually suggested ways in which state and federal laws might be prostituted to eliminate "troublemakers" from the valley. See Glassford to B. A. Harrigan, May 10, 1934, and Glassford to H. C. Gerrish, May 10, 1934, both in ibid.

88. Wyzanski to Glassford, April 16, 1934, in ibid.

89. Glassford to Wyzanski, April 28, 1934, in ibid.

90. Williams to Glassford, April 30, 1934, and American Civil Liberties Union Emergency Committee on Imperial Valley, "Goodwill Tour to the Other Half," *Bulletin No. 2*, n.d., both in ibid.; Williams to Wirin, May 1, 1934, in ACLU Papers, vol. 738.

91. Glassford to E. Raymond Cato, May 5, 1934; Cato to Glassford, May 5, 1934; Glassford to Secretary of Labor, Secretary of Agriculture, and Chairman, National Labor Board, May 6, 1934; Glassford to Wyzanski, April 30, 1934; all in Glassford Papers; testimony of Pelham Glassford, in La Follette Committee, *Hearings*, pt. 55, p. 20151.

92. *Open Forum*, May 12, 1934; Glassford to Marston, May 6, 1934, American Civil Liberties Union, press release, May 13, 1934, and Wirin to Glassford, May 25, 1934, all in Glassford Papers; Richard Bransten, "Glassford in the Imperial Valley," *New Masses* 11 (May 15, 1934):10–12; and the following items in ACLU Papers, vol. 738: Williams to Wirin, May 1, 1934; Wirin to Williams, May 4, 1934; Ward and others to Roosevelt, May 11, 1934; Ward and others to Frances Perkins, Henry A. Wallace, and Robert F. Wagner, May 12, 1934; Ward and Baldwin to Homer S. Cummings, May 12, 1934; and American Civil Liberties Union, press release, May 23, 1934.

93. Glassford to Wirin, May 30, 1934, in Glassford Papers.

94. Wirin to Glassford, May 25, 1934, and Glassford to Wirin, May 30, 1934, both in ibid.; Wirin to Glassford, June 7, 1934, in ACLU Papers, vol. 738.

95. Marston to Perkins, May 12, 1934, and Marston to Glassford, May 14,

1934, in Glassford Papers. See also Marston to Wirin, May 9 and May 15, 1934, in ACLU Papers, vol. 738.

96. Glassford to John Phillips, May 9, 1934, and Glassford, "Summary of the Situation in Imperial Valley," May 21, 1934, both in Glassford Papers.

97. For the correspondence documenting Glassford's unsuccessful efforts to reform the working and living conditions of farmworkers in the valley, see Folder 9, Box 25, Glassford Papers. See also Glassford to Wyzanski, May 31, 1934; Glassford to Jack, May 17, 1934; and Jack and Swink to Glassford, all in La Follette Committee, *Hearings,* pt. 71, Exhibit 12946, pp. 26167–68; Moore, "Labor Tie-up," p. 7.

98. Glassford, "Summary." See also the correspondence between Glassford and growers in Folder 11, Box 25, Glassford Papers.

99. Glassford to Wyzanski, May 27 and May 31, 1934, in Glassford Papers.

100. Glassford to Pierson M. Hall, May 23, 1934, in ibid.

101. "Assault on Attorney Ernest Besig of Los Angeles," June 8, 1934; Glassford to Marston, June 12, 1934; Glassford to John Beardsley, June 18, 1934; Glassford to Wyzanski, June 14, 1934; all in ibid.

102. "Information Authorized for Immediate Release by General Pelham D. Glassford," June 13, 1934, in Glassford Papers.

103. Ibid., June 14, 1934.

104. Ibid., June 15, 1934.

105. Glassford to Imperial County Board of Supervisors, June 23, 1934, in Glassford Papers.

106. Glassford to Wyzanski, June 20 and June 23, 1934, and Glassford to Taft, June 18, 1934, all in ibid.

107. Wirin to Glassford, June 18, 1934, in ACLU Papers, vol. 738.

108. Testimony of Pelham Glassford, in La Follette Committee, *Hearings,* pt. 55, pp. 20136–37.

109. *Agricultural Worker,* February 20, 1934; Jamieson, *Labor Unionism,* p. 110.

110. *Western Worker,* April 16 and April 23, 1934; Jamieson, *Labor Unionism,* p. 111.

111. Jamieson, *Labor Unionism,* p. 111.

112. *Main Resolution of 2nd Annual Convention of C.A.W.I.U.,* pp. 1–6, in Federal Writer Project Collection.

113. *Western Worker,* June 11, June 18, and June 25, 1934; *Oakland Tribune,* June 5, 1934; *Labor Clarion,* June 15, 1934; and the following material in La Follette Committee, *Hearings:* testimony of Charles B. Weeks, pt. 49, pp. 18020–24; Associated Farmers of California, Inc., "Radical Efforts to Precipitate Strike of Workers in Orchards and Packing Plants in Brentwood, Contra Costa County, Apricot District," n.d., pt. 49, Exhibit 8283, pp. 18115–57; Guernsey Frazer to James True Associates, June 22, 1934, pt. 73, Exhibit 13548, pp. 26911–12; and Walter E. Garrison to Frazer, June 28, 1934, pt. 73, Exhibit 13549, pp. 26912–14.

114. The origins, structure, purposes, and financing of the Associated Farmers of California are described in La Follette Committee, *Report,* pt. 4, pp. 573–636; Clarke A. Chambers, *California Farm Organizations* (Berkeley: University of California Press, 1952), pp. 39–45; Carey McWilliams, *Factories in the Field* (Boston: Little, Brown, 1939), pp. 230–32; Richard L. Neuberger, "Who Are the Associated Farmers?," *Survey Graphic* 28 (September 1939):517–21, 555–57.

115. La Follette Committee, *Report,* pt. 4, pp. 617–36; Chambers, *California Farm Organizations,* p. 42.

116. Frazer to Moore, March 7, 1935, in La Follette Committee, *Hearings,* pt. 72, Exhibit 13359, p. 26624; Associated Farmers of California, Inc., "Aspects of the Agricultural Labor Problem in California," in La Follette Committee, *Hearings,* pt. 51, Exhibit 8556, pp. 18992–94; La Follette Committee, *Report,* pt. 4, p. 630.

117. "Report of Guernsey Frazer, Executive Secretary, to Executive Committee Meeting of Associated Farmers of California, Inc.," June 25, 1934, in La Follette Committee, *Hearings,* pt. 67, pp. 24493–98; *Minutes of the Executive Committee Meeting of Associated Farmers of California, Inc.,* July 23, 1934, in ibid., pp. 24499–503; Jamieson, *Labor Unionism,* p. 113; Ella Winter, "Where Democracy Is a 'Red Plot,'" *New Republic* 79 (June 6, 1934):94–96; Caroline Decker, "California's Terror Continues," *New Masses* 12 (August 28, 1934):9; Ella Winter, "On the Western Front," *Common Sense* 3 (June 1934):6–8.

118. Wirin to Baldwin, August 3, 1934, in ACLU Papers, vol. 734; *San Francisco News,* August 21, 1934; *Daily Worker,* October 27, 1934. For clippings, reports, and correspondence relating to the red scare in California in mid-1934, see ACLU Papers, vols. 722 and 724.

119. *Western Worker,* August 1, August 8, August 16, August 20, and August 23, 1934; *Sacramento Bee,* July 21, 1934; *Sacramento Union,* July 21, 1934; "The West Goes Red Hunting," *Nation* 139 (August 1, 1934):116; "Terrorism in California," *New Republic* 79 (August 1, 1934):305–6; Jack Warnick, "Criminal Syndicalism in California," *New Republic* 81 (November 14, 1934):20; Martin Wilson, "'When in Doubt—Try Kidnapping,'" *Labor Defender* 10 (November 1934):8, 21. For additional reports and correspondence relating to the cases, as well as a copy of the grand jury indictment, see ACLU Papers, vol. 739.

120. La Follette Committee, *Report,* pt. 4, pp. 631–32, 694–95; Frazer to Frisselle, August 30, 1934, and January 15, 1935, in La Follette Committee, *Hearings,* pt. 69, Exhibit 11800, p. 25322, and Exhibit 11804, pp. 25323–24; Chambers, *California Farm Organizations,* p. 108.

121. Frazer to Dr. George P. Clements, January 5, 1935, in La Follette Committee, *Hearings,* pt. 55, Exhibit 8864, p. 20257.

122. People v. Chambers, 22 Cal. App. (2d) 687, 72 Pac. (2d) 746 (1937). Beyond the trial transcript, which is available at the California State Archives in Sacramento, information relating to the criminal syndicalism cases is available in illuminating detail in the following: *Western Worker,* January–April 1935; *Sacramento Bee* and *Sacramento Union,* January–April 1935; La Follette Committee, *Report,* pt. 4, pp. 632–33; Wilson, "'When in Doubt,'" pp. 8, 21; *Labor Defender* 10 (December 1934):9; Bruce Minton, "1512 Years For Organizing Unions," *Labor Defender* 10 (April 1935):10, 23; Norman Mini, "That California Dictatorship," *Nation* 140 (February 20, 1935):224–26; Travers Clement, "Red-Baiters' Holiday in Sacramento: The Criminal Syndicalism Trial," *Nation* 140 (March 13, 1935):306–8; Bruce Minton, "The Battle of Sacramento," *New Republic* 82 (February 20, April 10, and April 24, 1935):37–39, 227, 296; Bruce Minton, "Trial by Vigilantes," *New Masses* 14 (February 19, 1935):9–10; Lawrence Wilson, "California's Red Trial," *Christian Century* 52 (March 13, 1935):330–32; Lawrence Wilson, "California Convicts Itself," *Christian Century* 52 (April 17, 1935):506–8; Michael Quin, *The C.S. Case against Labor* (San Francisco: International Labor Defense, Northern California District, n.d. [1935]); Herbert Solow, *Union-*

Smashing in Sacramento: The Truth about the Criminal Syndicalism Trial (New York: National Sacramento Appeal Committee, 1935). For information on defense strategy and other aspects of the trial, see ACLU Papers, vols. 830 and 831.

123. A Lozovsky, "The Next Tasks of the International Revolutionary Trade Union Movement," *Communist International* 11 (May 20, 1934):317–26; William Z. Foster, *From Bryan to Stalin* (New York: International Publishers, 1937), pp. 268–77; Irving Howe and Lewis Coser, *The American Communist Party: A Critical History (1919–1957)* (Boston: Beacon Press, 1957), pp. 319–86.

124. "Directive on Work within the A.F. of L. and Independent Trade Unions," *Communist* 13 (January 1934):113–15; "Thesis of the Thirteenth Plenum of the Executive Committee of the Communist International," ibid. (February 1934):131–44; Jack Stachel, "Lessons of the Economic Struggles, and the Work in the Trade Unions," ibid. (March 1934):272–301; "Lessons of Economic Struggles, Tasks of the Communists in the Trade Unions: Resolutions of the Eighth Convention of the Communist Party of the U.S.A.," ibid. (May 1934):456–76; Jack Stachel, "Some Problems in Our Trade Union Work," ibid. (June 1934):524–35; B. Sherman, "The Eighth Convention of the Communist Party of the U.S.A. and Some Conclusions," *Communist International* 11 (June 20, 1934):390–94; Sam Brown, "Notes on the Strike Wave in the U.S.," *Communist International* 11 (September 5, 1934):563–68; *Western Worker,* April 9, 1934; Foster, *From Bryan to Stalin,* pp. 268–77; *Labor Fact Book,* vol. 3 (New York: Labor Research Association, 1936), p. 101.

125. Caroline Decker, "Why the Cry—'Keep the Party Out?'—How to Work in Mass Organizations," *Western Worker,* April 9, 1934, p. 2.

126. Interview with Sam Darcy, November 22, 1974.

127. H. Puro, "The Farmers Are Getting Ready for Revolutionary Struggles," *Communist* 13 (June 1934):571–72.

8. *Passage to No Man's Land*

1. U.S. Congress, Senate, Committee on Education and Labor, *Hearings on S. 2926, a Bill to Create a National Labor Board,* 73d Cong., 2d sess. (Washington, D.C.: Government Printing Office, 1934), pt. 1, p. 1 (hereafter cited as Senate, *Hearings on S. 2926*).

2. Ibid., p. 239. See also ibid., pt. 3, p. 695.

3. Ibid., pt. 2, pp. 473–74. See also *American Farm Bureau Federation Official News Letter* 13 (April 17, 1934):2. On the Farm Bureau's political influence during the New Deal era, see Grant McConnell, *The Decline of Agrarian Democracy* (Berkeley: University of California Press, 1953), especially pp. 66–96; Regional Oral History Office, "Paul Schuster Taylor: California Social Scientist," Earl Warren Oral History Project, Bancroft Library, University of California (Berkeley, 1975), 2:44–47 (hereafter cited as Taylor interview); Christiana M. Campbell, *The Farm Bureau and the New Deal* (Urbana: University of Illinois Press, 1956); transcript of Philip S. Bancroft interview, p. 336, in Bancroft Library, University of California, Berkeley.

4. Fred Brenckman to David I. Walsh, April 9, 1934, in Senate, *Hearings on S. 2926,* pt. 3, p. 1000. See also "Collective Bargaining among Farm Labor," *National Grange Monthly* 31 (May 1934):9.

5. National Labor Relations Board, *Legislative History of the National Labor*

Relations Act, vol. 1 (Washington, D.C.: Government Printing Office, 1949), pp. 1099, 1102. See also Austin P. Morris, "Agricultural Labor and National Labor Legislation," *California Law Review* 54 (December 1966):1952–53.

6. NLRB, *Legislative History,* vol. 2, p. 2306. See also Gardner Jackson to James Myers, January 25, 1935, in Gardner Jackson Papers, Franklin D. Roosevelt Library, Hyde Park, N.Y.; Taylor interview, vol. 2, p. 46.

7. NLRB, *Legislative History,* vol. 2, pp. 2936–37.

8. Ibid., pp. 3201–2.

9. Testimony of William T. Ham, in U.S. Congress, Senate, Subcommittee of the Committee on Education and Labor, *Hearings on S. Res. 266, Violations of Free Speech and Rights of Labor,* 74th Cong., 2d sess. (Washington, D.C.: Government Printing Office, 1941), Supplementary Hearings, pt. 1, pp. 117 (hereafter cited as La Follette Committee, *Hearings*); "The Fair Labor Standards Act in Relation to Agricultural Labor," in ibid., pt. 3, pp. 1009–40; Morris, "Agricultural Labor," pp. 1954–63. See also Taylor interview, vol. 2, pp. 41–42; Leif Dahl, "Agricultural Labor and Social Legislation," *American Federationist* 44 (February 1937):137–45.

10. Gardner Jackson to Pelham Glassford, November 9, 1934, in Jackson Papers. See also Jackson to Simon J. Lubin, January 19 and February 1, 1935, both in ibid.

11. Taylor interview, vol. 2, pp. 25–32. See also the following material in La Follette Committee, *Hearings,* pt. 62: Conference on Housing of Migratory Agricultural Laborers, *Proceedings* (October 12, 1935), Exhibit 9577-C, pp. 22592–609; Conference on Housing of Migratory Agricultural Laborers, *Proceedings* (November 18, 1935), Exhibit 9577-D, pp. 22609–38; "Statement of Regional Office of Resettlement Administration on Possible Establishment of Migrant Camps," Exhibit 9577-E, pp. 22638–42; California Conference of Agricultural Workers, *Transcript of Proceedings* (Stockton, Calif., June 6–7, 1936), Exhibit 9580, pp. 22685–89, 22699–700; and Walter J. Stein, *California and the Dust Bowl Migration* (Westport, Conn.: Greenwood Press, 1973), pp. 140–215; Sidney Baldwin, *Poverty and Politics: The Rise and Decline of the Farm Security Administration* (Chapel Hill: University of North Carolina Press, 1968), pp. 221–22; State Relief Administration of California, *Migratory Labor in California* (San Francisco, 1936), pp. 80–95.

12. On the attitudes of migrant workers toward the FSA camps, see "Program of the John Steinbeck Committee to Aid Agricultural Organization on Housing, Health and Relief for Agricultural Workers," October 29, 1938, typescript in Jackson Papers. See also Dr. Omer Mills, "Farm Labor Programs of the Farm Security Administration," in La Follette Committee, *Hearings,* pt. 59, Exhibit 9376, pp. 21924–26.

13. Stein, *California and the Dust Bowl Migration,* p. 151; Carey McWilliams, *Factories in the Field* (Boston: Little, Brown, 1939), p. 303.

14. Stanley V. White to Dr. J. R. Steelman, n.d. [December 1938], Records of the U.S. Conciliation Service, Record Group 280, File no. 195-815, National Archives (hereafter cited as RG 280, USCS); J. H. Fallin to P. D. Glassford, May 3, 1934, in the Pelham D. Glassford Papers, Graduate Research Library, University of California, Los Angeles; and the following material in La Follette Committee, *Hearings*: testimony of Theodore R. Rasmussen, pt. 60, p. 22069; W. V. Allen, "Agriculture and Its Employment Problems in California" (1935), pt. 62, Exhibit

9579-A, pp. 22666–73; U.S. Farm Placement Service, "Comments on Agriculture and Agricultural Labor in California" (1937), pt. 62, Exhibit 9579-B, pp. 22674–78; E. F. Loescher, "Important Farm Labor Developments during 1937," n.d., pt. 68, Exhibit 11353, p. 24885; R. N. Wilson to Anonymous, July 11, 1936, pt. 68, Exhibit 11381, pp. 24929–30; W. V. Allen to Lincoln McConnell, September 23, 1935, pt. 63, Exhibit 9629, p. 22988.

15. For examples of employers' objections to federal relief policies, see L. D. Ellett to Franklin D. Roosevelt, October 21, 1933, and L. A. Burtch to Roosevelt, October 22, 1933, both in File no. 176-635, RG 13, USCS; meeting of the Agriculture, Horticulture, and Livestock Committee of the Los Angeles Chamber of Commerce, *Minutes,* November 8, 1933, in La Follette Committee, *Hearings,* pt. 63, Exhibit 9599, pp. 22958–59.

16. Lorena A. Hickok to Aubrey Williams, August 17, 1934, "California—Field Reports, 1933–34," in Harry L. Hopkins Papers, Franklin D. Roosevelt Library, Hyde Park, N.Y.; Bonnie Fox Schwartz, "Social Workers and New Deal Politicians in Conflict: California's Branion-Williams Case, 1933–1934," *Pacific Historical Review* 42 (February 1973):53–73.

17. Clarke A. Chambers, *California Farm Organizations* (Berkeley: University of California Press, 1952), pp. 82–97; Ray Laughlin to Franklin D. Roosevelt, September 10, 1935, File no. 182-763, RG 13, USCS; and the following material in La Follette Committee, *Hearings*: Leigh Athearn, "Unemployment Relief in Labor Disputes—A Study of the Policies and Actions of the California State Emergency Relief Administration from 1935 to 1939 Regarding Aid to Persons Engaged in Labor Disputes," October 1939, pt. 62, Exhibit 8539, pp. 22751–68; State Emergency Relief Administration, "Agricultural Migratory Laborers in the San Joaquin Valley, July and August, 1937," December 1937, pt. 62, Exhibit 9578, pp. 22642–66; Frank F. Merriam to Walter E. Garrison, September 8, 1937, pt. 68, Exhibit 11604, p. 25181.

18. Los Angeles Chamber of Commerce, *Report of Special Labor Committee,* November 22, 1935, in La Follette Committee, *Hearings,* pt. 63, Exhibit 9599, pp. 22963–64. See also Committee on Farm Labor of the California State Chamber of Commerce, *Farm Labor Bulletin No. 1,* April 16, 1936, and *Farm Labor Bulletin No. 4,* August 27, 1934, both in ibid., pt. 68, Exhibits 11361 and 11364, pp. 24895–98, 24903–5; "Report to Statewide Agricultural Committee," November 19, 1936, in ibid., Exhibit 11384, p. 24932; Special Farm Labor Meeting of the California State Chamber of Commerce, *Minutes,* March 5, 1936, in ibid., pt. 67, Exhibit 11327-D, pp. 24802–7.

19. Farm Security Administration, "Narrative Report on Farm Labor, Region IX," n.d. [1938], in File no. 195-123, RG 280, USCS. See also Stein, *California and the Dust Bowl Migration,* p. 83; Chambers, *California Farm Organizations,* p. 86; McWilliams, *Factories in the Field,* pp. 285–96.

20. *Rural Worker* 1 (September 1936):4; ibid. (November 1936):2.

21. On the A.F. of L. debates regarding agricultural unionism, see *Report of Proceedings,* Fifty-fourth Annual Convention of the American Federation of Labor (San Francisco, 1934), pp. 58, 323–24, 668–72; ibid., Fifty-fifth Convention (Atlantic City, 1935), pp. 370–71, 689–92, 723; ibid., Fifty-sixth Convention (Tampa, 1936), pp. 222, 583–92.

22. Testimony of Samuel Parker Frisselle, in La Follette Committee, *Hearings,* pt. 49, p. 17946. For additional evidence of Scharrenberg's and Vandeleur's

opposition to farmworker organization and their close relations with farm employers, see Executive Committee Meeting of Associated Farmers of California, Inc., *Minutes,* April 30, 1934, in ibid., pt. 67, Exhibit 11327-B, pp. 24483–84; Guernsey Frazer to Frisselle, July 17 and July 18, 1934, in ibid., pt. 69, Exhibits 11752 and 11754, pp. 25292, 25295; Frazer to Edward Vandeleur, July 15, 1934, in ibid., Exhibit 11753, pp. 25292–95; Fred Goodcell to Col. Walter E. Garrison, May 29, 1936, in ibid., Exhibit 11722, pp. 25275–76; Bancroft interview, pp. 395–97; John Phillips, "Agriculture Meets the Issue," speech before the Twelve High Club, Stockton, Calif., May 14, 1934, pp. 3, 10, transcript in the Claude B. Hutchison Papers, Bancroft Library, University of California, Berkeley; Ralph H. Taylor, "California's Embattled Farmers," address before the Commonwealth Club of California, San Francisco, June 8, 1934, p. 21, typescript in Hutchison Papers; Philip S. Bancroft, "The Farmer and the Communists," address before the Commonwealth Club of California, April 26, 1935, typescript in Federal Writers Project Collection; Caroline Decker, "California's Terror Continues," *New Masses* 12 (August 28, 1934):9; McWilliams, *Factories in the Field,* p. 271.

23. *New York Times,* January 20, 1935, sec. 4, p. 1.

24. Vandeleur to William Green, June 22, 1936, in La Follette Committee, *Hearings,* pt. 68, Exhibit 11631, pp. 25201-2. See also California State Chamber of Commerce Committee on Farm Labor, *Farm Labor Bulletin No. 2,* May 5, 1936, in ibid., Exhibit 11362, pp. 24898–900.

25. Goodcell to Garrison, May 29 and June 27, 1936, in ibid., pt. 69, Exhibits 11722 and 11632, pp. 25275–76, 25202–3; Assistant Secretary to C. H. Breon, December 31, 1936, in ibid., pt. 68, Exhibit 11626, p. 25199; McWilliams, *Factories in the Field,* p. 270.

26. California Conference of Agricultural Workers, *Transcript of Proceedings* (Stockton, June 6–7, 1936), in La Follette Committee, *Hearings,* pt. 62, Exhibit 9580, p. 22697.

27. Goodcell to Garrison, May 29, 1936, in La Follette Committee, *Hearings,* pt. 69, Exhibit 11722, pp. 25274–75; Bancroft interview, p. 395.

28. California Conference of Agricultural Workers, *Transcript of Proceedings,* p. 22681. See also McWilliams, *Factories in the Field,* p. 270; Associated Farmers of California, Inc., "From Apathy to Action," June 6–7, 1936, in La Follette Committee, *Hearings,* pt. 62, Exhibit 9580, pp. 22704–7.

29. Goodcell to Garrison, June 27, 1936, in La Follette Committee, *Hearings,* pt. 68, Exhibit 11632, pp. 25202–3; Associated Farmers of California, "From Apathy to Action," June 6–7, 1936, p. 22707.

30. *Rural Worker* 2 (February 1937):6; ibid. (May 1937):3; McWilliams, *Factories in the Field,* p. 271. See also "Outline of Program of the California State Federation of Labor for the Organization of Agricultural Workers," February 28, 1937, in La Follette Committee, *Hearings,* pt. 62, Exhibit 9581, pp. 22708–11.

31. *Rural Worker* 2 (May 1937):3; McWilliams, *Factories in the Field,* p. 271.

32. J. B. Nathan to Gardner Jackson, June 17, 1937, in Jackson Papers; *Rural Worker* 2 (July 1937):3; Philip Bancroft, "The Agricultural Labor Situation," in Seventieth Convention of California Fruit Growers and Farmers, *Proceedings* (December 8, 1937), pp. 119–24; A. E. Eames to Garrison, June 21, 1937, in La Follette Committee, *Hearings,* pt. 68, Exhibit 11668; *The Reminiscences of Gardner Jackson* (Oral History Research Office, Columbia University, 1959), pp. 698–99.

33. Stuart Jamieson, *Labor Unionism in American Agriculture,* U.S. Bureau of Labor Statistics Bulletin no. 836 (Washington, D.C.: Government Printing Office, 1945), p. 149; Bancroft interview, pp. 392–95. On the ILWU's organizing campaign, see Harvey Schwartz, *The March Inland: Origins of the ILWU Warehouse Division, 1934–1938* (Los Angeles: Institute of Industrial Relations, University of California, 1978).

34. *Rural Worker* 2 (July 1937):3.

35. First National Convention of Agricultural, Cannery, and Fruit and Vegetable Packing House Unions, press release, July 1, 1937, in Jackson Papers; First National Convention of the United Cannery, Agricultural, Packing and Allied Workers of America *Official Proceedings* (Denver, July 9–12, 1937); *Reminiscences of Gardner Jackson,* pp. 704–13.

36. Henry A. Wallace to Secretary of Labor, June 4, 1937, File no. 195-123, RG 280, USCS.

37. White to Steelman, "Preparatory Steps for Our Work in the Agricultural Union Field," September 1, 1937, File no. 195-123, RG 280, USCS.

38. Jonathan Garst to Jackson, September 21, 1937, in Jackson Papers.

39. Stuart H. Strathman, "Organization Letter," August 12, 1937, in La Follette Committee, *Hearings,* pt. 68, Exhibit 11540, pp. 25138–39.

40. S. H. Strathman, "Organization Letter—Confidential," n.d., in La Follette Committee, *Hearings,* pt. 68, Exhibit 11542, pp. 25140–41. See also Executive Committee Meeting of the Associated Farmers of California, Inc., *Minutes,* July 31, 1937, in ibid., pt. 67, Exhibit 11327-B, pp. 24564–66; Associated Farmers of California, "From Apathy to Action," no. 56 (December 14, 1937), in ibid., pp. 24591–95; Loescher, "Important Farm Labor Developments," pp. 24888–89; Bancroft, "Agricultural Labor Situation," pp. 122–24.

41. Garrison to Perkins, October 9, 1937, in La Follette Committee, *Hearings,* pt. 69, Exhibit 11770, p. 25306.

42. *Rural Worker* 1 (November 1936), p. 2. See also Stanley White to Pierce Williams, July 14, 1937, File no. 195-123, RG 280, USCS; and the following items in Jackson Papers: Nathan to Jackson, June 17 and August 2, 1937; Nathan to Comrade [H. L. Mitchell], August 16, 1937; Mitchell to Nathan, August 19, 1937; Jackson to Nathan, August 30, 1939; Employees' Security Alliance of Fresno, "An Open Letter to the Agricultural Workers," n.d.; and "Convention Call to First National Convention of Agricultural, Cannery and Packinghouse in Unions," July 19, 1937.

43. White to Steelman, September 1, 1937, File no. 195-123, RG 280, USCS. See also Victor B. Nelson-Cisneros, "UCAPAWA and Chicanos in California: The Farm Worker Period, 1937–1940," *Aztlán* 7 (Fall 1976):453–77.

44. Jamieson, *Labor Unionism,* pp. 149–50.

45. For details of the Stockton strike, see La Follette Committee, *Hearings,* pt. 50, pp. 18242–324, 18354–416; U.S. Congress, Senate, Subcommittee of the Committee on Education and Labor, *Report, Violations of Free Speech and Rights of Labor,* report no. 1150, 77th Cong., 2d sess. (Washington, D.C.: Government Printing Office, 1942), pt. 8, pp. 1385–1406 (hereafter cited as La Follette Committee, *Report*); Jamieson, *Labor Unionism,* pp. 151–52; McWilliams, *Factories in the Field,* pp. 259–60.

46. Jamieson, *Labor Unionism,* pp. 152–55. On the close cooperation that developed between A.F. of L. conservatives and canning industry employers, see

the following materials in La Follette Committee, *Hearings*: Vandeleur statement, pt. 60, pp. 22058–59; R. L. Adams to F. J. Palomares, March 10, 1937, pt. 72, Exhibit 13329, p. 26583; Executive Committee Meeting of the Associated Farmers of California, Inc., *Minutes*, July 31 and September 24, 1937, pt. 67, Exhibit 11327-B, pp. 24561–67, 24571–78; Garrison to California Wool Growers Association, March 5, 1937, pt. 68, Exhibit 11555, pp. 25150–51; C. H. Kinsley to Garrison, March 9, 1937, pt. 68, pp. 25152–53; Lewis M. Foulke to Associated Farmers, March 10, 1937, pt. 68, p. 25153; Goodcell to Garrison, May 6, 1936, pt. 68, p. 25201; Goodcell to James C. Morton, September 10, 1937, pt. 68, pp. 25242–43; and Loescher, "Important Farm Labor Developments," pt. 68, p. 24888. See also "Report of Agricultural Field Labor Submitted to Dr. J. R. Steelman, Director of Conciliation, Department of Labor, January 18, 1938, by E. H. Fitzgerald and Walter G. Mathewson, Commissioner of Conciliation, Department of Labor," File no. 196-266, RG 280, USCS (hereafter cited as USCS Report).

47. Jamieson, *Labor Unionism*, pp. 149–79; USCS Report; "Narrative Report on Farm Labor, Region, IX," pp. 8–12; Vandeleur statement, in La Follette Committee, *Hearings*, pt. 60, p. 22059; Annual Convention of the California State Federation of Labor, *Proceedings* (1938), pp. 41–45; *CIO News*, December 12, 1938, p. 3; Associated Farmers of California, Inc., "Aspects of the Agricultural Labor Problem in California," n.d., in La Follette Committee, *Hearings*, pt. 51, Exhibit 8556, pp. 18996–99.

48. For a poignant statement of the despair that caused migratory farmworkers to strike despite the overwhelming odds against them, see Austin Killen to Roosevelt, October 12, 1938, in File no. 195-123, RG 280, USCS.

49. Jamieson, *Labor Unionism*, pp. 165–79; Stein, *California and the Dust Bowl Migration*, pp. 243–74; testimony of Theodore Rasmussen, in La Follette Committee, *Hearings*, pt. 60, pp. 22069–70.

50. District 2, United Cannery, Agricultural, Packing and Allied Workers of America, *Official Report* (December 1938), p. 46, Federal Writers Project Collection.

51. "Narrative Report on Farm Labor, Region IX," p. 9.

52. Testimony of Elizabeth Sasuly, in Cotton Picking Wage Hearings, *Minutes* (Fresno, September 28–29, 1939), reprinted in La Follette Committee, *Hearings*, pt. 52, Exhibit 8568, p. 19205.

53. Vandeleur statement, in La Follette Committee, *Hearings*, pt. 60, pp. 22061–62.

54. Second Constitutional Convention of the Congress of Industrial Organizations, *Daily Proceedings* (San Francisco, October 10–13, 1939), p. 222.

55. Ibid., pp. 219–20.

56. On this point see R. L. Burgess to Anonymous, November 25, 1936; White to Steelman, December 16, 1937, October 26, 1938, and November 9, 1938; William T. Ham to Steelman, July 10, 1939; all in File no. 195-123, RG 280, USCS; and White to Steelman, n.d. [marked "Confidential Memorandum"], File no. 195-815, RG 280, USCS. See also Taylor interview, vol. 2, pp. 39–49.

57. White to Steelman, July 17, 1939, File no. 195-123, RG 280, USCS.

58. For an interesting commentary on the background of *The Grapes of Wrath*, see Daniel Aaron, "The Radical Humanism of John Steinbeck," *Saturday Review*, September 28, 1968, pp. 26–27, 55–56.

59. On the La Follette Committee's activities in California, see Jerold S. Auer-

bach, *Labor and Liberty: The La Follette Committee and the New Deal* (Indianapolis: Bobbs-Merrill, 1966), pp. 177–96.

60. La Follette Committee, *Report,* pt. 1, p. 37.

61. Heber Blankenhorn to The [National Labor Relations] Board, March 6, 1939, in Heber Blankenhorn Papers, Archives of Labor History and Urban Affairs, Wayne State University.

62. Donald Henderson, "Agricultural Workers," *American Federationist* 43 (May 1936):488.

Index

Index

Index

Wheatland hop pickers' strike (1913), 88–94

Wickson, Edward, 41

Wilson, Clarence, 182

Wirin, A. L., 230–31

Wobblies. *See* Industrial Workers of the World.

Workers' International Relief, 116, 137

Workers Union of the Imperial Valley (Unión de Trabajadores del Valle Imperial), 108–9, 111, 225

Works Progress Administration, 271–72

Wright, Jack, 178–79

Wyzanski, Charles E., Jr., 242–44, 247

Young, Clement C., 119

Young Communist League, 131, 148, 224